NEW AUTHORITARIAN PRACTICES IN THE MIDDLE EAST AND NORTH AFRICA

Edited by
Özgün E. Topak,
Merouan Mekouar
and Francesco Cavatorta

EDINBURGH
University Press

Edinburgh University Press is one of the leading university presses in the UK. We publish academic books and journals in our selected subject areas across the humanities and social sciences, combining cutting-edge scholarship with high editorial and production values to produce academic works of lasting importance. For more information visit our website: edinburghuniversitypress.com

Edinburgh University Press Ltd
The Tun – Holyrood Road
12 (2f) Jackson's Entry
Edinburgh EH8 8PJ

Typeset in 11/14pt Adobe Garamond by
Cheshire Typesetting Ltd, Cuddington, Cheshire, and
printed and bound by CPI Group (UK) Ltd,
Croydon, CR0 4YY

A CIP record for this book is available from the British Library

ISBN 978 1 4744 8940 9 (hardback)
ISBN 978 1 4744 8943 0 (webready PDF)
ISBN 978 1 4744 8942 3 (epub)

CONTENTS

NOTES ON CONTRIBUTORS

Francesco Cavatorta is Professor of Political Science and Director of the *Centre Interdisciplinaire de Recherche sur l'Afrique et le Moyen Orient* (CIRAM) at Laval University, Quebec, Canada. His research focuses on the dynamics of authoritarianism and democratisation in the Middle East and North Africa. His current research projects deal with party politics and the role of political parties in the region. He has published several journal articles and books.

Giulia Cimini is a Junior Assistant Professor in Comparative Politics at the University of Bologna and a Gerda Henkel Research Fellow. Prior to her current position, she was a Teaching Assistant of Politics at Università L'Orientale of Naples, and Visiting Fellow at both the International University of Rabat (UIR), and at the Middle East, Central Asia and Caucasus Studies Institute at the University of St Andrews in Scotland. Her research interests include Maghrebi political parties, security assistance, dynamics of contention, and environmentalism. She has published in several academic journals, including The Journal of Intervention and Statebuilding, Contemporary Politics, Middle Eastern Studies, and The Journal of North African Studies.

Irene Costantini is a Postdoctoral Researcher in Politics and International Relations at Università L'Orientale, Naples. Her research interests include the politics of international interventions, the political economy of conflict and post-conflict transition, and processes of state transformation in the Middle

East and North Africa (MENA) region, focusing on Iraq and Libya. She has published in several academic journals, including *International Peacekeeping*, *Ethnicities*, *Ethnopolitics*, the *International Spectator* and *International Migration*, and she is the author of *Statebuilding in the Middle East and North Africa: The Aftermath of Regime Change* (2018).

May Darwich is Associate Professor in International Relations of the Middle East at the University of Birmingham in the United Kingdom. She is author of *Threats and Alliances in the Middle East: Saudi and Syrian Policies in a Turbulent Region* (2019).

Christopher Davidson is a British academic with a long-standing interest in the comparative politics of the Gulf states. He is an associate fellow of the Henry Jackson Society, and was previously a reader at Durham University and an assistant professor at Zayed University in the UAE. His books include *The United Arab Emirates: A Study in Survival* (2005); *Dubai: The Vulnerability of Success* (2008); *Abu Dhabi: Oil and Beyond* (2009); *Persian Gulf and Pacific Asia: From Indifference to Interdependence* (2010); *After the Sheikhs: The Coming Collapse of the Gulf Monarchies* (2013); *Shadow Wars: The Secret Struggle for the Middle East* (2016); and, most recently, *From Sheikhs to Sultanism: Statecraft and Authority in Saudi Arabia and the UAE* (2021).

Hilla Dayan is a political sociologist and lecturer at a liberal arts college, Amsterdam University College. Her earlier research focused on the Occupied Palestinian Territories and Israel's regime of separation and is featured in *The Power of Inclusive Exclusion: Anatomy of Israeli Rule in the Occupied Palestinian Territories* (2009). Other work includes surveillance in the context of the global authoritarian turn (2017), and reflection on 'Occupation Studies' (2018). Dayan is a co-founder of *gate48* platform for critical Israelis in the Netherlands and *academia for equality*, for the democratisation of Israeli academia and society.

Islam Amine Derradji is a Ph.D. candidate in the Department of Political Science at the Université de Montréal. His Ph.D. project examines protest coalitions in Algeria during the 'Arab Spring' mobilisations. He has recently published 'Le Hirak algérien: un laboratoire de citoyenneté', with Amel

Gherbi, in *Métropolitiques*, and 'Une si longue absence? Notes sur la politicité de la rue en Algérie, with Ratiba Hadj-Moussa', in *Maghreb-Machrek*.

Vincent Durac is Associate Professor in Middle East Politics at University College Dublin, Ireland and is a visiting professor at Bethlehem University. He is co-author (with Francesco Cavatorta) of *Politics and Governance in the Middle East* (2015) and of *Civil Society and Democratization in the Arab World: The Dynamics of Activism* (2010). His work has been published in *Democratization, Mediterranean Politics, Orient, Global Discourse, the British Journal of Middle Eastern Studies, the Journal of North African Studies* and the *Journal of Contemporary African Studies*.

Saeid Golkar is an Assistant Professor in the Department of Political Science and Public Service at the University of Tennessee at Chattanooga. His first book, *Captive Society: The Basij Militia and Social Control in Post-revolutionary Iran* (2015), was awarded the Washington Institute silver medal prize. His publications can be found in *Middle East Journal; Armed Forces & Society; Politics, Religion & Ideology; Middle East Journal; Middle East Policy; Journal of Contemporary Islam; and Middle East Quarterly*.

Yousif Hassan is a scholar of Science and Technology Studies (STS) in the STS department at York University and a fellow in the Harvard Kennedy School's Program on Science, Technology and Society. His areas of interests are the political economy of technoscience, critical race theory, Black/African studies, critical innovation studies, and information and communication studies. His research focuses on the social, economic and political implications of technology. His work has appeared in several academic publications, including *Information Polity*.

Kira Jumet is Associate Professor of Government at Hamilton College. Her research focuses on protest mobilisation leading up to and during the 2011 and 2013 Egyptian uprisings. She is the author of *Contesting the Repressive State: Why Ordinary Egyptians Protested during the Arab Spring* in 2017.

Alainna Liloia is a Ph.D. candidate at the University of Arizona. Her dissertation research examines the gendered political initiatives of the Qatari state and Qatari women's strategic negotiation of political, religious and social norms and expectations in the context of rapid development and social change. Her article 'Gender and Nation Building in Qatar: Qatari Women Negotiate Modernity' was published in the *Journal of Middle East Women's Studies* in 2019.

Driss Maghraoui is an Associate Professor of history and international relations at the School of Humanities and Social Sciences at Al Akhawayn University in Ifrane, Morocco. He is the co-editor of *Reforms in the Arab World: The Experience of Morocco* (*Mediterranean Politics* special edition, 2009), the editor of *Revisiting the Colonial Past in Morocco* (Routledge, 2013) and, more recently, co-editor with Noureddine Harrami and Khalid Mouna of *L'immigration au Maroc: les défis de l'intégration* (Fondation Heinrich Bölland Rabat Social Studies Institute, 2017). His publications are found in several international academic journals and edited books.

Merouan Mekouar is Associate Professor in the Department of Social Science at York University, Canada. Most of his writing has focused on social movements, authoritarianism and democratisation in the Middle East and North Africa (MENA), as well as the diffusion of social norms. His first book, titled *Protest and Mass Mobilization: Authoritarian Collapse and Political Change in North Africa*, was published by Routledge in 2016. He has received numerous awards and grants including the Abner Kingman Fellowship, the German Academic Exchange Service (DAAD) Grant, the Social Sciences and Humanities Research Council of Canada (SSHRC) Connection Grant, SSHRC Small Fund, York University Faculty Association Teaching Grant and the Faculty of Liberal Arts and Professional Studies Seed Grant, among others.

Curtis R. Ryan is a Professor of Political Science at Appalachian State University in North Carolina. He has written extensively on international relations in the Middle East, on inter-Arab relations and alliance politics, and on Jordanian domestic politics and foreign policy. He has published articles in several reviews, including, among others, *Middle East Journal*, *Middle East Policy*, *British Journal of Middle East Studies* and *Middle East Review of International Affairs*, and online with *Foreign Policy*, the *Washington Post* and *Middle East Report Online*. Dr Ryan is also the author of three books: *Jordan in Transition: From Hussein to Abdullah* (2002), *Inter-Arab Alliances: Regime Security and Jordanian Foreign Policy* (2009) and, most recently, *Jordan and the Arab Uprisings: Regime Survival and Politics beyond the State* (2018).

Ronald Bruce St John is an independent scholar specialising in the political economies of developing states. He has served as a commentator on Alhurra TV, Al Jazeera International, BBC World Service, CNN News and NBC News, as well as as a consultant to the US government and several Fortune 500 companies. He has published twenty-five books and monographs and contributed to thirty-four others, and has authored more than 400 articles and reviews. Recent publications include *Libya: Continuity and Change* (2nd edition, 2015) and *Libya: From Colony to Revolution* (3rd edition, 2017).

Ala'a Shehabi is the Deputy Director of the Institute for Global Prosperity at University College London. She is a trans-disciplinary researcher working on alternative ways of thinking about development and prosperity in the Middle East. Most recently she was the co-investigator for the Citizen Assembly on Energy Justice in Lebanon and sits on the planning committee for the Social Science Research Council's Transregional Collaboratory on the Indian Ocean. She is the co-editor of *Bahrain's Uprising: Resistance and Repression in the Gulf* (2015).

Özgün E. Topak is an Associate Professor in the Department of Social Science at York University, Canada, where he is primarily affiliated with the Criminology undergraduate programme and the Socio-legal Studies graduate programme. His degrees are from Istanbul University (BA), the Middle East Technical University of Turkey (MA) and Queen's University of Canada (Ph.D.). Dr Topak is an interdisciplinary social scientist interested in topics of surveillance, authoritarianism, migration and human rights. He has published extensively in these areas. He was awarded the 2019 Surveillance Studies Network Early Career Researcher Prize, and is currently an Associate Editor of *Surveillance & Society*.

Robert Uniacke is a political analyst and researcher specialising in authoritarian politics, disinformation and civil–military relations in the Arab World – primarily in the Gulf, Libya and Tunisia. He holds an MA in Arab Studies from Georgetown University's Center for Contemporary Arab Studies. His work on online authoritarian strategies in the Gulf has appeared in the *British Journal of Middle Eastern Studies*.

ACKNOWLEDGEMENTS

This work was supported by a grant (number 611-2019-0360) from the Social Sciences and Humanities Research Council of Canada. We would like to thank the Department of Social Science and the Faculty of Liberal Arts and Professional Studies at York University for their support. We would also like to acknowledge the helpful comments of the editorial team and the anonymous reviewers selected by Edinburgh University Press. Last, but certainly not least, we especially wish to acknowledge the outstanding work completed by our contributors. All were exceptionally patient with us throughout the three years needed to complete this project. We are truly grateful for their commitment, the thoughtful comments shared during our discussion workshop, and their excellent research.

FOREWORD

May Darwich

When Mohammed Bouazizi, in late December 2010, set himself alight in front of the governorate of Sidi Bouzid in Tunisia, sparking revolutions across the Arab world, euphoria and wishful thinking spread that the Middle East and North Africa was finally on the path to a democratic transition. A decade later, it has become evident that the Arab uprisings were not only more complex and bloodier than initially expected, but that they set the region even further away from democratisation. If anything, the 2009 Green Movement in Iran, the 2011 Arab uprisings and the 2013 Gezi protests in Turkey resulted either in states collapsing and descending into civil wars, or in authoritarian regimes surviving waves of protests, calibrating their tools of repression and holding a tighter grip over their societies. This substantial authoritarian reversal was only possible through a combination of traditional means of repression and innovative techniques for controlling younger generations relying on Twitter, WhatsApp and Facebook for social and political dissent. People, activists and academics are more than ever disillusioned with the prospects of democratisation in the Middle East and North Africa, relentlessly emerging as a region in transition to 'nowhere'.

The year 2011 was not the first instance of scholarship looking for signs of transformation of the MENA region into models of Western liberal democracies. During the heyday of Modernisation Theory in the 1950s, scholars looked at MENA as a region on the path to catching up with liberal models. However, this optimism was confronted with the depressing reality of outbreaks of civil wars, cold wars, coups d'état, and abolition of multi-party systems in favour of either absolute monarchies or single-party systems. In the 1990s, scholarship moved to focus on detecting early signs of democratisation, as it was believed that MENA would soon follow Eastern Europe and Latin America. High and optimistic expectations during the 1990s were soon replaced with disappointment and frustration. The Middle East seems to go in full-circle movements between hopes for democratisation and authoritarian retrenchment in a one-step-forward, two-steps-backward pattern. For decades, social scientists were concerned with the question of why the Middle East remained resistant to democratisation despite waves of changes, often implying some sort of uniqueness about the region. 'Robustness', 'resilience', 'endurance', 'durability' and 'upgrade' of authoritarianism have become timeless keywords in the study of the MENA region.

Instead of going along with this rather pessimistic account of authoritarianism in the MENA region as doomed to wander in futile circles, it is in both change and continuity that authoritarianism can be studied, examined and assessed. The recent flow of democratic changes followed by ebbs of authoritarianism does not imply that the last decade should be written off as a pure replay of past waves dismissed for not having lived up to their hope. Transitions are far from linear processes. Through a systematic study of authoritarian practices, old and new, the essays collected in this volume illuminate elements of continuity and change in authoritarian strategies to curb social and political dissent in the MENA region and show that authoritarian survival is often a process of change and counter-change. While there are structural conditions making the MENA region a fertile ground for authoritarian survival – such as external alliances, economic inequalities, civil–military relations – regimes also adopt micro-practices of repression. These practices are often vital in quashing dissent, controlling societies, and curbing demands for equality, human rights and freedom. New forms of protest, social media activism and critical journalism have evolved with the advent of technological advancement and globalisation. Yet, authoritarian regimes have equally adapted and learned innovative techniques to ensure their survival. Authoritarian regimes are now supressing growing dissent using not only physical violence, coercion and traditional surveillance, but also digital surveillance on social media, malicious software, mobilisation of troll armies and dissemination of fake news. This volume is a testament that focusing solely on the structural conditions of authoritarianism in the MENA region does not capture authoritarian reversals in the region. Instead, a study of the micro-dynamics of 'everyday authoritarianism' provides a window into the machinery of authoritarian survival and resilience across the region. The study of micro-practices of authoritarianism shows that global capitalism is at the heart of authoritarian globalisation, making the region appear far from exceptional. Authoritarian regimes in MENA survived as they relied on experiences from their past, learned from each other, and acquired innovative technologies from China, Russia and Israel.

The contributions in this edited book, covering many countries across the Levant, the Gulf, the Arabian Peninsula and North Africa, discuss the histories and legacies of current authoritarian practices and trace the innovations over time. These authoritarian practices are present across various countries regardless of the diversity in the regime type, the degree of pluralism and the presence (or lack thereof) of strong state institutions. Authoritarian practices are not akin to purely autocratic regimes, but they are also present in pluralistic regimes, such as Morocco, Jordan, Tunisia, Iraq, Turkey and the Palestinian Occupied Territories. In these contexts, the regimes combined some 'old' authoritarian practices including physical violence with some refashioned authoritarian practices using new digital surveillance tools. The non-pluralistic regimes, such as Egypt, Saudi Arabia, the United Arab Emirates, Iran, Sudan and Algeria, have exhibited a more intensive use of traditional means of physical repression, but innovative techniques and practices were also used to cope with younger generations with growing demands for freedom, social equality and economic redistribution. Some of the contributions in the volume also show that authoritarian practices are not only present in countries with a predominant regime in power. Authoritarian practices outlive authoritarian regimes. In cases of regime collapse, as in Libya and Yemen, authoritarian practices continue to haunt their societies; rival actors inherit and adopt these practices in trying to take control of territories and societies. In their quest for survival, MENA regimes have intensified the use of traditional practices and upgraded the apparatus of repression by integrating innovative techniques to cope with dissent.

The volume presents how MENA regimes exhibited high manoeuvrability in dealing with recurring protests, dissent and contestation. Authoritarian practices were revised, recalibrated and re-invented to ensure the survival of regimes in power. Authoritarian regimes have traditionally relied on the police, surveillance and the law to intimidate and criminalise dissent. Various contributions highlight the central role of police forces in quashing dissent and ensuring control over the masses. Various processes of police profes-sionalisation that took place across the MENA region in the past decade did not translate into 'reforms', and instead allowed the regimes to rebrand their tools in facing growing dissent relying on technology and social media. The chapters on Algeria, Egypt, Turkey, the UAE, Saudi Arabia and Israel show how police forces are often the regimes' first line of defence during moments of protest. Even in highly polarised societies – Yemen and Libya – police forces become autonomous actors used by rival factions in the civil conflict. In addition, authoritarian practices are often couched in judicial and legal laws. Repression, physical violence and imprisonment are legalised under the state of emergency, repressive laws and the suspension of human rights laws. During the last decade, MENA regimes have adapted and re-invented their judicial tools to cope with innovative modes of dissent. Various contributions show that MENA regimes re-invented their judicial practices, by adopting new, repressive internet, media and civil society laws, for example. Also, the regimes adopted digital surveillance techniques to cope with new forms of communication and collaboration facilitating social and political dissent. These practices vary from internet shutdown and censorship to new forms of surveillance and control, such as new hacking tools and software, new inter-net laws criminalising dissent, new restrictions for digital platforms — such as Facebook, Twitter and WhatsApp — and the use of predictive analytics to monitor and shape public feelings and activities.

The deployment of new authoritarian practices in the MENA region is far from exceptional. These practices are embedded in international trends in technology and data proliferation, showing the dark face of globalisation at the service of authoritarian diffusion. By tracing those new authoritarian practices, the volume shows how technologies combined with judicial meas-ures have created robust authoritarian survival, and should this technology exist elsewhere in the absence of the rule of law and accountability, similar authoritarian dynamics would evolve.

Authoritarianism has been a perpetuating and reproducing structure that has defined not only structural conditions in MENA but also the everyday lives of its people, who have endured repression, imprisonment, persecution, exile and estrangement. Scholars of MENA authoritarianism have come to take for granted the notion that the spread of democracy in the region will come in waves with bursts of progress. Henceforth, during waves of protest and contestation, scholars focus on elements of change, and during periods of ensuing frustration and disappointment scholarship has been very much regime-centred and has devoted most attention to the structural conditions of authoritarian durability. This edited collection offers a path in revisiting the authoritarian resilience paradigm in the study of MENA. Authoritarian regimes not only survive waves of change due to external alliances, control over resources and military dominance, but they also survive through adaptation, learning, and mixing both traditional and innovative techniques of repression and surveillance to control their populations. Authoritarian regimes are flexible in using their repression tools, amenable to changes, and adaptable to containing new forms of dissent and protests. The focus on everyday authoritarian practices provides a window into the durable nature of authoritarianism in the MENA region beyond any fallacies of exceptionalism.

Change versus continuity, revolutionary waves versus authoritarian reversal, old versus innovative repressive techniques – these themes define the experiences, aspirations and disappointments of people in the MENA region. With perceptiveness and authority, this edited volume presents an outstanding coverage of old and new authoritarian practices across the MENA region. The essays collected here illuminate the new practices of authoritarianism and place them in the context of the history of the region, establishing their resonance and relevance to future research on authoritarianism.

1

INTRODUCTION: NEW AUTHORITARIAN PRACTICES IN THE MENA REGION: KEY DEVELOPMENTS AND TRENDS

Özgün E. Topak, Merouan Mekouar and Francesco Cavatorta

Introduction

The brutal murder of the Saudi dissident journalist Jamal Khashoggi in October 2018 and the events leading up to his death illustrate the combined use of traditional and new authoritarian practices in the Middle East and North Africa (MENA). On 2 October 2018 Khashoggi entered the Istanbul Consulate of Saudi Arabia where he was tortured, killed and his body dismembered. Research by the University of Toronto's Citizen Lab (2018, 2019) and statements made by Omar Abdulaziz (Loveday and Zakaria 2018), another Saudi dissident and friend of Khashoggi, showed the key role played by Pegasus, a malicious tracking software developed by the Israel-based NSO Group, in the events leading to the murder of the Saudi journalist. The investigation Citizen Lab conducted showed that Abdulaziz's phone was infected with the spyware, which would have allowed Saudi officials to access his private conversations with his contacts, including Khashoggi. Abdulaziz revealed that he was in regular phone contact with Khashoggi about organising social media activism to counter the influence of Saudi pro-government trolls on the internet.

Extra-judicial killings of dissidents, alongside surveillance, imprisonment, intimidation, torture and ill-treatment of dissidents, as well as other practices to suppress dissent and control activists, opposition parties, the judiciary and the media, have long existed in the region. The chapters in this book demonstrate that, even if they may not be as spectacularly violent as in the Khashoggi killing, many MENA regimes continue to deploy tried-and-tested authoritarian practices to control society and suppress dissent. However, these historically-established practices have also been refashioned, often in innovative ways, by MENA regimes to respond to growing dissent in their societies. These refashioned authoritarian practices are often enabled by new digital surveillance tools. While the killing of Khashoggi, which combines murder and dismemberment with digital spying, is one of the most shocking examples of the mixed nature of contemporary authoritarian practices, other MENA regimes are also increasingly relying on new digitally-based authoritarian practices such as social media surveillance, the use of malicious software, the mobilisation of troll armies and dissemination of fake news on broadcast and social media. As a result, MENA regimes often use a mix of historically-established practices and new authoritarian ones in conjunction with one another to form what Topak (2019; this book 2022) calls an 'authoritarian assemblage'. This, for instance, combines police violence against street protesters with surveillance of dissenters on social media. Repressive legislation, some of which has long existed and some of which is newly made, may also be deployed to criminalise offline and online dissent, thus complementing the other elements of the assemblage.

The various contributions of this book show that established authoritarian practices have not disappeared. Rather, they continue haunting their societies and can be redeployed, often in combination with new practices, whenever local regimes need to use them. A case in point is the state of emergency, an age-old instrument employed in Egypt, Sudan, Turkey and Tunisia, which is used again to allow for the deployment of historically-established practices (e.g. purges in state bureaucracy and civil society) but also new ones (e.g. repressive internet surveillance). In some extreme cases, emergency rule is embedded in the very fabric of social life and empowered with new digital practices. A key example from the book is Israel's practices in the Occupied Palestinian Territories (OPT). MENA regimes can also articulate various excuses (some long-existing, some new), such as a coup attempt, a security threat or the Covid-19-induced health crisis, to legitimise these practices. Thus 'old' authoritarian practices remain part of the authoritarian toolbox of MENA regimes, to be redeployed whenever there is a need to suppress emerging threats of dissent or whenever new technological advances make them more potent. For instance, while Morocco has used sexual blackmailing in the past to intimidate activists or force political concessions from members of the opposition, new digital tools expanded the regime's ability to access private material and use 'revenge-porn' (*The Economist* 2021) to hurt its opponents (from this book see Maghraoui 2022). Thus, the 'new' practices highlighted in this book are not necessarily novel. New forms of dissent (such as social media activism) are met with new practices of repression (such as social media surveillance and troll armies) but also with old-established ones (jailing, torture and murder) as well as with assemblages combining various old and new repressive tools.

These mechanics of repression/dissent and the accompanying deployment of authoritarian assemblages can be observed clearly in the responses MENA regimes provided to the various episodes of social protest that have emerged in the region since the early 2000s. The book chapters demonstrate that MENA regimes have upgraded and intensified their use of authoritarian practices in response to these movements, including the 2009 Green Movement in Iran, the 2011 Arab Uprising and the 2013 Gezi protests in Turkey. In fact, even Tunisia, the birthplace of the 2011 Arab uprisings, has seen its democratic institutions muzzled by the country's president in July 2021. Other countries in the region either failed to consolidate their tentative democratic steps or became scenes of brutal civil wars such as occurred in Syria, Libya and Yemen. In fact, even during Tunisia's democratic experiment between 2011 and 2021, the quality and depth of the democratic transformation was tainted by residual authoritarian practices, and persisting 'authoritarian nostalgia' for past practices (see Cimini 2022 in this book). The survival of authoritarian practices across the MENA region illustrates how regime type might not necessarily tell us very much about the intensity, variety and depth of the broader apparatus of repression and how social and political dissent is dealt with.

The very term 'authoritarian practices' deceptively suggests that the tools and discourses of repression discussed in this book relate only to authoritarian regimes. Although the intensity and depth of such practices might indeed be stronger in authoritarian states, the contributions in this book clearly illustrate that they are present across regimes. In addition to Tunisia, it is apparent that the authoritarian assemblage has survived in Iraq, as Costantini explains in her chapter. While the Iraqi political system is pluralistic and 'free', dissent is still largely dealt with through the widespread use of violence usually accompanied by new practices of repression. The same is also true in Turkey, where the nominally pluralistic political system is not immune – far from it – to the use of authoritarian practices to stamp out dissent and prevent challenges against the dominant AKP and its leader. Although Morocco cannot be defined as a democratic country, it still has a pluralistic political system that, since the arrival of Mohammed VI to the throne, has attempted to present an image of progressive liberalisation and democratisation. It is true that the monarch is still the real wielder of power, but it had seemed to many that the style of governance and the use of authoritarian practices that Hassan II had employed were consigned to history. This has only partially been the case. While there have not been episodes of widespread indiscriminate violence, the Moroccan regime has adapted traditional authoritarian practices and added new ones to its survival toolkit. For its part, Israel has been central to both the employment and the export of new tools of authoritarian control. In addition to testing such instruments and practices in the Occupied Palestinian Territories (OPT), the Israeli authorities have increasingly used some of them at home against Israeli citizens and, crucially, exported them to a number of countries in the region, suggesting that historical rivalries might not be as important as previously thought. The non-pluralistic regimes of Saudi Arabia, Bahrain, the United Arab Emirates (UAE), Iran and Egypt display, of course, more intense authoritarian practices because they do not have to deal with domestic pluralism – not even a façade pluralism – and do not worry much about projecting liberal legitimacy abroad, although, in somewhat different ways ranging from the creation of a loyal civil society in Iran to the extensive use of social media surveillance in Saudi Arabia, these regimes have been able to efficiently marry older practices solidly based on the threat and use of physical force with newer practices of control usually aimed at monitoring and discrediting dissidents. Finally, states in transition or in the throes of civil war – scenarios where one would have expected fissures and flux – have also been at the forefront of both new and old authoritarian practices, even though, as in the case of Yemen and Libya, it might not be a sovereign state, or only a state actor implementing them. In these contexts where national sovereignty no longer exists, authoritarian practices are 'simply' put in place in specific enclaves by rival actors who try to dominate and rule the territory they control.

From the analyses that all the contributors have put forward, two points emerge clearly. The first is that, regardless of regime types, authoritarian practices are increasing and being adapted to the necessities of the regimes in place. It follows quite clearly that regime type is not really an indicator of authoritarian practices, although their intensity and depth may indeed vary according to regime type. The second point is that the Israel case indicates that authoritarian practices are not the monopoly of Muslim majority states and are therefore disconnected from the orientalist cultural explanations that see Islam as the root of all that is wrong in the MENA region. Furthermore, it should be emphasised that Western geopolitical interests in the region have fuelled authoritarian practices. These interests have led to imperialist and (neo)colonialist interventions, Western support for MENA authoritarian regimes, and the implementation of increasingly authoritarian border control practices at the Europe/MENA border areas to prevent refugees from reaching Western territories (see e.g. Gregory 2004; Brownlee 2012; Khalili 2012; Topak 2014; Yom 2016; Lemberg-Pedersen 2019).

Objectives of the Book

This edited collection provides the first comprehensive, systematic and comparative assessment of new authoritarian practices in the MENA region. This book's explicit focus on authoritarian practices provides a more balanced view of the structural and macro-institutional factors explaining the persistence of authoritarian rule in the MENA region. In explaining such persistence in the post-2011 uprising context, the bulk of the scholarship has focused on the mechanisms that have allowed the majority of regimes in the MENA to remain insulated from the demands for greater political pluralism, accountability and, crucially, economic opportunities (Teti et al. 2019). These macro-level and structural mechanisms include rent distribution (Brynen et al. 2013), elite co-optation (Brynen and Mekouar 2013; Mekouar 2014), foreign alliances (Heydemann and Leenders 2011; Yom and Gause 2012), the military's political role (Koehler 2017), the strength of the coercive apparatus (Bellin 2012; Mekouar 2017), the use of sectarianism by the ruling elites (Mathiesen 2013), the role of Islamists in politics (Seniguer 2017), the rules supporting voting procedures (Brown 2013) and inequalities generated by neoliberalism (Tuğal 2016). While such studies are necessary, there is a tendency to under-emphasise specific authoritarian practices targeting social dissent. The constant necessity to revisit the paradigm of authoritarian resilience (Anderson 2006; Hinnebusch 2006; Heydemann 2007) would not be so pressing if it were not for the recurrent and widespread outbursts of protests, usually rooted in demands for greater socio-economic benefits, individual freedoms and collective rights (Chalcraft 2016).

This is a paradox that needs to be better engaged with, because macro-level and structural factors do not alone capture the rapidity and intensity with which social dissent (via street protests, critical journalism, social media activism or in other ways) demanding human rights, democracy and social change are met by regimes in the region with specific authoritarian practices. It is thus necessary to examine the micro-practices of repression and the specific innovative means that are employed to quell dissent in their respective contexts. What are the specific practices that are employed? What are the historical continuities and discontinuities in authoritarian practices? What are the new authoritarian practices? In what ways do new laws, technologies, actors and platforms enable such practices? It is by focusing on micro-practices of repression that this book aims at explaining how authoritarian regimes are *in fine* able to remain in power despite widespread social discontent and opposition, and how pluralistic regimes respond to the challenges of dissent. This emphasis on the micro-practices of authoritarianism is informed by Foucault's call to study power in its micro-physical forms. Foucault advanced the idea that rather than being something that is simply possessed by powerful groups or structures, power should be analysed as something that operates through specific 'dispositions, maneuvers, tactics, techniques' (Foucault 1991: 26).

MENA regimes implement authoritarian practices in their own particular ways, which the readers will find in individual chapters. However, there are also commonalities in the types of practices, their trajectories, and their aims and consequences. The following section presents an overview of these commonalities.

Established Authoritarian Practices

The MENA scholarship has examined in great detail the long and painful histories of wars, massacres, occupations, torture, political trials and imprisonments, abusive policing and surveillance, *mukhabarat* (secret police) activities, extra-judicial killings, enforced disappearances, and other practices violating human rights, particularly of dissidents and minorities in the region (e.g. Abdel-Malek 1968; Zureik 1979; Heydemann 2000; Sassoon 2011; Guirguis 2017). These practices of 'the coercive apparatus' (Bellin 2004) were conducted by various military, police, paramilitary, surveillance and intelligence agents, and left an enduring mark in MENA societies (e.g. Khalili and Schwedler 2010; Golkar 2015). Indeed, they are not things of the past; they persist, even if under different formats and through different mediums.

Thus, different contributions in this book discuss the histories, legacies and current operations of these established authoritarian practices. In Bahrain, Shehabi (2022) shows how the British colonial tradition of repression has continued from the violent response to the 1960s March Intifada to the response to the 2011 uprisings with arbitrary arrests, political show trials, torture and extra-judicial killings of protesters. In the UAE, Davidson (2022) discusses the historical continuities in authoritarian practices by emphasising in particular the UAE's – still in force – 1980 Law on Governing Publications and Publishing and its contemporary implications for press censorship. Davidson also notes the continuation of more 'straightforward coercive tactics' (Davidson 2022: 5) such as arrests and imprisonments of political dissidents. In the Qatar chapter, Liloia discusses Qatar's long reliance on preventive authoritarian practices to maintain the status quo and 'to limit the development of an active civil society' (Liloia 2022: 10). In Saudi Arabia, Khashoggi's brutal extra-judicial killing illustrates the intensification and redeployment of specific authoritarian practices. While Saudi Arabia has a long history of executing members of the opposition domestically, the Khashoggi murder in Istanbul and the targeting of dissidents abroad illustrate how established authoritarian practices have continued and even intensified in new ways under the command of the Crown Prince Mohammed bin Salman (MbS). An example is MbS's new 'al-Ajrab' security force, which, in combination with other security and intelligence services, has targeted dissidents and opposing intellectuals, journalists, women's rights activists, royals and oligarchs with mass arrests and detention (Uniacke 2022: 5).

In her chapter on Israel/Palestine, Dayan shows the continuation of warfare against civilian populations in the Occupied Palestinian Territories (OPT) with mass incarcerations, arbitrary detentions and raids, and overall 'routine lethal physical violence and destruction' (Dayan 2022: 7). In Iran, Golkar identifies the Basij force, an extensive para-statal organisation founded by Ayatollah Khomeini in 1981, as the primary actor of established authoritarian practices and discusses the deepening of its social control powers in response to the post-2009 Green Movement (Golkar 2022). In the chapter on Turkey, Topak draws parallels between the 'state of emergency' treatment of Kurdish and leftist dissidents in 1980s and 1990s and the contemporary political trials, purges and imprisonments targeting dissident/opposing

Kurdish politicians, and leftist journalists, academics and civil society leaders by the AKP regime (Topak 2022). With respect to Egypt, Jumet provides a historical overview of established authoritarian practices, through the rules of Presidents Gamal Abdel Nasser, Anwar Sadat and Hosni Mubarak. Like other contributors, she emphasises that the new regime of Abdel Fattah Al-Sisi mobilised and intensified these established practices, including 'press censorship, torture, and enforced disappearances' (Jumet 2022: page X). In Yemen and Libya, Durac and St John both emphasise the continuities in established authoritarian practices (including arrests, kidnapping, torture and assassination of political opponents and espionage) from the pre-2011 context through the post-2011 context, in terms of conflict-ridden and increasingly fragmented sovereignty environments (Durac 2022; St John 2022). In Iraq, Costantini focuses on the continuities in authoritarian practices in post-2003 Iraq despite the fall of Saddam Hussein's brutal regime. She notes that the US invasion of the country led to high levels of civilian deaths and overall political violence. Costantini thus shows that the democratic demands of protesters expressed since the beginning of the Arab uprisings were met with violent authoritarian practices rooted in the past and ranging from targeted killings and disappearances of activists, harassment, arbitrary arrest and detention of independent journalists to censorship of the press (Costantini 2022), reminiscent of those used in previous decades. In Sudan, Hassan examines the brutal authoritarian practices of the Bashir regime which lasted for three decades and ended with the December 2018 uprising. Hassan emphasises that some of the established authoritarian practices of the Bashir regime continued in the transitional period. He notes, for instance, the continuing power of the Rapid Support Forces (RSF), a paramilitary force established by Bashir, in the transitional period, and discusses how the RSF targets and imprisons dissidents (Hassan 2022). In the Jordan chapter, Ryan discusses the continuities in established authoritarian practices, including arrests of dissidents and pressures on the media, alongside the development of new ones, in response to the 2011 protests and the protests which followed them (Ryan 2022).

The Algerian and Moroccan chapters also illustrate how difficult it is for the countries of the region to break away from past authoritarian practices even with a relatively strong commitment from local governments. In Algeria, Derradji and Mekouar's chapter (2022) shows that while the Algerian police sector has been trying to professionalise since the early 2000s, and to move away, with some success, from direct violence against protesters, police violence has persisted (either state-sanctioned or from individual policemen). Similarly, in Morocco, Maghraoui's piece (2022) shows that, despite King Mohamed VI's attempts to distance himself from his father's brutal reign and strengthen the rule of law in the country, the decade following the start of the Arab uprisings witnessed a return to old repressive practices, including the closure of independent media, the jailing of journalists and dissidents, and frivolous lawsuits against activists, as well as 'sexual blackmailing' against critical voices.

Even in Tunisia, the country where the democratic experiment went the furthest in the region, authoritarian practices persist. Despite significant democratic progress since the fall of President Zine El Abidine Benali in 2011, the loss of trust in the political system, the growing economic crisis and the country's security challenges have opened the way for what Cimini (2022) refers to as authoritarian nostalgia. This is not simply a popular feeling about the fact that 'things were better under Ben Ali', but something that is transformed into a set of practices rooted in the authoritarian past to deal with current challenges. The persistence of heavy-handed police repression of demonstrations, and arbitrary arrests of activists and bloggers, as well as the July 2021 suspension of parliament by the country's president, illustrates how difficult it is to break away from authoritarian heritage.

Protests and Policing

The largely unexpected revolt of ordinary people against authoritarian regimes during the Arab uprisings drew attention from political theorists who were not usually interested in the politics of the region. Anticipating a fundamental democratic transformation, many of these scholars made exaggerated and unsubstantiated arguments. Badiou (2012) argued, for instance, that the protests gave rise to 'the rebirth of history' by showing that radical emancipatory alternatives are possible beyond the Fukuyamian end of history. Žižek followed Badiou and described 2011 as 'the year of dreaming dangerously' (2012). Castells (2012) celebrated the use of information and communication technologies (such as Twitter) during the uprisings, emphasising that new technologies are mediums for expressing 'outrage and hope' and creating online as well as offline collectivity. Kaldor (2011) spoke of the Arab world's '1989 moment' in reference to the collapse of communism in Eastern Europe.

The authors of this book do not understate the power of protests for democratic change and creating new forms of collectivity, nor do they imply an inevitability of authoritarianism in the MENA region (Achcar 2013). However, rather than providing assumptions in a top-down manner, they follow a bottom-up approach focusing on the application and development of authoritarian practices before, during and after different episodes of social protest. Thus, chapters of this book discuss the specific authoritarian polic- ing tactics during protests such as the use of tear gas and lethal force and imprisonment of protesters. They also demonstrate how protests served as a catalyst for the expansion of both historically-established and new authoritar- ian practices.

Even though police violence has been a major catalyst of the 2011 pro- tests in Egypt,[1] Tunisia and other countries of the MENA region, and despite some timid attempts at police reform since 2011 (Sayigh 2015, 2016), the professionalisation of the police sector in the MENA region has remained at best incomplete, if not a total failure. In Turkey, for instance, some of the most heightened episodes of police violence (particularly during the Gezi park protests) occurred as the country was hosting European-sponsored pro- grammes aimed specifically at reducing the Turkish police's use of force against civilians (Babül 2013). Later, the powers of the Turkish police to search, arrest, use lethal weapons and conduct surveillance have only increased (see Topak 2022). Even in Tunisia, police–citizen relations have been marred by significant episodes of police brutality, and regular death-while-in-police- custody cases (HRW 2018; Cordall 2021).

Most contributions in this book highlight the central role played by local police forces for authoritarian resilience. In her chapter on Egypt, Jumet examines the role of the police in historical perspective and highlights the continuation (if not intensification) of violent policing tactics going back to President Mubarak's regime. Whereas the police force in Egypt has long been a major tool of for regime resilience, the expansion of its mandate in recent years has increased its direct control of the population. The same can be said about Iraq, where Constantini highlights the continuities of authoritarian practices before and after the fall of Saddam Hussein's regime, as well as Jordan and Morocco, where Curtis and Maghraoui show that local police forces continue to serve as a major stabilising tool for the two monarchies.

Other contributions focus on the expansion of the set of tools at the disposal of local police forces. In countries with high capacity such as the

UAE, Saudi Arabia and Israel, local police forces have been able to deploy and/or benefit from new digital tools while evading judicial oversight. These new capacities allow the police forces to spy on, track, unmask and punish citizens deemed disloyal more easily while better complementing the work of other security forces. In other cases, the formally differentiated role of the police is another tool at the disposal of the regime. In the Iranian chapter, for instance, Golkar emphasises the importance of the police force for the resilience of the Iranian regime. In particular, Golkar shows that the national police is the first line of the regime's defence against would-be opponents and works closely with more ideologically-oriented security forces such as the Basij, whose mandate is less about policing and more concerned with the defence of the regime.

As regards deeply fractured states, the chapters on Yemen and Libya highlight the broken and largely autonomous nature of police forces in post-conflict contexts. In Yemen, as Durac shows, the police forces have split along tribal/sectarian lines while turning into tools at the service of local powerbrokers. The same occurred in Libya, where the collapse of the police sector led to its quasi-disappearance behind local religious militias, ethnic/tribal groups and other local bodies. Finally, even in cases like Algeria, where the professionalisation of the police sector seems to have been conducted in earnest, Derradji and Mekouar show that the purpose of the professionalisation was not to consolidate the country's democratic institutions, but reduce the risks linked to uncontrolled social protests sparked by police brutality. Far from being an institution at the service of the people, the professionalised Algerian police are instead another tool at the service of the regime.

Legalising Authoritarian Practices

Authoritarian practices have an intimate relationship with law: they are often either legalised and facilitated by repressive laws or made possible through the suspension of human rights laws. Indeed, critical scholarship has long emphasised that exceptional authoritarian practices which violate human rights can be legalised under situations of a state of emergency, which not only includes situations of war, coups or public health crises, but may include any fabricated threats to 'national security' such as public dissent or the sole existence of a minority group (Agamben 2005). In some regimes, such 'exceptional' logic is deeply embedded in the system of sovereign rule, in which case there is not even a need to rely on emergency situations, rationales and justifications. As with other authoritarian practices, the embeddedness, as well as the broad and arbitrary implementation of states of exception and repressive laws, are not unique to the MENA region. However, they have a long history in various MENA regimes (e.g. Abujidi 2009; Bezci and Öztan 2016; Ardovini and Mabon 2020), and are increasingly becoming the norm in the post-uprisings environments (e.g. Capasso 2013; Topak 2017; Pratt and Rezk 2019). Thus, many chapters of this book examine the implementation of new repressive security, internet, media and civil society laws, either under conditions of formally declared states of emergency or more generalised systems of autocratic rule.

In the chapter on Egypt, Jumet (2022) first examines the state of emergency declarations and their facilitation of authoritarian practices and human rights violations by the Sadat and Mubarak regimes. She later focuses on the contemporary Al-Sisi regime's reliance on state of emergency powers and Emergency State Security Courts to criminalise dissent. Jumet also emphasises that the new 2015 Anti-Terror law further broadened the definition of terror (even compared to the previous law of the Mubarak regime) and enabled increased repression of dissidents and the media. In the chapter on Turkey, Topak (2022) examines the implications of the 2016 state of emergency rule, declared by the current AKP regime in response to the Gulenist coup attempt. He demonstrates how under Erdogan's command the AKP regime used the coup attempt as an excuse to broadly criminalise dissent and further increase pressures on the media and civil society. He notes how the transition to a presidential system solidified the state of emergency rule, thus turning the state of emergency into a more generalised regime of governance. Other examined cases of state of emergency include chapters on Sudan and Tunisia. Hassan (2022) examines the furthering of authoritarian practices enabled by Bashir's declaration of a state of emergency in response to the 2018 protests. In the Israel/Palestine chapter, Dayan discusses the extreme levels of legalised authoritarian violence perpetrated by the IDF in the OPT against Palestinian populations. Dayan draws on Fraenkel's concept of the 'Prerogative State' which is characterised by extreme violence in the absence of human rights laws.

Many other book chapters discuss the wide application of anti-terror laws to criminalise the regime's critics as a normalised form of legal violence. For instance, Uniacke discusses the amended 2014 counter-terror law of Saudi Arabia which considers acts including 'disrupting public order', 'harming the security and stability of the community', 'risking national unity' and 'harming the reputation or status of the country' as terror acts (Uniacke 2022: x). Many other chapters also discuss new laws designed in the aftermath of the 2011 uprisings to restrict protest rights, such as Egypt's 2013 Protest Law and Turkey's 2015 Internal Security Package. Internet and social media are other venues which are increasingly subject to repressive laws. In addition to Turkey's and Egypt's repressive internet laws, there are various other examples in the book. For instance, Davidson discusses the UAE's 2012 federal Law on Combating Cybercrimes, and Liloia discusses Qatar's 2014 Cybercrime law and its 2020 security amendment. Not all repressive laws are new. As with other established authoritarian practices, many existing laws were refashioned and re-applied to respond to increasing dissent in MENA societies. For instance, Liloia and Davidson respectively discuss the contemporary repressive application of Qatar's 1979 Publications and Publishing Law of 1979 and the UAE's 1980 Law on Governing Publications and Publishing.

Authoritarian Practices Shaping Civil Society and the Media

Due to the weakness of political parties, authoritarian rulers have traditionally focused their attention on civil society as the main site of potential dissent. It is for this reason that, since the 1990s, MENA regimes have begun to sponsor organisations and associations favourable to their policies, while infiltrating and harassing genuine oppositional ones (Wiktorowicz 2002). In particular, the 2011 uprisings showed that demands for greater rights and democratic reforms coming from civil society in the post-2011 uprisings period could no longer be countered simply through brute force or through the mobilisation of pro-regime actors. Thus, the regimes of the region engaged in much greater efforts to create a loyalist civil society, which does not solely comprise ad hoc organisations and actors as in the past. These new efforts seek to place the whole of society at the service of the goals – and the ultimate survival – of the regime, recalling the early days of totalitarianism. This is most evident in the Iranian case, as Golkar outlines clearly in his chapter. Through the concept of 'deep society', he explains how the mobilisation of pro-regime organisations results in a wide network demanding 'allegiance' to the rulers because every aspect of the life of individual Iranians comes to depend on this. Another notable example from the book is the Bashir's Tamkeen policy in Sudan. This policy used tactics ranging from purges to economic pressures to create a fully loyalist state bureaucracy and civil society, including private businesses. Although not to the same extent, similar processes are at work in other MENA regimes, where, on the one hand, oppositional civil society organisations are pressured by the regime and, on the other, loyalist organisations are created or supported. As with other authoritiaran practices, the depth and durability of such efforts should not be overstated. Consider that Bashir was ousted despite his three-decade Tamkeen policy, even though he left an extremely weak civil society as a legacy.

A specific authoritarian practice aimed at shaping civil society is informant surveillance or snitching. In this respect 'civil society' is a site of denunciation of suspected regime opponents. Informant surveillance is not a new practice in the region. Notably, the late Ottoman Sultan Abdulhamid II (r. 1876–1909) possessed a very large network of informants and spies across vast parts of today's MENA region (Koloğlu 1987; see Topak 2019: 466–7). While traditional snitching continues (as with Iran's Basij [see Golkar (2022)], in Bahrain [see Shebabi (2022)] or Morocco's *Muqaddem* system – a wide network of government-paid territorial informants), it is the digitally mediated form of snitching that is increasingly applied by pro-regime supporters. Notable examples discussed in the book include the Kulluna Aman ('we are all security') app of Saudi Arabia (Uniacke 2022), the use of Facebook by the GSS (General Security Service) of Israel to recruit informants (Dayan 2022) and the increasing cyber-informant work in Turkey (Topak 2022).

A key indicator of a strong civil society is the existence of an independent media. According to the World Press Freedom Index, the MENA region ranks last in the world in press freedom (RSF 2021). Indeed, different book chapters discuss the persisting and increasing pressures over journalists and media outlets, and other practices intended to fully monopolise information, including through censorship and fake news in respective MENA regimes, and to delegitimise independent journalists. A notable example is Morocco where the regime uses sensationalistic online platforms to settle scores with investigative journalists and intimidate independent voices. Other examples include Qatar, Egypt, Bahrain and Turkey. In the Qatar chapter, Liloia discusses the environment of self-censorhsip in Qatar despite the regime's attempts to promote itself as a progressive state in the MENA region. In the Egypt chapter, Jumet discusses the increasing environment of media censorship and attacks against independent journalists. In the Bahrain chapter, Shebabi notes the spread of fake news by the regime through tactics such as photoshops and false confessions. Topak also discusses the reliance by the regime on fake news to discredit and delegitimise protesters, framing them as against 'national values'. Indeed, the representation of dissidents as traitors to the country or sell-outs to foreign interests is widespread in the state-controlled media in all MENA regimes. Given that the traditional media organisations are controlled by states, many activists and dissidents are turning to social media to access reliable information and to communicate freely. Yet, this sphere is also increasingly controlled by the states, as we examine below.

Digital Surveillance

New digital technologies, particularly the internet, have substantially transformed societies through enabling both new forms of communication and collaboration and invasive state surveillance (Lyon 2001; Gillom and Monahan 2012; Diamond and Plattner 2012). MENA societies are not exempt from this global trend. Indeed, this dual use of digital technologies, and their liberating and constraining dimensions, has been noted by scholars who have examined the uprisings in the region (e.g. Golkar 2011; Lynch 2011; Tufekci 2017). On the one hand, the internet, social media and instant messaging apps have enabled activists to quickly communicate and organise, and share videos showing police brutality (e.g. Arda 2015; Ruijgrok 2017). On the other, activists have been confronted by state-sanctioned internet shutdowns and censorships, and new forms of surveillance and intimidation in social media, some of them leading to arrests and imprisonments. It is, sadly, the latter control dimension that has become dominant in the post-uprisings context. MENA regimes have upgraded their digital surveillance capacities with new technologies, actors, laws and restrictions including the use of new monitoring and hacking tools, mobilisation of trolls in the social media, new internet laws to legalise targeting of dissident users, and new restrictions for digital platforms such as Facebook, Twitter and messaging apps (e.g. Jones 2015, 2019; Topak 2017; 2019; Al-Rawi 2019; Akbari and Gabdulhakov 2019; Saka 2019; Uniacke 2020).

Most chapters in this book discuss these new forms of digital surveillance, applied both in the heat of the uprisings and gradually in their aftermath, as new authoritarian practices. Following Deibert (2015), these practices can be categorised as first, second and third generations of digital controls. First-generation controls are 'defensive' and include blocking access to digital information through filtering systems or outright bans (Deibert 2015: 65–6). Second-generation controls are 'deepening' in that they extend digital surveillance into the very fabric of the society. They include new laws and technologies implemented to expand the surveillance powers of the security agencies to monitor and collect data about dissidents, which may then lead to their arrest and imprisonment (Deibert 2015: 66–7). Third-generation controls are 'offensive' and include the use of hacking tools and mobilisation of pro-regime agents (such as trolls) over social media to target dissidents (Deibert 2015: 68–9).

The book chapters demonstrate that, in their different ways, MENA regimes use one or a combination of these digital control methods. The chapters on the GCC countries provide details about some of the most sophisticated methods of digital surveillance in the MENA region. In the Saudi Arabia chapter, Uniacke (2022) discusses the use of spyware (such as NSO's Pegasus spying software) to target Saudi dissidents, the mobilisation of Twitter bots to silence dissent and disseminate fake news on social media, and the use of the *Kulluna Aman* mobile app to facilitate digital snitching. He further emphasises that the MBS regime aspires to become a global leader in digital surveillance technology, and not only a regime that passively imports surveillance technology from major players such as Israel and China. In the UAE chapter, Davidson discusses the rapid advancement of digital surveillance by the Abu Dhabi regime with the implementation of the 2012 Cybercrime law, the use of advanced spyware technologies and manipulation by Twitter bots (Davidson 2022). In the chapter on Bahrain, Shehabi discusses Bahrain's increasing digital repression capacity and the use of spyware programs, which led to she herself being targeted alongside other dissidents. Shebabi further notes the regime-organised misinformation campaigns, involving bots, on Twitter (Shehabi 2022). In the Qatar chapter, Liloia emphasises the persistent, and even increasing, practices of criminalisation of regime criticism in social media and digital content censorship, despite the regime's attempts to establish itself as a progressive hub in the MENA region (Liloia 2022). For instance, she discusses how the 2014 Cybercrime Prevention Law uses the fight against 'fake news' and protection of Qatar's 'social values' and 'general order' as excuses to target a wide range of dissident views (Liloia 2022).

In the chapter on Turkey, Topak demonstrates that the state's attempts to pre-empt another Gezi-like uprising found their way into the new digital repression tactics of the AKP regime. These include the new internet and cybercrime laws which extended security agencies' surveillance powers, digital content removals, the targeting and imprisonment of dissident social media users, the mobilisation of pro-government trolls and the use of spyware (Topak 2022). Sudan is another context where all three digital forms of controls were implemented. Hassan discusses the now-overthrown Bashir regime's internet blocking and censorship practices alongside more offensive strategies of targeting and hacking dissident users and spreading government propaganda on social media. He notes that the latter practices were organised by the Cyber Jihad unit which was established in the aftermath of the Arab Uprising protests (Hassan 2022). In the Egypt chapter, Jumet traces the development of Egypt's digital surveillance capacities from Mubarak to the Sisi regime. Like other contributors, she emphasises that the mass protests led to the establishment of more pervasive and sophisticated digital surveillance practices of monitoring, targeting and hacking dissidents and targeted blocking of online content. In the chapter on Iran, Golkar discusses how the Islamic Revolutionary Guard Corps (IRGC) was organised to digitally repress the Green Movement from the outset, by shutting down the internet and SMS services, and later blocking access to Twitter and YouTube, among other websites which publish politically sensitive material (Golkar 2022). Golkar also discusses the adoption of more proactive controls by the Iranian regime through the creation of new units (such as the IRGC Cyber Defense Command and Cyber Basij) to monitor and target dissident users.

In Libya, St John discusses how the post-Gaddafi conflict in Libya was spread to the online sphere. He particularly notes the role of Russian-linked companies in manipulating Libya's information space with fake news and propaganda (St John 2022). In another conflict-ridden setting, Yemen, Durac notes the use of drone surveillance and warfare by opposing actors as a key digital repression mechanism. Other notable practices of digital repression discussed in the book include internet shutdowns in Iraq in response to the wave of protests from 2018, social media monitoring and preventive arrests conducted by the Cybercrime squads of Bab Ezzouar in Algeria, and Morocco's massive deployment of NSO's spying software to intimidate and/ or concoct evidence leading to the incrimination of investigative journalists and dissenting voices.

Finally, the case of Israel is significant for not only the high levels of digital repression practices against Palestinians but also the country's leading role in exporting surveillance technologies to other regimes. In her chapter,

Dayan builds on Zureik et al. (2011) to emphasise that Israel's surveillance technologies, including biometrics, drones and spywares, were first 'tried-and-tested' in the OPT and later exported to other authoritarian regimes in the region, through companies such as the NSO group.

Authoritarian Learning and Alliances

There is a large literature examining the international dimension of authoritarianism in the Arab world (Brownlee 2007, 2012; Cavatorta 2009). Both authoritarian states and democracies in fact have tended to support authoritarianism to ensure 'stability'. Whether out of economic, strategic or ideological interests, the United States, Russia, the European Union and China have all preferred to avoid the potential pitfalls of democratisation and have been reluctant to prevent the tools and technologies of control from reaching authoritarian regimes in the region.

This emerges quite clearly in the chapters in this book. The cases of Bahrain and the UAE are notable for demonstrating the employment of former officers of Western armies and intelligence services. The cases of Libya and Yemen are significant for showing the involvement of global and regional powers in MENA conflicts through supporting their preferred sides with warfare and surveillance tools. Many chapters note that the monitoring and hacking tools provided by Western and Israeli companies, such as Finisher/FinSpy (provided by a German company), Sandvine (an American/Canadian Company) and Pegasus (an Israeli company), find their ways into the hands of the MENA regimes, such as in Morocco, Egypt, Turkey, the UAE and Saudi Arabia. Other examples include the international diplomatic cover for MENA regimes for their repressive activities (the cases of Morocco and Jordan are particularly telling). These examples underline that MENA regimes develop their practices while embedded in an international network of alliances.

In addition, authoritarian regimes in the region have often collaborated with and learned from each other, ensuring therefore that innovative practices can be transferred easily from one regime to the other. Shortly after the 2011 uprisings, Heydemann and Leenders (2011) argued convincingly that Arab authoritarian regimes had been learning from one another regarding what worked and what did not in containing social protests. Since then, this process of authoritarian learning as a pillar of authoritarian resilience has further deepened. The involvement of the GCC Peninsula Shield Force

(GCCPS), which is composed of troops from Saudi Arabia and the UAE, in suppressing the protests in Bahrain is a striking example of direct collaboration in the GCC. Another notable example is the involvement of regional powers (Saudi Arabia, the UAE, Iran and Turkey) in conflicts in the MENA (such as in Yemen and Libya), alongside international actors. Interestingly, Israel has become a crucial nexus of authoritarian learning. Through its leading role in the development and export of surveillance technologies, and the brutal practices it has deployed in the OPT, Israel enjoys a position of 'privilege' in the new authoritarian practices that Arab countries have put in place.

Gender and the Double-authoritarian Burden

Scholars have established a correlation between authoritarianism and increased forms of gender-based violence and discrimination (e.g. Al-Ali 2019; Adra et al. 2020). Discriminatory attitudes towards women are by no means limited to the MENA region. Authoritarian or semi-authoritarian countries such as Russia, where President Putin successfully watered down laws protecting women (Thornton 2021), India, where President Modi fought against provisions to criminalise marital rape (ibid.; Rana 2015), and the Philippines, where President Duterte encouraged troops to rape 'up to three women with impunity' (Beinart 2019), have all exhibited violent attitudes towards women. Even in the European Union, authoritarian-leaning member states such as Poland and Hungary have been successful in scaling back women's rights (Baczynska 2021), and in liberal Western states gender inequalities and gender-based violence against women persist despite legal improvements.

In the MENA region, women have long faced gender-specific forms of violence. While diverse and changing, and subject to political contestation (see e.g. Hasso and Salime 2016), these forms of violence have intensified in recent years. They include state-sanctioned sexual harassment of female human rights activists during protests, smear campaigns, sexual violence and rape, virginity tests and male-guardianship systems, as well as governmental 'revenge porn', all of which are deployed against women *in addition to* the general set measures targeting the general population. While the nature of gender-based violence is often dependent on the cultural, political and social context of each country, the different contributions in this book show that gender-specific forms of violence target women following two broad logics: *gender-violence as an end*, which is designed to hurt women activists, and *gender-violence as a means to an end*, which targets non-politicised women in order to punish male activists and/or send a message to the general population.

In the Bahrain chapter, Shehabi (2022) shows, for instance, how the government has been using sexual abuse and rape to torture women activists such as Najah Yusif, a civil servant and mother of four who was jailed and raped for protesting against the organisation of a motor-racing event in the country. Similarly, Hassan (2022) examines the 3 June 2019 Khartoum Massacre during which seventy people (the vast majority of them women) were raped by the military in a clear attempt to terrorise the population as a whole. Finally, Morocco remains perhaps one of the countries where gender-based violence as a means to an end has been systematised the most. As Maghraoui (2022) shows, the country's intelligence services routinely invent fake sexual accusations and force women to testify against local activists targeted by the authorities. The regime has also been collecting intimate videos and using revenge porn to punish figures deemed disloyal, and discarding women as mere collateral damage.

Resistance

Despite the ferocity of authoritarian practices in the MENA region, different forms of social resistance continue to exist and even thrive. In some cases, organised forms of protest (such as street marches, strikes and demonstrations) were able to achieve some important victories ranging from the resignation of president Bouteflika in Algeria to the withdrawal of unpopular tax provisions in Jordan. In particularly telling cases such as Iraq, demonstrators were able to achieve important results, such as the resignation of Prime Minister Adil Abdul Mahdi despite fierce pushback from the security forces, who killed more than five hundred protesters in early 2020 (El Yaakoubi and Awadalla 2020). The same argument can be made with respect to Sudan, where brutal cases of state crackdown such as the Khartoum Massacre, during which army soldiers killed 128 protesters (Walsh 2019) and raped seventy men and women (Saliah and Burke 2019), did not break the determination of the local civil society, which has been able to impose major political power-sharing concessions on the army. Social resistance seems, however, to be more muted in cases where state repression is more digitally advanced. In a typical Foucauldian fashion, 'invisible' digital surveillance appears to have disciplinary effects on the entire society, thus pre-empting any revolt.

Finally, while the fairness and independence of elections in the MENA region are questionable, there is nevertheless the potential of electoral victories acting as forces of resistance in more pluralistic regimes. A notable example here is Turkey (Topak 2022). In 2019 the opposition party CHP won the Ankara and Istanbul municipalities, despite efforts by the governing AKP to rig the elections (including through a cancellation and re-run of the Istanbul elections). Yet, neither 'successful' elections nor protests necessarily result in a weakening of the authoritarian practices. As Dayan (2022) notes in her chapter on Israel, the Balfour demonstrations and the replacement of Netanyahu with Bennett are more likely to deepen the authoritarian practices against Palestinians.

Conclusion

The focus the book has placed on authoritarian practices in the MENA is warranted insofar as it contributes to the ongoing debate on authoritarian resilience in the region a decade after the uprisings. However, it should be made clear that the MENA is not an isolated case when it comes to a resurgence of authoritarian practices, both established and new. The contributions in this edited collection have demonstrated that such practices have become an increasing asset to different regime types, and it is therefore crucial to underline that this applies well beyond the MENA region and non-Muslim majority states. As a number of scholars have noted, the last years have seen the resurgence of authoritarianism globally, and the MENA is not an outlier when it comes to the use of authoritarian practices (e.g. Khalili 2012; Kumar 2012; Diamond et al. 2016, Murakami Wood 2017; Hintz and Milan 2018). Authoritarian practices, including the use of excessive force against protesters, mass and indiscriminate surveillance of online activities, torture, secret rendition, indefinite detention, extra-judicial killing, undue pressures on media outlets, and violent treatment of racial, ethnic, religious and gender minorities, women, migrants, refugees and terror suspects, are also adopted by many liberal-democratic states of the West as well as elsewhere. Ironically and tragically, Muslims are one of the major groups of sufferers from authoritarian practices both inside MENA and in Western territories.

While the degree of the intensity of repression and surveillance might change across regime types and across the different regions of the world, the trend is towards the greater use of authoritarian practices as tools for governance. This is is something that should be clearly highlighted, particularly at a time where the Covid-19 pandemic has provided the opportunity for many governments – both authoritarian and pluralistic inside and outside the MENA – to continue or to extend practices that prevent social and political mobilisation. In conclusion, the book should be seen as an attempt to discuss, through the case of MENA countries, the dangerous global trend of the 'convergence of governance' when it comes to monitoring and preventing social and political dissent.

Note

1 The torture and brutal murder of Khalid Said while in police custody in Alexandria in 2010 was, for instance, one of the major catalysts of the 2011 protests in the country.

References

Abdel-Malek, A. (1968). *Egypt: Military Society*. New York: Random House.

Abujidi, N. (2009). 'Palestinian States of Exception and Agamben', *Contemporary Arab Affairs* 2(2): 299–319.

Achcar, G. (2103). *The People Want*. Los Angeles: University of California Press.

Adra, N., N. Al-Ali, S. Farhat, D. Joly, P. Larzillière and N. Pratt (2020). 'Women, Violence and Exiting from Violence with a Gendered Approach: Mena Region and Diaspora', *International Panel on Exiting Violence, hal-02498142*. https://hal.archives-ouvertes.fr/hal-02498142/document

Akbari, A. and R. Gabdulhakov (2019). 'Platform Surveillance and Resistance in Iran and Russia: The Case of Telegram', *Surveillance and Society* 17(1/2): 223–31.

Al-Ali, N. (2019). 'Iraq: Gendering Violence, Sectarianisms and Authoritarianism', in D. Kandiyoti, N. Al-Ali and K. Spellman (eds) *Gender, Governance & Islam*. Edinburgh: Edinburgh University Press.

Al-rawi, a. (2019). 'Cyber Conflict, Online Political Jamming & Hacking in the Gulf Cooperation Council', *International Journal of Communication* 13: 1,301–322.

Anderson, L. (2006). 'Searching Where the Light Shines: Studying Democratization in the Middle East', *Annual Review of Political Science* 9: 189–214.

Arda, B. (2015). 'The Construction of a New Sociality through the Social Media: The Case of Gezi Uprising in Turkey', *Conjunctions* 2(1): 65–99.

Babül, E. (2017). 'Gezi Resistance, Police Violence, and Turkey's Accession to the European Union'. *Jadaliyya*, 7 October. https://www.jadaliyya.com/Detai ls/29604

Baczynska, G. (2021). 'Poland, Hungary Block "Gender Equality" from EU Social

Summit'. Reuters, 7 May. https://www.reuters.com/world/europe/poland-hung arypush-against-gender-equality-eu-social summit-2021-05-07/

Badiou, A. (2012). *The Rebirth of History. Times of Riots and Uprisings*. London: Verso.

Beinart, P (2019). 'The New Authoritarians Are Waging War on Women', *The Atlantic*, January/February. https://www.theatlantic.com/magazine/archive/20 19/01/authoritarian-sexism-trump-duterte/576382

Bellin, E. (2004). 'The Robustness of Authoritarianism in the Middle East: Exceptionalism in Comparative Perspective', *Comparative Politics* 36(2): 139–57.

Bellin, E. (2012). 'Reconsidering the Robustness of Authoritarianism in the Middle East: Lessons from the Arab Spring', *Comparative Politics* 44(2): 127–49.

Bezci, E. B. and Öztan, G. G. (2016). 'Anatomy of the Turkish Emergency State: A Continuous Reflection of Turkish Raison d'État between 1980 and 2002', *Middle East Critique* 25(2): 163–79.

Brown, N. (2013). 'Egypt's Failed Transition', *Journal of Democracy* 24 (4): 45–58.

Brownlee, J. (2007). *Authoritarianism in an Age of Democratization*. Cambridge: Cambridge University Press.

Brownlee, J. (2013). *Democracy Prevention: the Politics of the US–Egyptian Allliance*. Cambridge: Cambridge University Press.

Brynen, R. (2012). *Beyond the Arab Spring: Authoritarianism & Democratization in the Arab World*. Boulder, CO: Lynne Rienner.

Brynen, R., P. W. Moore, B. F. Salloukh and M. J. Zahar (2013). *Beyond the Arab Spring: Authoritarianism and Democracy in the Arab World*. Boulder, CO: Lynne Rienner.

Brynen, R. and M. Mekouar (2013) 'North Africa: Algeria, Egypt, Libya, Morocco, Tunisia', in R. Brynen, P. Moore, B. F. Salloukh and M. J. Zahar (eds) *Beyond the Arab Spring: Authoritarianism and Democratization in the Arab World*. Boulder, CO: Lynne Rienner.

Capasso, M. (2013). 'Understanding Libya's "Revolution" through Transformation of the Jamahiriyya into a State of Exception', *Middle East Critique* 22(2): 115–28.

Cavatorta, F. (2009) *The International Dimension of the Failed Algerian Transition*. Manchester: Manchester University Press.

Chalcraft, J (2016). *Popular Politics in the Making of the Modern Middle East*. Cambridge: Cambridge University Press.

Cimini, G. (2022). 'Authoritarian Nostalgia and Practices in Newly Democratising Contexts: The Localised Example of Tunisia', in Ö. E. Topak, M. Mekouar and F. Cavatorta (eds) *New Authoritarian Practices in the Middle East and North Africa*. Edinburgh: Edinburgh University Press, pp. 276–95.

Citizen Lab (2018). 'The Kingdom Came to Canada. How Saudi-Linked Digital Espionage Reached Canadian Soil'. https://citizenlab.ca/2018/10/the-kingdom-came-to-canada-how-saudi-linked-digital-espionage-reached-canadian-soil/

Citizen Lab (2019). 'The Dangerous Effects of Unregulated Commercial Spyware'. https://citizenlab.ca/2019/06/the-dangerous-effects-of-unregulated-commercial-spyware/

Cordall, S. (2021). 'Protests over Police Violence Spread through Tunisian Capital'. *The Guardian*, 15 June. https://www.theguardian.com/global-development/2021/jun/15/protests-over-police-abuses-continue-in-tunisian-capital

Costantini, I. (2022). 'Silencing Peaceful Voices: Practices of Control and Repression in post-2003 Iraq', in Ö. E. Topak, M. Mekouar and F. Cavatorta (eds) *New Authoritarian Practices in the Middle East and North Africa*. Edinburgh: Edinburgh University Press, pp. 112–30.

Davidson, C. M. (2022). 'The United Arab Emirates: Evolving Authoritarian Tools', in Ö. E. Topak, M. Mekouar and F. Cavatorta (eds) *New Authoritarian Practices in the Middle East and North Africa*. Edinburgh: Edinburgh University Press, pp. 320–39.

Dayan, H. (2022). 'Israel/Palestine: Authoritarian Practices in the context of a Dual State Crisis', in Ö. E. Topak, M. Mekouar and F. Cavatorta (eds) *New Authoritarian Practices in the Middle East and North Africa*. Edinburgh: Edinburgh University Press, pp. 131–51.

Deibert, R. (2015). 'Authoritarianism Goes Global: Cyberspace under Siege', *Journal of Democracy* 26(3): 64–78.

Derradji, I. A. and M. Mekouar (2022). 'Maintaining Order in Algeria: Upgrading Repressive Practices Under a Hybrid Regime', in Ö. E. Topak, M. Mekouar and F. Cavatorta (eds) *New Authoritarian Practices in the Middle East and North Africa*. Edinburgh: Edinburgh University Press, pp. 30–50.

Deutsche Welle (2019). 'Militiamen in Sudan Raped Men and Women, Says Eyewitness'. https://www.dw.com/en/militiamen-in-sudan-raped-men-and-women-says-eyewitness/a-49120693

Diamond, L. and Plattner, M. (2012). *Liberation Technology: Social Media and the Struggle for Democracy*. Baltimore, MD: Johns Hopkins University Press.

Diamond L., M. Plattner and C. Walker (2016) *Authoritarianism Goes Global: The Challenge to Democracy*. Baltimore, MD: Johns Hopkins University Press.

Durac, V. (2022). 'Authoritarian Practice and Fragmented Sovereignty in Post-Uprising Yemen', in Ö. E. Topak, M. Mekouar and F. Cavatorta (eds) *New

Authoritarian Practices in the Middle East and North Africa. Edinburgh: Edinburgh University Press, pp. 340–57.

El Yaakoubi and Awadalla (2020). 'Violence Escalates in Iraq as Government Pushes to End Protests', Reuters, 27 January. https://www.reuters.com/article/us-iraq -protests-idUSKBN1ZQ0XP

Foucault, M. (1991). *Discipline and Punish: The Birth of the Prison*. London: Penguin.

Gilliom, J. and Monahan, T. (2012). *SuperVision: An Introduction to the Surveillance Society*. Chicago, IL: University of Chicago Press.

Golkar, S. (2011). 'Liberation or Suppression Technologies? The Internet, the Green Movement and the Regime in Iran', *International Journal of Emerging Technologies and Society*, 9(1), 50–70.

Golkar, S. (2015). *Captive Society: The Basij Militia and Social Control in Iran*. New York: Columbia University Press.

Golkar, S. (2022). 'Deep Society and New Authoritarian Social Control in Iran after the Green Movement', in Ö. E. Topak, M. Mekouar and F. Cavatorta (eds) *New Authoritarian Practices in the Middle East and North Africa*. Edinburgh: Edinburgh University Press, pp. 92–111.

Gregory, D. (2004) *The Colonial Present: Afghanistan, Palestine, Iraq*. Oxford: Blackwell.

Guirguis, L. (2017). *Copts and the Security State: Violence, Coercion, and Sectarianism in Contemporary Egypt*. Stanford: Stanford University Press.

Hassan, Y. (2022). 'The Evolution of the Sudanese Authoritarian State: The December Uprising and the Unraveling of a "Persistent" Autocracy', in Ö. E. Topak, M. Mekouar and F. Cavatorta (eds) *New Authoritarian Practices in the Middle East and North Africa*. Edinburgh: Edinburgh University Press, pp. 252–75.

Hasso, F. S. and Z. Salime (2016). *Freedom without Permission: Bodies and Space in the Arab Revolutions*. Durham, NC: Duke University Press.

Herman, S. (2011). *Taking Liberties. The War on Terror and the Erosion of American Democracy*. Oxford and New York: Oxford University Press.

Heydemann S. (2000). *War, Institutions, and Social Change in the Middle East*. Berkeley: University of California Press.

Heydemann, S. (2007). 'Upgrading Authoritarianism in the Arab World', Analysis Paper #13. Washington, DC: Saban Center for Middle East Policy at the Brookings Institution.

Heydemann, S. and R. Leenders (2011). 'Authoritarian Learning and Authoritarian Resilience: Regime Responses to the "Arab Awakening"', *Globalizations* 8(5): 647–53.

Hinnebusch, R. (2006). 'Authoritarian Persistence, Democratization Theory and the Middle East: An overview and critique', *Democratization* 13(3): 373–95.

Hintz A. and S. Milan (2018). 'Through a Glass, Darkly: Everyday Acts of Authoritarianism in the liberal West', *International Journal of Communication* 12: 3,939–59.

Human Rights Watch (2018). 'Tunisia: Abusive Treatment during Protests Investigate Abuse by Police; End Prosecutions for Criticism of Government'. https://www.hrw.org/news/2018/01/31/tunisia-abusive-treatment-during-protests

Jones, M. O. (2015). 'Social Media, Surveillance and Cyber-Politics in the Bahrain uprising', in A. Shehabi and M. O. Jones (eds) *Bahrain's Uprising: Resistance and Repression in the Gulf*. London: Zed Books, 239–62.

Jones, M. O. (2019). 'Propaganda, Fake News, and Fake Trends: The Weaponization of Twitter Bots in the Gulf Crisis', *International Journal of Communication* 13: 1,408–9.

Jumet, K. D. (2022). 'Authoritarian Repression Under Sisi: New Tactics or New Tools?', in Ö. E. Topak, M. Mekouar and F. Cavatorta (eds) *New Authoritarian Practices in the Middle East and North Africa*. Edinburgh: Edinburgh University Press, pp. 73–91.

Kaldor, M. (2011) 'Civil Society in 1989 and 2011', *Open Democracy*, 7 February. https://www.opendemocracy.net/en/civil-society-in-1989-and-2011/

Khalili, L. and J. Schwedler (2010). *Policing and Prisons in the Middle East: Formations of Coercion*. New York: Columbia University Press.

Khalili, L. (2012). *Time in the Shadows: Confinement in Counterinsurgencies*. Stanford, CA: Stanford University Press.

Koehler. K. (2017). 'Political Militaries in Popular Uprisings: A Comparative Perspective on the Arab Spring', *International Political Science Review* 38(3): 363–77.

Koloğlu, O. (1987). *Abdülhamit Gerçeği* [*The Truth about Abdülhamit*]. İstanbul: Gür.

Kumar, D. (2012). *Islamophobia and the Politics of Empire*. Chicago, IL: Haymarket.

Lemberg-Pedersen, M. (2019). 'Manufacturing Displacement. Externalization and Postcoloniality in European Migration Control', *Global Affairs* 5(3): 247–71.

Liloia, A. (2022) 'New Authoritarian Practices in Qatar: Censorship by the State and the Self', in Ö. E. Topak, M. Mekouar and F. Cavatorta (eds) *New Authoritarian Practices in the Middle East and North Africa*. Edinburgh: Edinburgh University Press, pp. 208–27.

Loveday, M. and Z. Zakaria (2018). 'Secret Recordings Give Insight into Saudi Attempt to Silence Critics', *The Washington Post* https://www.washingtonpost.com/world/secret-recordings-give-insight-into-saudi-attempt-to-silence-critics/2018/10/17/fb333378-ce49-11e8-ad0a-0e01efba3cc1_story.html

Lynch, M. (2011). 'After Egypt: The Limits and Promise of Online Challenges to the Authoritarian Arab State', *Perspectives on Politics* 9(2): 301–10.

Lyon, D. (2001). *Surveillance Society: Monitoring Everyday Life*. Buckingham and Philadelphia, PA: Open University.

Maghraoui, D. (2022) '"The Freedom of No Speech": Journalists and the Multiple Layers of Authoritarian Practices in Morocco', in Ö. E. Topak, M. Mekouar and F. Cavatorta (eds) *New Authoritarian Practices in the Middle East and North Africa*. Edinburgh: Edinburgh University Press, pp. 189–207.

Mathiesen, T. (2013). *Sectarian Gulf*. Stanford: Stanford Briefs.

Mekouar, M. (2014). 'No Political Agents, No Diffusion: Evidence from North Africa', *International Studies Review* 16(2): 206–16.

Mekouar, M. (2017). 'Police Collapse in Authoritarian Regimes: Lessons from Tunisia', *Studies in Conflict & Terrorism* 40(10): 857–69.

Murakami Wood, D. (2017). 'Editorial: The Global Turn to Authoritarianism and After', *Surveillance & Society* 15(3/4): 357–70.

Pratt, N. and D. Rezk (2019). 'Securitizing the Muslim Brotherhood: State Violence and Authoritarianism in Egypt after the Arab Spring', *Security Dialogue* 50(3): 239–56.

Rana, P. (2015). 'Modi Government's Reasons Why Marital Rape Is Not a Crime', *The Wall Street Journal*, 30 April. https://www.wsj.com/articles/BL-IRTB-29243

RSF (2021). '2021 World Press Freedom Index', Reporters Without Borders. https://rsf.org/en/2021-world-press-freedom-index-journalism-vaccine-against -disinformation-blocked-more-130-countries

Ruijgrok, K. (2017). 'From the Web to the Streets: Internet and Protests under Authoritarian Regimes', *Democratization* 24(3): 498–520.

Ryan, C. (2022). 'Jordan: A Perpetually Liberalizing Autocracy', in Ö. E. Topak, M. Mekouar and F. Cavatorta (eds) *New Authoritarian Practices in the Middle East and North Africa*. Edinburgh: Edinburgh University Press, pp. 152–70.

Saka, E. (2019). *Social Media and Politics in Turkey: A Journey through Citizen Journalism, Political Trolling, and Fake News*. New York: Lexington.

St John, R. B. (2022). 'Libya: Authoritarianism in a Fractured State', in Ö. E. Topak, M. Mekouar and F. Cavatorta (eds) *New Authoritarian Practices in the Middle East and North Africa*. Edinburgh: Edinburgh University Press, pp. 171–88.

Saliah, Z. M. and J. Burke (2019). 'Sudanese Doctors Say Dozens of People Raped during Sit-in Attack', *The Guardian*, 11 June. https://www.theguardian.com /world/2019/jun/11/sudan-troops-protesters-attack-sit-in-rape-khartoum-doct ors-report

Sassoon, J. (2011). *Saddam Hussein's Ba'th Party: Inside an Authoritarian Regime*. New York: Cambridge University Press.

Sayigh, Y. (2015). 'Missed Opportunity: The Politics of Police Reform in Egypt and Tunisia'. *Carnegie Middle East Center*. https://carnegie-mec.org/2015/03/17/missed-opportunity-politics-of-police-reform-in-egypt-and-tunisia/i5hy

Sayigh, Y. (2016). 'Dilemmas of Reform: Policing in Arab Transitions'. *Carnegie Middle East Center*. https://carnegie-mec.org/2016/03/30/dilemmas-of-reform-policing-in-arab-transitions-pub-63090

Seniguer, H. (2017). 'Les Islamistes ont-ils évolué? Retour critique sur une idéologie résiliente', *Confluences Méditerranée* 100(1): 159–75.

Shehabi, A. (2022). 'The Authoritarian Topography of the Bahraini State: Political Geographies of Power and Protest', in Ö. E. Topak, M. Mekouar and F. Cavatorta (eds) *New Authoritarian Practices in the Middle East and North Africa*. Edinburgh: Edinburgh University Press, pp. 51–72.

Teti, A, P. Abbott and F. Cavatorta (2019) 'Do Arabs Really Want Democracy? Evidence from Four Countries', *Democratization* 26(4): 645–65.

The Economist (2021). 'Sex, Lies and Videotape: Morocco's Regime Is Accused of Blackmailing Critics'. *The Economist*, 30 January. https://www.economist.com/middle-east-and-africa/2021/01/28/moroccos-regime-is-accused-of-blackmailing-critics

Thornton, L. (2021). 'Opinion: How Authoritarians Use Gender as a Weapon'. *The Washington Post*, 7 June. https://www.washingtonpost.com/opinions/2021/06/07/how-authoritarians-use-gender-weapon/

Topak, Ö. E. (2014). 'The Biopolitical Border in Practice: Surveillance and Death at the Greece-Turkey Borderzones', *Environment and Planning D: Society and Space* 32(5): 815–33.

Topak, Ö. E. (2017). 'The Making of a Totalitarian Surveillance Machine: Surveillance in Turkey Under AKP Rule', *Surveillance & Society* 15(3/4): 535–42.

Topak, Ö. E. (2019). 'The Authoritarian Surveillant Assemblage: Authoritarian State Surveillance in Turkey', *Security Dialogue* 50(5) 454–72.

Topak, Ö. E. (2022) 'An Assemblage of New Authoritarian Practices in Turkey', in Ö. E. Topak, M. Mekouar and F. Cavatorta (eds) *New Authoritarian Practices in the Middle East and North Africa*. Edinburgh: Edinburgh University Press, pp. 296–319.

Tufekci, Z. (2017). *Twitter and Tear Gas: The Power and Fragility of Networked Protest*. New Haven: Yale University Press.

Tuğal, C. (2016). *The Fall of the Turkish Model: How the Arab Uprisings Brought Down Islamic Liberalism*. Brooklyn: Verso.

Uniacke, R. (2020) 'Authoritarianism in the Information Age: State Branding, Depoliticizing And "De-Civilizing" of Online Civil Society in Saudi Arabia and the United Arab Emirates', *British Journal of Middle Eastern Studies*, doi: 10.1080/13530194.2020.1737916.

Uniacke, R. (2022) 'Digital Repression for Authoritarian Evolution in Saudi Arabia', in Ö. E. Topak, M. Mekouar and F. Cavatorta (eds) *New Authoritarian Practices in the Middle East and North Africa*. Edinburgh: Edinburgh University Press, pp. 228–51.

Yom, S. (2016). *From Resilience to Revolution: How Foreign Interventions Destabilize the Middle East*. New York: Columbia University Press.

Yom, S. and G. F. Gause (2012). 'Resilient Royals: How Arab Monarchies Hang On', *Journal of Democracy* 23(4): 74–88.

Walsh, D. (2019). 'Sudan Power-Sharing Deal Reached by Military and Civilian Leaders'. *The New York Times*, 4 July. https://www.nytimes.com/2019/07/04/world/africa/sudan-power-sharing-deal.html

Wiktorowicz, Q. (2002). 'The Political Limits to Nongovernmental Organizations in Jordan', *World Development* 30(1): 77–93.

Zureik, E. T. (1979). *Palestinians in Israel: A Study of Internal Colonialism*. London: Routledge & Kegan Paul.

Zureik, E., D. Lyon and Y. Abu-Laban (2011). *Surveillance and Control in Israel/Palestine: Population, Territory and Power*. Abingdon: Routledge.

2

MAINTAINING ORDER IN ALGERIA: UPGRADING REPRESSIVE PRACTICES UNDER A HYBRID REGIME

Islam Amine Derradji and Merouan Mekouar

Introduction

The Arab uprisings of 2011 increased scholarly interest in the relationship between security forces and citizens in hybrid regimes (Barany 2011; Cook 2011; Haas and Lesch 2013; Kandil 2016; Lutterbeck 2013). On the one hand, deviant practices by members of the security apparatus nourished popular grievances and undermined citizens' trust in public institutions. While members of the police are supposed to maintain public order, police brutality cases have shown that security agencies could become the primary producers of 'public disorder' (Dias Felix 2020). On the other hand, the way in which security agencies answer the challenges created by mass mobilisations has a direct effect on the regime's survival as well as the ability of protesters to achieve their demands (Goodwin 2001; Goldstone 2014; Goldstone and Ritter 2019; McAdam, Tarrow and Tilly 2001; Slater 2010).

During the Arab uprisings of 2011, the Tunisian and Egyptian security forces were quickly dispatched to prevent the diffusion of demonstrations (Hmed 2015). The strategies employed included the indiscriminate arrest of ordinary citizens, the surveillance and infiltration of dissident groups and the use of 'thugs' or *agents provocateurs* to disturb and discredit the protests. More importantly, security agents used lethal force against the protesters (Mekouar 2016). In the two cases, senior military members decided to deploy troops in the streets to stop the security agencies' exactions and preserve social peace. These interventions precipitated the downfall of Ben Ali and Mubarak.

In Algeria, the 2011 demonstrations and the 2019–20 *Hirak* protests did not follow the same scenario. Although activists and journalists faced legal harassment,[1] intimidation and pre-emptive arrests, the use of large and indiscriminate lethal force remained limited. In fact, crowd management strategies have evolved since the early 2000s, when episodes of sustained popular mobilisation would still lead security agencies to open fire on citizens. What made these changes in policing strategies possible? Despite the 'theoretical centrality of coercion' (Greitens 2016: 5) to explain the regime's stability, variations in repressive practices have remained less studied (Chen and Moss 2018; Davenport 2007; Levitsky and Way 2012). We know that rulers can adapt to the new liberal order by diverting institutions to their benefit, multiplying channels of patronage and renewing legitimisation sources (Heydemann 2007), but what about repression? Building on an in-depth analysis of local legislation, expert reports, journalistic investigations, secondary literature and interviews conducted with activists, this chapter reflects on the evolution of coercive practices in Algeria. It shows that state capabilities building and new technologies of information and telecommunication, as well as the transnational diffusion of policing doctrines and know-how, implied a gradual transition from a repertoire of repression that relied on lethal force, large-scale torture and courts of limited jurisdiction to one that neutralises challengers mainly through pre-emptive arrests and legal harassment, bureaucratic obstruction, social network surveillance and 'democratic crowd management' techniques.[2] Faced with multiple protests, and eager to decrease the material and symbolic costs of maintaining public order,[3] the Algerian authorities adapted by upgrading their repressive practices.

A study of contentious episodes: cases, variables and concepts

This study is based on a diachronic comparison of two contentious episodes in Algeria: the riots of October 1988 and the 'Arab Spring' mobilisations of 2011. We reconstitute the conflictual processes to identify the forces at work, the crowd composition, and the repertoires of action mobilised by the protesters. We also describe the police units, gendarmerie units or troops mobilised, and the strategies deployed to face the challengers. We select these cases for two reasons. The first is the variations that they allow on both the dependent variable (coercive practices) and the independent variables used to explain coercion: macro-level factors like regime type (Waddington 1998; Chen and Moss 2018) or security agencies' cohesion and institutional design

(Greitens 2016), meso-level variables like police capabilities and training procedures (Fillieule and della Porta 2006), and micro-level factors like interactions between protesters and law enforcement forces, as well as the latter's perception of the former (della Porta and Reiter 1998; Lacey et al. 1990). These perceptions are usually based on crowd composition (gender, race, social class or ethno-linguistic background) and their repertoires of action (peaceful or violent).[4] The second reason is data availability. The two episodes have been extensively documented. In addition, we managed to conduct interviews with activists who were protagonists of the two cycles of protests. These interviews were critical to understanding the lived experience of repression and the evolution of policing practices.

Finally, we mobilise the concept of *repertoire* to interpret the authorities' lines of conduct. Tilly first introduced the concept of a *repertoire of contention* to describe 'a limited set of routines that are learned, shared and acted out through a relatively deliberate process of choice. Repertoires are learned cultural creations, but they do not descend from abstract philosophy or take shape as a result of political propaganda; they emerge from struggle' (Tilly 1995: 42). We extend this idea to show that the Algerian authorities enacted a routinised set of practices that systematically included the public disqualification of mobilised groups, the search for scapegoats or internal enemies and the designation of external enemies. However, the repertoire of repression evolved[5] over time. Violence has been relatively 'euphemized' (Fillieule and della Porta 2006) or 'cleaned' (Rejali 2007) to decrease the cost of crowd control and better suit a liberal discourse.

Maintaining Order during the Single Party Era: The Logics of Threat Eradication

The 1980s Algerian regime was quite different from what it is now. Although the political landscape was already diverse, with a myriad of leftist and Islamist groups, a Berber movement committed to the defence and promotion of the Amazigh language and culture (Sini 2015) and a vocal women's movement denouncing the family code (Lalami 2012), these actors shared a defining experience: clandestinity. The National Liberation Front (FLN) was the only legal political party. The regime was also relying on a handful of mass organisations to co-opt interest groups of workers (UGTA), women (UNFA) and youth (UNJA) in what looked like an ideal type of authoritarian corporatism (Werenfels 2007). Although some dissident groups ran magazines or newspapers, these were shared with caution, since the state-run RTA (Algerian Radio and Television) and some newspapers (*El Naasr, El Djeich, El Moudjahid*) were the only media allowed (Brahimi 2012). These outlets delivered official discourses and served as propaganda tools for the regime.

Without the recognition of the state, dissident organisations were considered illegal, and their activity was subject to crackdowns by the Military Security (secret police) or the National Security Directorate (police). Agents would infiltrate dissident groups to gather information or fuel conflict between competing factions, conduct illegal home searches to find evidence of activism and practice torture to punish and terrorise opponents, obtain confessions of guilt or gather intelligence. One of our informants recalls:

> I got involved in the student movement first in the 1970s. I became one of the local leaders, and that's where you learn the principles of clandestinity, working in secret . . . I got arrested for the first time in 1971 . . . Then I was tortured. I won't describe how, but they would try to break your mind, make you question your beliefs, ask you to give them the names of your friends, offer you to become an informant. (K., interview conducted in Oran, April 2016)

In some cases, activists were subjected to the special jurisdiction of the *Cour de Sûreté de l'État*. The verdicts show that dissidents' journals, obtained after home searches, were used as evidence to press charges for 'offence against the authority of the State' (Collectif contre la répression en Algérie–France 2008). Moreover, the verdicts were based on police reports, and the court would use them even if confessions were obtained under duress. In other cases, for example the September 1986 Constantine Student movement, security agencies would also detain the presumed leaders in special camps. Here, detainees were subjected to torture, including 'absorption of Crésyl [a creosol-based disinfectant], beatings and stapling of fingers' (Nesrouche 2006).

The political, mediatic and coercive state apparatuses strived to maintain a façade of *unanimity* that did not, however, resist growing expressions of popular discontent. The national context, particularly tense in the mid-1980s, was marked by falling hydrocarbon prices, growing pressure on public finances and rising food prices. The international context was also defined by pro-democracy revolutionary movements in Eastern Europe. These conditions exacerbated factional struggles within the regime and fuelled social unrest that culminated in the 1988 riots.

The riots of October 1988[6]

On the evening of 4 October 1988, protesters from the popular neighbourhoods of Bab-El-Oued and El-Harrach attacked state stores, public buildings and the luxurious shopping and cultural centre of Ryad-el-Feth. The rioters were 'mainly young people aged 12 to 20 years, high school students, college students, unemployed . . . They lived in the underprivileged neighbourhoods of the capital and were from the working classes' (Aït-Aoudia 2015: 60). Frédéric Fritscher, a correspondent for *Le Monde*, observed that law enforcement agencies did not intervene immediately. It was only the day after 'around 1 pm that they took up positions in the town to protect the buildings of the RTA, the Presidency and the Ministry of Defense' (Aggoun and Rivoire 2005: 116). Surprised by the scale of the protests and faced with 'the inability of the usual law and order forces – police and gendarmerie – to cope with the situation, the authorities asked the army to intervene' (General Benyelles in Barrat, Bensmaïl and Leclère 2002, 7 min. 30 to 8 min. 12).

On the evening of 5 October, a state of siege had been decreed. Following the provisions of Article 119 of the constitution, all 'civil, administrative and security authorities were placed under the control of the army' (Aït-Aoudia 2015: 61). Gatherings were prohibited and a curfew was imposed. The military head of staff deployed counter-insurgency tactics that included the use of propaganda and disinformation to attribute the protest's responsibilities to internal (leftist groups) and external (Western countries) enemies; the deployment of combat units in Algiers to control the main city roads; the use of lethal force to neutralise protesters; and mass arrests and large-scale torture to punish challengers, obtain confessions of guilt or terrorise the population.

All these practices constituted a repertoire of repression that was in fact learned through an accumulation of past experiences and professional training. General Nezzar, commander of the land forces, declared in an interview:

> I designed my approach based on the foreign textbooks I had studied and the notions I had kept from them. I went to their schools; I knew the policing system. I know that the military must support the police in a state of emergency and that it secures the powers of the police in a state of siege by using weapons when necessary. The president did not have that knowledge. (Bourdon and Comte 2001)

On 6 October, clashes broke out between rioters and soldiers, resulting in the troops opening fire on the crowd. In an interview, General Nezzar justified the use of lethal force by arguing that it was the only means of answering an insurgency:

> In case of an insurrection, there is only one way . . . to maintain order; it is to use the troops. The president decreed the state of siege and declared me responsible for Algiers . . . There was a ban on gatherings. The use of fire-arms was only allowed to disperse people and was tightly regulated. (Barrat, Bensmaïl and Leclère 2002, 8 min. 15 to 8 min. 25)

Frédéric Fritscher, *Le Monde* correspondent, stated, however, that 'soldiers, many of whom came from the military region of Béchar, obeyed orders. They fired savagely at other Algerians, with pistols, shotguns, sniper rifles, and machine guns' (Aggoun and Rivoire 2005: 117).

Lethal force was also used against other actors. More peaceful rallies organised by imams to denounce state repression also led to mass shootings. The death toll thus mounted to 500 (Aït-Aoudia 2015: 65). The summer camp of Sidi Fredj was also transformed into a torture centre. General Benyelles stated that 'some security services, having been unable to point fingers at the culprits of these riots and being convinced that there was a foreign hand behind these events, have carried out mass arrests and have tried to make people talk under torture' (Barrat, Bensmaïl and Leclère 2002, 11 min.). Repression also fell on intellectual circles, trade union activists and clandestine far-left organisations. Confessions of guilt were then used to support the thesis of a conspiracy conducted by alleged 'enemies of the State'. As the security forces were crushing the demonstrations, the country's official media[7] nourished the state's efforts to delegitimise protesters. The regime's daily *El Moudjahid* presented the youth as a threatening 'horde'. At the same time, the coverage of foreign journalists was portrayed as a manoeuvre designed to destabilise Algeria. The military command added to the assertions by claiming that 'young people, manipulated by the enemies of the Algerian people and its revolution, ransacked public buildings, looted public and private property, violated homes and damaged the very symbols of our national heritage' (Aït-Aoudia 2015: 65).

In sum, the Algerian authorities responded to the riots of 1988 following a repertoire of actions constrained by the state's available material (riot units and troops) and symbolic (media and justice) resources. Still, they included media disqualification of protesters, searching for culprits or scape-goats and the public designation of internal and external enemies. Faced with the inability of specialised riot units to respond to the unrest, military troops were also deployed, which led to the use of lethal force against civilians, mass arrests and large-scale torture, following previously learned strategies of counter-insurgency.

State Capabilities Building and Police Learning

October 1988 proved to be a critical juncture. In a speech to the nation, President Chadli Bendjedid announced major political and economic reforms. A new constitution came into force in February 1989 and enshrined freedom of expression and association while opening the way to a multi-party system. The written press also experienced a golden age. Privately-owned dailies, some of which were particularly critical of the regime, gradually appeared. Clandestine opposition parties were legalised, and new ones were created. Autonomous trade unions emerged to defend the workers' interests, while various advocacy associations were formed to protect citizens' rights.

After the victory of the Islamic Salvation Front in the first round of the December 1991 legislative elections, the army chief of staff interrupted the electoral process, worried that the FIS would threaten the republican nature of the Algerian State. This interruption caused the failure of the Algerian democratic transition. Algeria then fell into a civil war that contributed to the strengthening of the state's coercive apparatus, a more pronounced division of labour in the security sector and a renewed inclination to regulate public spaces (street and cyber-domain). New laws and administrative provisions were then introduced to criminalise dissent and curb the constitutional rights conceded during the liberalisation.

Containing the oppositions: legal frameworks and administrative control

Following the constitutional reform, the organisation of public meetings or events became subject to a declaratory regime under the provisions of Law 89-28 of 31 December 1989. Five days before the holding of an event, organisers had to announce their intention to the prefect, and specify the routes to be taken and the means used to ensure the event's smooth running (Art. 17).

The law was, however, modified in December 1991 and placed further restrictions on public demonstrations. The organisation of public events was now subjected to a regime of administrative authorization rather than a regime of declaration (Art. 15). Following the amendment of the law, unauthorised demonstrations were labelled as unarmed gatherings and were punishable by up to twelve months in prison. On the basis of these legal provisions, local authorities could use their discretionary power to neutralise dissenting voices. Although the constitution guarantees multi-party politics and freedom of association, the laws governing the creation of political parties and civil society associations also evolved to ensure better administrative control of the opposition. In fact, without official state recognition, a political party cannot legally raise funds, rent premises or hold conventions. Different strategies can then be deployed to prevent activists from obtaining accreditations: repeated refusals, unanswered requests and tedious bureaucratic procedures. This in turn keeps them in a situation of illegality. Thus, the failure to comply with the legal framework creates risks of judicial proceedings as well as financial penalties.

The authorities responded also to the emergence of the cyber-domain with new legal provisions, allowing for its regulation and policing. Although the new judicial articles were meant to fight cybercrime, they can be interpreted in ways that contribute to silencing political dissent. Law 09-04 of 2009 specifies that 'in order to protect public order . . . technical devices may be put in place to monitor electronic communications, collect and record their contents in real-time, and carry out searches and seizures of IT systems' (Art. 3).

Enhancing crowd management and cyber-policing

The 1990s and 2000s were also marked by the gradual development of more specialised units to fight crime, counter terrorism and ensure public order: the Mobile Judicial Police Brigades (1995); the Research and Intervention Brigade (2005) and Special Operations Group (2016); the Republican Security Units (1995); and the Law Enforcement Units (2014). Specialised cybercrime units were also set up by the Algerian police and gendarmerie, such as the cybercrime brigade, which reports to the Bab Ezzouar[8] criminal police station, or the Center for the Prevention and Fight against Computer Crime and Cybercrime (2009). The number of police officers increased significantly from 35,000 in the mid-1990s to 209,000 in 2014 (L.M 2014). The authorities also expanded the fleet of vehicles, acquired new infrastructure and modernised the security agencies' armaments (Tlemçani 2010). As a result, the World Internal Security and Police Index ranked Algeria fifth in the world in 2016 for its police and security force capacities (Abdelmottlep and International Science Assocation IPSA 2016: 29). In fact, the Algerian police's modernisation became a strategic priority for senior members of the Direction Générale de la Sûreté Nationale (DGSN). Material investments were then coupled with the establishment of police institutes and schools designed to increase courses and training[9] in crowd management and cyber-policing.

In 2008, the director of the DGSN, Ali Tounsi, declared to the Algerian press service that the DGSN gave priority to training because it 'increases police efficiency and allows for the use of sophisticated techniques to fight crime . . . Forensic science currently allows legal and scientific evidence to convict a criminal without even having to brutalize or threaten him . . . We no longer need these methods to get confessions.' In the same interview, he added that 'even if cybercrime is not very widespread, we prefer to take the lead' (Mokhtaria 2008). In April 2012, Major General Abdelghani Hamel, head of the DGSN, stated that the police forces had gone beyond 'the role of maintaining and restoring order by moving towards the democratic management of crowds, with the aim of preserving citizens' safety . . . The techniques in question consist of containing the demonstrators and channeling them without the slightest attack on their dignity' (Bourihane 2012). The same year, he further clarified the police's doctrine by stating that 'democratic crowd management was a deliberate choice to avoid bloodshed' (Benrahal 2012). This doctrinal inflection was motivated by the need to increase policing efficiency rather than effectiveness. However, it is important to note that the security co-operation between Algeria and Western countries also made these changes possible.

The transnational diffusion of know-how and doctrines

After the civil war, Algeria emerged as an essential security partner for the European Union, particularly in the fight against terrorism, organised crime and illegal migration, and bilateral co-operation agreements were adopted, such as the one between Algeria and France in 2005 (Assemblée nationale 2004). Algeria also took part in regional security forums and co-operation projects, including the Euromed police partnership, which aims at building institutional capabilities in neighbouring countries (CEPOL 2019). Although the Franco-Algerian Cooperation Agreement was initially intended to strengthen exchanges on terrorism and illegal migration, it covers a wide range of areas, including crowd management. Article six specifies that the purpose of technical co-operation is: 'general and specialized training; exchange of information and professional experience; technical advice; exchange of specialized documentation; and, where appropriate, the reciprocal hosting of officials and experts' (Assemblée nationale 2004: 6). Thus, French police experts provided training to their Algerian counterparts on how to resist provocations during demonstrations or engage in crowd channelling. Algerian police officers were also invited to attend training sessions in France.

Cyberspace was also a domain of police co-operation. As early as 2008, the DGSN sent agents to Switzerland for six months of training in cyber-crime investigation and forensics (Mokhtaria 2008). More recently, the EU/MENA counter-terrorism training partnership allowed the Algerian police to gain state-of-the-art training in cyber-surveillance.[10] The investigation led by Privacy International revealed the course content of the European agency for law enforcement training (CEPOL). In 2019, CEPOL experts went to Algiers to share OSINT techniques and teach how to create sock puppets (Privacy International 2020). Police capabilities building and the transnational diffusion of police doctrines and know-how contributed to the evolution of the coercive repertoire. Although training was provided by the European counterparts to fight crime and maintain order, the acquired surveillance techniques and policing strategies have been effectively used for political purposes: containing the opposition and mitigating threats to the regime.

Maintaining Order in the Hybrid Regime: The Logics of Mitigation

Since President Abdelaziz Bouteflika came to power in 1999 Algeria has experienced multiple instances of social conflict. The turn of the century saw major riots in Kabylia. The ensuing repression left hundreds of people dead and thousands injured. A report by the LADDH stated that the *gendarmes* used heavy weapons and subjected demonstrators to physical abuse and torture (LADDH 2002). From the mid-2000s onwards, however, policing strategies underwent significant changes nourished by the capacity building of police units and the gradual introduction of new law enforcement doctrines and trainings. While popular demonstrations have become a routinised form of expression of popular discontent in the last fifteen years (Brown 2011; Bennadji 2011), the increase in the number of social protests was paradoxically accompanied by a reduction in the use of lethal force.

Although Algerian authorities continue to answer challengers by relying on a set of routinised discursive practices that include the public disqualification of mobilised groups and the designation of internal or external enemies, these framing processes became more complex with the liberalisation of the media. However, the public space was still tightly controlled and highly monitored. Within the cyber domain, surveillance techniques are deployed to conduct pre-emptive arrests against opponents, gather material evidence to convict them, or spread propaganda and disinformation through fake accounts and bots. In the streets, legal regulations, bureaucratic obstruction and police 'democratic crowd management' practices are used to maintain order while avoiding excessive bloodshed.

The Arab Spring mobilisations

At the beginning of January 2011, Algeria saw the opening of a new protest cycle. The increase in food prices was the immediate detonator of riots in which young people, mainly from working-class backgrounds, participated. They blocked roads, ransacked public buildings and threw stones and glass bottles at the police (AFP 2011). Anti-riot units were deployed to disperse the crowd using tear gas and water cannon. The confrontations resulted in five deaths among the protesters and nearly 800 injured, 300 of whom were police officers. One thousand two hundred young people were also arrested and brought before the courts for disturbing public order (Dridi 2011). One of our informants gave us insights into both crowd management techniques and social media usage by activists to publicise repression, which showed marked differences with October 1988:

> Riots started in my neighbourhood. I was posting information, photos on the Facebook page of the Algerian Special Envoys . . . On the ground, I would sometimes talk to some cops who were sent to negotiate with the young people . . . He would come and say, 'OK, here we are, we've been ordered to disperse you, you'd better go home' . . . In my neighbourhood, they fired tear gas. There was one dead man. The next day, the Minister of the Interior said that it was a young thug, a delinquent, and that the police had not killed him. It wasn't true. (A., interview conducted in Algiers, September 2015)

The Interior Minister described the rioters as 'criminals with a vengeful instinct' (Rouadjia 2011). Denying the revolt's political motivation, he framed it as juvenile deviance, covered by criminal law. Although the public television channel contributed to the amplification of the authorities' message by broadcasting scenes of destruction, a counter-discourse developed in the written press due to some daily newspapers' relative autonomy. Opposition parties, unions, associations and public figures also formed the National Coordination for Change and Democracy (CNCD), which then called for the organisation of rallies on 12 and 19 February (Baamara 2012). Thirty thousand police officers were called on to deal with peaceful middle-class activists and a heterogeneous crowd of two to three thousand protesters (Chebellah 2011). For Major General Abdelghani Hamel, the use of lethal force was no longer an option. He explained that he wanted to 'deploy a large number of police officers so as not to have to use water cannons, tear gas or other weapons' and added that it was necessary to 'show strength so as not to have to use it' (Flici 2011). Human and technical intelligence was also used to spot protesters before events began. One activist, for instance, stated:

> There were people . . . who attended the meetings and told the police who was who, who the leaders were . . . But the repression had changed forms. It consisted mainly of arrests and questioning. In most cases, people were released from police stations. In some cases, they were put on trial. It seemed to us that the authorities didn't want to make martyrs and that they had accumulated the material and human resources and the knowledge to . . . do what they call 'democratic crowd management.' So, they managed to break the actions without making victims. In any case, it was incomparable with 1988 or with 2001. (Ba., interview conducted in Oran, January 2016)

Cybercrime squads of Bab Ezzouar in Algiers also carried out social media monitoring to conduct preventive arrests. Activists were summoned for comments they had made on social networks and convicted for contempt towards state figures or institutions (the President or the army), defamatory statements or incitement of unarmed gatherings. Material evidence of guilt was found online and considered sufficient to press charges. The cyber squad activities were thus a testimony to the resources' fungibility and know-how transferability from fighting crime to constraining political opponents.

The state bureaucracy also increased its efforts to avoid granting authorisations for demonstrations, arguing that the latter might constitute a risk for the safety and security of citizens. Failure to obtain this permission would then justify the deployment of police units to disperse illegal gatherings. In some cases, real bargaining took place to offer protesters alternatives, which would then mitigate the risk perceived by the authorities of losing control. In fact, the authorities sought to manage and restrict planned demonstrations by offering protesters the possibility of indoor gatherings instead of outdoor rallies. Not only was it easier to control a fixed crowd, but by 'enclosing' demonstrators in conference rooms, the authorities attempted to decrease the signalling effect of the demonstrations (T., interview conducted in Oran, April 2016).

The media's strategy to disqualify the leading figures of the opposition was twofold. First, the public media ignored the protests or dismissed activists as political actors without popular support. Second, they sought to turn the pro-democracy activists into malicious actors, committed to destabilising the country and determined to make it relive the civil war's darkest days. Emphasis was also placed on some divisive or controversial opposition figures, to either repel them or exacerbate tensions within the collectives. As for the lesser-known participants, rumours were spread to frame them as agents of foreign secret services. The pressure on the activists was even more significant, as this media harassment aroused fear, suspicion or paranoia in their entourage. One activist explained:

> There are things that you should not touch if you want to be in politics. These are customs, religion, or the relationship to Morocco or Israel. They start a rumour that you are connected to one of these elements, and you are finished politically, it's not very complicated. (B. interview conducted in Oran, January 2016)

Disinformation, propaganda and coercive practices went hand in hand with other strategies designed to demobilise or co-opt individual or collective actors. The oil rent made it possible to grant interest-free loans to young people; the authorities announced the lifting of the state of emergency to meet some of the demands of the *Coordination Nationale pour le Changement et la Démocratie* (CNCD), and the President announced constitutional reforms. As a result, the Algerian regime has many institutional levers with which to respond to social conflicts. It can announce early elections or constitutional changes to regain momentum. It can also push for the resignation of ministers, or even the President. As in a chess game, several pieces can be sacrificed to preserve the authority of the state and the army as its guardian.

Conclusion

The purpose of this chapter has been to examine the evolution of coercive practices in Algeria. How did the authorities respond to the challenges created by social movements and political opponents? To what extent has repression evolved with façade political liberalisation? We have shown that the authorities continue to enact a routinised set of practices that systematically includes the public disqualification of mobilised groups, the search for scapegoats or internal enemies and the designation of external enemies. However, violence has been relatively 'euphemized' (Fillieule and della Porta 2006), 'civilized' (Giustozzi 2011) or 'cleaned' (Rejali 2007) to decrease the cost of population surveillance and control.

The cycle of contention opened by the *Hirak* mobilisations in 2019 reinforced several of our observations. Because of the number of people mobilised, the unity of the movement and its duration, the *Hirak* represented a more significant challenge to the Algerian regime than the previous cases of popular mobilisation. However, it did not lead to the use of lethal force against civilians in the street. On the one hand, the police forces started by relying on 'democratic crowd management' strategies. The crowd's composition (i.e., the diversity of its social categories and age groups and the presence of families), as well as the pacifism of the protesters, might have prevented an escalation of violence. The rallies organised on Tuesdays by students were nonetheless repressed more violently, which testifies to the *heuristic fertility* of the micro-sociological level of social interactions and the need to better study, at the meso-sociological level, the police categories of crowd perception and evaluation.

On the other hand, the authorities deployed routinised discursive practices, aimed at disqualifying opponents. The public media and the private channels close to the regime at first ignored the marches, before relaying a bellicose discourse suggesting that malicious parties wanted to infiltrate the mobilisations (Dziri 2020). Social networks were also inundated with false accounts and bots designed to delegitimise specific opposition figures or to relay the regime's propaganda (Bendjoudi 2020). Internet surveillance by cyber-crime squads eventually led to the arrest of journalists and activists whose public statements were used as evidence in trials for damage to the army's morale, damage to the unity of the nation, or incitement of unarmed assembly (Lamriben 2019).

Ironically, the regular organisation of presidential elections was one of the main strategies used to ensure the survival of the regime. Well-known figures of the regime were the most serious contenders for the presidency, while some opposition leaders like Karim Tabbou were detained. The *Hirak* activists called for the boycott of the elections under these circumstances and doubted that the presidential contest would change anything regarding the tutelary position of the military, the extra-constitutional power that it held (even more so during a political crisis) and the informality of politics. The continuity of the mobilisation, despite the institutional solutions put forward by the regime, led to more repression, including the heavy censorship of some electronic media (Maghreb Emergent, Radio M), mass arrests and long-term pre-trial detentions.

While these violations of civil and political rights raise the question of authoritarian reversal, the relationship between the nature of the political regime and repressive practices is not straightforward (Davenport 2007). Under democratic regimes, law enforcement agencies should in theory refrain from using disproportionate force against citizens. In practice, this is not always the case. In 2001, the Swedish police, in panic, opened fire on anti-globalisation demonstrators in Gothenburg. In the same year in Genoa, demonstrators against the G8 were subjected to physical abuse, bullying and humiliation by the gendarmerie. Beyond these moments of intense mobilisation, interactions between police and citizens can also be marked by acts of police brutality, as the murder of George Floyd in the United States reminds us.

The use of force raises questions about the state as much as about political regimes. It is possible to imagine states abandoning the use of brute force as they develop more efficient instruments of control, surveillance and confinement of populations. Logics of institutional isomorphism would then imply that democratic and authoritarian states become similar in their techniques and repertoires of repression regardless of their political regimes. More studies, however, are needed to clarify these possible evolutions.

Notes

1 See also the 'Legalising Authoritarian Practices' section in the Introduction, which provides an overview of key examples from the book chapters (Topak et al. 2022).

2 It is important to note, however, that these are ideal types of repressive repertoires. To be sure, acts of torture are still occurring in Algeria according to human rights organisations. Although brutal practices did not disappear following the development of new surveillance and control strategies, the intensity and scope of state-sanctioned torture have decreased in comparison to the late 1980s and the 1990s. In the 1990s, the context of the civil war and the deployment of counter-terrorism strategies were conducive to large-scale torture, forced disappearances and extra-judicial killings. Moreover, we do not imply a linear or teleological movement towards a new repertoire. Not only can old practices exist with new ones, but 'regression' to brutality is always possible. Finally, we focus mainly on the police. It is possible that policing doctrines, training and know-how evolve in some security agencies but not others, or at a different pace.

3 Destructions and casualties, naming and shaming campaigns, risks of RtoP foreign interventions.

4 Obviously, the three levels can combine in many ways. By example, Crowd's perception is dependent on its composition, the police organisational culture, and broader social systems of domination and discrimination like racism.

5 Another examination of the evolution of policing in this book can be found in Golkar (2022).

6 Reconstruction of the contentious episode is based on Aggoun and Rivoire 2005; Aït-Aoudia 2015; Charef 1990.

7 For an overview of similar practices in other examined MENA contexts in this book, see the 'Authoritarian Practices Shaping Civil Society and the Media' section in the introduction (Topak et al. 2022).

8 An Algiers suburb.

9 In 2016, the Algerian police force had fourteen institutes and schools, including the Dar El-Beida school, which offered specialised training in law enforcement.

10 Other examined cases of cyber-surveillance in this book include the UAE (Davidson 2022), Saudi Arabia (Uniacke 2022), Bahrain (Shehabi 2022), Qatar (Liloia 2022), Israel (Dayan 2022), Turkey (Topak 2022), Morocco (Maghraoui 2022) and Sudan (Hassan 2022).

References

Abdelmottlep, M. and International Science Assocation IPSA (2016). 'World Internal Security & Police Index'. Florida, USA: Institute for Economics & Peace. http://www.ipsa-police.org/Images/uploaded/Pdf%20file/WISPI%20Report.pdf

AFP (2011). 'En Algérie, premières victimes après les émeutes'. *AFP*, 7 January 7.

https://www.lemonde.fr/afrique/article/2011/01/07/les-manifestations-ont-rep ris-en-algerie-apres-une-matinee-calme_1462547_3212.html

Aggoun, L. and J. B. Rivoire (2005). '5 Octobre 1988, le tournant'. In *Françalgérie, crimes et mensonges d'États*, 116–34. Poche/Essais. Paris: La Découverte. https:// www.cairn.info/francalgerie-crimes-et-mensonges-d-etats--9782707147479-p- 116.htm

Aït-Aoudia, M. (2015). 'Des émeutes à une crise politique: les ressorts de la politisa- tion des mobilisations en Algérie en 1988', *Politix* 112(4): 59–82.

Assemblée Nationale (2004). *Projet de Loi Autorisant l'approbation de l'accord Entre Le Gouvernement de La République Française et Le Gouvernement de La République Algérienne Démocratique et Populaire Relatif à La Coopération En Matière de Sécurité et de Lutte Contre La Criminalité Organisée*. https://www.assemblee-nat ionale.fr/12/pdf/projets/pl1861.pdf

Baamara, L. (2012). '(Més) aventures d'une coalition contestataire: le cas de la Coordination nationale pour le changement et la démocratie (CNCD) en Algérie', *L'Année du Maghreb* VIII, October, 161–79.

Barany, Z. (2011). 'Comparing the Arab Revolts: The Role of the Military'. *Journal of Democracy* 22(4): 24–35.

Barrat, P., M. Bensmaïl and T. Leclère (2002). *Algérie(s) – 1. Un Peuple sans Voix*. France: Article Z. http://www.film-documentaire.fr/4DACTION/w_fiche_fi lm/11315_1

Bendjoudi, A. (2020). *14. Les «mouches électroniques» de la police politique sur les réseaux sociaux. Hirak en Algérie*. Paris: La Fabrique Éditions.

Bennadji, C. (2011). 'Algérie 2010: l'année des mille et une émeutes', *L'Année du Maghreb* VII, December, 263–9.

Bourdon, W. and A. Comte (2001). 'Les événements d'octobre 1988 – Algeria-Watch'. https://algeria-watch.org/?p=19292

Bourihane, N. (2012). 'Des CIR Pour Le Maintien de l'ordre: La DGSN Privilégie Le Recours Aux Techniques sans l'usage de La Violence', *Horizons*, 10 April. https://www.djazairess.com/fr/horizons/102562

Brahimi, B. (2012). *Le Pouvoir, La Presse et Les Droits de l'homme En Algérie*. Alger: ENAG Editions.

Brown, J. (2011). 'Algeria's Midwinter Uproar', *Middle East Report Online* (blog). 20 January. https://merip.org/2011/01/algerias-midwinter-uproar/

CEPOL (2019). 'Algerian Delegation Visits CEPOL for the First Time'. *CEPOL* (blog). 23 October. https://www.cepol.europa.eu/media/news/algerian-delegat ion-visits-cepol-first-time

Chebellah, A. (2011). '»Ce n'est qu'un début»: les manifestants à Alger défient le pouvoir'. La Presse, 12 February. https://www.lapresse.ca/international/dossiers

/crise-dans-le-monde-arabe/autres-pays/201102/12/01-4369665-ce-nest-quun -debut-les-manifestants-a-alger-defient-le-pouvoir.php

Chen, X. and D. M. Moss (2018). 'Authoritarian Regimes and Social Movements', in D. Snow, S. A. Soule, H. Kriesi and H. J. McCammon (eds) *The Wiley Blackwell Companion to Social Movements*, 666–81. New York: John Wiley.

Collectif contre la répression en Algérie (France) (2008). *Au nom du peuple!: le procès de la Ligue des droits de l'homme: Cour de sûreté de l'état, décembre 1985*. Alger: Koukou.

Cook, S. (2011). 'The Calculations of Tunisia's Military', *Foreign Policy: The Middle East Channel* (blog), 20 January. https://foreignpolicy.com/2011/01/20/the-cal culations-of-tunisias-military/

Davenport, C. (2007). 'State Repression and the Tyrannical Peace', *Journal of Peace Research* 44(4): 485–504.

Davidson, C. M. (2022). 'The United Arab Emirates: Evolving Authoritarian Tools', in Ö. E. Topak, M. Mekouar and F. Cavatorta (eds) *New Authoritarian Practices in the Middle East and North Africa*. Edinburgh: Edinburgh University Press, pp. 320–39.

della Porta, D. and H. Reiter (1998) 'The Policing of Protest in Western Democracies', in D. della Porta and H. Reiter (eds) *The Policing of Mass Demonstrations in Contemporary Democracies*, 1–34. Minneapolis: University of Minnesota Press.

Dias Felix, A. (2020). 'La police «démocratique» comme productrice de (dés)ordres sociaux: les cas du Brésil et du Mexique', *Lien social et Politiques* 84: 260–83.

Dridi, D. (2011). 'CNCD, Pouvoir, agenda du changement: Me Bouchachi s'explique sur tout', *Maghreb Emergent*, 9 March. Algeria-Watch. https://algeria -watch.org/?p=34274

Dziri, H. (2020). *13. La couverture très orientée du hirak par les médias algériens. Hirak en Algérie*. Paris: La Fabrique Éditions.

Fillieule, O. and D. della Porta. (2006.) *Police et manifestants. Maintien de l'ordre et gestion des conflits*. Paris: Presses de Sciences Po.

Flici, N. (2011). 'Les Explications Du Général Hamel: Déploiement Des Policiers Lors Des Marches'. *L'Expression*, 8 March. Djazairess. https://www.djazairess .com/fr/lexpression/129425

Giustozzi, A. (2011). *Art of Coercion: The Primitive Accumulation and Management of Coercive Power*. New York: Columbia University Press.

Goldstone, J. (2014). *Revolutions: A Very Short Introduction*. Oxford and New York: Oxford University Press.

Goldstone, J. and D. Ritter (2019). 'Revolution and Social Movements', in D. Snow, S. A. Soule, H. Kriesi and H. J. McCammon (eds) *The Wiley Blackwell Companion to Social Movements*. New York: John Wiley.

Golkar, S. (2022) 'Deep Society and New Authoritarian Social Control in Iran after the Green Movement', in Ö. E. Topak, M. Mekouar and F. Cavatorta (eds) *New Authoritarian Practices in the Middle East and North Africa*. Edinburgh: Edinburgh University Press, pp. 92–111.

Goodwin, J. (2001). *No Other Way Out: States and Revolutionary Movements 1945–1991*. Cambridge: Cambridge University Press.

Greitens, S. (2016). *Dictators and Their Secret Police*. Cambridge: Cambridge University Press.

Haas, M. and D. Lesch (2013). *The Arab Spring: Change and Resistance in the Middle East*. Boulder, CO: Westview Press.

Hassan, Y. (2022) 'The Evolution of the Sudanese Authoritarian State: The December Uprising and the Unraveling of a "Persistent" Autocracy', in Ö. E. Topak, M. Mekouar and F. Cavatorta (eds) *New Authoritarian Practices in the Middle East and North Africa*. Edinburgh: Edinburgh University Press, pp. 252–75.

Hmed, C. (2015). 'Répression d'État et situation révolutionnaire en Tunisie (2010–2011)', *Vingtieme Siecle: Revue d'histoire* 128(4): 77–90.

Kandil, H. (2016). *The Power Triangle: Military, Security, and Politics in Regime Change*. New York: Oxford University Press.

Lacey, N., C. Wells and D. Meure (1990). *Reconstructing Criminal Law: Critical Perspectives on Crime and the Criminal Process*. London: Weidenfeld & Nicolson.

Ligue Algérienne de Défense des Droits de l'Homme (LADDH) (2002). 'Rapport Algérie: La Répression Du Printemps Noir, Avril 2001–Avril 2002'. https://algeria-watch.org/pdf/pdf_fr/Algerie330.pdf

Lalami, F. (2012). *Les Algériennes contre le code de la famille*. Paris: Presses de Sciences Po.

Lamriben, H. (2019). 'Surveillance Électronique, Arrestations et Incarcérations: Sale Temps Pour Les Militants Du Hirak'. https://www.elwatan.com/a-la-une/surveillance-electronique-arrestations-et-incarcerations-sale-temps-pour-les-militants-du-hirak-05-09-2019

Levitsky, S. and L. Way (2012). *Competitive Authoritarianism: Hybrid Regimes after the Cold War*. Cambridge: Cambridge University Press.

Liloia, A. (2022). 'New Authoritarian Practices in Qatar: Censorship by the State and the Self', in Ö. E. Topak, M. Mekouar and F. Cavatorta (eds) *New Authoritarian Practices in the Middle East and North Africa*. Edinburgh: Edinburgh University Press, pp. 208–27.

Lutterbeck, D. (2013). 'Arab Uprisings, Armed Forces, and Civil–Military Relations', *Armed Forces & Society* 39(1): 28–52.

McAdam, D., S. Tarrow and C. Tilly (2001). *Dynamics of Contention*. Cambridge: Cambridge University Press.

Maghraoui, D. (2022) '"The Freedom of No Speech": Journalists and the Multiple Layers of Authoritarian Practices in Morocco', in Ö. E. Topak, M. Mekouar and F. Cavatorta (eds) *New Authoritarian Practices in the Middle East and North Africa*. Edinburgh: Edinburgh University Press, pp. 189–207.

Mekouar, M. (2016). *Protest and Mass Mobilization: Authoritarian Collapse and Political Change in North Africa*. London: Taylor & Francis.

Mokhtaria, B. (2008). 'Cybercriminalité: Des techniciens de la DGSN en Suisse pour une formation'. *Le Quotidien d'Oran*, 22 July. https://algeria-watch.org/?p=24626.

Nesrouche, N. (2006). 'Il y a 20 Ans, Les Émeutes de Constantine'. *El Watan*, 14 November. https://www.djazairess.com/fr/elwatan/53870

Privacy International (2020). 'Revealed: The EU Training Regime Teaching Neighbours How to Spy'. *Privacy International* (blog), 10 November. http://privacyinternational.org/long-read/4289/revealed-eu-training-regime-teaching-neighbours-how-spy

Rejali, Darius (2007). *Torture and Democracy*. Princeton, NJ: Princeton University Press.

Rouadjia, Ahmed (2011). 'La Révolte «criminelle Des Jeunes Algériens»en Algérie et Le Soulèvement Populaire En Tunisie | El Watan', 18 January. https://www.elwatan.com/archives/idees-debats/la-revolte-criminelle-des-jeunes-algeriensen-algerie-et-le-soulevement-populaire-en-tunisie-18-01-2011

Shehabi, A. (2022) 'The Authoritarian Topography of the Bahraini State: Political Geographies of Power and Protest', in Ö. E. Topak, M. Mekouar and F. Cavatorta (eds) *New Authoritarian Practices in the Middle East and North Africa*. Edinburgh: Edinburgh University Press, pp. 51–72.

Slater, D. (2010). *Ordering Power: Contentious Politics and Authoritarian Leviathans in Southeast Asia*. New York: Cambridge University Press.

Tilly, C. (1995). *Popular Contention in Great Britain: 1758–1834*. Cambridge, MA: Harvard Universiy Press.

Tlemçani, S. (2010). 'Il l'a modernisée et disciplinée malgré des erreurs de gestion: L'empreinte de Ali Tounsi à la tête de la police'. *Algerie360*, March. https://www.algerie360.com/il-la-modernisee-et-disciplinee-malgre-des-erreurs-de-gestion-lempreinte-de-ali-tounsi-a-la-tete-de-la-police/

Topak, Ö. E., M. Mekouar and F. Cavatorta (2022) 'Introduction', in Ö. E. Topak, M. Mekouar and F. Cavatorta (eds) *New Authoritarian Practices in the Middle East and North Africa*. Edinburgh: Edinburgh University Press, pp. 1–29.

Uniacke, R. (2022) 'Digital Repression for Authoritarian Evolution in Saudi Arabia', in Ö. E. Topak, M. Mekouar and F. Cavatorta (eds) *New Authoritarian Practices in the Middle East and North Africa*. Edinburgh: Edinburgh University Press, pp. 228–51.

Waddington, P. A. J. (1998). 'Controlling Protest in Contemporary Historical and Comparative Perspective', in D. della Porta and H. Reiter (eds) *The Policing of Mass Demonstrations in Contemporary Democracies*, 111–40. Minneapolis: University of Minnesota Press.

Werenfels, I. (2007). *Managing Instability in Algeria: Elites and Political Change since 1995*. London: Routledge.

3

THE AUTHORITARIAN TOPOGRAPHY OF THE BAHRAINI STATE: POLITICAL GEOGRAPHIES OF POWER AND PROTEST

Ala'a Shehabi

Introduction

The idea of 'monarchical exceptionalism' in the Gulf, first posited after the Arab Spring, implied that the mode of hereditary absolute rule in Bahrain, Morocco and Jordan had its own inherent legitimacy enabling it to withstand popular opposition movements (Yom and Gause 2014). This was used to explain why the Gulf Cooperation Council (GCC) states seemed to be 'immune' to regime change. Rather than focusing on the concept and operationalisation of legitimacy, this chapter analyses the new authoritarian practices the Bahraini state used to maintain its matrix of domination, to reconstitute privileges and oppression in a sectarian racialised system. This occurred within the structural domains of the law, the media and economic wealth. The chapter further focuses on the disciplinary mechanisms that pin this matrix down. In turn, it demonstrates that monarchical exceptionalism does not exist, and that the Bahraini state has no inherent legitimacy as an absolute monarchy, but has instituted persistent structures of oppression within its matrix of power. Sectarianism here is not an essentialist paradigm, but serves as a disciplinary mechanism enforcing the violent hierarchy of racialised life in Bahrain.

A Tradition of Pre- and Post-colonial Authoritarian Practices

The Al-Khalifa ruling family, a Bedouin tribe from the Arabian Peninsula, conquered Bahrain in 1783 and has ruled through primogeniture ever since, warding off foreign competition through a protection treaty with Great Britain signed in 1820 and lasting until 1971. The ruling family relied on the protection of the British against foreign attacks, as the island's sovereignty had been contested by neighbouring powers for decades. Bahrain was a 'colony' in everything but name. Britain would remove rulers as it did in 1923, and acted as judge and arbiter in a mediated relationship between the Al-Khalifa princes and the indigenous Baharna population up until the official British withdrawal in 1971. The Al-Khalifa tribe's rule against the Baharna was characterised by routine and systematic sectarian violence for as long as historical records go back. The Baharna, a Shia Arab population, had lived in villages on fertile coastal land for centuries, worked the land, fished from the sea and produced basic goods from weaving or pottery.

The sheikhs of the Al-Khalifa tribe appropriated ownership of entire villages and enriched themselves through the collection of feudal rents (*Raqabiyya*) and forced labour (*sukhra*) on land they appropriated from villagers. Opposition movements in Bahrain date back to at least the 1920s. On 21 December 1921 a large group of Baharna presented a petition to the British Political Agency, stating that 'the Shi'ah Community is in a state of great humiliation and subject to public massacre. They have no refuge, the evidence of none of them is accepted, their properties are subject to plunder and themselves liable to maltreatment every moment. Injustice is increasing everyday' (Aljamri 2013). In the 1950s, popular cross-sect committees were formed, inspired by Nasserist socialist and anti-colonial fervour. The leaders of these committees were imprisoned and exiled. In the 1960s, in what became the March Intifada, strikers at the Bahrain Petroleum Company (BAPCO) demanded the ending of British rule and the mass lay-off of 450 plant workers at the main oil plant. They were heavily repressed. When the British left in 1971, they pushed for constitutional reforms 'in order to help "guard against revolutions"' (Jones 2020). A new constitutional monarchy was established with a constitution designed by an elected committee. This introduced a short-lived parliamentary experiment in 1973 that lasted two years. The Emir disbanded the parliament in 1975 when the latter decided to issue an eviction notice to an American military base and questioned the Emir's powers of arbitrary arrests. For the next twenty-five years, Bahrain was ruled under the state security law, conceived by Colonel Ian Henderson, an advisor to the Emir, which gave the Emir unprecedented powers of arrest and detention. This period coincided with the oil boom, with the ruling family overseeing an expansion of public services and urban infrastructure development. The national oil company – BAPCO – was nationalised, retaking control from the American companies, which had enjoyed cheap concessions for decades. The 1980s witnessed another cycle of protests and crackdowns in the aftermath of the 1979 Islamic revolution in Iran. Finally in 1992, over two hundred notables signed a national petition calling for the return of the 1973 constitution and another popular uprising ensued shortly afterwards. The twentieth-century repression–protest cycle is symptomatic of a volatile social contract between the Al-Khalifa, the British colonial agent and the indigenous subjects which they govern. Violence and colonial modernisation through policing and administrative reform continued long into the postcolonial period and shaped the process of nation-building.

The current King, Hamad bin Salman Al-Khalifa, ascended to the throne in 1998. By 2000 he had introduced a National Action Charter (*mithaq al'amal alwatani*) that promised a return or a 'constitutional monarchy', namely the re-promulgation of the 1973 constitution. The 'state' would become a 'Kingdom' and the 'Emir' would become the 'King'. In 2001, a national referendum resulted in a 98.4 per cent vote for the Charter in a show of rare national unity. By 2002, however, the King had introduced a constitution with nearly forty amendments that severely limited the power of a bicameral parliament.

Colonial Policing and Modernisation of the State

Bahrain, similar to the UAE (see Davidson 2022 in this volume), is a country where international support for authoritarianism is easily observable.[1] A few notable British agents and officers played very prominent roles in the authoritarian practices that we see today, none more so than Colonel Ian Henderson (in Bahrain from 1966 to 2013). After independence, he moved to Bahrain to work for the Emir after a stint in Kenya in which he played a role in suppressing the Mau uprising. A notorious shadowy figure known as the 'Butcher of Bahrain', he built the security apparatus – the current Ministry of the Interior – and the National Security Agency. We therefore see the continuation of the long history of British security support for the regime post-independence (Jones 2020). In addition to upgrading the security infrastructure, the British reformed the legal system, including ending slavery and the exploitative *sukhra* tax, a form of feudal control, whilst at the same time allowing Bahrain's rulers to receive a quarter of the country's wealth. Jones

(2020) notes: 'reform sought not only to defuse oppositional tension but to improve the long-term survivability of the regime. Reform can actually be, in some cases, a most insidious form of repression.'

Henderson died in 2011, but by then the Ministry of the Interior had come to rely even more on British and American 'freelance' security advisors, namely John Yates (former head of the Metropolitan Police in the UK) and John Timoney, both recruited in 2011 to oversee police 'reform'. The newer 'reforms' they introduced are closely modelled on British security systems, but lacked independence, or democratic oversight. Since 2011, these reforms have included mass CCTV surveillance installed across the country, a prison inspectorate modelled on the British Inspectorate of Prisons, which oversees prison conditions, an ombudsman in the Ministry of the Interior to investigate claims of torture, and community policing. In 2020, they introduced 'alternative punishments', which include 'community service' as an alternative to prison detention, and a proposal for 'open prisons' where inmates can leave and return. While some political prisoners have been released under these schemes, they have had to sign a statement saying they would refrain from criticising state institutions as a condition of release. Finally, scores of policemen and judges have been sent for human rights training in the UK and Europe. While positive on the surface, none of these reforms addresses structural problems: the lack of an independent judiciary, police accountability and the release of prisoners of conscience. These 'reforms' continue previous colonial traditions of upgrading the security apparatus as well as renewing the entanglements with Bahrain's British allies in which British advisors continue to profit financially, while twinning it with a discourse of liberal reformist modernisation. All this did/does not change the level of actual repression and the de-democratisation actually taking place under the guise of British-supported 'reform'. The British, in this way, also continue seeing Bahrain's authoritarianism as an opportunity for 'trade' for British security companies: a protection racket of sorts.

Another structural feature of colonial design is the way the police force itself has been built on an 'ethnic' policing model whereby 'a minority within a colony was utilized as police against the majority. The British disseminated an ideology of martial races and criminal tribes in order to maintain the minority's sense of superiority over the majority' (Strobl 2018). Following the 1920s' protests and petitions, the British chose to adopt an ethnic policing model and dropped all Persian and Baharna personnel from the police force. This tradition continues to characterise the police force today, in which the upper echelons continue to be manned by Al-Khalifa members and their close Sunni loyalist tribes, while riot police units are manned by thousands of foreign mercenary recruits from Pakistan, Yemen and Jordan. Tens of thousands of these policemen have been given Bahraini citizenship and benefit from social housing. This became particularly contentious in 2011, when a largely naturalised foreign police force was tasked with repressing the indigenous population, who are in turn punished through the revocation of their citizenship. It brings to the fore questions of identity, belonging and sectarian hierarchies in the way citizenship is used as an authoritarian tool.

Citizenship and Statelessness

The question of citizenship has closely been tied to patterns of sectarian demographic engineering. This came to a critical political juncture in 2006, when a senior foreign government advisor leaked government documents, in what became known as the 'Bandargate Report', revealing intricate state plans for mass naturalisation of foreign Sunnis (Frayer 2006). This is in contrast to other Gulf states, where citizenship is largely restricted to certain groups of particular tribal lineage and historical presence. While mass naturalisations proliferated as a mechanism of 'sunnification', the transverse practice of rendering political opposition leaders 'stateless' by revoking their citizenship as a form of punishment has also increased. In one day alone in 2019, 138 people were stripped of their citizenship, bringing the total number to over a thousand since 2020 (*BBC News* 2019). The decision to revoke citizenship also affects the citizen's rights and the state entitlements of their families. It may well be the case that the Shia are now no longer a majority due to this demographic engineering, but there is no way of verifying this statistically. In this way, the ruling family would tackle its long-standing 'minority rule' status (minority group governing a majority without consent).

The Counter-revolutionary Response to the 2011 Uprising

The first wave of uprisings in Tunisia, Egypt, Bahrain, Libya and Syria was promising in both form and scale. Collective imagining and collective action were quickly translated into events like the 'day of rage', and slogans of 'Justice, freedom and liberty' and 'The people want the downfall of the regime', together with occupying public space. New forms and expressions of emancipatory enactments that challenged dominant logics of power under-pinned those vivid moments of collective effervescence. In Bahrain, nearly a third of Bahrainis took to the streets over a three-week period, occupying a key site in central Manama, the iconic Pearl Roundabout, setting up a small self-governed colony and constructing within it the new world that they dreamed of.

Within a few months if not weeks, each country's protests took a different trajectory depending on the state's response. Similar to other MENA regimes examined in this book,[2] in Bahrain, the government's immediate response was to use violence and to clear the 'square', forcibly removing the protesters occupying the Pearl Roundabout. Interestingly, after a first failed attempt, the state realised it could not do this alone. After convening a meeting with GCC leaders, the King 'invited' the GCC Peninsula Shield Force (GCCPS), a previously little-known military entity consisting of around 1,000 troops from Saudi Arabia and the UAE, to enter Bahrain on 13 March. According to recently released American emails, the King of Bahrain told King Abdullah of Saudi Arabia to use a policy of 'shoot to kill, if needed, to aid overwhelmed Bahraini security forces in dispersing anti-government demonstrators' ('Clinton emails Ref C05787272' 2011). Protesters considered this an illegal military 'invasion', shouting a slogan of 'Bahrain is free, is free. Peninsula Shield get out'. The Saudi military intervention made international headlines, and even though we now know US and UK allies were neither informed nor consulted, they avoided public condemnation. A foreign invasion was needed to quell the uprising because the Bahraini forces were overwhelmed. They had attempted to clear the main square a few weeks earlier on 17 February, killing five protesters, but then withdrew after they shot and killed another protester (Abdulredha Buhmaid) who was marching to the square again. The video of his death went viral and was reported internationally, encouraging protesters to resume the occupation of the Pearl Roundabout. Ultimately, Saudi forces thus bolstered the Bahraini ones and ended the protests. At the same time this also certainly sent a signal. It indicated that the GCC was capable of and just beginning a journey of unilateral military intervention without Western military support and it could be used as leverage for action in other countries like Libya, Yemen or Syria where the GCC had particular interests in overthrowing regimes. The intervention in Bahrain was a harbinger of the new, overt interventionist approach that Saudi and the UAE would play in those other countries.

These forces spread across the country setting up checkpoints at key sites, clearing the Pearl Roundabout, and taking over the main public hospital, which it accused protesters of occupying, and arresting doctors and medical staff. It was not enough to reclaim the space; the state physically destroyed the Pearl monument altogether. Ironically, the monument was originally built to commemorate the establishment of the Gulf Corporation Council in 1981 and here the GCC forces were destroying it.

On state television, the King's son declared that 'there was nowhere anyone could hide on this island'. On a daily basis, security forces raided villages, arresting anyone who had been identified in the protests. State media launched a daily show that identified all the key figures who were seen at protests as part of a campaign to vilify and accuse the protesters of being Iranian agents. Those who appeared on state TV would either be quickly arrested or would immediately be sacked. Approximately 4,000 people were indeed fired from their jobs in the public sector. It was by far the biggest and bloodiest crackdown in Bahrain's contemporary history in terms of death toll and arrests.

The state justified its militarised response as necessary to avoid 'instability', 'chaos' and 'turmoil' in the country, and to protect against an 'Iranian takeover' and argued that the 'current social order is infallible' (Jones 2020). The regime ramped up old and new forms of information control to galvanise this narrative. What we now call 'fake news' was a well-documented programme of disinformation. Jones outlines four main modes of disinformation. The first mode, censorship and insulation to limit information, included shutting down the only opposition newspaper, *Alwasat*, arresting journalists and preventing the entry of hundreds of foreign correspondents. Secondly, there was increasing propaganda, through the official news agency, Bahrain News Agency (BNA), the state television channel and six newspapers. This would include forced confessions by key activists, open disparagement, and fictional dramatisation of alleged crimes, among other things. State propaganda, aimed at domestic loyalists, fed a barrage of what Jones (2020) calls 'strategic disinformation'. Some examples of this were the use of photoshopped images of protesters, false confessions of crimes, such as the murder of police, obtained under torture, videos of allegedly seized military-grade weapons, stories of Iranian ships smuggling weapons into Bahrain, Iranian drones and Iranian tunnels. Daily and weekly programmes were aired as part of a campaign to justify the crackdown, vilify protesters and cement patriotic loyalty and support for the King. Thirdly, the regime hired the services of Western PR companies, spending $35 million between 2011 and 2012 alone. Their role included threatening news platforms like the *Guardian*, CNN and *The Independent* with legal action, resulting in articles being taken down and documentaries being pulled. This campaign targeted even Wikipedia edits (Jones 2020). Finally, social media offered a new frontier for the info-war. Early in 2011, anonymous accounts like @7areghum were accused in the BICI report of using sectarian hate speech and inciting violence. The situation developed further when, in 2016, strange hashtags started trending around the time of big security encounters, such as the raid in Duraz in 2017. Marc Owen Jones' analysis revealed that 51 per cent of tweets on these hashtags were from bots aimed at 'spreading propaganda' and 'drowning out legitimate or critical information' (Jones 2020).

This information warfare ran parallel with security operations. As in many other MENA regimes which rely on informant surveillance,[3] regime supporters were urged to inform on neighbours, colleagues or even family members who took part in protests. This was another way of expanding surveillance, crowdsourcing the work of the intelligence services and ensuring their loyalty to the regime in support of its crackdown. These collaborators were rewarded in different ways depending on their request or needs; it could be in the form of taking over the manager's position if they were fired for protest participation, getting ownership of a government housing plot, or strategic jobs in government institutions. This had a lasting effect on social relations, leading to deep sectarian rifts in which one group benefited from the oppression of the other. Benefits would include job promotion (if colleagues got sacked for taking part in protests), priority in government posts or scholarships.

During the first three months of military curfew, the state tried civilians (protesters and non-protesters) in summary show trials in military courts. National-security-related charges would go to the upper court, and protest-related charges would go to the lower court. Indeed, I observed several of these military trials as a relative of some of those arrested. Without a modicum of due process, these trials would last for fifteen minutes and with no lawyers present in most cases and would result in severe sentences, from one year for each count of 'illegal gathering'/'spreading false information' to life imprisonment for 'plotting to overthrow the regime'. The latter was based on an obscure 'terrorism' law within which 'harming national unity' is a crime.

The unannounced execution of three protesters by firing squad in January 2017 (*BBC News* 2017a), a year after Saudi Arabia executed forty-seven prisoners including a religious cleric, Nimr Al-Nimr (Reuters 2016), sent shock-waves domestically. It followed a pattern: group executions of protesters (who had previously been convicted of 'police murders' in summary trials and sentenced to death) in the middle of the night without the prior knowledge of families or those being executed. Bodies were buried in secret to avoid any public funeral or commemoration. The executions received little international attention, let alone condemnation. The secretive but clearly planned and premeditated nature of these executions and the scale of them in small close-linked communities sent reverberations across Bahrain's small villages. Executions are rarely enacted or signed off by the King, but they do occur when pressure arises from hardline factions of the Bahraini and Saudi governments. The last execution of a political prisoner that had taken place was that of Isa Qambar in 1996. The 2017 group executions are part of a historic pattern in the authoritarian response to Bahrain's episodic uprisings as an exceptional, singular act within the arc of the authoritarian response, and one that has been used to violently mark the apex in power consolidation in the knowledge of complete state impunity at the international level.

The project to cement the matrix of power in every structural domain continued relentlessly. The security and financial cost of consolidating regime power, however, was much higher than in the past. 'Stability' comes at the expense of a higher level of security and military investment in more surveillance and 'crowd control' weapons. At one point in 2011–13, security forces were using up to 2,000 tear gas canisters across small villages as a form of collective punishment, bigger prisons, bigger PR efforts, bigger surveillance systems and bigger budgets. Leaked defence procurement documents showed the government was stockpiling 1.8 million tear gas canisters (Kerr and Mundy 2013). At the same time in this period, the state spent $32.5 million on Western PR firms between 2011 and 2012 (Jones 2020: 300). The latter was fuelled by the desire to counter the critical coverage the Bahraini state was receiving in the international media – in other words, to hide the violence. Public relation companies offered 'reputation management services' that tried either to minimise coverage or to force state narratives onto the media 'as another point of view' that required equal reporting, often threatening news outlets with legal action, inviting selected journalists into the country. In this battle over narrative, oppositional forces, more than in previous episodes, used an international human rights discourse that focused on freedom of speech and freedom of assembly, while documenting social media cases of torture, death in custody and protest repression. We explore this more in the next section.

The Arab Spring and the Rise and Fall of the Human Rights Discourse

In Bahrain, some of the most popular leaders of the 2011 Arab Spring movement were human rights activists like Nabeel Rajab and the Khawaja family, who used liberal human rights discourse to criticise the sectarian violence of the state. In response, the state set up several Gongos (government NGOs), while shutting down political societies, and eliminated all vestiges of independent civil society. It sent large delegations to Geneva to confront human rights activists pushing for accountability through mechanisms like the Universal Periodic Review. To subvert this, the Bahraini King was strongly advised by his American allies to invite Professor Cherif Bassiouni, a prominent human rights lawyer, to chair the Bahrain Independent Commission of Inquiry (BICI). This was unprecedented. While the state officially denied any wrongdoing, Bassiouni's Commission spent three months and gathered testimonies and evidence of police killings of thirty-six protesters, and 'systematic torture' in custody. Bassiouni's report ran to several hundred pages and was presented to the King at a lavish party in his palace. The report did not contain recommendations for reparative justice or accountability, although Bassiouni did go on the record later to say that it was those in the highest echelons of the Interior Ministry who should be held accountable. Again, while a novel and reformist act like an independent human rights report allowed international praise to be heaped on the King, the material conditions of repression remained. Many political prisoners are still detained at the time of writing, and no compensation was offered to the families of those killed. This situation echoes across the region; Morocco, Egypt and Bahrain share the closest comparative experience of the absence of restorative justice – a notion that can be engaged within authoritarian structures that depend on different forms of violence.

While the main actors of the street protests were youth groups mobilising at the village level and congregating centrally at Manama or other landmarks, the main opposition groups were pursuing different strategies. Some political groups, such as Al-Wafa and HAQ, called for a *Jumhuriyaa* or 'republic' in Bahrain, as their interpretation of the slogan 'the downfall of the regime' was to remove the ruling family from power. In my interviews with some of the leaders of these groups, I understood that this was a strategy to escalate demands so that the more 'moderate' groups would not settle for half-baked reforms that would not give equal voice and representation to the Baharna. The Al-Wefaq political society (a Shia political party) and Wa'ad (a leftist party), which had, prior to 2011, taken part in elections and had won just under half the seats in Parliament, were reluctantly forced to resign their parliamentary seats and join the street protest movement. The leaders of both parties, Sheikh Ali Salman and Ebrahim Sharif, were later arrested and imprisoned alongside more radical political opposition leaders who had, prior to 2011, taken stringent positions on boycotting all parliamentary elections. Ten years later, all these leaders, with the exception of Ebrahim Shareef who was released after five years' imprisonment, are still in jail or in exile.

Gendered Authoritarianism

Since the focus of this volume is on specific ruptures in modes of authoritarian practice, attention should shift to what Hasso (2016) refers to as the 'sex-sect-police nexus' in the post-revolutionary era in Bahrain, Egypt and other countries. In response to the increase in female participation, and the way new formations of activism disputed the gender order, states increasingly focused on the gendered dimension of state violence (Hasso and Salime 2016).[4] A river of black abaya-clad women from conservative backgrounds, visible in much of the iconic imagery of mass protests, stood alongside men. Women continued to be constantly cast in relation to men – where men are at the centre in media headlines, which included lines such as 'women stood behind' or 'beside men', emphasising their roles as mothers, wives and sisters over their involvement as citizens. The uprising produced a set of iconic and heroic female figures, who challenged social norms while leading protests against the state. Many names come to mind, with the Yemeni activist Towakkul Karman even receiving a Nobel Peace Prize (even as she later became a proponent of the Saudi-led war on Yemen). In Bahrain, female doctors, nurses, teachers and mothers were central to the organisation of street protests in direct and indirect ways. I noted at the time that necessity as well as new-found agency drove participation: "'It wasn't a social decision, it was out of need – women maintained the struggle, women maintained the *resistance*'" (quoted in Fielding-Smith 2011); as more men were arrested, women's responsibilities increased.

The more women became active, the harsher the strategies used to alienate them from their activism. In this mode, assaults and harassment on the streets, sexual abuse in prisons and other forms of violence against female political activists are meant to contain women's revolutionary acts and exclude them from power politics. Over time, we have seen how these actions alienate and displace women from their political role and from the revolution they helped create. This renders them more vulnerable to further violence.

Many prominent examples are now on the record. Female doctors and nurses, who were part of a group of fifty medical staff detained during the military takeover of the main public hospital, were arrested and tortured, with the accusation that they had attempted to overthrow the regime, and were eventually sentenced to fifteen years' imprisonment. The case of the doctors being tried in military courts attracted global attention. Other prominent cases also demonstrated the diversity of targets: the arrest of the journalist Nazeeha Saeed, who reported being forced to get down on all fours and bark like a dog; the poet Ayat Al-Qurmuzi, who reported having a toilet brush pushed down her mouth; female staff members who worked at the Formula 1 track who were dragged from their office building to detention facilities. Female academics were also arrested in their homes in their dressing gowns as punishment for the student protests on the University of Bahrain campus.

Although the use of torture was not new, reports of sexual abuse and rape were much greater than in the past. In a recent BBC documentary, Najah Yousif, another activist, broke down as she described the sexual abuse she had suffered in prison. This form of torture is, however, not only directed against women. The BICI report stated: 'there were numerous allegations of sexual abuse of detainees at various locations including the NSA building, Asri, Al Naim, Al Riffa, Al Qudaibiya, Al Wista, Sitra, Hamad Town and Isa Town . . . Two detainees alleged that hoses and other objects were inserted into their anus and that guards groped their genitalia aggressively.' Sexual abuse against female detainees can be and has been directed by both policemen and -women. Similarly, in Saudi Arabia, the prominent women's rights activist Loujain Al-Hathloul also reported sexual abuse in detention (Michaelson 2019). Given the sensitivity of this topic, very little research, beyond human rights documentation, has explored the use of sexual abuse as a torture method by authoritarian states and the long-term psychological effects on victims. The use of rape as a weapon of war has been documented in places like Iraq, focusing on ISIS fighters and the rape of Yazidi women, but much less in authoritarian contexts like Egypt, where it has also been used by security forces against political dissidents.

Much of the research on authoritarianism, repression and policing has missed out the crucial dimension of gendered policies and policing. Strobl's research specifically traces the establishment of the female contingent of the Bahraini police force back to British colonial rule and argues that 'the very introduction of policewomen in the Gulf region is a colonial imposition' (Strobl 2008). As of 2005, it was estimated that policewomen formed approximately 10 per cent of the force and that 98 per cent were Sunni. It is hard to tell if this composition has changed. During the 2011 protests, female police units were used to carry out all arrests of female protesters. Women were also on the receiving end of male police violence, for instance during house raids, during interrogation, or during the breaking up of protests. Indeed, one of the first women killed, Bahiyya Alaradi, was shot in the head at a petrol station by military forces the day after the GCC Peninsula Shield entered the country. Male police also conducted interrogations and took part in the torture and sexual assault of women in custody.

State propogandists also played a significant role in vilifying female protesters in particular through codes of honour and shame. During the second clearing of the roundabout, state media produced images claiming that underwear and other items were found in one of the tents, insinuating that protesters were having illicit sexual relations in the tents. This also carried sectarian tropes in reference to protesters being *'awlad al-mut'aa'* (illegitimate children, in reference to temporary marriages sanctioned in Shia Islam). While this did not go as far as the 'virginity testing' that took place in Egypt, it was designed to question the honour of women and, in doing so, dehumanising and justifying attacks on them. Socially, the religious Shia establishment also tried to dissuade women from protesting, citing safety concerns.

This brief outline of visible gendered state violence against women after 2011 increasingly looks like the state punishing women for their more prominent role and the increasing radical feminist discourse that is being adopted. The uprisings disrupted a pattern of modernisation spearheaded by 'state feminists' – usually the first lady (e.g. Suzanne Mubarak in Egypt, Asma al-Assad in Syria, Sabeeka Al-Khalifa in Bahrain, Reema bin Bandar Al Saud in Saudi Arabia). This allowed the soft face of authoritarianism to emerge through performative acts filling up a calendar of annual events such as the opening ceremonies of female-run businesses, participation in international/multilateral conferences, especially UN initiatives, or the seeking of the appointment of UN Goodwill Ambassadors. There is an important contradiction here, because while the project of modernisation is crucial to upgrading authoritarianism, 'saving women's bodies' has also been used as a justification in the West for waging wars in the Middle East, such as those in Iraq and Afghanistan, by both liberals and neo-conservatives. The West, in its soft-power dealings with dictatorships, legitimises state feminists as political representatives of Arab women, while failing to listen to, amplify or support Arab women calling for democratic rights in these same countries.

The Political Economy of Authoritarianism

In the Gulf, the economically dominant class comprises of the core ruling family members as well as their tribal support network, interlocutors or brokers (Hertog 2011). 'The state' is often used interchangeably with the ruling family given its political and economic dominance across state machinations (the daily administration of the state), structural domains (law, media, the economy) and disciplinary mechanisms (the army, the police, the judiciary). The relationship between state extraction of oil rent capital and the political order was originally theorised by Beblawi and Luciani (1987) in their rentier state theory. In simple terms, this theory says that there is a social contract between the oil-producing state and its citizens whereby individual welfare services provided by the regime are reciprocated through people's loyalty and consent to the regime. Authoritarian power is gleaned from an 'oil-stability nexus': the ability to extract, sell and allocate a country's resources in order to build state capacities, social spending and disciplinary mechanisms of surveillance, policing and coercion. Smith (2017) posits the idea of 'rent leverage' and looks at state capacity (the state's ability to collect resources and allocate them, e.g spending on domestic coercion) to emphasise the complexities of the political influence of oil. The GCC states' oil revenues fund exorbitant military expenditure on defence and security.

In Bahrain, another political economy of land was created by the King of Bahrain, Hamad bin Isa Al-Khalifa. In 1991, the King issued a royal decree to give himself the sole prerogative to gift land, disallowing other senior members to do so as they had done in the past. A couple of years later, Bahrain witnessed an accelerated process of land reclamation from the sea. Bahrain benefits from shallow waters and cheap dredging costs. Over 65 square kilometres of land were reclaimed from the sea and transferred to companies owned by the King. Between 2003 and 2014 the King also built a parallel portfolio of over £1 billion of real estate in London, which was revealed in a *Financial Times* investigation in 2014. The country's land mass, which mushroomed into the sea from the northern coast, became the new means of capital accumulation, replacing oil rent. Sea plots were commodified and sold to foreign investors, and there is plenty of sea, just like there was plenty of oil once. This created a new political economy, of real estate developers, lawyers, bankers, commercial and retail property owners and, more importantly, spatial reconfigurations as new gated cities occupied by the rich are increasingly served by an underclass of low-paid workers. Much of this development caters for Western expatriate communities, other Gulf citizen investors and the younger generation of Bahrainis from notable merchant families who form an oligarchic class. The class divisions among Bahraini society roughly align with sectarian lines in the sense that relative poverty and unemployment afflict the Baharna Shi'a disproportionately and discriminatorily, particularly in high-level government jobs. Other forms of discrimination in public services include access to state housing, university scholarships and investment in local leisure infrastructure, and occur indirectly in business transactions such as building permits (through the application of arbitrary zoning laws) and government procurement contracts.

This extractivist rentier political economy causes great inequality and environmental devastation. The nature of the island, its palm groves, natural oases, fertile land and coral reefs which were cultivated by indigenous communities for centuries, have today been destroyed. It was this accelerated land grab that led to the uprising in 2011 after a parliamentary investigation in 2006 published its report detailing this process of massive coastal land grabs by the ruling family. Initially, many of the artificial islands that were being dredged on the coastal path of ancient villages of the northern shore had promised to contain crucial social housing for those on housing waiting lists in these villages. Protests in Duraz, for example, were called off after these promises were made. However, it later emerged from plans and from what we see after the completion of the construction of these islands that they are made up of luxury private resorts for a privileged few. Foreign investors are given residencies and voting rights in municipal elections in Bahrain to encourage investment. Resurgent interest in urban studies has brought interest in how space is reconfigured to fragment, control, create enclaves, and exacerbate class inequalities as cities of the Gulf grow (see Al-Nakib 2016).

The Regional Arc of Autocracy – Deeper Alliances and New Accords

Authoritarianism is internally and externally contingent; contingent on the level of state power (governmentality in the Foucauldian sense) over bodies within the state's territories, and contingent on classic Westphalian notions of sovereignty (i.e., political recognition by other states in the form of alliances and support). Current and historical colonial entanglements, kinship, inter-marriages and tribal loyalties and rivalries, as well as the blurred boundaries between the physical and the digital, complicate the territorial boundary of the state. The internet has become a major frontier in understanding authoritarianism and explains the desire by states to enact increasing repression.[5] Bahrain post-2011 in particular has become more intertwined with, and strongly beholden to, Saudi Arabia through very deep economic and political dependency and loyalty. It is the affliction of being a small, relatively poorer state next to big richer neighbours. What the events of 2011 did was to tie in and lock the ruling family in an unwritten pact with Saudi Arabia. The ruling family even initially called for a 'confederation' between the two states. Bahrain in turn lent its full and unquestioned support to Saudi's regional decisions. What started out as proxy conflicts in several countries (Syria, Libya, Yemen) has turned into full-blown civil wars. The Saudi/UAE/Bahrain blockade of Qatar in 2017 took a much more vindictive and personalised character, steeped in the ancient tribal rivalry between the Al-Khalifas and Al-Thanis. This had looked like it had been settled after the land-dispute ruling at the Hague in 2000 and the rulers of both states embarked on ambitious joint plans such as the Qatar–Bahrain Causeway (now on hold). With those conflicts still raging, this chasm has been pushed further by the so-called Abraham Accords and the official normalisation of relations between the UAE and Bahrain and Israel that was signed in September 2020. At the same time this cemented the anti-Iran axis of countries led by the UAE and Saudi Arabia in the region.

There was always the suspicion that secret relations between GCC and Israel existed, but this was confirmed when Israeli media reported that a secret Israeli office had been operating in Bahrain since 2009 under a commercial guise. For the UAE, the urgency came in the form of a $23 billion arms deal for the sale of powerful F-35 fighter jets that Israel had previously been blocking (*US plans sale of F-35 fighter jets to UAE in $23B arms deal* 2020). Following on from the signing ceremony at the White House, relations are being forged at all levels; from education to knowledge exchange about water desalination techniques, to, as Israeli media report, 'learning from Bahrain's experience of land reclamation' (Kerr 2020).

For several years, the GCC states – bar Kuwait and Qatar – have worked towards integrating their surveillance and intelligence infrastructure with that of Israel. As the contribution by Davidson (2022) in this volume makes clear, the UAE has been working closely with Israeli surveillance firms at least as far back as 2008 (Donaghy 2015), and examples have been revealed slowly (Blau and Scharf 2019). For example, in 2019 the UAE had purchased spy planes from an Israeli firm with which to monitor Iran. The spectre of the Iranian threat has then been used to purchase further surveillance for the internal monitoring of citizens. Since 2015, authoritarian states, including Saudi Arabia (see also Uniacke 2022 in this volume) and Bahrain, have been using one of Israel's most sophisticated digital surveillance tools for targeted surveillance, Pegasus, a spyware developed by the NSO Group that can enable a target's phone remotely. The NSO is a company set up for members of Unit 8200, part of the Israeli Defence Force. Pegasus can hack into Windows, Linux and Apple hardware and Facebook software via 'zero-day' vulnerabilities in their operating systems. Bill Marczak first discovered that Pegasus was being used in the UAE in 2015 against Ahmed Mansour, a human rights activist who is now serving a ten-year prison sentence. This forced Apple to issue an urgent iOS global update. Since then, Marczak's team has discovered that 'at least six countries with significant Pegasus operations have previously been linked to abusive use of spyware to target civil society, including Bahrain, Kazakhstan, Mexico, Morocco, Saudi Arabia, and the United Arab Emirates' (Marczak et al. 2018).

The use of commercial digital interception tools in Bahrain was in fact detected just after the Arab Spring. In 2012 and prior to the NSO discovery, Marczak uncovered the use of German–British spyware called FinFisher that was sent to my personal email and was the first specimen of software that security analysts had gained access to (Marquis-Boire and Marczak 2012). Bahrain began building digital intelligence capacities through a dedicated 'anti-cybercrime directorate' much earlier. This directorate, would purchase and deploy the tools against dissidents (both within the country and abroad) while receiving significant operational support from the foreign spy company, in Bahrain's case Gamma International or the NSO Group.

Nationalism, the Far Right and its Forked Media Tongue

While the uprising in Bahrain was the largest in the country's modern history, the counter-revolution was the most brutal. During the violence, the ruling family's loyalists increased their support for the measures of repression used against fellow citizens. The regime used ultra-nationalist and populist rhetoric that appealed to ethno-sectarian fears and rallied anti-Shia and anti-Iranian xenophobic vilification. This nationalism become compelling to loyalists who felt existentially threatened by the Trojan Horse of an Iranian takeover on the one hand and, on the other, the constant portrayal of Bahraini Shi'a as a fifth column. Information coming from the BBC, Aljazeera or the mainstream media about Bahrain became less trustworthy. Authoritarianism cannot accomplish its goals through the use of police intimidation alone. Distorting information becomes an important tool, and though the use of state propaganda is not new, but what is now referred as 'fake news' refers to deliberate disinformation campaigns disseminated faster and farther through social media networks. The early disinformation campaign relied on loyalist accounts, Information Affairs Authority employees, and even intelligence officers who would tweet about pending arrests before they occurred. Marc Owen Jones first noticed the shift to larger-scale disinformation when pro-government hashtags began to trend following the raid and arrest of Ayatollah Sheikh Issa Qassim in the village of Duraz in Bahrain in 2017. Careful analysis revealed these were mostly 'bots', or fake accounts (Jones 2020). Owen Jones noted a similar pattern in pro-MBS hashtags after the Khashoggi murder. The detection of fake accounts from real accounts and the role that states play in 'platform manipulation' on a mass scale is now believed to be a global problem for social media companies, in some cases affecting electoral outcomes in the West. The purpose of platform manipulation is to undermine/disrupt the public conversation; artificial amplification of certain accounts; getting hashtags to trend; or aggressive trolling. This is not only done through fake accounts. A New York Times investigation described a media operation inside the royal court in Saudi Arabia that includes a 'troll farm' in which hundreds of youth are directed '*via group chats in apps like WhatsApp and Telegram, sending them lists of people to threaten, insult and intimidate; daily tweet quotas to fill; and pro-government messages to augment*' (Benner *et al.* 2018). More recently, regimes have shifted to the use of 'social media influencers', people who have built significant profiles to promote their policies, from health (e.g. Covid-19 campaigns, or pro-Israel messaging). Authoritarian states across the world, beginning with some of the Gulf states, are investing and extending their tools to the internet in new and innovative ways that we are only just beginning to understand.

Conclusion

The 2011 uprisings were a sequence of related non-violent political ruptures of historical significance. The counter-revolutions that followed were the antithesis of these ruptures and sought to restore the status quo. Research into the former focused on social movements and valorised resistance theory, but interest in authoritarian practices has waned in liberal academic spaces. Sites of research like Bahrain are often dismissed for their small size or marginality or framed simply as places with sectarian conflict. This misses the deeper and more interesting insights that are relevant globally.

The early authoritarian response was reactionary and focused on standard disciplinary approaches: elimination of overt opposition and dissent. The punitive and vindictive nature of the clamp-down on opposition leaders, trade unionists and human rights activists, as well as teachers, doctors and athletes, among others, harks back to the periodic cycles of protest, repression and appeasement of previous decades. At the same time, features of new authoritarian methods such as surveillance and information control also emerged. Major disinformation campaigns on social media platforms, used to foment xenophobic nationalism and distort narratives, and censor and curtail support for opposition movements, relied on fake news and fake bots on such a large scale as to influence narratives. Ultimately, though, the geopolitical arc of autocracy will continue to entrench authoritarian practices and reveal contradictions that will produce the inevitability of another uprising.

Notes

1 See also the 'Authoritarian learning and Alliances' section in the Introduction (Topak et al. 2022).

2 For an overview see the 'Protests and Policing' section in the Introduction (Topak et al. 2022).

3 On other cases of informant surveillance examined in this book see the 'Authoritarian Practices Shaping Civil Society and the Media' section in the Introduction (Topak et al. 2022).

4 See also the cases of Morocco (Maghraoui 2022) and Sudan (Hassan 2022) discussed in this book, and the 'Gender and the double-authoritarian burden' section in the Introduction (Topak et al. 2022).
5 See the 'Digital Surveillance' section in the Introduction for an overview of internet surveillance practices used by MENA regimes examined in this book, from other Gulf States to Egypt, Turkey and Sudan.

References

Aljamri, A. (2013). 'A Chasm without Karama', *Islander's Oasis*, 27 June. https://ali aljamri.com/2013/06/27/chasm-without/

Al-Nakib, F. (2016). *Kuwait Transformed: A History of Oil and Urban Life*. Stanford: Stanford University Press.

AP News (2002). 'US Plans Sale of F-35 Fighter Jets to UAE In $23b Arms Deal'. https://apnews.com/article/bahrain-israel-iran-united-arab-emirates-middle-ea st-822123a6e70cd6154dfd6433c9fcf610

BBC News (2019). 'Bahrain Revokes Citizenship of 138 People After Mass Trial'. https://www.bbc.co.uk/news/world-middle-east-47947036

Beblawi, H. and G. Luciani (2015). *The Rentier State*. London: Routledge.

Benner, K. *et al.* (2018). *Saudis' Image Makers: A Troll Army and a Twitter Insider – The New York Times*. https://www.nytimes.com/2018/10/20/us/politics/saudi -image-campaign-twitter.html

Blau, U. and A. Scharf (n.d.). 'Mysterious Israeli Businessman behind UAE Spy Planes Mega-deal', *Haaretz.com*. https://www.haaretz.com/middle-east-news/ .premium-israel-businessman-uae-spy-planes-iran-saudi-arabia-1.7696711

Davidson, C. M. (2022). 'The United Arab Emirates: Evolving Authoritarian Tools', in Ö. E. Topak, M. Mekouar and F. Cavatorta (eds) *New Authoritarian Practices in the Middle East and North Africa*. Edinburgh: Edinburgh University Press, pp. 320–39.

Donaghy, R. (2015). *Falcon Eye: The Israeli-installed Mass Civil Surveillance System of Abu Dhabi, Middle East Eye*. http://www.middleeasteye.net/news/falcon-eye-isr aeli-installed-mass-civil-surveillance-system-abu-dhabi

Fielding-Smith, A. (2011). *The Face of Freedom*. https://www.ft.com/content/988a3 a20-1fc1-11e1-9916-00144feabdc0

Frayer, L. (2006). 'Al-Bandar Ejection Exposes Bahrain Split', *AP News*, 2 October. https://apnews.com/article/fd8c82c255790fb034a12f1dec61c2b8

Hassan, Y. (2022). 'The Evolution of the Sudanese Authoritarian State: The December Uprising and the Unraveling of a "Persistent" Autocracy', in Ö. E. Topak, M. Mekouar and F. Cavatorta (eds) *New Authoritarian Practices in the Middle East and North Africa*. Edinburgh: Edinburgh University Press, pp. 252–75.

Hasso, F. S. and Z. Salime (2016). *Freedom without Permission: Bodies and Space in the Arab Revolutions*. Durham, NC: Duke University Press.

Hertog, S. (2011). *Princes, Brokers, and Bureaucrats: Oil and the State in Saudi Arabia*. Ithaca: Cornell University Press.

Jones, M. O. (2020). *Political Repression in Bahrain*. Cambridge: Cambridge University Press.

Kerr, S. (2020). 'Israel Expects $500m in Deals with Bahrain and UAE', *Financial Times*, 15 September. https://www.ft.com/content/d554cc7c-5c49-46dd-ae2b -fb1bbc74a117

Kerr, S. and S. Mundy (2013). 'Bahrain Boosts Supplies of Tear Gas as Instability Continues', *Financial Times*. https://www.ft.com/content/67a619e2-397d-11 e3-a3a4-00144feab7de

Maghraoui, D. (2022). '"The Freedom of No Speech": Journalists and the Multiple Layers of Authoritarian Practices in Morocco', in Ö. E. Topak, M. Mekouar and F. Cavatorta (eds) *New Authoritarian Practices in the Middle East and North Africa*. Edinburgh: Edinburgh University Press, pp. 189–207.

Marczak, B. et al. (2018) *HIDE AND SEEK: Tracking NSO Group's Pegasus Spyware to Operations in 45 Countries*. https://citizenlab.ca/2018/09/hide-and-seek-track ing-nso-groups-pegasus-spyware-to-operations-in-45-countries/

Marquis-Boire, M. and B. Marczak (2012). *From Bahrain with Love: FinFisher's Spy Kit Exposed, The Citizen Lab*. https://citizenlab.ca/2012/07/from-bahrain-with-l ove-finfishers-spy-kit-exposed/

Michaelson, R. (2019). '"What They Did to Me Was So Horrific": Brutal Silencing of a Saudi Feminist', *The Guardian*. https://www.theguardian.com/global-devel opment/2019/may/24/what-they-did-to-me-was-so-horrific-brutal-silencing-of -a-saudi-feminist-loujain-al-hathloul

Shehabi, A. (2016). 'Inviolable Sheikhs and Radical Subjects: Bahrain's Cyclical Sovereignty Crisis', *Arab Studies Journal* 24(1): 228–53.

Shehabi, A. and M. O. Jones (2015). *Bahrain's Uprising: Resistance and Repression in The Gulf*. London: Zed Books. https://www.amazon.co.uk/Bahrains-Uprising -Resistance-Repression-Gulf/dp/1783604336

Smith, B. (2017). 'Resource Wealth as Rent Leverage: Rethinking the Oil–Stability Nexus', *Conflict Management and Peace Science* 34(6), pp. 597–617.

Strobl, S. (2008). 'The Women's Police Directorate in Bahrain: An Ethnographic Exploration of Gender Segregation and the Likelihood of Future Integration', *International Criminal Justice Review* 18(1): 39–58.

Strobl, S. (n.d.) *Sectarian Order in Bahrain: The Social and Colonial Origins of Criminal Justice*. https://rowman.com/ISBN/9781498541602/Sectarian-Order -in-Bahrain-The-Social-and-Colonial-Origins-of-Criminal-Justice

Topak, Ö. E, Mekouar, M and Cavatorta, F (2022). 'Introduction', in Ö. E. Topak, M. Mekouar and F. Cavatorta (eds) *New Authoritarian Practices in the Middle East and North Africa*. Edinburgh: Edinburgh University Press, pp. 1–29.

Uniacke, R. (2022). 'Digital Repression for Authoritarian Evolution in Saudi Arabia', in Ö. E. Topak, M. Mekouar and F. Cavatorta (eds) *New Authoritarian Practices in the Middle East and North Africa*. Edinburgh: Edinburgh University Press, pp. 228–51.

Yom, S. L. and G.F. Gause (2014). 'Resilient Royals: How Arab Monarchies Hang On', in L. Diamond and M. Plattner (eds) *Democratization and Authoritarianism in the Arab World*. Baltimore, MD: Johns Hopkins University Press.

4

AUTHORITARIAN REPRESSION UNDER SISI: NEW TACTICS OR NEW TOOLS?

Kira Jumet

Introduction

In the decades prior to the 2011 Arab uprisings, scholars of the Middle East and North Africa produced a plethora of literature on the persistence of authoritarianism in the region (Bellin 2004; Makiya 1998). From clientelism and elite cohesion to personalised regimes and hereditary succession, research topics reflected a state-centred approach to explaining domestic political dynamics while marginalising non-state actors that were deemed peripheral to the circles of the politically relevant elite. Those exploring the role of civil society wrote about the weakness of political parties and their co-optation or the limits of non-governmental organisations, associations and unions (Heydemann 2007; Schlumberger 2007). Because specialists focused on formal institutions, they missed the new wave of informal networks and mobilisation movements that were emerging in the years leading up to 2011. Thus, when citizens took to the Egyptian streets in 2011, most academics were surprised (Gause 2011).

By 2014, however, when Abdel Fattah al-Sisi formally assumed presidential powers in Egypt, the possibility of a democratic transition in the country was a distant reality. Academics who had written about 'people power' only a couple of years previously shifted their focus to the strength of Egypt's deep state, the economic and political power of the military and the re-emerging prominence of the security services.

Alongside the re-emergence of authoritarianism came its familiar corollary: repression. This chapter contributes to the literature on Egypt's 'new authoritarianism' by posing the question: are the repressive tactics employed by Sisi to support his autocratic government really new or are they simply a continuation and enhancement of an authoritarian style that reaches back through a series of presidencies? Focusing on media censorship, cyber-surveillance and legislation, I contend that these particular tools used by Sisi are intensified versions of those employed by previous Egyptian presidents, even if enhanced by procurement of new surveillance technologies and techniques from other countries and foreign private companies.

Repression: Theory and History

On 25 January 2011, Egyptians took to the streets to protest against police brutality, corruption and the poor state of the economy. After eighteen days and a turn-out unprecedented in modern Egyptian history, Mubarak stepped down from power, leaving the military's Supreme Council of the Armed Forces (SCAF) to lead the year and five months of the political transition to presidential elections. In June 2012, Mohamed Morsi of the Muslim Brotherhood became Egypt's first democratically-elected president. However, Egyptians soon became disenchanted with Morsi, and on 30 June 2013 millions of Egyptians took to the streets calling for him to step down; on 3 July 2013, the Egyptian military removed Morsi from office and took him to an undisclosed location. Adly Mansour, the head of the Supreme Constitutional Court, was installed as Egypt's interim president until new elections could be held. In reality, Sisi and SCAF informally held authority. Sisi's leadership was formalised in May 2014 when he won the presidential elections. Many agree with the claim that 'Egypt under President Sisi is more autocratic and repressive than at any other point in the country's history' (Mandour 2015).

Repression is a common tactic employed by autocrats to maintain power, although it is not always overt. Sullivan (2016) determined that suppressing dissent by targeting clandestine mobilisation activities is more effective than overt police responses to demonstrations and riots because 'coercion undermines the capacity of the organisation to co-ordinate collective action and incentivize participation', whereas overt repression 'leaves challenger organizations intact to publicize abuse and to deliver the selective incentives necessary to promote further challenges' (Sullivan 2016: 647). On the other hand, scholars have uncovered such glaringly repressive methods as engaging in torture to 'solicit confessions . . . or simply to teach respect for authority' (El-Dawla 2009: 123), using repression apparatuses that include 'judges, lawyers, informers, doctors, and many others' (Henderson 1991: 123).

Beyond repressive tactics targeting specific individuals and/or groups, prominent examples of mass repression through indiscriminate violence in the Middle East region include the June 1996 Abu Salim Massacre in Libya under Muammar al-Qadhafi, when up to 1,200 prisoners were killed (HRW 2006); Saddam Hussein's chief enforcer Ali Hassan al-Majid's murder of 5,000 Kurdish civilians in Halabja by poison gas in 1988 (Cockburn 2010); and the 1982 Hama Massacre in Syria, when Hafez al-Assad deployed the Syrian army to quash a Syrian Muslim Brotherhood uprising by bombarding the city of Hama, leading to thousands of deaths (Lefèvre 2013).[1]

Since the 1952 Free Officers coup d'état, Egyptian presidents have engaged in repression to maintain control. Although President Gamal Abdel Nasser was known for his 'Arab socialism' and populist economic policies, he did not remain in power by depending solely on popular support for his socio-economic policies and Arab/Egyptian nationalist, anti-colonial/non-aligned ideology. He also employed repression to consolidate his position. In 1954, an assassination attempt believed to be orchestrated by the Muslim Brotherhood led Nasser to imprison and torture over a thousand of its members, execute six leaders of the group (Zakaria 2004: 12) (Zolner 2019) and denounce its Supreme Guide Hassan al-Hudaybi. In addition, he used 'censorship and state propaganda to silence and discredit his enemies, and established the aggressive police state we see at work in Egypt today' (Smith 2016). Wickham argues that Nasser 'preempted the rise of opposition activism by subordinating potential agents, sites, and targets of mobilization to state control' (Wickham 2002: 21) by banning all opposition groups and co-opting educated lower-middle-class youth.

When Anwar Sadat assumed the presidency in 1970, he moved away from Nasser's Arab socialism and developed a new economic *infitah* (open/open door) policy, leading to an open-market economy that relied on Egyptian business elites and relations with oil-producing Gulf states, rather than the masses, to underpin his authoritarian regime. Sadat's economic liberalisation did not result in political liberalisation. On 16 January 1977, the elimination of subsidies on food staples, as required by terms of an agreement with the International Monetary Fund, led to bread riots. Sadat deployed the armed forces to crush the rioters, and in addition to the thousands imprisoned, a state of emergency was declared and a curfew imposed (Abul-Magd 2016: 76–7).

Under Mubarak, the State of Emergency provided 'police and security agencies with powers to prohibit demonstrations, censor newspapers, monitor personal communications, detain people at will, hold prisoners indefinitely without charge, and send defendants before special military courts to which there [was] no appeal' (El-Dawla 2009: 120). Since Sisi assumed power, Egypt has seen increased levels of repression and human rights abuses. In addition to intensifying the use of historic repressive methods, such as press censorship, torture and enforced disappearances, the state has increased its capabilities in the area of cyber-surveillance and expanded Mubarak's repression of civil society through legislation broadening the definition of terrorism. Sisi's repressive tactics are not new, but as a reaction to the protests that led to the 2011 and 2013 coups they specifically target protesters and the independent media and activists who mobilise them by providing information that stokes grievances against the state.

Freedom of the Press

Egypt has a long history of restrictions on press freedom.[2] The charter of the state-operated public broadcaster Egyptian Radio and Television Union (ERTU), drafted in 1979, gave 'almost absolute power to the minister of information' (Abdulla 2014). It allowed the state to monopolise broadcasting by requiring ERTU to broadcast anything the government desired, and it gave sole rights to ERTU to broadcast in Egypt. Even when the state decided to permit Egyptian-owned private satellite broadcasting, the networks were still subject to state regulations and censorship, and those who benefited were businessmen close to Mubarak (i.e., Ahmad Baghat and Naguib Sawiris) (Sakr 2007: 28–9).

Print and online journalists have also faced restrictions on reporting. In May 1995, Mubarak's government revised the national press law to allow for five-year prison sentences 'for the publication of "false or biased rumors, news and statements or disconcerting propaganda . . . if it offends social peace, arouses panic amongst the people, harms public interest or shows contempt for the state institutions or officials"' (Turner 1995). The law did not apply to television, which was already monopolised by the state, and the government said it would not enforce the law against reporters in Egypt who worked for foreign publications (Turner 1995). However, it did impose 'fines and prison sentences from 5 to 15 years for journalists for a range of vaguely worded crimes' (Napoli 1995). A July 2006 press law submitted to the People's Assembly included heavy fines and jail sentences for offences including 'the production, publication or possession of material that could "harm the national reputation"' (Sakr 2007: 42), and in 2008, Ibrahim Eissa, editor-in-chief of the independent daily *Al-Dustur*, was sentenced to two months in jail for reporting on the president's health (France 24 2008). A 2010 Human Rights Watch (HRW) report described security officers targeting journalists and bloggers who exposed human rights violations, and it criticised government policies and the sentencing of 'journalists to prison terms under penal code provisions that criminalize defamation' (HRW 2010). For the year preceding Mubarak's ouster, Egypt ranked 127 on the Reporters Without Borders World Press Freedom Index (RSF 2010).

The 29 December 2013 arrests of the English Al Jazeera journalists Mohamed Fadel Fahmy, Peter Greste and Baher Mohamed, and the cameraman Mohamed Fawzy, on charges of harming national security, distorting the country's image abroad, fabricating news to aid the Muslim Brotherhood and supporting terrorists (Cunningham 2013; Fadel 2014), along with their June 2014 sentencing to seven years in the maximum security Tora Prison (Kingsley 2014), portended the approach that Sisi would take to freedom of the press. Following the July 2013 coup, Al Jazeera Mubasher Misr, the Egyptian Arabic-language branch of the Al Jazeera channel, was banned from Egypt because of its perceived support for the Muslim Brotherhood, a group classified as a terrorist organisation in December 2013 (Al Jazeera 2013). Those who were familiar with the imprisoned Al Jazeera journalists could attest that they had no personal connection with Islamist groups, but their attempts at independent journalism that included interviewing members of the outlawed Muslim Brotherhood landed them in prison. Even Bassem Youssef, host of one of the most popular satirical television programmes, shut down his *al-Bernameg* show out of fear for the safety of his family (BBC 2014); to ensure his security he left Egypt for Abu Dhabi a few hours before the airing of his first post-coup season's first episode, which poked fun at the military (Abdellatif 2013). While Youssef's mockery of Morsi was accepted, jokes about the military, which could be perceived as undermining its status, were dangerous.

The list of journalists in Egypt who have been targeted by the state since Sisi came to power is long and includes well-known cases such as the arrest and five-year imprisonment of the Egyptian photojournalist Mahmoud Abou Zeid (a.k.a. Shawkan) for covering the 2013 crackdown on anti-military protests (Raghavan and Mahfouz 2019a), the 2015 arrest of the independent journalist and founder of the Egyptian Initiative for Personal Rights (EIPR) Hossam Baghat for 'publishing false news that harms national interests and disseminating information that disturbs public peace' (Khalil and Black 2015) and the home raid and arrest in 2020 of the brother of Mohamed el-Garhy, a journalist known for criticising the regime (Associated Press 2020). Foreign journalists whom the state deems hostile to Egypt's image abroad have also been prevented from entering the country or have been deported, including Times (of London) journalist Bel Trew, arrested in February 2018 while reporting from Cairo's Shubra neighbourhood and deported (Michaelson 2018), David Kirkpatrick, former Cairo bureau chief for the New York Times, who was denied entry in 2019 and sent back on a flight to London (Walsh 2019), and the Italian journalist Francesca Borri, who was also denied entry in 2019, probably because of her reporting on the torture and killing of Italian graduate student Giulio Regeni by Egyptian security agents (Middle East Eye 2019). In addition to the individual journalists caught in the cross-hairs of the state, the offices of independent media outlets, such as *Mada Masr*, have been raided and editors detained (Samaan, Paget and Kottasova 2019).

Reporters Without Borders ranked Egypt 166th out of 180 countries in its 2020 Press Freedom Index, and the country continues to be one of the world's top jailers of journalists (Samaan, Paget and Kottasova 2019). In its *Freedom in the World 2020* report, Freedom House categorised Egypt as 'Not Free', and its score dropped from 22/100 to 21/100, with civil liberties such as press freedom described as 'tightly restricted' (Freedom House 2020). In fact, since the 2013 coup, the number of journalists under attack in Egypt has sky-rocketed to unprecedented levels, and in 2019 alone twenty-six journalists were imprisoned in the country (CPJ 2019).

Authoritarian regimes are known to repress freedom of speech. Although the Mubarak government engaged in media censorship and co-optation (Sakr 2007: 22–3), as long as citizens and journalists refrained from publicly criticising prominent political figures or the president, including his family, they were allowed to vent about some socio-economic and political issues to let off steam (Hassanin 2014: 122). Even Mubarak's 1995 amendments to the press law insulated foreign journalists against prosecution. In contrast, Sisi leaves little room for open political discussion or debate on any topic, foreign journalists are fair game for arrest and deportation, and now almost all the Egyptian media are owned directly by the state or state-controlled through the purchase of independent media outlets by the intelligence services using the company Eagle Capital (Shea 2019).

Cyber-surveillance and Online Censorship[3]

To 'surveil' is to 'closely monitor or observe' (Oxford English Dictionary 2020). Surveillance is practised by both democracies and autocracies, but authoritarian surveillance is aimed at repression 'to create a climate of fear' (Henderson 1991: 122). Michaelsen argues:

> Surveillance represents an inherent element of authoritarian rule. Confronted with a 'twin problem of uncertainty', authoritarian power holders can never be fully sure about potential threats to regime stability and their actual success in preventing such threats. From the totalitarian dictatorships of the twentieth century to today's 'networked authoritarians', these regimes have monitored their populations to detect dissent, discern dissatisfaction and preempt challenges. (Michaelsen 2017: 465)

In 2011, international media began referring to the uprisings in Egypt as the 'Facebook Revolution', in reference to activists' use of the social media platform for mobilisation. The misinformed enthusiasm for the internet and social media as a democratising tool had been acknowledged a few years prior by Ronald Deibert, who contended that while it was long assumed that the absence of a central control biased the internet towards democracy and freedom of speech, 'pressures from the security and commercial sectors to regulate and control the Internet are beginning to alter its basic material framework in ways that may undermine not only the activities of global civic networks, but the long-term prospects for an open global communications environment as well' (Deibert 2003: 501–2). Social media did not cause the 2011 uprisings, but they did serve as one of the most prominent mobilising tools, and authoritarian regimes in the region took note. As Vasileios Karagiannopoulos observed: 'The democratising and revolutionizing potential of the Internet for these struggles can also be doubted due to the regimes' capacity to infiltrate and manipulate information production and exchange, therefore transforming the Internet from a tool of dissent to a tool of oppression' (Karagiannopoulos 2012: 165).

'The Internet as an international structure offers boundless opportunities for dissent, but domestic regimes restrict such opportunities based on desire and ability' (Jumet 2018: 64). Under Mubarak, the state attempted to track down online opposition activists, but government methods were described as 'rudimentary'. A 2009 report by OpenNet Initiative claimed there was no evidence of internet filtering in Egypt and, according to Freedom House, the 'authorities typically employ[ed] "low-tech" methods such as intimidation, legal harassment, detentions, and real-world surveillance of online dissidents' (Freedom House 2011: 1). All internet users were required to register their personal information with the ISP operator, and those who purchased a USB modem had to 'fill out a registration form and submit a copy of their national identification card' (Freedom House 2011: 6). Additional methods of monitoring included the 2005 requirement for internet café managers and owners to record their customers' names and ID numbers (The Arabic Network for Human Rights Information 2005), which in 2008 was broadened to include email addresses and phone numbers of clients before they were permitted to use the Internet (AFP 2008). However, enforcement capabilities were low, and many establishments flouted the rules.

Between 2011 and 2013, the Egyptian state had already initiated its cyber-surveillance programme, procuring Remote Control System (RCS/DaVinci) malware from the Italian company Hacking Team and surveillance assistance from an affiliate/branch of American cyber-surveillance company Blue Coat (FIDH 2018: 20), in part as a reaction to the January 2011 Uprising and subsequent protests that had been organised and/or mobilised online. After Sisi officially came to power in 2014, the Ministry of the Interior (MOI) intensified its online monitoring, sought an intelligence system capable of surveilling social media (i.e., Facebook, Twitter and YouTube) and began intercepting private messaging (i.e., LinkedIn, Google, Viber and WhatsApp) through the MOI program 'Social Networks Security Hazard Monitoring Operation (public opinion measurement system)' (AFTE 2018: 21; Ezzat 2014).

In addition to monitoring social media sites and surveilling private communications, in May 2017 the state began blocking websites, including the *Mada Masr* and al Jazeera news sites. By June 2017, the state was blocking not only news websites but also sites offering Virtual Private Networks (VPNs) (TunnelBear, CyberGhost, Hotspot Shield, TigerVPN and ZenVPN) in order to counter use of VPN services to circumvent the state's online censorship. By 2018, there were reports that Egypt was seeking training from China on cyber-surveillance (Radu 2018).

Also in 2018, the parliament passed a cybercrime bill, which was the country's first law to regulate social media content. The legislation 'set a precedent in regulating web censorship', and there were harsh penalties and fines for violators, including '29 penalties sentencing offenders to up to five years in prison and/or fines of between LE10,000 and LE20 million' (al-Abd 2018). According to the 2018 Freedom on the Net report, Egypt was rated 'Not Free' because it blocked political/social content and arrested bloggers/ICT users (Freedom on the Net 2018), and a 2018 Citizens Lab report found that Egypt was using technology produced by the American company Sandvine to 'block dozens of human rights, political, and news websites' (Marczak, et al. 2018: 33). Website blocking reached unprecedented levels between 1 June 2017 and 31 May 2018, especially surrounding the time of the March 2018 presidential elections. Journalists, bloggers and activists were arrested and/or held in arbitrary detention for non-violent political, social or religious posts on social media, and parliament considered and passed a number of laws that criminalised the spread of 'false' news, censored news sites and created provisions to register popular social media users (Freedom on the Net 2018).

In 2019, Sisi pursued amending the constitution to allow for the extension of his presidency to 2034. Activists who opposed the change posted a petition on voiceonline.net for Egyptians to express publicly their disagreement with the legislation. After the number of signatures had reached 60,000 within hours of the petition's online publication, the state used its authority to direct almost all Egyptian internet service providers (Vodafone, Orange, Raya and Telecom Egypt) to block the website (Masri 2019). However, people were still able to access the site from abroad or through VPN. The *Batel* (null and void) campaign, which contested not only the constitutional amendments extending Sisi's presidency but also the position of the military in politics and limits on the autonomy of the judiciary, led the government to block over 34,000 internet domains that challenged the constitutional referendum (Mada Masr 2019).

Mubarak's lack of sophistication when it came to controlling online dissent and mobilisation was revealed during the 2011 Uprising, when he was unable to target particular individuals and groups online to prevent them from mobilising protests against him. He was forced to implement a five-day shutdown of the entire internet, costing the Egyptian economy over

$18 million per day (Olson 2011). Sisi has upgraded Egypt's online repression, as demonstrated by his order to internet service providers to block particular websites rather than shut down the entire country's internet access and his acquisition of website blocking, cyber-surveillance and communications interception technologies from abroad.

Suppressing Activism: Laws, Detentions and Violence[4]

After two coups by way of protest in two years, SCAF (led by Sisi) recognised protest as a primary threat to its power. In November 2013, a new protest law was passed (Law 107) banning overnight sit-ins and requiring activists to acquire seven separate permits before they could organise a demonstration, with the security services having the final say. Petitions that were rejected could be appealed to the courts, controlled by a state that was hostile to protests. As with previous emergency laws, unsanctioned gatherings of more than ten people (in public or private) were banned, and violators incurred heavy fines and/or long prison sentences (HRW 2013). Early casualties of the law included the co-founder of the April 6th Youth Movement Ahmed Maher and the activist Alaa Abdul Fattah, who were fined and imprisoned for protesting against it (TIMEP 2013).

In 2016, Egypt saw nationalist protests to contest the transfer of the Tiran and Sanafir islands to Saudi Arabia, journalists' protests against police raids on the Journalists Syndicate, and doctors' protests to express outrage over the assault on two doctors by police at the Matariya Public Hospital. However, the protest law was most seriously challenged in 2019. On 2 September 2019, the Egyptian actor-turned-construction-contractor Mohamed Ali, whose company had previously held construction contracts with the military, began posting a series of videos on social media from his self-imposed exile location in Spain that heavily criticised the Sisi government and prominent members of the military (Al Jazeera 2019; MEMO 2019). The attacks spoke to specific incidents of government waste and corruption, including Sisi's construction of five villas for his colleagues and a palace for himself. Criticism of the regime's financial corruption resonated with a public negatively impacted by the faltering economy. By 20 September, Ali's appeals for protests against Sisi had mobilised Egyptians onto the streets of Cairo, Alexandria, Suez and Mahalla el-Kubra (Walsh 2019).

The government responded to the numerous days of protests with tear gas, birdshot and mass arrests (Yee and Rashwan 2019a). Major squares were heavily policed, the metro stations surrounding Tahrir Square were closed and pro-government rallies were organised (Michaelson 2019; Raghavan and Mahfouz 2019b). Two weeks following the initiation of demonstrations on 20 September at least 2,285 Egyptians caught in the crackdown remained incarcerated (Yee and Rashwan 2019b).

Sisi's deployment of tear gas (a chemical weapon) and birdshot against citizens was not unprecedented. During the 2011 Uprising, Egyptians experienced moral shock over the televised use of tear gas, bullets and other forms of violence against thousands of peaceful protesters demanding their rights (Jumet 2018). It was not the first time Mubarak had violently assaulted his own people. Voter intimidation by security forces in the 2000 elections included shooting potential voters with rubber bullets and throwing pepper sauce in voters' eyes (Kassem 2004: 67). Large protests during Mubarak's time were rare, and when activists did try to mobilise they were quickly arrested, as in the 2008 case of fifty people, including journalists, arrested before the start of a Kefaya-organised protest against the abolition of ration cards (Rabie 2008). In 2003, security forces attacked hundreds of anti-Iraq war demonstrators with water cannon, clubs, dogs and stones, before arresting and torturing many of them (HRW 2003).

Legislating Terror

From Ethiopia to Egypt, authoritarian regimes have defined terrorism in ambiguous ways in order to create legal justification for the imprisonment of their opponents (Grinberg 2017: 436).[5] Over-broad definitions have negative implications for civil society and everyday citizens' rights. Chiha (2013) found the following:

> The Mubarak Regime designed such a broad definition to ensure that the Egyptian legal system contained permanent tools to restrict the fundamental rights and freedoms of its citizens, in particular the freedoms of speech and association. Relying on that definition and a strong secret police apparatus, Mubarak's regime was able to weaken political opposition and civil society groups for decades. Such groups were forced into silence for fear of being prosecuted as terrorists. (Chiha 2013: 93)

Egypt's history with anti-terror laws dates back to the 1980s when Mubarak authorised 'the imprisonment of "anyone against whom there is credible evidence or is under suspicion of any activity that compromises public security or public order or threatens national unity or social stability"' (Al-Sadany 2014). Egypt officially introduced terrorism as a crime in 1992 through the passage of its first formal anti-terror legislation (Law no. 97), which amended the Penal Code and Criminal Procedures Code (Al-Sadany 2014). In March 2007, the Egyptian constitution 'was amended to incorporate Article 179 that set forth a constitutional obligation to combat terrorism, giving the government free rein to crack down on anything it deemed to be terrorism, without respect for human and civil rights' (Al-Sadany 2014).

When Sisi took power following the 2013 coup, he continued with Mubarak's policies and intensified them. After the Muslim Brotherhood's 2013 designation as a terrorist organisation, members of the group were subjected to mass trials, including, for example, that of Supreme Guide Mohamed Badie along with 681 other members tried in March 2014 and the sentencing to death of 529 other Muslim Brotherhood supporters that same month (Kamal 2014). The heavy repression of the Muslim Brotherhood was reminiscent of 1954, when Nasser banned the group, arrested over 4,000 of its members and executed some of its leaders (Onians 2004: 78), as well as Sadat's coup accusation against Muslim Brotherhood General Guide Tilmisani, leading to Tilmisani's arrest, along with hundreds of activists, and the dissolution of ten Islamist societies (Sattar 1995: 19).

In 2015, Egypt implemented strict anti-terror laws that allowed for fast-track trials of suspected militants in special courts, a ten-year prison sentence for those found guilty of joining a militant group, life sentences (25 years) for financing militant groups, five- to seven-year sentences for inciting violence or creating websites deemed to spread terrorist messages, and fines of 200,000–500,000 EGP for journalists who contradicted official accounts of militant attacks (BBC 2015). At the time, human rights groups warned correctly that 'the legislation will be used by Mr. Sisi to crush dissent' (BBC 2015).

Since October 2017, Sisi has used a state of emergency to transfer some 'terrorism' cases to Emergency State Security Courts, part of a parallel judicial system that fails to guarantee fair trials and whose decisions cannot be appealed (HRW 2018).[6] Cases referred to the Supreme State Security Prosecution, which handles terrorism cases, included the arrest of political activist Amal Fathy on charges of 'membership of a terrorist group', after she publicly criticised the government's failure to tackle sexual harassment (Amnesty International 2018), and the imprisonment of satirist and video blogger Shady Abu Zeid for 'joining a terrorist group and spreading false news' after he and the actor Ahmed Malek had posted an online video of their walking around Tahrir Square giving police officers inflated condom balloons 'decorated with the phrase "From the youth of Egypt to the police on January 25"' (Egyptian Streets 2020).

Egypt faces real terror threats, particularly from Wilayat Sinai (Islamic State-Sinai Province, WS). However, as Nadim Houry, HRW's terrorism/ counterterrorism director, explained, 'While Egypt faces security threats, the government of President Abdel Fattah al-Sisi has exploited these threats cynically as a cover to prosecute peaceful critics and to revive the infamous Mubarak-era state security courts' (HRW 2018). The designation of the Muslim Brotherhood as a terrorist organisation was a tactic used to prevent the organisation's return to politics or operation as a civil society organisation following the 2013 coup, and the expansion of the definition of terrorism beyond Mubarak's already broad definition and the new 2015 terror legislation are among many methods the regime has employed to suppress anti-regime activists and independent media.

Conclusion

Both Mubarak and Morsi were deposed by military intervention following protests, and Sisi's enhanced repression is, in part, a result of his fear of suffering a similar fate. While Sisi has taken a different approach to authoritarianism from his predecessors, including reconfiguring the political system, many of his methods of repression are similar to those of previous Egyptian presidents, diverging more in intensity and sophistication than in method or intent. In addition to increased use of torture and enforced disappearances, Sisi has further restricted press freedom to prevent criticism of his regime, with the Committee to Protect Journalists (CPJ) ranking Egypt third-worst jailer of journalists worldwide in 2020. Sisi has attempted to curb domestic anti-regime activists through legislation, including the 2013 protest law and the 2018 cyber-crime bill, and by increasing cyber-surveillance capabilities, gained through partnerships with foreign countries (e.g. China) and companies situated in Europe and the United States.

In 2014, Sisi argued that Egypt required a strong military man to rule the country to prevent chaos and combat terrorism. Since then, terrorist attacks in the country have accelerated. Rather than succeed in countering terrorism, Sisi has used the war on terror as a pretext to stamp out dissent through terror laws that target journalists and civil society activists.

Egypt's recent history is replete with examples of tactics that make use of repressive measures to shore up authoritarian regimes. Sisi's repressive tactics are 'new' primarily in the way they take advantage of new tools to achieve his desired goal. Egypt's use of tools such as cyber-surveillance is a response to forms of communication that have only appeared in recent decades, and although capabilities to surveil social media and intercept WhatsApp messaging may not be new on the international stage, they are recent to Egypt. Sisi's 'new authoritarianism' does not include innovative repressive tactics, or at least not tactics innovated by Sisi's regime, but instead relies on access to new, foreign surveillance technologies that address the ever-changing online challenges to authoritarian rule.

Notes

1 See also the 'Established Authoritarian Practices Section' in the Introduction, which provides an overview of key examples from the book chapters (Topak et al. 2022).
2 For an overview of similar practices in other examined MENA contexts in this book, see the 'Authoritarian Practices Shaping Civil Society and the Media' section in the Introduction (Topak et al. 2022).
3 See the 'Digital Surveillance' section in the Introduction (Topak et al. 2022) for similar digital practices (of varying degrees) in other MENA regimes, particularly the Gulf States such as Saudi Arabia (Uniacke 2022) and the other regional powers, Turkey (Topak 2022) and Iran (Golkar 2022).
4 See the 'Protests and Policing' section in the Introduction (Topak et al. 2022) for similar practices targeting social movements in other MENA regimes.
5 See the 'Legalising Authoritarian Practices' section in the Introduction (Topak et al. 2022) for similar authoritarian legal practices in other MENA regimes.
6 Other examined states of emergency in the book include Sudan (Hassan 2022), Turkey (Topak 2022) and Tunisia (Cimini 2022).

References

Abdellatif, R. (2013). 'Comedian Bassem Youssef's Return to TV Comes to a Quick End', *The Wall Street Journal*, 2 November.
Abdulla, R. (2014). 'Egypt's Media in the Midst of Revolution', Carnegie Endowment for International Peace, 16 July.
Abul-Magd, Z. (2016). *Militarization the Nation: The Army, Business, and Revolution in Egypt*. New York: Columbia University Press.
AFP (2008). 'Egypt Demanding Data from Cyber Cafe Users: NGO', *AFP*, 9 August.

AFTE (2018). 'Decision from an Unknown Body: On Blocking Websites in Egypt'. *AFTE*, 1 February. https://afteegypt.org/en/right_to_know-2/publicationsright _to_know-right_to_know 2/2017/06/04/13069-afteegypt.html

al-Abd, R. (2018). 'Cybercrime Bill Nears Committee Approval with Harsher Penalties for Website Admins, Protection for Bona Fides', *Mada Masr*, 16 April.

Al-Sadany, M. (2014). 'Legislating Terror in Egypt', *Tahrir Institute for Middle East Policy*, 19 July.

Al Jazeera (2019). 'Egyptian Contractor Targeted over Sisi Allegations', *Al Jazeera*, 5 September.

Al Jazeera (2013). 'Egypt's Military Shuts Down News Channels', *Al Jazeera*, 4 July.

Amnesty International (2018). 'Free Sexual Harassment Survivor Amal Fathy'. Amnesty International. https://www.amnesty.org/en/get-involved/take action/ w4r-2018-egypt-amal-fathy/

Arabic Network for Human Rights Information (2005). 'Egypt: Increasing Curb over Internet Usage Harrassments against Net Cafes Should Immediately End', www.anhri.net, 23 February.

BBC (2014). 'Egypt Satirist Bassem Youssef Confirms End of Show', *BBC*, 4 June.

BBC (2015). 'Egypt's al-Sisi Imposes Strict Anti-Terrorism Laws', *BBC*, 17 August.

Bellin, E. (2004). 'The Robustness of Authoritarianism in the Middle East', *Comparative Politics* 36: 139–57.

Chiha, I.I. (2013). 'Redefining Terrorism under The Mubarak Regime: Towards a New Definition of Terrorism in Egypt', *The Comparative and International Law Journal of Southern Africa* 46(1): 90–120.

Cimini, G. (2022). 'Authoritarian Nostalgia and Practices in Newly Democratising Contexts: The Localised Example of Tunisia', in Ö. E. Topak, M. Mekouar and F. Cavatorta (eds) *New Authoritarian Practices in the Middle East and North Africa*. Edinburgh: Edinburgh University Press, pp. 276–95.

Cockburn, P. (2010). '"Chemical Ali", the Killer of 5,000 Kurds, Is Executed', *Independent*, 26 January.

CPJ (2019). 'Egypt/Middle East and North Africa', *Committee to Protect Journalists*, 11 December. https://cpj.org/reports/2019/12/journalists-jailed-china-turkey -saudi-arabia-egypt/

Cunningham, E. (2013). 'Four Al Jazeera Journalists Detained in Egypt, Accused of Illegal Ties to Muslim Brotherhood', *The Washington Post*, 30 December.

Deibert, R. J. (2003). 'Black Code: Censorship, Surveillance, and the Militarisation of Cyberspace', *Millennium: Journal of International Studies* 32(3): 501–30.

Egyptian Streets (2020). 'Egypt Releases Satirist and Vlogger Shady Abu Zeid After 2 Years', *Egyptian Streets*, 18 October.

El-Dawla, A. (2009). 'Torture: A State Policy', in R. El-Mahdi and P. Marfleet (eds) *Egypt: The Moment of Change*. London: Zed Books, pp. 120–35.

El-Dine, C. C. (2016). 'Egypt: From Military Reform to Military Sanctuarization', in H. Albrecht, A. Croissant and F. Lawson (eds) *Armies and Insurgencies in the Arab Spring*. Philadelphia: University of Pennsylvania Press, pp. 185–202.

Ezzat, A. (2014). '"You Are Being Watched!" Egypt's Mass Internet Surveillance', *Mada Masr*, 29 September.

Fadel, L. (2014). 'Detention of Al-Jazeera Journalists Strains Free Speech in Egypt'. *NPR*, 29 January.

FIDH (2018). *Egypt: A Repression Made in France*. Paris: FIDH. https://www.fidh .org/IMG/pdf/382873255-egypt-a-repression-made-in-france.pdf

France 24 (2008). 'Journalist Jailed for Writing about President Mubarak's Health'. *France 24*, 28 September.

Freedom House (2011). *Freedom on the Net 2011*. Freedomhouse.org

Freedom House (2020). *Freedom in the World 2020*. Washington, DC: Freedom House. https://freedomhouse.org/country/egypt/freedom-world/2020

Freedom on the Net. 2018. *Egypt Country Report*. Freedom on the Net. https://freed omhouse.org/report/freedom-net/2018/egypt

Grinberg, D. (2017). 'Chilling Developments: Digital Access, Surveillance, and the Authoritarian Dilemma in Ethiopia', *Surveillance & Society* 15(3/4): 432–8.

Hassan, Y. (2022). 'The Evolution of the Sudanese Authoritarian State: The December Uprising and the Unraveling of a "Persistent" Autocracy', in Ö. E. Topak, M. Mekouar and F. Cavatorta (eds) *New Authoritarian Practices in the Middle East and North Africa*. Edinburgh: Edinburgh University Press, pp. 252–75.

Hassanin, L. (2014). *Egypt: 2014-Communications Surveillance in the Digital Age*. Global Information Society Watch (GISWatch). https://www.giswatch.org/en /country-report/communications-surveillance/egypt

Henderson, W. (1991). 'Conditions Affecting the Use of Political Repression', *The Journal of Conflict Resolution* 35(1): 120–42.

Heydemann, S. (2007). *Upgrading Authoritarianism in the Arab World*. Analysis paper, Washington, DC: The Saban Center for Middle East Policy at The Brookings Institution.

Human Rights Watch (2003). 'Egypt: Crackdown on Antiwar Protests', 23 March.

Human Rights Watch (2006). 'Libya: June 1996 Killings at Abu Salim Prison', 27 June.

Human Rights Watch (2010). *Egypt: Events of 2009*. New York: Human Rights Watch.

Human Rights Watch (2013). 'Egypt: Deeply Restrictive New Assembly Law Will Enable Further Crackdown, Stifle Electoral Campaigning', 26 November.

Human Rights Watch (2014). *All According to Plan: The Rab'a Massacre and Mass Killings of Protesters in Egypt*. New York: Human Rights Watch.

Human Rights Watch (2018). 'Egypt: Intensifying Crackdown Under Counterterrorism Guise', 15 July.

Jumet, K. (2018). *Contesting the Repressive State: Why Ordinary Egyptians Protested During the Arab Spring*. New York: Oxford University Press.

Kamal, T. (2014). 'Brotherhood Head, 682 Others Tried in Egypt After Mass Death Sentence', Reuters, 25 March.

Karagiannopoulos, V. (2012). 'The Role of the Internet in Political Struggles: Some Conclusions from Iran and Egypt', *New Political Science* 34(2): 151–71.

Kassem, M. (2004). *Egyptian Politics: The Dynamics of Authoritarian Rule*. Boulder, CO: Lynne Rienner.

Khalil, J. and I. Black (2015). 'Anger as Egypt Detains Campaigning Journalist', *The Guardian*, 9 November.

Kingsley, P. (2014). 'Al-Jazeera Journalists Jailed for Seven Years in Egypt', *The Guardian*, 23 June.

Lefèvre, R. (2013). *Ashes of Hama: the Muslim Brotherhood in Syria*. New York: Oxford University Press.

Mada M. (2019). 'Egypt Blocks Over 34,000 Websites in Attempt to "Shut Down"', 16 April.

Makiya, K. (1998). *Republic of Fear: The Politics of Modern Iraq*. Berkeley: University of California Press.

Mandour, M. (2015). 'Repression in Egypt from Mubarak to Sisi'. Carnegie Endowment for International Peace, 11 August.

Marczak, B., J. Dalek, S. McKune, A. Senft, J. Scott-Railton and R. Deibert. 2018. *Bad Traffic: Sandvine's PacketLogic Devices Used to Deploy Government Spyware in Turkey and Redirect Egyptian Users to Affiliate Ads?* Research Report. Toronto: The Citizen Lab.

Masri, L. (2019). 'Egypt Blocks Campaign Site Opposing Constitutional Changes', Reuters, 10 April.

McManus, A. (2020). 'ISIS in the Sinai: A Persistent Threat for Egypt', *Center for Global Policy*, 23 June. https://cgpolicy.org/articles/isis-in-the-sinai-a-persistent -threat-for-egypt/

MEMO (2019). *Egypt Contractor Accuses Army of Squandering Public Funds amid Austerity*, 6 September. https://www.youtube.com/watch?v=Oj29oZRQsUE

Michaelsen, M. (2017). 'Far Away, So Close: Transnational Activism, Digital Surveillance and Authoritarian Control in Iran', *Surveillance & Society* 15(3/4): 465–70.

Michaelson, R. (2018). 'Egypt Expels British Journalist, Raising Fears for Press Ahead of Election', *The Guardian*, 23 March.

Michaelson, R. (2019). 'Hundreds of Egyptians Arrested in Latest Wave of Protests against Sisi', *The Guardian*, 22 September.

Middle East Eye (2019). 'Egypt Deports Italian Journalist After Brief Detention at Cairo Airport', 12 October.

Napoli, J. (1995). 'New Press Law Alienates Mubarak's Media Supporters'. *Washington Report on Middle East Affairs*, July/August.

Olson, P. (2011). 'Egypt's Internet Blackout Cost More than OECD Estimates'. *Forbes*, 3 February.

Onians, C. (2004). 'Supply and Demand Democracy in Egypt', *World Policy Journal* 21(2): 78–84.

Rabie, P. (2008). '50 People, Including Journalists, Arrested Before Kefaya Protest Begins', *Daily News Egypt*, 17 January.

Radu, S. (2018). 'China's Web Surveillance Model Expands Abroad', *U.S. News*, 1 November.

Raghavan, S. and H. Farouk Mahfouz (2019a). 'Egyptian Photojournalist Released After More Than 5 Years in Prison'. *The Washington Post*, 4 March.

Raghavan, S. and H. Farouk Mahfouz (2019b). 'In Egypt, Dissent Is Silenced by Masked Men, Riot Police and Blocked Roads', *The Washington Post*, 27 September.

Reporters Without Borders (2010). '2010 World Press Freedom Index'. https://rsf .org/en/ranking/2010

Sakr, N. (2007). *Arab Television Today*. London; New York: I. B. Tauris.

Samaan, M., S. Paget and I. Kottasova (2019). 'Egypt Raids One of Its Last Independent News Publications, and Detains Some of Its Journalists', *CNN*, 24 November.

Sattar, N. (1995). '"Al Ikhwan Al Muslimin" (Society of Muslim Brotherhood) Aims and Ideology, Role and Impact', *Pakistan Horizon* 48(2): 7–30.

Schlumberger, O. (2007). *Debating Arab Authoritarianism: Dynamics and Durability in Nondemocratic Regimes*. Stanford: Stanford University Press.

Shea, J. (2019). 'Egypt's Online Repression Thwarts Both Growth and Democracy', *The Tahrir Institute for Middle East Policy*, 16 August.

Smith, A. (2016). 'Egypt's Nasser: Beneath the Nostalgia, a Repressive Ruler', *The New Arab*, 27 September.

Spencer, R. (2019). 'Egypt Arrests Brother of Key Revolutionary Figure', *The Times*, 20 September.

Sullivan, C. (2016). 'Political Repression and the Destruction of Dissident Organizations: Evidence from the Archives of the Guatemalan National Police', *World Politics* 68(4): 645–76.

TIMEP (2013). 'April 6 Youth Movement Activists Sentenced to Three Years in Prison', *Tahrir Institute for Middle East Policy*, 22 December.

Topak, Ö. E. (2022). 'An Assemblage of New Authoritarian Practices in Turkey', in Ö. E. Topak, M. Mekouar and F. Cavatorta (eds) *New Authoritarian Practices in the Middle East and North Africa*. Edinburgh: Edinburgh University Press, pp. 296–319.

Topak, Ö. E., Mekouar, M and Cavatorta, F (2022). 'Introduction', in Ö. E. Topak, M. Mekouar and F. Cavatorta (eds) *New Authoritarian Practices in the Middle East and North Africa*. Edinburgh: Edinburgh University Press, pp. 1–29.

Turner, C. (1995). 'Mubarak Tries to Muzzle Egypt Press – But He May Get Bitten', *Los Angeles Times*, 17 June.

Uniacke, R. (2022). 'Digital Repression for Authoritarian Evolution in Saudi Arabia', in Ö. E. Topak, M. Mekouar and F. Cavatorta (eds) *New Authoritarian Practices in the Middle East and North Africa*. Edinburgh: Edinburgh University Press, pp. 228–51.

Walsh, D. (2019). 'Egypt Turns Back Veteran New York Times Reporter', *The New York Times*, 19 February.

Wickham, C. Rosefsky (2002). *Mobilizing Islam: Religion, Activism, and Political Change in Egypt*. New York: Columbia University Press.

Yee, V. and N. Rashwan (2019a). 'In Egypt, Scattered Protests Break Out for Second Week', *The New York Times*, 27 September.

Yee, V. and N. Rashwan (2019b). 'Egypt's Harsh Crackdown Quashes Protest Movement'. *The New York Times*, 4 October.

Zakaria, F. (2004). 'Islam, Democracy, and Constitutional Liberalism', *Political Science Quarterly* 119(1): 1–20.

Zolner, B. (2019). 'Surviving Repression: How Egypt's Muslim Brotherhood Has Carried On', Carnegie Middle East Center, 11 March.

5

DEEP SOCIETY AND NEW AUTHORITARIAN SOCIAL CONTROL IN IRAN AFTER THE GREEN MOVEMENT

Saeid Golkar

Introduction

What keeps dictators up at night? Sources of a dictator's anxiety include coups, foreign interventions and revolutions. Dictators therefore work hard to nullify all these threats through the creation of institutions and the implementation of multiple preventive policies. In the early 2000s, coloured revolutions with civil society at their core overthrew some of the dictators in Eastern Europe and Central Asia. Middle Eastern dictators, for their part, seemed to have been successful in immunising their regimes by suppressing civil society organisations. However, since 2009, ordinary people, starting with the 2009 Iranian Green Movement, followed by the 2011 Arab uprisings and the Gezi protests in Turkey in 2013, have defied these dictators. While these protests were not entirely successful in overthrowing the dictatorships in many of these countries, they challenged the assumption of authoritarian survivability in the Middle East and North Africa (MENA).

In response to these protests, authoritarian MENA regimes have upgraded their survival strategies. In addition to suppressing active opposition and distracting apolitical groups, they learned the need to actively organise and mobilise their own social bases, securing their loyalty through patron–client networks and mobilising them against their enemies. While the Islamic Republic of Iran (IRI), as a revolutionary populist regime, has relied on mass mobilisation since 1979, it was only after 2009 that it started to cohere and mobilise its supporters more aggressively by creating what I call a 'deep society'. Since 1979, the Islamic Republic has gradually lost its legitimacy among citizens and alienated several social and political groups. As a counter-strategy to the growth of internal opposition, the regime has transformed the Islamic Revolutionary Guard's corps (IRGC)'s civil militia branch – the Basij – into a deep society. Through this civilian mass organisation, the IRI has recruited and organised more than 2 million Iranians from different social strata and professions. The regime also uses deep society to share the rent and co-opt Iranians, especially youth, to become part of the regime. For its members, being part of this community means having more opportunities and privileges in all aspects of life, including education and career. Deep society also helps the regime to put Iranians who are effectively growing more dissatisfied under its gaze. By creating a chilling atmosphere, the members of deep society intimidate their peers, disseminating the regime's misinformation and disinformation, spying and identifying the regime dissidents and trolling activists in both physical and online spaces. This chapter briefly discusses the transformation of Iranian society from mass to civil and then to deep society in post-revolutionary Iran, focusing on the concept of 'deep society', and its role in the regime's resilience despite massive internal and external crises.

Civil Society vs Deep Society: From Democratisation to the Authoritarian Survival

Civil society is one of the main concepts in transitology, especially in the literature on the third wave of democratisation. This wave, which began in the mid-1970s, continued into the 1980s and 1990s (Huntington 1991). Among the factors responsible for democratisation, civil society played a prominent role (Haggard and Kaufman 2016). As Diamond (1997: 3) clearly states: 'civil society serves as the buffer zone between the state and its citizens to protect the individual from state power. Civil society provides multiple avenues for "the people" to express their interests and preferences, to influence policy, and to scrutinise and check the exercise of state power.' That is why civil society helps to transition from dictatorship and contributes further to the expansion and consolidation of democracy. Without a functioning civil society and stable, transparent institutions, attempts at overthrowing authoritarianism fail to bring about liberal democracy (Fukuyama 2014).

Since the early 2000s, civil society has held an even more significant role, as the colour revolutions suggest, and authoritarian regimes in the Middle East and North Africa did indeed perceive such revolutions as a Western plot in which civil society had a central role. Since 2000 several non-violent mass uprisings against entrenched leaders have occurred in East Europe and Central Asia: Georgia's Rose Revolution in 2003, Ukraine's Orange Revolution in 2004 and Kyrgyzstan's Tulip Revolution in 2005. As non-violent mass uprisings emerged after fraudulent elections, coloured revolutions led to a transition in some of the political regimes in a number of post-Soviet states.

Faced with the threat of a colour revolution, authoritarian incumbents in the MENA and elsewhere developed a series of strategies to neutralise it, including isolation, marginalisation, rent distribution, repression or persuasion (Evgeny and Brudny 2012). Some authoritarian regimes also supported the emergence of government-organised non-governmental organisations (GONGOs) to legitimise their rule. Co-optation of civil society is part of the repertoire of authoritarian regimes' strategies to attract young people and technocrats outside formal state structures (Aarts and Cavatorta 2013), pre-empting their potential discontent and providing them with a stake in the survival of the regime. In addition, by representing the regime in international gatherings, these institutions serve the regime's propaganda, creating an illusion of civil liberties. Although dummy civil society organisations are useful for circumcising genuine grass-roots civil society, painting the regime as quasi-democratic and legitimising it in the international arena, they are not very useful when the regime faces mass uprising. In short, they are important for a regime's window-dressing and for representing it in international meetings, but they are not exactly mass-mobilising instruments for the regime's supporters.

Authoritarian regimes usually have small social bases, mostly because they do not rule through popular consent. At the same time these regimes also have little active visible opposition, because of the brutal suppression of dissidents who dare to challenge them. Timur Kuran's (1995) theory of preference falsification explains why most people intentionally hide their true beliefs and preferences under social and political pressures. Most people in a dictatorship are not regime supporters or opponents, but apolitical individuals uninterested in being involved in politics, out of fear of the potential costs of political participation. The regime thus faces a tipping point only when the people in this vast grey zone join the opposition at times of crisis. To neutralise society's threats during such crises, dictators need a strategy to mobilise their small social base to control the overwhelmingly young, unemployed and frustrated citizens, and to help security forces suppress the opposition.

One new strategy to accomplish these tasks is the creation of a deep society, a concept similar to 'parallel society', which was initially outlined by the Czech philosopher Václav Benda in the late 1970s. For Benda, the goal of creating a *parallel society under* a totalitarian regime was 'taking over . . . every space that state power has temporarily abandoned or which it has never occurred to it to occupy in the first place' (Bron 2004). The concept of parallel society later lost its original connotation and has been used by European sociologists to denote segregated communities of immigrants, who voluntarily abstain from social and political participation in mainstream society.[1]

Deep society is different from 'parallel society', in terms of its relations with the state. Unlike 'parallel society', which is based on social groups, a deep society is a regime's creation and dictators employ it to protect the regime against a growing alienated and dissatisfied people. Deep society thus replaces civil society. It organises, mobilises and indoctrinates its members, it distributes rent among them, it surveils the population, and it suppresses the opposition.

While civil society is responsible for organising citizens and furthering their civil education, deep society is accountable for recruiting, managing and indoctrinating the regime's supporters. While people in civil society are often educated, members of deep society are indoctrinated to obey authority

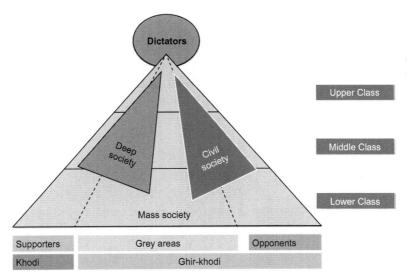

Figure 5.1 Dictators' support and opposition from society

without question. The purpose of indoctrination is to guarantee that people will abide by commands. In short, the regime legitimises itself and creates social conformity among its followers.

In the transition from civil society to a deep society, the control of social institutions becomes concentrated in the hands of regime's elites. The population is grouped into closed organisations and indoctrinated with the regime's values. The result is the weakening of civil sectors of society, and the increased capability of the regime to suppress and control dissidents.

From Mass Society to Civil Society in Post-revolutionary Iran

As Kamrava (2005: 165) writes, 'despite the new political environment that emerged starting in the late 1980s, it was not until the presidential elections of 1997, that discussions of civil society moved out of small intellectual circles and assumed national political center'. This transition mostly took place under the influence of democratisation processes in Eastern Europe after the collapse of the Soviet blocs in the late 1980s. Civil society became one of the main slogans Iranian reformists employed when Mohammad Khatami came to power in 1997. Twenty years after the revolution, and one decade after the ending of the Iran–Iraq war, Khatami won his presidential campaign, which focused on political progress and promises of easing state control over society. The reformists' goal was to strengthen the regime by increasingly channelling the new middle-class demands and giving them a voice.

During the Reform Period from 1997 to 2005, social and political developments followed the so-called Reconstruction Period from 1989 to 1997, which 'had to a certain degree paved the way for a slow transition from mass society to a segmented civil society' (Bashiriyeh 2010). Khatami's government set up an administrative and bureaucratic apparatus for promoting a network of loyalty, mostly from the new modern middle class, and political support for reform as well as improving Iran's international and diplomatic position (Rivetti 2012). Under Khatami, the number of civil society organisations rapidly increased to around fifteen thousand NGOs and charities (Namazi 2005). Iranian conservatives, headed by the Iranian Supreme Leader, had always perceived projects for the expansion of civil society organisation as a threat to their power, but Iranian civil society came under more severe pressure as colour revolutions occurred internationally between 2001 and 2005. In addition, the US invasion of Afghanistan and Iraq in 2001 and 2003 respectively, together with the inclusion of Iran in the 'Axis of Evil' and the allocation in the United States of a considerable budget for 'democracy promotion in the Middle East and North Africa', led to the intensification of pressure over Iranian civil society organisations on the part of the regime (Fathollah-Nejad 2013). These US foreign policy initiatives and the expansion of colour revolutions led to more pressure on the reformists, who had already been criticised by Iranian youth for being ineffective.

Hardline Government and Suppression of Civil Society 2005–2009

With the emergence of a hardline candidate, Mahmood Ahmadinejad, in the 2005 presidential election, the regime began a new cultural revolution to put the country on the 'right' path created by the 1979 revolution. Ahmadinejad's presidential campaign, based on social justice, fighting the oligarchy running the regime and the redistribution of wealth, appealed to the poor and the lower classes in urban areas and to peasants in the rural ones.

Ahmadinejad's victory paved the road for the securitisation and IRGC-isation (Islamic Revolutionary Guard Corps) of the Iranian regime. The IRGC became the most powerful bloc within the regime, and its personnel occupied many key positions in the state bureaucracy. The IRGC has become an essential player in security and military policymaking. Concerned by the colour revolutions in Eastern Europa and Central Asia, the IRGC focused on neutralising the threat of a possible colour revolution in Iran. This led to the securitisation of civil society and the perception of civic activism as a national security threat. From the Islamic Republic's perspective, the ideas that civil society promoted were a security threat to the regime's existence and were propagated to create the conditions for a colour revolution in Iran. That is why the IRGC intelligence deputy was charged with neutralising the expansion of civil society organisations in Iran through surveillance and the suppression of civil society activities.

As a pre-emptive policy, the IRGC has repressed civil society organisations and arrested civil and political activists since 2006, including Iranian internationally, such as Ramin Jamenbegloo, an Iranian Canadian scholar, Haleh Esfandiari, the director of the Middle East Program at the Woodrow Wilson International Center for Scholars in Washington, DC, and Kian Tajbakhsh, a scholar of urban planning and politics and a consultant to the Open Society Institute. They have been accused of empowering civil society organisations for staging a colour revolution and overthrowing the regime (Ansari 2019). Although many of active independent civil society organisations were suppressed during Ahmadinejad's administration, civil and political activists were involved in shaping and spreading the Green Movement, which started after the disputed 2009 presidential election. Many Iranians questioned the results of the 2009 election, sparking a series of protests known as the Green Movement, which was the most serious popular unrest the regime had experienced since its establishment in 1979 (Golkar 2020).

The regime perceived the Green Movement as a classic 'colour revolution' scenario – a popular revolt triggered after rigged elections, having a symbolic colour and being non-violent – and suppressed it brutally. The IRGC had in fact started warning about a colour revolution a few days before the election took place (Milani 2009). The IRGC began its campaign against the Green Movement even before election day by cutting off the internet and SMS services and immediately arresting political activists. It was the largest internet interruption since 2001, when the Islamic Republic began its online censorship. The IRGC's security headquarters cut off SMS services a day before the election, reduced internet speeds and filtered and blocked many websites. During the Green Movement, website filtering became more extensive; accessing most political websites and social networks such as YouTube and Twitter became impossible. Even public sites like Yahoo and Google and their email services were inaccessible (Golkar 2011a). In addition, the IRGC Cyber Defense Command (IRGCG-CDC), created in 2006–7 to monitor Iranian cyberspace, extended its powers to suppress the activities of Iranian online activists who had moved to cyberspace after the regime had brutally suppressed them on the streets.

The Green movement led to a more aggressive policy in suppressing civil society organisations, as numerous NGOs were shut down and many activists were arrested and others silenced, while some fled the country altogether. Following this repressive turn, many activists began focusing on much less politicised domains, such as environmental issues and charity work. The Islamic Republic used severe repression against civil society, and security forces directly attacked and closed down some organisations. Around 800 civil society activists were sentenced to prison by the judiciary or freed on bail (Razzaghi 2010). The regime also isolated itself by limiting foreign NGOs' ability to operate in Iran and denying visas to journalists. The regime also increased its efforts to reward its supporters by distributing rents such as pensions to families of martyrs and veterans (Tezcür 2012).

While the regime was successful in controlling and ultimately suppressing the Green Movement in the space of few months, the strength and widespread appeal of the Green Movement were a wake-up call for the Islamic Republic, which had alienated vast swathes of the modern Iranian middle class that had emerged after the Iran–Iraq war. Thus, in addition to the suppression of civil society, the regime realised that organising its supporters effectively was necessary for maintaining social and political order.

The Islamic Republic and the Mobilisation of its Social Base

As an aspirational totalitarian regime, the Islamic Republic has tried relentlessly to control all aspects of the life of its citizens, including private life. The Islamic Republic has a long history of manipulating ideas through propaganda and censorship. It also regulated the Iranian body through morality policing, sex segregation and mandatory Islamic dress code. In addition to these policies, the Iranian regime has manipulated emotions by intentionally depressing Iranian society. Elsewhere, the regime's cultural policy of intentionally depressing or saddening youth as a strategy for reducing their energy has been documented (Golkar 2016). Like other totalitarian regimes, it has systematically divided Iranians into *khodi* (insider, ally, one of us) and *ghyer khodi* (them, not a partner, outsiders), mostly on the basis of loyalty to the regime, its ideology and its supreme leader (Rivetti 2020). Insiders are considered trustworthy and shape the regime's social base. They usually occupy critical jobs in the state bureaucracy, including security, while outsiders are not trusted to hold essential positions and occupy less sensitive state bureaucracy posts.

Insiders and outsiders can be seen among all social classes, including the upper, middle and lower classes. However, while there are many exceptions, insiders belong to the more religious and traditional part of society whereas outsiders are more 'secular', believe in the separation of religion and state and have a more personal interpretation of the faith. This is because the critical component of the ideology of the Islamic Republic is political Shi'ism. Since 1979, the regime has simultaneously atomised outsiders through suppression, creating a mass society, and organising the insiders in pro-regime organisations, including Islamic associations (*Anjoman-e hay-e Eslami*) and the Basij (mobilisation).

The Basij Militia and Mobilising the Regime's Supporters

The Basij militia, founded by Ayatollah Khomeini in 1981, became one of the ten units of the IRGC, helping to maintain the regime in power in 1982. As a popular force, the Basij recruited and trained 100,000 Iranians, mostly teenagers or the elderly, and deployed them to the front against Iraq. Because of the lack of military training and experience, most Iranian casualties during the eight-year war with Iraq were Basij members. For Khomeini (1998: 190), 'the Basij . . . was blessing favored by God to the Islamic Revolution which . . . ensured the country and the Islamic Revolution through . . . sacrifice, sincerity, devotion, and martyrdom'.

In 1990, Ayatollah Seyed Ali Khamenei, the regime's new Supreme Leader, ordered the militia's promotion from unit to a conventional military force. The Basij unit was upgraded to the Basij Resistance Force (BRF) and became one of the five main branches of the IRGC, which include the Ground Force, Navy, Air Force and Quds Force. It constitutes a parallel to the IRGC Ground Force. Since 1990, Basij has expanded vertically by creating a unit in each province, a regional branch for each city, and units for neighbourhoods. As the Basij opened up new organisations, it also developed economic activities, moral policing, and physical repression activities during riots. This was most evident during the early years of repression of unrest in undeveloped areas between 1993 and 1994 when the Basij battalions, including Ashura (male) battalions, were used as anti-riot forces (Afshon 2014).

During the reform era (1997–2004), conservatives used the Basij to confront the reform movement and hinder Khatami's programme. Since 2001, the Basij has been used as the linchpin of hardliners, including Ahmadinejad's electoral success in 2005, as the militia worked to 'get out the vote' in conservative strongholds. Ahmadinejad was a Basij member and a strong supporter of the Supreme Leader and moved the country towards a more conservative approach. With the support of the Ahmadinejad administration the Basij expanded dramatically, and its members occupied many positions in the state bureaucracy. During this time, the Basij force was used to suppress civil society activities, while the regime also allocated a considerable budget to the Basij as the most prominent NGO in Iran (Mohebi 2014).

The Basij members and other security forces, such as the police, suppressed the Green Movement after the disputed presidential election in 2009 in Tehran and other large cities (Khosrokhavar 2011). According to Iran's domestic security doctrine, the Basij is the second layer of the regime's defence after the national police, a centralised armed force under Iran's Ministry of the Interior (Golkar 2018). Because of the Green movement's broader reach and the inability of the police to suppress the protests, the Basij forces and units were deployed in the streets to suppress the demonstrations. The regime's use of the Basij militia to quell the unrest led to it losing credibility and legitimacy in the eyes of millions of Iranians.

Basij as Deep Society

Since 2009, the Basij has become more than just an instrument of suppression for the Islamic Republic. The regime transformed the militia into what I call deep society, as its aim is to protect the regime against people. To achieve this goal, the Basij Resistance Force was officially transformed from a military force into a more civilian mass organisation. Its name changed from the Basij Resistance Force into the Organization for the Mobilization of the Oppressed (OMO) in 2009. General Mohammad Reza Naqdi was appointed President of DBO rather than Basij commander. The aim was to focus more on social control by expanding the Basij social strata organisation and exerting a more stable form of control.

The DBO was shaped to incorporate many of the regime's supporters (potential or active) into the organisation. Through mass membership of the regime's supporters, the organisation shows its strength in numbers, and intimidates non-members. Since 2010, the DBO has vertically expanded its branches and created more than twenty-two sub-organisations to cover vast swathes of society. Historically, the Basij focused on recruiting and organising people on the basis of their residency in urban and rural bases. It has created more than twenty-two different branches for recruiting and managing Iranians into various social strata and professions since 2010. The Basij introduced many new chapters, including the Workers Basij Organisation, Employees Basij Organisation, Guilds (*Asnaf*) Basij Organisation, Medical Society Organisation, Engineers Basij Organisation, Lawyers Basij Organisation, Artists Basij Organisation, Sports Society Basij Organisation, Cultural/Teachers Basij Organisation, Lecturers Basij Organisation, Clergies and Islamic Students Basij Organisation, Panegyrists (religious singers; *Maddah*) Basij Organisation, and Media/Journalists Basij Organisation.

The Basij has extended its reach into all aspects of Iranian society and population through the creation of the Babies Basij Organisation for members aged between three and seven and the Retirement Basij Organisation for the elderly. The militia has also established branches specifically geared towards women and professionals in the education system. The Women's Society Basij Organisation appeals to women who support the regime's conservative ideals. The Baby Basij Organisation was created under the Women's Society Basij Organisation's supervision, responsible for organising pro-regime Iranian women. Basij members were trained as kindergarten teachers to educate children according to religious principles. They provide free or cheaper day-care, mostly for Basij members. The Basij also established various education-related branches, including the Students Basij Organisation, Pupils Basij Organisation, Teachers Basij Organisation and Cultural/Lecturers Basij Organisation (mentioned above), to organise students of all ages and faculty at all levels. These groups are useful because they use peer pressure to encourage non-members in a specific profession or company to join the militia for the benefits they might derive even if they do not ideologically support it. For example, there is a 40 per cent quota for active Basij members looking to attend Azad University.

In academia, the Basij created an extensive control network through three main branches: staff, professors' and students' Basij organisations. For example, student activists are simultaneously under the gaze and surveillance of their Basij classmates, instructors and university staff. These organisations work hand in hand with other repressive organisations at the university, including Herast, a branch of the Ministry of Security and Intelligence present on each campus. Some of these Basij students then spy on their university professors and report to security organisations, including the IRGC intelligence organisations. As a reward, students loyal to the regime get scholarships or are hired as faculty members at university. For example, during the Ahmadinejad era, the Basij members, most of them without the necessary academic qualifications, received more than 2,000 Ph.D. scholarships. Active Basij membership also provides a political security net, thanks to which they cannot be fired despite their incompetence.

The regime has expanded the Basij vertically and horizontally. Vertically, the Basij spread from the top down and, ultimately, into each neighbourhood, school, university and state bureaucracy. Thus, the Basij has more than 54,000 offices throughout the country. Horizontally, it also spread and penetrated all sectors of society, covering almost all professions, to replace civil society and integrate the regime's supporters. The Basij, like the Party in Mussolini's political thought, is the 'capillary' via which the dictatorship's blood is diffused throughout society (*Gandhi and Przeworski* 2006: 15).

Deep Society Membership

Through this complex institution, the Islamic Republic has recruited a large number of its supporters and people in the 'grey' zone. However, not all these people have the same status in terms of training, loyalty and connections to the regime. For example, the first and largest level is called the Regular Basijis (*Basij-e Adei*) and includes members who have been ideologically/politically trained at the most basic level. Legally, anyone who wants to become a Regular Basiji can do so regardless of gender, age, religion, ethnicity or education status.

Second-level Basijis, known as Active Basijis, must undergo more extensive ideological/political training and are, therefore, given more responsibility and authority within the militia. Active Basijis pass ideological and security background checks to ensure that they are loyal members and supporters of the regime. This is done to prevent anti-regime citizens from secretly infiltrating the militia.

The third level of Basij membership includes the cadre. Active Basij members may be promoted to this third rank after passing more intense ideological and political training. They become the central part of the Basij base. This means they are full-time Basij members and on the payroll. These members also form the main Basij structure and its military units.

The fourth and final membership level is the Special Basijis, which requires the most rigorous military and ideological training. They are hired by the IRGC for military operational zones, such as borders, to work under the IRGC ground force. Special Basijis are considered full-time employees; they are formal members of the IRGC and receive a salary.

The recruitment and promotion in deep society are directly related to the indoctrination of deep society's members. The Basij has gradually developed a pervasive system of ideological and political training, in which every member has to pass several courses to absorb the regime's Islamic ideology. Another post-2009 change in the Basij was the evolution of the system for organising its members. According to this new plan, all Basij and IRGC members should be organised in 'ideological circles' (*Haleghehay-e Eteghadi*).

All Basij members, from the first level to special membership, are organised on the basis of age and education into different 'righteousness circles' (*Haleghehay-e Salehin*). The aim is to indoctrinate Basij members and bind them more effectively through social pressure. Basij members of the same ideological learning circles will have spent more time together.

Deep Society and Enforcing an Islamic Social Lifestyle

Organising the Basij members in ideological circles puts them under peer pressure to conform to the Islamic Republic's system. Simultaneously, the members of these circles are forced to conform to the Islamic social lifestyle and its culture: what has been labelled a 'religious-Hezbollahi' culture. The regime firmly supports the religious and Hezbollahi (Arzeshi/Basiji) lifestyle, which is mostly based on political Shi'ism. In this lifestyle, religion (in the official Shia interpretation) forms the central plank, defining all social, personal, public and private life elements.

The regime promotes this religious and Hezbollahi lifestyle as an alternative against the hybrid-postmodern lifestyle which most Iranians follow. Based on a liberal interpretation of Islam and acceptance of modernity, this new lifestyle is more focused on materialistic values and consumption. People in the hybrid-postmodern subculture have a greater acceptance of cultural and moral relativism and believe that liberty and freedom are simply as essential as religion. As Golkar (2018b) summarises the matter, 'most Iranians have accepted both Islam and consumerism and are pursuing hedonism, leisure and gratification while simultaneously remaining mindful of otherworldly asceticism'.

Deep Society and the Co-optation of Insiders

While members of the Basij come from all walks of life and all socio-economic classes, including the upper middle class, most of them belong to lower-middle-class families who join for many reasons including religious, ideological and, crucially, material incentives. Joining deep society helps the regime's supporters move up the social ladder rapidly, even without qualifications. Inside this society, as mentioned earlier, there are four layers of membership, which one can climb after proving loyalty to the regime and successfully completing the ideological and political training.

Also, the regime uses deep society to distribute rent among its supporters. As Roozbeh and Sabet (2010) argue, 'Basij membership entails a wide range of benefits including jobs, preferential loans, a quota in universities, access to facilities (health clinics, sports clubs, etc.), paramilitary training and much more, thus improving living standards and facilitating social mobility'. While the cadre and special Basij members are specifically on the Islamic Republic's payroll, the Basij works as a network to find jobs for its members and introduce them to other state bureaucracies for jobs. For example, Iran's police – NAJA – usually encourage and support Basij members to join the force, mostly because they have some military training and have more security qualifications than non-Basij members.

In addition to the police, Basij members have priority in obtaining jobs in all Iranian security and military organisations, including the conventional army, the IRGC and the Ministry of Security and Intelligence. For example, almost all IRGC members are drawn from the active Basij membership. At the same time, Basij members prioritise being hired by the Iranian conventional army and the police. The state bureaucracy also gives priority to active Basij members for recruitment. There is an official quota for recruiting upper-echelon Basij members, and unofficially, they receive support from their Basij comrades. In this sense, Basij works as a social club.

Deep Society and Controlling Others

Unlike civil society, which aims to work as a buffer zone and protect the individual against the state, deep society was developed to protect the regime against increasingly dissatisfied people detached from the regime and its ideology. The Basij has always been the regime's tool for maintaining social and political order. For example, it served as the regime's moral police, which was based on the idea of *Amr be Maruf va Nahy az Monkar* (commanding the right and forbidding the wrong), in line with the Islamic Republic's ideology. Since the early 1990s, the Islamic Republic has used Basij members as legal judiciary officers. It has relied on them ever since to intimidate society, discipline offenders and impose Islamic codes of behaviour and dress, including forcing women to wear the *hijab* and preventing male–female interactions in public places (Golkar 2011b).

Moreover, from its inception, the Basij tried to control public spaces, surveil, and suppress dissidents. Their bases are the lowest organisational level and are the most accessible part of the Basij's hierarchical structure. Many of the bases are placed in convenient locations for all Iranians, such as mosques, residential neighbourhoods, factories, offices and schools.

Therefore, the bases should be considered the real backbone of the Militia (Golkar 2015).

The bases in each neighbourhood serve the regime in the same way as Jeremy Bentham's panopticon building, in which people believe they are always observed by the authorities (Foucault 1977). For example, during the 2009 Green Movement, when people chanted slogans on their roofs, these bases were used to identify the people on the roofs. Many people received warnings from the Basij bases in their neighbourhoods to stop chanting anti-regime slogans.

The Basij bases' success in controlling and surveilling society convinced the regime to expand the Basij bases dramatically following the 2009 Green Movement. The Basij bases have increased in number from 36,000 to 54,000 throughout the country in rural and urban areas. The Islamic Republic tries to preventively crack down on protests by establishing the Basij bases in public squares or mosques in the main street.

The Basij has also helped the regime's security apparatus since its inception in 1981. As the regime's security system's eyes and ears, the Basij is responsible for watching online and offline spaces, gathering intelligence, identifying troublemakers and reporting these people to its security services. However, the Basij surveillance mission has dramatically expanded since 2009, under a newly-shaped body called the IRGC Security and Intelligence Organisations. Many members of Iran's deep society have been encouraged to spy on their friends and family members.

After 2009, some Basij members also acted as informers (*Mokhber Basiji*) to provide the regime with 'intelligence coverage' (*Ashraf Etlaati*). Some Basij members have organised a network called *Ayon*, meaning eyes, to identify people who defy the Islamic social order covertly. They take down the licence-plate numbers of cars whose drivers have broken Sharia law, such as by taking off their hijab in the car, playing music too loudly or having an improper hijab. They keep watch over neighbourhoods to identify and report any suspicious 'non-Islamic' activities, like house parties or home churches (Golkar 2015). This has had a chilling effect on Iranians, who feel constantly watched.

The Green Movement has been labelled a Twitter revolution, and the internet and social media have played an important role in continuing the protests and spreading the news (Keller. 2010). With the Green Movement in the streets suppressed, many activities have relied more and more on the internet and social media for disseminating information. This is why the regime, like other MENA regimes examined in this book,[2] has invested heavily in modern technologies to control cyberspace. The Islamic Republic has also increased the militia's presence in cyberspace through the creation of new cyber branches like the Cyber Basij organisation, which is responsible for educating and equipping Basij members for monitoring online spaces. The Basij has provided training and facilitated its members' presence on the internet so as to produce pro-regime content, distribute the regime's propaganda, and identify and troll the activists (Article 19, 2017). In one instance, in Tehran, the Basij created 144 cyber units for fighting enemies online, according to Brigadeer General Mohammadreza Yazdi, commander of the IRGC Mohammad Rasulallah Division (Iran International 2020).

By using deep society members in physical space and cyberspace in an integrative way, the Islamic Republic has perfected what Ozgun Topak (2019) has labelled the authoritarian surveillant assemblage (ASA) in his study of Turkey's authoritarian state surveillance regime (see also Topak 2022 in this volume). Compared to Turkey's case, however, deep Iranian society is more institutionalised and more deeply rooted in the regime's fabric.

Conclusion: Deep Society and Regime Survival in Iran

Since 2009, a new wave of mass uprisings has shaken the Middle East and North Africa and brought a moment of optimism that the winds of change were blowing through the region. Although the Tunisian transition has apparently been successful, MENA dictatorships have remained entrenched and have upgraded their survival toolkit. Learning from other regimes' experiences and their own, they have started a new wave of authoritarian upgrading in the region, such as through more online suppression. In the Iranian case, the Islamic Republic has actively tried to organise and mobilise its small social base against Iranians' growing dissatisfaction, equipped with modern information and communications technologies. In addition to expanding its policing capacity, and investing more resources in military and security forces, the Islamic regime has upgraded and transformed its militia force into a more civilian organisation to shape what I have called a deep society. The Basij militia has grown gradually since its inception in 1980, both organisationally and in its presence throughout society. Following the 2009 Green Movement, the militia has created more than twenty-two branches to incorporate all social groups. Through these organisations, the regime has organised, indoctrinated and hegemonised its supporters to make sure they will be attached to the regime and to insulate it against increasingly unattached Iranians. More importantly, deep society has been used to provide the regime with more loyal human capital, thanks to unrelenting ideological education, peer pressure and surveillance. While members of the deep society prioritise joining the state bureaucracy, the deep state (the supreme leader, its networks and the IRGC) has mostly relied on the deep society for human capital.

In addition to its supporters, the regime uses the deep society to absorb and co-opt the people in a grey area or prevent them from joining the active oppositions. Through the provision of legal and material support, deep society is an attractive community even for non-ideological Iranians. The members of deep society also are employed to control and suppress dissent through intimidation of their peers in social organisations, dissemination of the regime's propaganda, spying on and identification of regime dissidents, trolling of activists online and in society, and, ultimately, suppression through naked force.

The creation of a deep society was one reason why the Islamic Republic was successful in maintaining power and tackling the frequent uprisings that have emerged in recent years, such as in 2017–18, 2019 and 2020. However, there is no guarantee that the deep society can neutralise the threat of future mass uprising if the regime cannot provide basic goods for Iranians. Attitudes inside Iran show that the likelihood of the balance of power remaining the same is slim. There is only so much repression, especially when it is committed by peers through government manipulation, that people can take before repression itself becomes reason enough for change.

Notes

1 According to the supporters of this new interpretation, 'parallel societies' theory maintains that ethnic minorities develop social networks that do not interconnect with those of native Europeans. It is also claimed that the concurrent segregation within educational institutions and in the labour market and spatial segregation eventually develop institutions that reproduce the socio-economic isolation of migrant communities (Mueller 2006). According to the German political scientist Thomas Meyer, a social group must fulfil five criteria to be classified as a parallel society: 'ethnic cultural or cultural-religious homogeneity; almost complete

everyday civil, societal and economic segregation; practically complete duplication of the institutions of the majority society; formal, voluntary segregation; and segregation in living quarters or social interaction' (Gorchakova 2011).

2 See the 'Digital Surveillance' section in the Introduction (Topak et al. 2022) for an overview of digital surveillance practices in other MENA regimes at varying degrees, particularly the Gulf States such as Saudi Arabia (Uniacke 2022), and other regional powers: Turkey (Topak 2022) and Egypt (Jumet 2022).

References

Aarts, P. and F. Cavatorta (2013). 'Introduction', in P. Aarts and F. Cavatorta (eds) *Civil Society in Syria and Iran: Activism in Authoritarian Contexts*. Boulder, CO: Lynne Rienner.

Arseh, S. (2010). 'Iran: Legalizing the Murder of Civil Society', *Arseh Sevom Peace Democracy*. https://www.arsehsevom.org/wp-content/uploads/2010/12/Danger -to-Civil-SocietyIran2.pdf

Article 19 (2017). 'Tightening the Net Part 2: The Soft War and Cyber Tactics in Iran'. https://www.article19.org/data/files/medialibrary/38619/Iran_report_pa rt_2-FINAL.pdf

Ansari, A. (2019). *Iran, Islam, and Democracy: The Politics of Managing Change*. London: Gingko.

Bron, M. Jr (2004). 'From "Parallel Society" to Civil Society: Surfacing from Authoritarianism', *Journal of Adult and Continuing Education* 6: 5–20.

Diamond, L. (1997). 'Civil Society and the Development of Democracy', Working Paper 1997/101.

Finkel E. and Y. M. Brudny (2012). 'No More Colour! Authoritarian Regimes and Colour Revolutions in Eurasia', *Democratization* 19(1): 1–14.

Fathollah-Nejad A. (2013). 'Iran's Civil Society Grappling with a Triangular Dynamic', in P. Aarts and F. Cavatorta (eds) *Civil Society in Syria and Iran: Activism in Authoritarian Contexts*. Boulder, CO: Lynne Rienner.

Foucault, M. (1977). *Discipline and Punish: The Birth of the Prison*. Trans. New York: Pantheon.

Fukuyama, F. (2014). *Political Order and Political Decay: From the Industrial Revolution to the Globalization of Democracy*. London: Profile.

Kamrava, M. (2001). 'The Civil Society Discourse in Iran', *British Journal of Middle Eastern Studies* 28(2): 165–85.

Keller, Jared (2010). 'Evaluating Iran's Twitter Revolution', *The Atlantic*, 18 June. https://www.theatlantic.com/technology/archive/2010/06/evaluating-irans-twi tterrevolution/58337/

Khomeini, R. (1988). 'Sahifeh-ye Imam' 21, 23 November, 189–91.

Khosrokhavar, F. (2011). 'The Green Movement', in E. Hooglund and L. Steinberg (eds) *Navigating Contemporary Iran: Challenging Economic, Social and Political Perceptions*. London: Routledge.

Kuran, T. (1995). *Private Truths, Public Lies: The Social Consequences of Preference Falsification*. Cambridge, MA: Harvard University Press.

Iran International (2020). 'Iran Commander Says He Has 144 Active Cyber-Battalions', 17 November. https://iranintl.com/en/world/iran-commander-says-he-has-144 active-cyber-battalions

Haggard, S. and R. Kaufman (2016). 'Democratization during the Third Wave', *Annual Review of Political Science* 19(1): 125–44.

Huntington, S. (1991). 'Democracy's Third Wave', *Journal of Democracy* 2(2): 12–34.

Gandhi, J. and A Przeworski (2006). 'Cooperation, Cooptation, and Rebellion under Dictatorships', *Economics & Politics* 18(1): 1–26.

Golkar, S. (2011a). 'Liberation or Suppression Technologies? The Internet, the Green Movement and the Regime in Iran', *International Journal of Emerging Technologies and Society* 9(1): 50–70.

Golkar, S. (2011b). 'Politics of Piety: The Basij and Moral Control of Iranian Society', *Journal of the Middle East and Africa* 2(2): 207–19.

Golkar, S. (2016). 'Manipulated Society: Paralyzing the Masses in Post-revolutionary Iran', *International Journal of Politics, Culture and Society* 29: 135–55.

Golkar, S. (2018a). 'The Evolution of Iran's Police Forces and Social Control', *Middle East Brief* 120, Crown Center for Middle East Studies, Brandeis University.

Golkar, S. (2018b). 'Cultural Heterogeneity in Post-Revolutionary Iran', *Policy Notes* 50, Washington Institute for Near East Policy.

Golkar, S. (2020). 'Protests and Suppression in Post-revolutionary Iran', *Policy Notes* 85, Washington Institute for Near East Policy.

Gorchakova, N. (2011) 'The Concept of Parallel Societies and its Use in the Immigration and Multiculturalism Discourse', University of Helsinki, unpublished. https://www.academia.edu/1175022/The_concept_of_Parallel_Societies_and_its_use_in_the_immigration_and_multiculturalism_discourse

Jumet, K. D. (2022). 'Authoritarian Repression Under Sisi: New Tactics or New Tools?', in Ö. E. Topak, M. Mekouar and F. Cavatorta (eds) *New Authoritarian Practices in the Middle East and North Africa*. Edinburgh: Edinburgh University Press, pp. 73–91.

Milani, A. (2009). 'Is Iran Heading Toward A Military Coup?', 18 June. https://www.cbsnews.com/news/is-iran-heading-toward-a-military-coup/

Mohebi, M. (2014). *The Formation of Civil Society in Modern Iran: Public Intellectuals and the State*. London: Palgrave Macmillan.

Mueller, C. (2006). 'Integrating Turkish Communities: A German Dilemma', *Population Research, and Policy Review* 25(5/6): 419–41.

Namazi, B. (2005). 'The State of Civil Society and NGOs under Iran's New Government', Middle East Program, Wilson Center.

Ostovar, A. (2013). 'Iran's Basij: Membership in a Militant Islamist Organization', *Middle East Journal* 67(3): 345–61.

Postel, D. (2010). 'Counter-Revolution and Revolt in Iran; An Interview with Iranian Political Scientist Hossein Bashiriyeh', *Constellations* 17(1): 61–77.

Razzaghi, S. (2010). 'State of Civil Society in Iran', Policy Paper. https://tavaana.org /sites/default/files/state_of_civil_society_in_iran_-_pdf_-_english.pdf

Rivetti, P. (2012). 'Coopting Civil Society Activism in Iran, in Civil Society in Syria and Iran', in P. Aarts and F. Cavatorta (eds) *Civil Society in Syria and Iran: Activism in Authoritarian Contexts*. Boulder, CO: Lynne Rienner.

Rivetti, P. (2020). *Political Participation in Iran from Khatami to the Green Movement*. London: Palgrave Macmillan.

Safshekan, R. and F. Sabet (2010). 'The Ayatollah's Praetorians: The Islamic Revolutionary Guard Corps and the 2009 Election Crisis', *Middle East Journal* 64(4): 543–58.

Tezcür, G. (2012). 'Democracy Promotion, Authoritarian Resiliency, and Political Unrest in Iran', *Democratization* 19(1): 120–40.

Topak, Ö. E. (2019). 'The Authoritarian Surveillant Assemblage: Authoritarian State Surveillance in Turkey', *Security Dialogue* 50(5): 454–72.

Topak, Ö. E. (2022). 'An Assemblage of New Authoritarian Practices in Turkey', in Ö. E. Topak, M. Mekouar and F. Cavatorta (eds) *New Authoritarian Practices in the Middle East and North Africa*. Edinburgh: Edinburgh University Press, pp. 296–319.

Topak, Ö. E., M. Mekouar and F. Cavatorta (2022). 'Introduction', in Ö. E. Topak, M. Mekouar and F. Cavatorta (eds) *New Authoritarian Practices in the Middle East and North Africa*. Edinburgh: Edinburgh University Press, pp. 1–29.

Uniacke, R. (2022). 'Digital Repression for Authoritarian Evolution in Saudi Arabia', in Ö. E. Topak, M. Mekouar and F. Cavatorta (eds) *New Authoritarian Practices in the Middle East and North Africa*. Edinburgh: Edinburgh University Press, pp. 228–51.

6

SILENCING PEACEFUL VOICES: PRACTICES OF CONTROL AND REPRESSION IN POST-2003 IRAQ

Irene Costantini

Introduction

On 6 July 2020, two gunmen shot dead Hisham al-Hashemi, a respected Iraqi researcher and analyst, outside his house in the Ziyouna district of Baghdad (*BBC News* 2020). On 19 August 2020, Riham Yacoub, a graduate in sports science who ran a women's health and fitness centre, was murdered by anonymous gunmen in Basra (Robin-D'Cruz 2020). These are only two cases of targeting killings in a list that is, unfortunately, much longer. In the period from 1 October 2019 to 9 May 2020 the United Nations Assistance Mission for Iraq (UNAMI) documented '31 incidents of attempted or completed killings of persons linked to the protests that resulted in 22 deaths (including three women) and the injury of 13' (UNAMI and OHCHR 2020: 33). The special Representative of the UN Secretary General for Iraq, Jeanine Hennis-Plasschaert, added that 'this is not random violence but a deliberate silencing of peaceful voices, coupled with the total impunity enjoyed by perpetrators' (UNAMI and OHCHR 2020: 3).

Iraqi citizens are not new to violence. At least since the US invasion of the country in 2003, Iraq has witnessed cyclical high levels of political violence. According to the Iraqi Body Count, the number of civilian deaths from violence peaked in 2006 and 2007 with the outbreak of the civil war, reaching, respectively, more than 29,000 and 26,000 registered deaths, a number that peaked again in 2014 with more than 20,000 deaths as the Islamic State advanced throughout the country. At its lowest level, between

2010 and 2011, the country was still counting more than 4,000 violent civil-ian deaths a year.[1] Forms of violence have changed according to the country's political circumstances, but its intensity has largely remained high. Against a background of latent violence cyclically turning into open conflict, Iraq has witnessed a parallel trend of violent repression, which is distinctively tied to the emergence and evolution of protest movements challenging the existing political establishment.

An Iraqi protest movement has appeared since at least 2010–11, coinci-dentally with the events occurring in other countries in the MENA region, although it has received far less attention than in other contexts across the region, at least until recently. Iraq has witnessed a number of episodes of social mobilisation, which testify to people's agency and power in a context of instability and violence (Costantini 2020). Amid a great variety of smaller protests scattered around the Iraqi territory, some episodes have had a pro-nounced impact on national politics. The 2012–13 round of protests, which were concentrated mainly in the Sunni-populated governorates of al-Anbar, Nineveh and Salah ad-Din, were violently crushed by the security forces, cre-ating a fertile ground for the strengthening of the Islamic State (Al-Marashi 2017). By the summer of 2015 people had taken to the streets and squares of southern Iraq and Baghdad, and they continued to do so throughout 2016. From the protest ranks emerged a new, and in some ways unexpected, political alliance between the leftist/secularist movement (headed by the Iraqi Communist Party) and the al-Sadr-led Shia block (Jabar 2018; Robin-D'Cruz 2019), whose electoral coalition gained the largest number of seats in Parliament in the May 2018 election. In the summer of the same year, protests erupted in Basrah, with large crowds demanding a number of socio-economic and governance reforms (Hasan 2018).

In October 2019, renewed popular protests shook Iraq once again. The Iraqi youth, which made up the bulk of the protesters and was exasperated by years of violence and poor socio-economic opportunities, mobilised in Baghdad and other cities in the south of the country to demonstrate against the government of Adil Abdul-Mahdi, which, like all its predecessors, had proved unable to formulate a political programme capable of reversing the negative spiral the country is in (Hasan 2019). The October 2019 protests surpassed the previous episodes in spontaneity and scale and were successful in obtaining the resignation of the prime minister only a year after his appoint-ment. The cost, however, was extremely high: the government's response has in fact been extremely violent. The crackdown has seen security forces crushing the protest by employing water cannon, live rounds and rubber bullets, causing a high number of casualties. The impetus of the protest waned only as the country, and the world, began to face the consequences of the Covid-19 pandemic in 2020.

To respond to different protest episodes, the Iraqi state oscillated between concessions and, increasingly, coercion, upgrading its mechanisms of control, surveillance and repression to stifle dissent, neutralise opponents and prevent further social mobilisation. The resorting to such practices questions the degree of change that the Iraqi political system went through over the last two decades. The post-2003 Iraqi governance system has been built in reaction to the brutal authoritarian regime of Saddam Hussein. The institutional architecture designed to govern the country following the US invasion and occupation included a number of mechanisms meant to guarantee group representation (power-sharing); minorities' protection and individual freedoms, as stated in the Constitution, in addition to checks and balances on the government's actions, including the role of parliament and various commissions, such as the Iraqi High Commission for Human Rights. From an institutional perspective, then, Iraq took a decisive step away from the previous regime. However, political and socio-economic developments following 2003 suggest a mismatch between these institutional guarantees and the way in which the political leadership has managed the transition.

The chapter proceeds as follows. The next section surveys the practices of control and repression employed to respond to the Iraqi protest movements, focusing mainly on the 2019 protests. The chapter then moves on to discuss these practices in light of the democratic credentials of the post-2003 Iraqi political system, its continuity with past modes of governance and the institutional changes brought about by regime change.[2] In particular, it relates the analysis of new authoritarian practices to the debate on power-sharing, seeking to assess whether the latter may be conducive to the former. It concludes by arguing that the formal institutional arrangements and the informal rules that shape post-2003 Iraq constitute an important obstacle to the risk of a relapse into an all-out form of authoritarianism; at the same time, however, the same formal institutional arrangements and informal rules are one of the primary sources for the survival of authoritarian practices in the country.

Practices of Repression and Control

As anticipated above, social mobilisation in post-2003 Iraq has been met with a mixture of concessions and coercion. The pendulum radically shifted towards the latter in response to the protests that occurred starting in October 2019. UNAMI/OHCHR records the death of at least 487 protesters, with 7,715 injured, between 1 October 2019 and 30 April 2020 (UNAMI and OHCHR 2020: 14). The Iraqi High Commission for Human Rights reports a higher number, totalling 541 demonstrators dead and 20,597 injured from the beginning of the protest up until 10 June 2020 (IHCHR 2020), while the government has not released official numbers. Various reports confirm that security forces resorted to live ammunition, tear gas canisters, stun grenades (often fired horizontally), shotgun cartridges containing buckshots and/or birdshot ammunition and air rifles to respond to the protesters, thus showing an intention to suppress rather than control the protest (UNAMI and OHCHR 2020; IHCHR 2020; HRW 2020).

Although the scale of violence against the protesters in 2019 has been particularly high, this is not the first time the Iraqi government has resorted to violence against social mobilisation. Notable, for instance, is the violent response of former Prime Minister Nuri al-Maliki against the 2012–13 protests. In January 2013, protesters were killed in Fallujah as security forces sought to break up a demonstration; in April of the same year violence erupted in al-Hawija where the security forces were deployed to dismantle a protest camp, resulting in at least fifty victims; and in December 2013, al-Maliki ordered the closure of the sit-in camp in Ramadi, another episode that turned particularly violent (Human Rights Watch 2014; Mabon and Royle 2017). Excessive violence against protesters was reported also in Basra in summer 2018 and in the Kurdistan region of Iraq, especially to face down the protests that erupted in 2018 across the Erbil, Duhok and Sulaymaniyah governorates (Van Der Toorn 2018).[3]

The repression of episodes of social mobilisation in Iraq demonstrates the ambiguous role of security providers in the country. In response to the October 2019 protests, a number of security forces were involved in the repression, most of them under the control of the Minister of Interior and operating according to the Law of Police Officers' Crime Prevention Duties, which dates back to 1980.[4] However, in addition to official forces, other unidentified armed groups were responsible for attacking protesters and activists.

This is a pattern already identified in the protests that erupted in the summer of 2018 in Basra, when some of the protesters violently clashed with some of the pro-Iranian militias within the Popular Mobilization Forces (PMF) (Hasan 2018). In 2018, and since October 2019, protesters have become more vocal against the role of militias in Iraq, in particular the pro-Iranian ones, and have targeted their offices together with those of the main political parties and government buildings. If not collusion, at best government forces have been unable to stop militias from employing violence against the protesters and have been unable to protect them.

More worryingly, violence against the protesters exited the protest sites and entered everyday life. As mentioned in the introduction, targeted killings have been another way of silencing the voice of those committed to the protest movement or expressing views critical of the existing political and security situation. The killings or attempted killings occurred in several governorates across Iraq, but were mostly concentrated in the southern ones, including Babil, Basra, Dhi Qar, Qadisiyah, Karbala, Maysan, Wasit and Baghdad. Various advocacy and human rights organisations have denounced this practice, which is arguably aimed at weakening the Iraqi protest movement by targeting its key figures. As Robin D'Cruz (2020) has noted, the assassinations target individuals who 'tend to be slightly older than many of the protesting youths (typically in their mid-to-late 20s or 30s), come from middle-class families, are university educated and in employment, and are disproportionately female'.

In addition to direct force against the protesters, a massive wave of arrests weakened the movement. Thousands were detained by security forces between 1 October 2019 and 30 April 2020 without judicial oversight and procedural guarantees (UNAMI and OHCHR 2020: 24). Furthermore, prominent activists, bloggers and lawyers were arrested at their homes or at checkpoints, with some of the arrests conducted by the militias. Cases of abductions have also been registered. Allegations of torture and/or ill-treatment of detainees abound. The arrests were carried out under the provision of the Iraqi Penal Code of 1969, another law that dates back to the prior regime. At the beginning of the October 2019 protests, the High Judicial Council even threatened the protesters by declaring that acts against the security forces could be treated under the Iraqi Federal Anti-terrorism Law, which contemplates the death penalty, but was later blocked by the Federal Cassation Court (UNAMI and OHCHR 2020: 7).

Intimidation and threats against the protesters were also widespread online. In Iraq, as elsewhere,[5] social media channels have been a primary instrument for organising demonstrations and gathering support from the wider public. However, they also became the venue for countering demonstrations, with unknown or fake profiles denigrating activists. Social media campaigns against protesters often resorted to a narrative depicting them as agents of or manipulated by Western countries. For instance, the killing of Riham Yacoub was preceded by the accusation that she was part of a US plot to instigate protests in the city of Basra (Robin-D'Cruz 2020). Female activists or sympathisers with the protests have been targeted in social media campaigns denouncing their immorality and resorting to public shaming. Many other similar cases of online intimidation have been reported in the country and some of the targeted assassinations occurred after the victims had received threats online.

The online social media space has become a terrain for a polarising Iraqi society. Controlling this space has become key to preventing online social activism from becoming offline street mobilisation and eventually turning into a genuine mass movement. It is thus not surprising that the Iraqi government imposed a full national shutdown of the internet between 3 and 8 October 2019, as the response against the demonstrations turned violent. Internet services were restored only partially at the beginning of November, but localised blockages have been imposed since, such as the one in Nasiriyah on 28–9 October following the death of twenty-four demonstrators. Cutting off the internet meant preventing access to most social media channels, rendering communication inside, to and from Iraq very limited (UNAMI and OHCHR 2020: 38). Partial and full internet shutdowns had occurred also in reaction to previous protest episodes, for instance to limit the spread of the protests in Basra in the summer of 2018.

Restrictions have been imposed also on television and radio channels covering the demonstrations. Security forces and other armed elements have harassed, attacked and arrested journalists as they were covering the events in the squares and streets of Iraq and they have stormed the headquarters of various TV channels. On 10 January 2020, for instance, a reporter for the TV channel Dijlah and his cameraman were killed in Basra after they had covered the resumption of protests in the country (RSF 2020). According to Reporters Without Borders, four journalists and two media assistants were killed in 2020. On 24 October 2019 the Ministry of Interior went so far as to prohibit live coverage of the protests (UNAMI and OHCHR 2020: 39) while media and press restrictions sought to control the content of the news. Already in June 2014, the Iraqi Communication and Media Commission, a regulatory body for broadcasting and telecommunication, had issued mandatory media guidelines during the campaign against the Islamic State, which were later updated in May 2019.[6] On 12 November of the same year, the Commission issued an order for the closure of eight TV channels and four radio stations and warned five others channels, as they were accused of violating the Commission's guidelines (Wille 2020: 28).[7]

In all, the high level of violence perpetuated by official and non-official security personnel against the protesters went largely unpunished. On 12 October, the government convened a Ministerial Investigative Committee to investigate the events of the first days of the 2019 protest, without, however, this being followed by judicial investigation or prosecution. In May 2020, with a new government in place headed by Mustafa al-Khadimi, a fact-finding committee was established to produce a list of victims whose families could claim compensation. As of August 2020, the list included 560 persons who have been declared martyrs, who include also security personnel (UNAMI and OHCHR 2020: 8). In addition, in July 2020, in reaction to the death of the well-respected researcher and analyst Hisham al-Hashemi, the High Judicial Council established a body to investigate cases of assassination in the country.

Authoritarian Practices in Post-2003 Iraq

The above-detailed practices of control and repression against the protest movement lead us to question the democratic credentials of the post-2003 Iraqi political system, its continuity with past modes of governance, and the institutional reforms brought about with regime change. In 2020, Freedom House listed Iraq as non-free, with particularly low scores on civil liberties (Freedom House 2020). The Democracy Index 2019 downgraded Iraq from a 'hybrid regime' to an 'authoritarian regime', with a score of 0 in the functioning of government categories and low scores on civil liberties (The Economist Intelligence Unit 2020). Overall, these assessments and country-based research point to an authoritarian tendency in the country (Dodge 2013; O'Driscoll 2017). In post-2003 Iraq, old practices of silencing dissenting voices through killings, arrests and torture resurfaced while combining with new practices targeting also the online space.

As argued elsewhere, the political developments in Iraq from 2003 can be explained by combining an analysis of external factors (foremost, the US-led process of state-building and the geopolitical competition between the US and Iran) and internal ones, including the positioning of a new political elite vis-à-vis the previous regime and society (Costantini 2018). After 2003 the Iraqi state did not entirely abandon previous modes of organisation and operation. It maintained a distribution of power focused on political-parties-centred networks of patronage that go beyond the structure of the state, sustained by a rentier political economy reliant on wealth distribution rather than wealth creation. While these traits were maintained, Iraq developed new state forms modelled upon the internationally-led state-building framework. These new forms did not materialise into legitimate and effective institutions, but rather produced the contours of an 'empty state', one that is built in forms, but not in practice (Richmond 2014). It is thus not surprising that some of the legal grounds within which contemporary practices of control and repression occur date back to the former regime (i.e., the 1969 Penal Code and the 1980 Law of Police Officers' Crime Prevention Duties), not-withstanding the massive institutional restructuring that Iraq went through beginning in 2003.

The examination of authoritarian practices thus needs to consider their development within the contours of a hybrid political order distinct from the full-scale authoritarianism of the past (Sassoon 2012), as yet not fully democratic, but pluralistic in nature. This does not equate to the concept of competitive authoritarianism (Levitsky and Way 2002), but rather considers a variety of state and 'non-state forms of order and governance [and] the combination of elements that stem from genuinely different societal sources' standing not in isolation, but rather permeating each other (Boege, Brown and Clements 2009: 17; see also Boege 2019). Accordingly, a problematic aspect when examining authoritarian practices is identifying their sources. As the above review shows, they were, for instance, employed by security actors who sit uneasily in the distinction between state and non-state, thus questioning the centrality of the state in the unfolding of authoritarian practices and its control over the security apparatus, as further discussed below.

The rise of a new form of authoritarianism in Iraq has been primar-ily associated with the contested figure of former prime minister Nuri al-Maliki (2006–14). Once granted authority through democratic elections, al-Maliki began to use state resources – financial and coercive – to shrink the political space and curb the opposition. He came to control key state institutions (including the country's independent commissions such as the High Commission for Human Rights and the Independent Electoral Commission) through the expansion of a network of relatives and loyal party members and monopolised the use of violence by personalising the security chain of command to the extent that, by his second term, he had concentrated a tremendous amount of power in his person (Dodge 2013). However, authoritarian practices persisted following his mandate, and spanned different governments. In 2019, under the premiership of Adil Abdul-Mahdi, Renad Mansour warned once again against an 'authoritarian turn' in the country (Mansour 2019b). The unfolding of authoritarian practices throughout different governments and among different political leaders calls into question the institutional architecture of the country, rather than its leadership, in contrast to other Middle Eastern contexts, such as Erdogan's Turkey, al-Assad's Syria, al-Sisi's Egypt or Mohammad Bin Salman's Saudi Arabia.

Looking at such architecture, the analysis of authoritarian practices connects with the debate on power-sharing, particularly as regards whether the latter may be conducive to the former. At first glance, power-sharing and authoritarian tendencies may be seen as mutually exclusive forms of political organisation. Drawing on the classical work of Arend Lijphart (1977), consociationalists put forward a model built upon: proportionality in the electoral system as well as in the distribution of resources and public positions; minorities' power of veto to guarantee the safeguard of minorities from the majority's decision; segmental autonomy, usually taking the form of federalism or autonomy; and the formation of inclusive grand coalition governments.[8] Consociationalism is a constraint on majoritarian democracy, and its constitutive elements, at least in theory, work against a concentration of power, as, contrastingly, does authoritarianism.

Power-sharing formulas have been regarded by the international community as most suitable for providing solutions for countries experiencing civil conflicts, especially in highly divided societies, although there exists no definitive evidence that they work (Jarstad 2015: 249). Within the broader agenda of democratisation (part and parcel of international intervention in conflict-affected countries), power-sharing mechanisms have been introduced in Iraq as well as in other contexts, such as Bosnia-Herzegovina or Lebanon. However, 'power sharing itself is not inherently democratic. In fact, most elements of power sharing do not require democracy to function' (Hartzell and

Hoddie 2015: 49). Indeed, as has been observed in different cases, conflict termination does not equate with democracy, and often 'the choice is between reforms to promote democracy versus efforts to secure peace' (Jarstad 2008: 18). In other words, power-sharing may serve a security-oriented objective, but in itself does not guarantee full adherence to democratic practices.

The model pursued in Iraq was grounded on liberal consociationalism, which, in contrast to the 'corporate' variant, does not accommodate groups according to predetermined criteria, but rather 'rewards whatever salient political identities emerge in democratic elections, whether these are based on ethnic or religious groups, or on subgroup or transgroup identities' (McGarry and O'Leary 2007: 675). However, in practice, the institutional arrangements of consociationalism triggered the consolidation of political identities around existing ethno-religious groups, which in turn engulfed power-sharing mechanisms, resulting in the primacy of *muhasasa ta'ifia'* (sectarian apportionment) as the key regulative mechanism in the country. As it developed in practice, liberal consociationalism in Iraq was similar to other forms of corporate consociationalism, and it 'gave rise to forms of sectarian representation, discourse, and rivalry similar to those in Lebanon' (Saouli 2019: 80).

Scholars have explained the rooting of such a corporate system from two different perspectives. On the one hand, Boogards (2019: 2) argues that 'the temporary and liberal nature of the main consociational provisions resulted in incomplete, informal, and increasingly voluntary power sharing and failed to provide Iraq with a stable framework for the accommodation of communal tensions'. 'Consociationalism light' – the model promoted in Iraq, according to Boogards – left power-sharing arrangements to the voluntary commitment of political elites and was never fully implemented, creating a degree of flexibility that left Iraq unable to address its transition (see also Horowitz 2008). On the other hand, rather than focusing on whether there was too much or too little consociationalism, scholars looked at the actual political developments in Iraq, noting how informal power-sharing arrangements have deeply affected the institutional architecture of the country. For instance, Dodge (2019) shows how informal rules and norms not only distribute state-level positions on the basis of ethno-sectarian allegiances, but extend also to ministerial posts and senior civil servants (see also Dodge and Mansour 2020).

Recent scholarship on power-sharing in the Middle East has begun to question its negative consequences, pointing at sectarianisation (Dixon

2020), its counter-revolutionary ethos (Halawi 2020) and even its transformation into zombie power-sharing (Nagle 2020). This chapter builds on
these views to argue, by taking a step further, that consociationalism in Iraq
developed two tendencies that can be related to the use of authoritarian practices to control and eventually repress the population. First, power-sharing
in Iraq led to a concentration of power in the executive – a worldwide trend
associated with democratic deconsolidation – with government coalitions
created through a painstakingly long process of formation to reflect the distribution of power between informal party-controlled networks, approaching
'government formation as a rent-seeking exercise' (Mansour 2019a: 6). The
rationale is that coalition governments tend to 'accommodate political differences; rest on negotiations and pacts; pursue more moderate programs;
enjoy wider electoral support; and are closer to the median voter than single-
party governments' (Maravall 2010: 84). However, this occurred more on
the ground of a distribution of institutional and bureaucratic positions than
on the convergence of political agendas and at the expense of the centrality
of Parliament, where opposition forces not organised along ethno-sectarian
lines find it difficult to hold the government accountable.

A second tendency is the high degree of 'immobility' that consociationalism generated, which translates into a very low level of governance
performance in the country. The solidity of government coalitions stands
on a delicate balance of representation, which prevents the formulation of a
courageous political programme capable of directing state resources to the
most-needed areas of interventions. Indeed, a corollary of power-sharing in
Iraq has been the conversion of political capital into economic and military
power as a way of maintaining the political salience of ethno-religious identities in society. This created the ground for a political system that, despite
the instrumental exploitation of societal demands, is geared towards maintaining the status quo, irrespective of its dysfunctionality, and where new
political forces have difficulties in finding representation at the institutional
level.

In light of these two tendencies, authoritarian practices to control and
eventually repress the population need to be understood as part of a defensive
strategy perpetuated by the Iraqi political elite to defend their intra-elite
political pact and shield themselves from demands emerging from society. The
Iraqi protest movement has predominantly remained peaceful and organised
around a reformist rather than a revolutionary ethos. But its development,

including the protests that began in October 2019, saw a progressive tendency towards demands for radical change. The political leadership interprets calls for reforms that cannot be met by makeshift arrangements or through a distribution of resources as threats to its very existence, against which it reacts through repressive means. Thus, authoritarian practices are not part of the unintended consequences of the convergence between institutional reforms (power-sharing) and informal political developments, but rather a constitutive feature of the Iraqi political system.

The actual working of power-sharing in post-2003 Iraq has then impacted the articulation of state power, with direct consequences for the practices of control and repression. This is notable when considering the security apparatus, in relation to which Iraq continues to be characterised by the presence of non-state providers of (in)security, ambiguously positioned vis-à-vis official security forces.[9] The presence of militias in repressing dissent has generated different patterns. As Mansour and D'Cruz (2019) have noted, 'the tight-knit relationship between Iraqi security forces, local tribes and militias' in Basra explains the more cohesive strategic model of repression in the governorate following the 2018 protests. However, this can hardly be extended nationwide, where cohesiveness is lost in favour of a rather uncoordinated response to the protests. Indeed, Prime Minister Adil-Abdul Mahdi ordered the security forces not to use live ammunition as protests erupted in October 2019, but to no avail. Similarly, Mohammed Tawfiq Allawi, nominated as Prime Minister in February 2020 (and later replaced by Mustafa al-Khadhimi), could not contain the use of force.

The absence of a hierarchical system of repression and control leaves a marginal space for protesters' actions, but at the same time increases the insecurity of the environment in which they operate. This is then complicated by the fact that the survival and contestation of the Iraqi political system cannot be isolated from international and regional factors. While the protest movement called for an end to all foreign meddling in the country, some of the protesters attacked the offices of pro-Iranian militias and the Iranian consulate in Kerbala and Najaf. From Iran came the accusation that the protests were, in turn, the result of American sedition (Al-Monitor 2019), which justified the active role of pro-Iranian militias in repressing the movement. Against them, Muqtada al-Sadr's armed 'blue hats', another militia, took on the task of protecting the protest sites until his U-turn against the demonstrators and his participation in repression practices. Heightened tensions between the United States and Iran, especially following the killing of Qasem Soleimani and Abu Mahdi al-Mohandes, deputy commander of the PMF, in a US airstrike, contributed to the protest being erroneously framed as part of this geopolitical rivalry, thus intensifying authoritiarian practices of control and repression.

Conclusion

As the overall critique of the American-led regime change in Iraq has extensively discussed, the state-building enterprise in the country fell short of realising that grandiose democratic revolution that was invoked by former President George W. Bush. If further evidence for this is needed, the practices of control and repression employed by the Iraqi political leadership and detailed in this chapter substantiate this reading. The current pluralistic nature of the Iraqi political system does not allow us to speak of continuity with the previous centralised and hierarchically organised regime of Saddam Hussein. At the same time, the perseverance with which the Iraqi political leadership has resorted to, among other things, direct oppression of the protesters, targeting killings, or measures that infringe civil and political freedoms both online and offline, does not allow us to speak of a complete rupture from the previous regime, either. To grasp such development, this chapter has discussed authoritarian practices in relation to the institutional architecture of the country, the position of the Iraqi political leadership in it, and its impact on the articulation of state power, foremost its monopoly over the legitimate use of violence.

In conclusion, the formal institutional arrangements and the informal rules that came to shape post-2003 Iraq constitute an important obstacle to the risk of a relapse to an all-out form of authoritarianism. At the same time, however, the formal institutional arrangements and the informal rules that came to shape post-2003 Iraq are one of the primary sources of authoritarian practices in the country. If authoritarian practices were a function of the strength of the regime of Saddam Hussein, they are now a function of the weakness of the new Iraqi political elite, including its inability to control the security apparatus. The Iraqi protest movement is the key target of such practices as well as the main challenger to them. While, so far, demands against the status quo have only been partially successful, the Iraqi protest movement has been successful in showing the link between the consociational structure of governance in the country and the everyday life of its citizens, by denouncing the high level of corruption and socio-economic mismanagement, as well as its violence.

Notes

1 'Iraq Body Count', https://www.iraqbodycount.org/database/
2 See also the 'Established Authoritarian Practices' section in the Introduction, which provides an overview of key examples from the book chapters (Topak et al. 2022).
3 Although actual problems in both the Kurdistan Region and the rest of the country are largely similar, social mobilisation is a product and reflection of its environment, and thus it responds to distinct socio-political and economic dynamics. Protests have been organised independently in the KRI with no spill-over effects. Triggered by socio-economic grievances and sustained by deep-seated distrust towards the authority, protests in the KRI have often turned into the expression of rivalries between existing Kurdish political parties.
4 They included: the Federal Police, the Emergency Response Division and the Facilities Protection Service; in some of the provinces where protests occurred, the local Police, SWAT forces, Emergency Response Units; and, in Basra, the Al Sadma force (or Shock Forces) (UNAMI and OHCHR 2020: 17).
5 Other examined cases of social media control in the book include Egypt (Jumet 2022), Turkey (Topak 2022), the UAE (Davidson 2022) and Qatar (Liloia 2022), among others.
6 The Commission's guidelines for the management of Iraqi mass media during the war on terror included provisions that, among others, instruct the media to refrain from 'broadcasting news material that may be interpreted against security forces', as well as inviting pro-government coverage of the fight against Islamic State, in particular, 'to focus on the security achievements of the armed forces, by repetition throughout the day, and highlighting them in special newscasts and coverage, praising the heroic acts performed by security personnel. And also to broadcast material showing the brutality of the enemy, and genuine news of the desperation and bankruptcy of the armed, terror groups' (HRW 2014).
7 The following are the outlets included in the Commission's decision: the Amman-based Dijlah TV and Anb TV, the Dubai-based Al-Sharqiya TV, the Saudi-funded Al-Arabiya Al-Hadath, the US-funded Radio Sawa, the Sulaymaniyah-based NRT News and Radio Nawa, and the Baghdad-based Al-Rasheed TV, Al-Fallujah, Hona Baghdad, Radio Al-Nas and Radio Al-Youm (CPJ 2019).
8 Advocates of the integrative power-sharing model call on Donald Horowitz (1985) and propose a system capable of mitigating the negative effects of pure consociationalism (Sisk 1996; Ben Reilly 2001; Reynolds 2002). They call for:

the introduction of centripetal institutional mechanisms that encourage moderation and avoid polarising tendencies in electoral campaigning (attracting votes from different constituencies); an arena of bargaining capable of creating space for compromise; and party or coalition politics of a centrist type. In particular, the integrative notion of consociationalism is strictly related to the presence of an ethnically-based political system that often has a centrifugal effect (Benjamin Reilly 2006).

9 For parallel discussions of the role of non-state actors see Durac 2022 (Yemen) and (St John 2022 (Libya).

References

Al-Marashi, I. (2017). 'Iraq and the Arab Spring: From Protests to the Rise of ISIS', In M. Haas and D. Lesch (eds) *The Arab Spring: Change and Resistance in the Middle East*. Boulder, CO: Westview Press.

Al-Monitor (2019). 'Tehran Decries Foreign Influence in Iraq Protests', 1 November. https://www.al-monitor.com/pulse/originals/2019/10/iran-media-claims-forei gn-influence-iraq-protests.html

BBC News (2020). 'Hisham Al-Hashimi: Leading Iraqi Security Expert Shot Dead in Baghdad', 7 July. https://www.bbc.com/news/world-middle-east-53318803

Boege, V. (2019). 'State Formation in the Context of Hybrid Political Orders', in N. Lemay-Hébert (ed.) *Handbook on Intervention and Statebuilding*. Northampton: Edward Elgar.

Boege, V., M. A. Brown and K. P. Clements (2009). 'Hybrid Political Orders, Not Fragile States', *Peace Review* 21(1): 13–21.

Bogaards, M. (2021). 'Iraq's Constitution of 2005: The Case against Consociationalism "Light"', *Ethnopolitics* 20(2): 186–202.

Costantini, I. (2018). *Statebuilding in the Middle East and North Africa: The Aftermath of Regime Change*. London: Routledge.

Costantini, I. (2020). 'The Iraqi Protest Movement: Social Mobilization amidst Violence and Instability', *British Journal of Middle Eastern Studies*, January, 1–18. https://doi.org/10.1080/13530194.2020.1715788.

CPJ (2019). 'Iraq Media Regulator Orders Closure of 12 Broadcast News Outlets', *Committee to Protect Journalists* (blog), 25 November. https://cpj.org/2019/11/ir aq-media-regulator-orders-closure-of-12-broadcas/

Davidson, C. M. (2022). 'The United Arab Emirates: Evolving Authoritarian Tools', in Ö. E. Topak, M. Mekouar and F. Cavatorta (eds) *New Authoritarian Practices in the Middle East and North Africa*. Edinburgh: Edinburgh University Press, pp. 320–39.

Dixon, P. (2020). 'Power-Sharing in Deeply Divided Societies: Consociationalism and Sectarian Authoritarianism', *Studies in Ethnicity and Nationalism* 20(2): 117–27.

Dodge, T. (2013). *From War to a New Authoritarianism*. London: The International Institute for Strategic Studies.

Dodge, T. (2019). 'Corruption Continues to Destabilize Iraq', Chatham House. 1 October. https://www.chathamhouse.org/2019/10/corruption-continues-de stabilize-iraq.

Dodge, T. and R. Mansour (2020). 'Sectarianization and De-Sectarianization in the Struggle for Iraq's Political Field', *The Review of Faith & International Affairs* 18(1): 58–69.

Durac, V. (2022). 'Authoritarian Practice and Fragmented Sovereignty in Post-Uprising Yemen', in Ö. E. Topak, M. Mekouar and F. Cavatorta (eds) *New Authoritarian Practices in the Middle East and North Africa*. Edinburgh: Edinburgh University Press, pp. 340–57.

Freedom House (2020). 'Freedom in the World 2020: Iraq', Freedom House. https://freedomhouse.org/country/iraq/freedom-world/2020.

Halawi, I. (2020). 'Consociational Power-Sharing in the Arab World as Counter-Revolution', *Studies in Ethnicity and Nationalism* 20(2): 128–36.

Hartzell, C. A. and M. Hoddie (2015). 'The Art of the Possible: Power Sharing and Post-Civil War Democracy', *World Politics* 67(1): 37–71.

Hasan, H. (2018). 'The Basra Exception', Carnegie Middle East Center, 19 September. http://carnegie-mec.org/diwan/77284?lang=en.

Hasan, H. (2019). 'Iraq Protests: A New Social Movement Is Challenging Sectarian Power', Carnegie Middle East Center, 4 November. https://carnegie-mec.org /2019/11/04/iraq-protests-new-social-movement-is-challenging-sectarian-pow er-pub-80256

Horowitz, D. (1985). *Ethnic Groups in Conflict: With a New Preface*. Berkeley: University of California Press.

Horowitz, D. (2008). 'Conciliatory Institutions and Constitutional Process in Post-Conflict States', *William and Mary Law Review* 49(4): 1,213–48.

HRW (2014). 'The Communication and Media Commission Guidelines for the Management of Iraqi Mass Media During the War on Terror', Human Rights Watch. 2 July. https://www.hrw.org/news/2014/07/02/communication-and-media-commission-guidelines-management-iraqi-mass-media-during-war

HRW (2020). 'World Report 2020, Iraq'. Human Rights Watch.

HRW (n.d.) 'World Report 2013: Iraq'. New York: Human Rights Watch.

HRW (2014). 'Iraq: Investigate Violence at Protest Camp', Human Rights Watch. 3 January. https://www.hrw.org/news/2014/01/03/iraq-investigate-violence-pr otest-camp

IHCHR (2020). 'Freedom of Opinion, Expression and Peaceful Demonstration', Special report V. Baghdad: Iraqi High Commission for Human Rights.

Jabar, F. A. (2018). 'The Iraqi Protest Movement: From Identity Politics to Issue Politics', LSE Middle East Centre Paper Series 25.

Jarstad, A. (2008). 'Dilemmas of War-to-Democracy Transitions: Theories and Concepts', in A. Jarstad and T. Sisk (eds) *From War to Democracy: Dilemmas of Peacebuilding*, 17–36. Cambridge: Cambridge University Press.

Jarstad, A. (2015). 'Sharing Power to Build States', in D. Chandler and T. Sisk (eds) *Routledge Handbook of International Statebuilding*. London: Routledge.

Jumet, K. D. (2022). 'Authoritarian Repression Under Sisi: New Tactics or New Tools?', in Ö. E. Topak, M. Mekouar and F. Cavatorta (eds) *New Authoritarian Practices in the Middle East and North Africa*. Edinburgh: Edinburgh University Press, pp. 73–91.

Levitsky, S. and L. Way (2002). 'The Rise of Competitive Authoritarianism', *Journal of Democracy* 13(2): 51–65.

Liloia, A. (2022). 'New Authoritarian Practices in Qatar: Censorship by the State and the Self', in Ö. E. Topak, M. Mekouar and F. Cavatorta (eds) *New Authoritarian Practices in the Middle East and North Africa*. Edinburgh: Edinburgh University Press, pp. 208–27.

Lijphart, A. (1977). *Democracy in Plural Societies: A Comparative Exploration*. New Haven: Yale University Press.

Mabon, S. and S. Royle (2017). *The Origins of ISIS: The Collapse of Nations and Revolution in the Middle East*. London; New York: I. B. Tauris.

Mansour, R. (2019a). 'Iraq's 2018 Government Formation. Unpacking the Friction between Reform and the Status Quo'. LSE Middle East Centre Report.

Mansour, R. (2019b). 'Iraq's New Republic of Fear', 23 November. https://www.fo reignaffairs.com/articles/iraq/2019-11-20/iraqs-new-republic-fear

Mansour, R. and B. Robin-D'Cruz (2019). 'The Basra Blueprint and the Future of Protest in Iraq', Chatham House. 8 October. https://www.chathamhouse.org /expert/comment/basra-blueprint-and-future-protest-iraq

Maravall, J. M. (2010). 'Accountability in Coalition Governments', *Annual Review of Political Science* 13(1): 81–100.

McGarry, J. and B. O'Leary (2007). 'Iraq's Constitution of 2005: Liberal Consociation as Political Prescription', *International Journal of Constitutional Law* 5(4): 670–98.

Nagle, J. (2020). 'Consociationalism Is Dead! Long Live Zombie Power-Sharing!', *Studies in Ethnicity and Nationalism* 20(2): 137–44.

O'Driscoll, D. (2017). 'Autonomy Impaired: Centralisation, Authoritarianism and the Failing Iraqi State', *Ethnopolitics* 16(4): 315–32.

Reilly, B. (2001). *Democracy in Divided Societies: Electoral Engineering for Conflict Management*. Cambridge: Cambridge University Press.

Reilly, B. (2006). 'Political Engineering and Party Politics in Conflict-Prone Societies', *Democratization* 13(5): 811–27.

Reynolds, A. (2002). *The Architecture of Democracy: Constitutional Design, Conflict Management, and Democracy*. Oxford: Oxford University Press.

Richmond, O. (2014). *Failed Statebuilding: Intervention and the Dynamics of Peace Formation*. New Haven: Yale University Press.

Robin-D'Cruz, B. (2019). 'Social Brokers and Leftist-Sadrist Cooperation in Iraq's Reform Protest Movement: Beyond Instrumental Action', *International Journal of Middle East Studies* 51(2): 257–80.

Robin-D'Cruz, R. (2020). 'Why Did They Kill Riham Yacoub? The Murder of a Civil Society Activist in Basra', *Middle East Centre* (blog), 24 August. https://bl ogs.lse.ac.uk/mec/2020/08/24/why-did-they-kill-riham-yacoub-the-murder-of -a-civil-society-activist-in-basra/

RSF (2020). 'Two Iraqi Journalists Shot Dead after Covering Protests in Basra | Reporters without Borders', RSF, 11 January. https://rsf.org/en/news/two-iraqi -journalists-shot-dead-after-covering-protests-basra

St John, R. B. (2022). 'Libya: Authoritarianism in a Fractured State', in Ö. E. Topak, M. Mekouar and F. Cavatorta (eds) *New Authoritarian Practices in the Middle East and North Africa*. Edinburgh: Edinburgh University Press, pp. 171–88.

Saouli, A. (2019). 'Sectarianism and Political Order in Iraq and Lebanon', *Studies in Ethnicity and Nationalism* 19(1): 67–87.

Sassoon, J. (2012). *Saddam Hussein's Ba'th Party: Inside an Authoritarian Regime*. Cambridge: Cambridge University Press.

Sisk, T. (1996). *Power Sharing and International Mediation in Ethnic Conflicts*. Washington, DC: United States Institute of Peace Press.

The Economist Intelligence Unit (2020). 'Democracy Index 2019: A Year of Democratic Setbacks and Popular Protest'. London: The Economist Intelligence Unit.

Topak, Ö. E. (2022). 'An Assemblage of New Authoritarian Practices in Turkey', in Ö. E. Topak, M. Mekouar and F. Cavatorta (eds) *New Authoritarian Practices in the Middle East and North Africa*. Edinburgh: Edinburgh University Press, pp. 296–319.

Topak, Ö. E., M. Mekouar and F. Cavatorta (2022). 'Introduction', in Ö. E. Topak, M. Mekouar and F. Cavatorta (eds) *New Authoritarian Practices in the Middle East and North Africa*. Edinburgh: Edinburgh University Press, pp. 1–29.

UNAMI and OHCHR (2020). 'Human Rights Violations and Abuses in the

Context of Demonstrations in Iraq October 2019 to April 2020'. Baghdad: UNAMI and OHCHR.

Van Der Toorn, C. (2018). 'Kurdistan Politics at a Crossroads', Carnegie Endowment for International Peace, 26 April. http://carnegieendowment.org/sada/76195

Wille, B. (2020). '"We Might Call You in at Any Time", Free Speech under Threat in Iraq', Human Rights Watch. https://www.hrw.org/report/2020/06/15/we-might-call-you-any-time/free-speech-under-threat-iraq

7

ISRAEL/PALESTINE: AUTHORITARIAN PRACTICES IN THE CONTEXT OF A DUAL STATE CRISIS

Hilla Dayan

Introduction

The state of Israel defines itself in ethno-national terms as 'Jewish and democratic', a construction that the late Baruch Kimmerling (1999) critiqued, arguing that the state is theocratic in its very foundation. The theological and ideological imperatives of Zionism, unlike other modern nationalisms, are to elevate and prioritise the status of all Jews in 'the Jewish state' and outside it above all others, while denying equal rights to the Palestinian citizens, the survivors and descendants of the survivors of the 1948 Nakba (Palestinian catastrophe). The hegemonic project of Zionism is dedicated to perpetually Judaising the land and constructing and maintaining a Jewish sovereign power for Jews only, erasing the Palestinian existence and national aspirations. Israel Harel, a publicist and spokesperson for the settler's movement, once likened Zionism to a bicycle ('once you stop pedaling, you fall'), illustrating the necessity for perpetually continuing the settlement project despite having the goal of sovereignty having long been achieved (Harel 2005).

While normally confident of its status as a 'Jewish democracy', the state of Israel is nevertheless sensitive to attacks on its basis of legitimacy in pursuing the national goal of asserting sovereignty over Palestinian territories it occupied in 1967. For over five decades, Israel has been ruling over around 4 million subjects in the West Bank and Gaza. Its ultimate strategic concern in recent decades has been to normalise its regime and prevent the state's deterioration into international pariah status. This chapter focuses on the repressive Israeli apparatuses, the prerogative part of the Israeli system of rule, henceforth 'the Prerogative State'. By 'Prerogative State' I mean the coercive apparatus as well as repressive authoritarian policies (Bellin 2004). I examine its relation to the normative part of the Israeli system of rule, henceforth 'the Normative State', by which I refer to institutions of the rule of law such as the parliament and courts, as well as citizenship statuses and protections and a functioning, open civil society. My account leaves out socio-economic and intra-Jewish structures of disenfranchisements, mass arrests, repression and the systematic discrimination of Palestinian citizens, who make up a fifth of Israel's citizen population, as well as the dynamic of Palestinian resistance.

A growing body of studies of the Israeli occupation has uncovered the myriad ways by which the normalisation of the occupation is pursued and achieved both domestically and internationally: for instance, through lucrative real-estate projects aimed at attracting non-ideological settlers to the Occupied Palestinian Territories (OPT) (Algazi 2006); through Israeli industries exporting OPT products as 'made in Israel' (Allegra et al. 2017); or, in another striking example, through the gradual expansion of Israeli academia to the OPT. The institution 'Ariel University', to elaborate briefly, was established beyond the green line in 1982 as a peripheral college branch in the illegal Ariel settlement in the West Bank and operated under the authority of the military government. In 2012 a controversy arose when the institution was declared a university by a decree of the military commander in charge of the occupied territories, bypassing normal academic accreditation processes. The specific 'academic higher council of Ayosh' – Ayosh is the Hebrew acronym for the OPT – was disbanded. The institution was subsequently absorbed into the national structures of the Council for National Higher Education (*Malag*). Both Israeli and international academia have since normalised scientific collaboration with Ariel.

Another well-known form of normalisation of the occupation is through the global spread of Israeli security know-how and technology. Thanks to massive military and state investments, by and large building on the machinery of repression in the OPT, the homeland security industry managed to position Israel as a 'start-up capital' of the world. Israeli security products are deployed indiscriminately by both authoritarian and non-authoritarian regimes. The products of the Israeli company Cellebrite, for instance, are used by police authorities in Scotland, UK, as well as by Hong Kong, Russian and Indonesian authorities who target and seek to eliminate political opposition. Neve Gordon (2008), Yotam Feldman (2013) and Elia Zureik et al. (2011) emphasise, in their studies of the global homeland security industry, that Israel's reputation as a technology-driven country is based on normalised and commercialised authoritarian repression. Zureik makes the point that although the technologies are developed under the extreme and specific conditions of 'tried and tested in the OPT lab', they nevertheless travel and 'normalise' as seamlessly transferrable tools for democratic governments, as the example of Canada's adoption of Israeli biometric technology for its own domestic needs demonstrates. In addition to the export of surveillance and cybertechnologies, Israeli 'smart' unmanned weapons and drones have become the decisive and most commonly used deadly weapons of twenty-first-century warfare. Most recently, Israeli-produced s-300 unmanned drones proved instrumental in Armenia's loss of the Nagorno Karabagh region to Azerbaijan (Kubovitz 2021). It was established that Saudi authorities used the NSO company's tool 'Pegasus' for the killing of the journalist Jamal Khashoggi (Kabir 2018), as Uniacke (2022) also details in his chapter in this volume. The UAE has used it to spy in neighbouring countries, for instance, on the commander of the national guard in Saudi Arabia, Qatar authorities and other opposition 'enemies' of the regime (Mazetti et al. 2019). It has become apparent, as cyber-tech blogger Thomas McCullan notes, that business is especially booming between Israeli companies and repressive Middle East regimes, and that this reality is already shaping the Middle East alliance (McCullan 2019). The chapters in this volume by Liloia (2022) and Davidson (2022) also deal with this aspect in detail and together they speak to the theme of the external dimension of repressive practices, as the introduction to this volume makes clear (Topak et al. 2022).

It is significant that Israel's tech sector operates in an open climate conducive to capitalist ventures and technological innovation, and that the international common sense about Israel is that it is a democratic high-capacity state and an 'innovation hub' (Tilly 2007). The Normative State is an essential factor in the prestige of the tech sector, which is almost never questioned. The marketing figure of speech 'start-up nation' has entered the Zionist lexicon, and Tel Aviv is considered a 'startup ecosystem' with one of the highest start-up densities in the world (over 2,500 start-ups for only around 435,000 inhabitants). Israeli cybersecurity start-ups collaborate with over thirty multinational corporations that have R&D centres in Tel Aviv.[1] The companies receive a protective shield from the institutions of the Normative State – the Ministry of Defence and Israeli courts, which systematically uphold the veil of secrecy on security R&D, innovation and exports, citing the necessity not to harm Israel's foreign and diplomatic interests. Not all Israeli high-tech is tied to the homeland security industry, but those companies that have emerged as the most successful globally do tend to be companies from the 'OPT lab'. The reason why they are particularly interesting to pay attention to is not just their role in global 'dirty operations', but their position at the nexus of the Prerogative State and the Normative State. In other words, their success is generated through the investment, personnel, know-how and experience gained in the framework of the Prerogative State, and their global operations are successfully whitewashed by the Normative State.

The theory through which we may understand the dynamic between the Normative and the Prerogative State is the dual state theory developed in the 1940s by the Jewish refugee from Nazi Germany and Frankfurt school legal scholar Ernst Fraenkel. Fraenkel, who studied the military occupation of the Rhineland by France and Belgium after World War I, postulated that in a dual state where a Normative State and a Prerogative State exist in tandem, and where a relatively free society and economy and a civilian rule of law exist, there is a *disequilibrium* between the prerogative and the normative, or between the occupying sovereign and a popular sovereign (Fraenkel 1940: 1941). By 'disequilibrium' Fraenkel meant to stress that the Normative State is both at the service of the Prerogative State and subservient to it. The Normative State, he argued, should not be confused with a 'democracy'. Rather, in his words, 'the Normative State is a necessary complement to the Prerogative State and can be understood only in that light' (Fraenkel 1941: 74). The theory of the dual state has seen a revival in the post-9/11 era. The dual state is known especially in the field of constitutional law and is normally applied on cases such as Putin's Russia (Trochev and Solomon 2018). The spectre of authoritarianism thus looms large here: prerogative power must not collapse the normative jurisdictions and the normative liberal façade on which it depends. It is not enough to have structures of a democratic state, as the political theorist Norberto Bobbio once argued: it is necessary that the people will not be governed despotically (Bobbio 1989: 156).

Unlike the Rhineland occupation, the military occupation of Palestine is not a temporary construction but a permanent one, and hence it can be construed as illegal under international law, as some Israeli legal scholars have argued (Gross et al. 2005). Nevertheless, it is crucial not to separate the occupation regime from the Normative State, and to understand and analyse Israel/Palestine as a single analytical unit. The dual nature of the state, ironically, finds expression in multiple forms of legal, social, economic, political and spatial separations and administrative differentiations (Ben Natan 2021; Mehozay 2016). Illegality is legalised in the context of the Normative State, and administrative differentiations produce a semblance of procedural continuity and 'checks and balances' in the context of the Prerogative State. This, as Smadar Ben Natan argues, is a condition reminiscent of colonial jurisdiction, in which 'the law is extended to enemies, without extending full legal protections' (Ben Natan 2020: 30). The approach that we ought to adopt in describing authoritarian practices in the Israel/Palestine context is, then, that of 'seeing Israel through Palestine' as Hawari et al. persuasively advocate (2018), and so with that in mind I turn to authoritarian practices in the OPT in order, first, to try to gauge any new developments.

Nothing New under the OPT Sun

Routine outbursts of extreme violence and killings, combined with creeping ethnic cleansing and territorial dispossession, are the most distinctive and well-known features of the Israeli regime in the OPT (Ophir and Azoulay 2012). When routine outbursts of extreme violence subside, the occupation returns to its 'normal' functioning as a matrix of control that has evolved into a regime of separation. A vast array of permits and restrictions separate populations and governs their daily lives in the OPT (Dayan 2009; Berda 2019). In a modern dictatorship, according to Andrew Arato (2003), a semblance of legality is essential. This semblance is kept through the bureaucracy of the occupation that is supposedly 'checked' administratively by Israeli military and civilian courts, the High Court of Justice (HCJ) chief among them. Under the Israeli permit system, for instance, individuals are formally classified as a 'security risk', which means being denied permits necessary for work, travel or medical treatment; in short, survival. The colonial legal apparatus manages lives under the jurisdiction of the coercive apparatus of the state. The coercive system works on a flat homogenising logic (everyone is suspect), yet it is also intricate in the ways it forces every individual to engage it for his or her basic needs. The bureaucracy of the occupation thus enforces dependency both on the military and the civil administration, and a semblance of legality is maintained.

To provide a concrete example of the level of penetration of Israeli bureaucracy, since 2019 Palestinian permit holders can download and use the app Elmonaseq (אלמונסק המנסק), 'the coordinator', in Arabic to access information related to their security and labour-permit status. With the advance of the Covid-19 pandemic in 2020 Palestinian labourers were instructed to download it, and to give authorisation to accessing of all the information stored in their cellphones, including contacts, messages and locations, which the IDF was authorised to transfer to other parties. Targeted cellphone surveillance is not a new practice, but soliciting authorisation from users in the context of the pandemic paved the way for a sudden expansion of cellphone surveillance. This was eventually 'checked' by the Normative State. In response to appeals by human rights organisations the IDF informed the HCJ that it will restrict the invasion to cellphone data to the minimum necessary to manage the Covid-19 crisis.[2] Whether this restriction was indeed applied or not is unclear. In any case, the Elmonaseq app clearly forces Palestinian permit holders into maintaining and even authorising 'interactive' relations with the occupier.

Palestinian permit holders are one of the most important lifelines of the OPT economy, and throughout the duration of the occupation the movement of labourers from the West Bank to Israel never ceased. The Covid-19 crisis brought a sudden change. Labourers were required not to travel back to the OPT and to stay overnight in Israel. This was a rather remarkable adaptation to the conditions of the global pandemic, because Palestinians had officially not been allowed to stay overnight within the Green Line since 1991. Prior to the emergence of the permit regime – the pre-Oslo era (1967–91) – Palestinians regularly crossed the Green Line, though these were hardly 'better times': their presence then was heavily policed, and they suffered from extreme exploitation and abuse, as well as racist violence (Grinberg 2016).[3] Israel appeared to be reluctant to sever economic ties despite the special circumstances, because of the economic implications for the construction sector, one of the few sectors relatively spared by the temporary crisis. The new guidelines regarding accommodation in Israel provide a good example for the nature of the apparatus of control: flexible, adaptable and totalitarian. It is a system which continuously seeks ways to eliminate means of *physical mediation* (e.g. via the new app, and earlier through biometric recognition devices in checkpoints), yet becoming not less but ever more penetrating in terms of intelligence gathering, and ever more restrictive.

Gaza is a somewhat different story. Since 2007 Israel has imposed a punishing siege after Hamas took over. Only 'humanitarian cases' are allowed to leave the strip through the Israeli-controlled crossings, mostly for medical purposes. Here again, a sudden condition forced an adaptation. According to Gisha, the Israeli legal centre for freedom of movement, Israel moved, as a Covid-19 safety measure, to apply a blanket 'double closure'. As a result, the number of so-called 'humanitarian permits' plummeted to 3 per cent of the normal rate. The state fought vigorously to deny virtually all 'humanitarian' appeals, enforcing the strictest closure since the siege was first imposed. The HCJ played its supporting role and backed the imposition of the double closure. It even intervened to overturn the handful of authorisations of movement won by Palestinians in lower Israeli courts (Galili 2021; Gisha 2021, PHR 2021). In 'normal times', between rounds of devastating military campaigns causing hundreds of civilian deaths and massive infrastructural destruction, draconian control of movements, bureaucratic torture and 'hermetic closures' constitute Israel's routine authoritarian practices in relation to the Gaza population. As a general rule, OPT policy is constantly subject to revisions, and these are immediately 'normalised': changes become new routine practices. The impetus for adaptations is normally incremental and ad hoc, sometimes satisfying the needs and imperatives of the Prerogative State as in the Elmonasaq app, and sometimes that of the Normative State as we saw in the labourers 'stay in' example.

A highly destabilising, carceral 'enemy penology' drives the military presence and military operations in the West Bank. Mass incarcerations and arbitrary administrative detentions without any charges occur at the rate of hundreds of cases a year, including minors and children. There are on average 200 military raids in private homes per month. The nightly IDF raids rob every Palestinian of a sense of security in their own private dwelling, inflicting collective trauma and disrupting people's normal daily functioning (Yesh Din 2019). The siege on Gaza and raids in the West Bank constitute forms of mass psychological warfare, whose overwhelming effect is a state of social implosion, which is particularly extreme in Gaza (Abdel-Wahab 2021). They are accompanied by routine lethal physical violence and destruction. Before the latest round of military campaigns in Gaza in May 2021, which left 227 civilians dead and 1,530 wounded and also destroyed the only Covid-19 centre in the strip, the statistics on routine military violence were assembled by the journalist Amira Has from various official sources: in 2019 there were more than 18,000 'violent incidents', around 1,800 a month from January to October. Violent incidents include shootings and killings, military raids on private homes, neighbourhoods and villages, arrests and detentions, uprooting of trees and destruction of crops, and daily vigilante actions of armed settlers that attack farmers, herders and entire villages. The year 2018 was the year of the 'Great March of Return' to the Gaza fence. Initially a peaceful grass-roots initiative, the peaceful marches met an IDF response of lethal violence, and scores of civilians (33 civilians, 44 alleged members of armed groups) died as a result of sniper shootings. That year more than 30,000 Palestinians were seriously wounded by the IDF. In a 'normal' year, serious injuries statistics are around 13,000 (Has 2021).

In the mid-2000s, when the separation wall was erected, the wall and the most notorious points of access in the West Bank – the Kalandia and the Bethlehem checkpoints – became icons of Palestinian humiliation and suffering. The years 2009 and 2010 marked the high point of checkpoints functioning as epicentres of military violence and collective punishment. Dozens of 'flying' and permanent checkpoints were temporarily or permanently constructed. As Hagar Kotef and Merav Amir showed in their study of the checkpoint phenomenon, their function at the time was not only to enforce 'enclaving', but to render Palestinians transgressors and thus facilitate military violence against them (Kotef and Amir 2011). Incidents of lethal violence at checkpoints have since significantly dropped. Infamous 'cattle scenes' – the cruel crowding of Palestinian in checkpoints – are still emblems of the violence and disenfranchisement under the occupation. But the installation of air-cooled transit halls and biometric machines had eased passage, creating more 'photogenic' crossings (Has 2019a, b). Palestinian movement through checkpoints is governed by the colonial logic of 'racialized time' (Lavie and Jamal 2019). The system, to give a concrete example, punishes Palestinians who are not abiding by the specific hours allocated to them for passing the checkpoints during morning rush hour. Time, as the journalist Amira Has once pointed out, is a vital resource stolen from Palestinians, a resource which no agreement could ever compensate for or return.

In Israel/Palestine, checkpoints constitute an elaborate domestic border regime. In 'Geography of the Occupation' the geographer Elisha Efrat points out that with very few exceptions, no other state in the world surrounds another state on all sides, controlling all exits and entrances, as Israel controls PA-administered areas in the West Bank (Efrat 2002: 196). Israel paved expensive access roads to marginal settlements locations serving a tiny population of settlers while deliberately ignoring the needs of the majority of the population in the area. This infrastructure is known as 'apartheid roads' (Efrat 2002: 151). The fortified mountain-top settlements, according to Eyal Weizman, are by design and in and of themselves 'optical devices . . . to exercise control through supervision and surveillance' (Segal and Weizman 2003: 86). According to Amira Has and Dror Etkes, an independent researcher specialising in the settlements, the 'greater Erez Ysrael' camp's dream of flooding the OPT with Jews never materialised. Ironically, the settlements failed demographically but succeeded geo-politically. They never became popular dwellings in the eyes of the majority of Israelis, but they manage nevertheless to destroy the fabric of life in the OPT, irrevocably disrupt its space, erase Palestinian history and, most importantly, normalise the brutal dispossession and the Jewish supremacy regime in Israel/Palestine as a whole as both inevitable and irrevocable (Has and Etkes 2016). Weizman's notion of a 'vertical apartheid' captures succinctly the big picture: there are layers and layers of administrative, geographical, infrastructural apparatuses of control in the OPT (Weizman 2017). These systems are so embedded in the environment and their presence is so ubiquitous that their dismantlement and disentanglement seem virtually impossible. Note especially the way the Normative and the Prerogative not only work in tandem but also normalise and regularise authoritarian practices, so that they become fully embedded and a part of routine of daily life. Authoritarian practices are thus 'logical' and 'necessary', a matter of policy, from the perspective of rulers, and of course an inescapable daily reality for the ruled.

This inevitably partial account has only dealt with the most well-known authoritarian practices in the OPT and cannot do full justice to either the experience or the reality of people living under this regime. One must bear in mind that authoritarian practices tell but one part of the story. The other part is the remarkable ability of individuals and communities to persevere despite and in the face of the disasters of the occupation (Shalhoub-Kevorkian 2008).

The New (Temporary) Emergency

The emergence of a new logic of emergency with the outbreak of the Covid-19 crisis in Israel in 2020 – a crisis that proved to be temporary yet very impactful – enables a peek into the 'normal' state of emergency and the 'normal' functioning of the dual state. There have been 112 Covid-19-related emergency decrees that came into effect within a period of eight months. The decrees themselves were subject to frequent changes and amendments. For example, one decree was amended thirteen times in nine months. Among them, a specific decree authorised the GSS (General Security Service) to lead command-and-control operations in an attempt to apply a central, mandatory mass surveillance modelled after China's. The public outcry that ensued in Israel over possible violations of the right to privacy brought to light the little-known fact that the GSS was already *legally* harvesting cellphone data from Israeli citizens under the operation codenamed 'The Tool'. Meantime, the HCJ rejected all appeals brought against the authorisation given to the GSS and made clear it would not intervene in government management of the health emergency. In typical 'liberal authoritarian' fashion (Kalyvas 2002), the HCJ retroactively legalised all previous government Covid-19-related emergency measures.

Typically, the Normative State is called to serve the Prerogative State. This time around, the Prerogative State was called to serve the Normative State. A new homeland security unit, 'Alon', was established to co-ordinate military operations assisting public health authorities. The health crisis thus amplified the condition that Yoav Mehozay depicts as 'fluid jurisprudence' (Mehozay 2012). This led some to speculate on the benefits of harnessing the capabilities of prerogative powers in the context of civilian social and health crises. Naftalie Bennett of the Jewish Home party tried to enlist the private surveillance company NSO (described by Edward Snowden as 'the worst of the worst') to implement a national system that ranks people's social behaviour and adherence to Covid-19 measures. This initiative never took off, but NSO was in a position to fill in a vacuum that occurred when the GSS appeared reluctant to deploy its full surveillance capabilities on citizens (Bendel 2020). Another 'bold idea' floated was to use GSS capabilities to suppress a rising level of criminality that has come to terrorise Arab communities in Israel (Barnea 2021).

Why was the GSS so reluctant to use its powers and apply its full capabilities in the framework of the Normative State? We can speculate that the GSS wanted to avoid further information spilling on 'The Tool', but also, interestingly, that it acted out of 'sensitivity to rights and privacy', as former General Giora Eiland put it.[4] The sensitivity has to do with the Prerogative State's dependency on the Normative State. It can be demonstrated by a similar 'sensitivity' shared by the Israeli private homeland security sector.

Cellebrite, for instance, was embarrassed by revelations that its product was used by Russia to hack opposition leader Alexi Navalny in the failed attempt to assassinate him in Germany. AnyVision, an offshoot of the Military unit 'Google Ayosh' that developed 'Better Tomorrow' – a facial-recognition software system – and operates hundreds of surveillance cameras in the OPT, was embarrassed when an NBC investigation uncovered that Microsoft is one of its investors, in violation of the six ethical codes Microsoft itself developed (Statt 2020).[5] Cellebrite, AnyVision and NSO – the three most famous and successful 'OPT lab' companies – could have had their 'tried-and-tested in Israel' moment. Yet this was carefully avoided, probably out of fear of being embroiled in 'sensitive' civilian operations. Contrary to common opinion, these companies do not develop their products to serve authoritarian practices particularly. Their business model is to 'roll out' products to the widest global clientele possible. The ever-growing demand for their products tends to be jeopardised by public exposure, as the case of Cellebrite withdrawal from Russia and Belarus clearly demonstrates (Yaron and Goychman 2021). The same business logic informs young entrepreneurs of the 'start-up nation', to provide a striking example, who begin their careers while still in their formal mandatory military service (as young as 18–21), setting up private ventures that successfully attract global investors. The story of Unit 81 of the IDF, with a hundred graduates, fifty companies and 10 billion dollars of investments, is a case in point (Shulman 2021).

The critical attention that the Israeli surveillance industry attracts is well-deserved, but Israel's intelligence-gathering practices in the OPT tend not to be primarily high-tech operations, and this is true across other cases explored in this volume whereby regime supporters operate within society to denounce potential opponents and, as Golkar (2022) shows in this volume in the case of Iran, fashion civil society activism entirely at the service of the regime. In Israel, the military and the GSS rely very heavily on old-fashioned human contacts: 'collaborators'. Unlike in the past, today's practices of soliciting collaboration are no longer shrouded by a veil of secrecy. Hillel Cohen's recent study documented how the GSS began to openly engage Palestinians through multiple Arabic-language Facebook pages, 'captain's pages' (the nickname for GSS operator in a given area), that have hundreds of thousands of followers (Facebook is immensely popular in the OPT with over 2 million users, around half the Palestinian population).[6] Facebook is hence another domain of psychological warfare sowing suspicion and encouraging opportunism. What we see with this striking example is how the Prerogative State frames itself as a normative 'service provider' in IDF parlance: through these pages – for example, the Facebook page of the office of the co-ordinator of government activities (COGAT) – Palestinians get information that is up to date and vital for conducting their activities. Using Facebook openly as a platform for both information and the soliciting of human intelligence is a relative novel practice. More frequently, however, the GSS and IDF rely on *traditional authoritarian methods*: military mass arrests, the threat of arrest, methods of permit allocations and denials, interrogations (including torture), extortions and intimidations, sometimes based on details concerning sexual conduct and identity, as has been revealed by dissenting intelligence officers (Cohen 2014).[7]

Drawing the story to a conclusion, despite the new layer of emergency, the situation in Israel during the Covid-19 crisis did not get out of control. There was no particular 'flow' of authoritarian methods and surveillance capabilities from the OPT to Israel. We can nonetheless point to some pressures generated by the state of emergency's erosion of rights and protections. The revelation that the GSS 'tool' applies to citizens was scandalous, and a 'technical glitch' that caused a leak of sensitive medical information on 140,000 Israeli citizens without their knowledge or authorisation from the Ministry of Health to the GSS raised further concerns. This mistake was corrected, but citizens now know that they too are under permanent GSS surveillance (Liss et al. 2021). In a more serious instance, it was revealed that using the new 'Covid-19 Law' the Israeli Police forced internet providers to install their servers with mechanisms to direct surfers' traffic through to a secret police-controlled system enabling the Police to perform traffic surveillance and even 'back-door' tinkering with individual accounts (Yaron 2020). This story broke in the midst of the harshest police repression of anti-Netanyahu demonstrations in the heart of Jerusalem.

Eventually, the Covid-19 emergency proved to be a temporary emergency. But the two-year-long emergency had a significant impact on a deeper level than the battle against the disease. The emergency exacerbated the racial exclusion of Palestinians (who had limited and late access to vaccines), and the unaccountability of governing institutions of the Normative State, exposing the dysfunction of government ministries and the fragility of the rule of law. Conditions of systemic chaos led to the accumulation of anger, frustration and desperation. Society was on the brink, ripe with tensions, especially between disenfranchised and nationally divided communities – conditions waiting to spiral out of control at any given moment. While authoritarianism in OPT proved during this period of time a remarkably stable and strong system, the Normative State was collapsing. One can describe it in stark terms as an opposition between a strong system and no-system or systemic chaos. Let us, then, turn to examine more closely the dynamic of the deep crisis and its relation to authoritarian practices in the OPT.

The Political Crisis

Benjamin Netanyahu's long tenure of power led to the erosion and weakening of liberal norms in Israel and his tenure was marked by anti-Arab and anti-democratic legislation, culminating in the 2018 'nationality law'. The nationality law has formalised Jewish supremacy and prompted a renewed interest in addressing the case of Israel as an 'apartheid state' (B'tselem 2020; Human Rights Watch 2021). Over the years, Netanyahu cultivated a cult of personality typical of authoritarian figures such as Viktor Orbán with his presidential illiberalism, and Recep Tayyip Erdoğan's anti-democratic populism (Rogenhofer and Panievsky 2020). Netanyahu's systematic attacks against institutions of the Normative State and against civil society, and a tendency to transgress the rules of the game, began to destabilise the Normative State already around 2011 (Dayan 2011). Following the announcement of charges of corruption pressed against him, 'Paris square' in Jerusalem filled, on 14 July 2020, with people calling for Netanyahu to go ('*Lech!*'). The anti-Bibi protest movement has been active since at least 2017. Despite their lack of unified leadership, the goal of disparate protest groups is nonetheless clear: 'to save democracy' and to hold Netanyahu accountable. The protesters were met with the heaviest means of crowd control at the Police's disposal. Every demonstration ended with mass and violent arrests. Water cannon vehicles (*Machtaziot*) were deployed (Hampel 2020; Carr 2020). These massive vehicles are especially popular with human-rights-violating regimes such as Honduras, Burundi, China, Indonesia and Zimbabwe. The black speakers, or sound cannons, capable of causing vomiting, disorientation, ear damage, sonic injury and deafness appeared in the OPT in the village of Bil'in in the early 2000s. They were used at the Kalandia checkpoint at the height of violence at checkpoints in the 2010s and during the 'Great March of Return' in Gaza in 2018. In 2020–1 they made an appearance in Paris Square, Jerusalem (Gill 2020).

As the weekly Balfour demonstrations continued, Netanyahu moved to ban demonstrations altogether. According to the civil rights advocate Gabi Laski, 600 demonstrators have been arrested and prosecuted for merely attending protests in violation of 'social distancing' rules, which was not a violation of any law. In addition, the police handed out heavy fines to protesters as a method of deterrence in times of severe economic crisis. The new Covid-19 law made 'resisting or disturbing police enforcement' – previously an administrative charge – into a criminal offence, and such criminal charges were immediately served against the leaders of the demonstrations. All the attempts to 'kill' the protest, however, failed. As Geoffrey Pleyers' comparative study shows, despite severe restrictions placed on social movements around the world, social protest was not stifled. Israel is certainly a case in point (Pleyers 2020).

The Balfour demonstrations were by and large a spontaneous affair. Yet the demand to oust Netanyahu was not coming only from the streets. It became evident, as the political crisis continued to escalate, that the question was *who* could remove Netanyahu and *how*, despite his still-formidable popularity. The political field began to form into a bloc of 'anti-Bibi' forces, including some of Netanyahu's sworn enemies on the Right. A 'change block' forced a deadlock: Netanyahu was no longer able to win elections decisively and form stable right-wing governments. Within less than two years, four election rounds were held (April 2019, September 2019, March 2020, March 2021). Many hawkish former IDF generals and high-ranking security services figures openly supported the demonstrations and the anti-Bibi bloc: Ehud Barak, Bogi Ye'elon, Carmi Gilon, Amir Haskal, to name a few leading figures. In the run-up to elections round # 3 in March 2020 the anti-Bibi bloc rallied behind former IDF chief Benny Gantz. In the run-up to election round #4 in March 2021, four other former military figures announced their candidacy. In round #4 Netanyahu failed yet again to form a government, and eventually the 'anti-Bibi' bloc formed the unlikely coalition of settlers' parties, Zionist left and centre parties, and the Islamic movement Raam Party led by Mansour Abbas. Many in the ranks of the Israeli global elites, particularly patriotic ex-military elites, consider Netanyahu a pariah and blame him for deteriorating Israel into a presidential-style dictatorship. Note that former top IDF officers who also have civilian careers in the homeland security and cybersecurity sector – a phenomenon known as the 'revolving door' (Hever 2008, 2019) – see Netanyahu as a patriotic nemesis because his conduct threatens the Normative basis that guarantees the social and economic power of elites in Israel.

Conclusion

Throughout this high-risk and chaotically managed crisis period, Netanyahu loyalists have only escalated their attacks on major institutions of the state: the parliament, the state attorney office, the press and the courts. As elsewhere around the world, the Covid-19 crisis has wreaked enormous social and economic havoc, but in Israel urgent social and economic issues were not addressed because of a severe political crisis and a crisis of governability. We may conclude by asking: how is this crisis of the Normative State connected to what is depicted above as a stable situation in the OPT? What would the pressures on the Normative State and continued political instability entail for the system in the OPT and the dual state as a whole? With a view 'from Palestine', it appears that the epicentre of the crisis is not the Prerogative State in the OPT, which appears extremely consistent, including the routine outbursts of violence and 'rounds of war' with Hamas in Gaza. It is, rather, the Normative State that destabilises the existing order. Under Netanyahu, to add another critical dimension to the crisis, the normalisation of the occupation has progressed to such an extent that a formal annexation of the OPT appears to be its only logical outcome. This, Netanyahu's political rivals fear, has the potential to spell the end of the Normative State.

My main contention is that the Normative State crisis is a major disruption with consequences that we cannot foresee. To recall, Israel/Palestine is a bifurcated case with a stable military dictatorship alongside a liberal order. Rather than pointing to a 'crisis of democracy', as the Balfour protest slogans go, I have tried to highlight the vested economic interests in keeping the Prerogative State 'checked' so as not to add additional pressures in an already fragile and tense situation generated by two years of a state of emergency that impacted everyone. Viewing the governability crisis in Israel through its authoritarian practices in the OPT, I also pointed at the hegemonic aspects of grass-roots mobilisations to oust Netanyahu. Democratising forces within Israeli society tend to be vested with social and economic powers. The struggle to 'save democracy' hence inevitably reaffirms a Zionist settler-colonial logic and is purposefully or inadvertently 'saving' an authoritarian status quo.

Using the Normative State and the Prerogative State as analytical tools, I have showed the delicate disequilibrium in the dual state system, and have accounted for the most serious challenge to the structure in decades. At the same time, social reality always defies our best attempts to grasp it as a structure or a totality. The dual state binary is a useful analytical tool with which to explain the current turbulence. Yet it cannot explain counter-powers, new practices of resistance and manifold unanticipated effects of state violence, for instance, a new-found unity of Palestinian struggles, new forms of repression and resistance inside 1948 borders, a re-invigoration of Jewish–Arab solidarity and a genuine common craving by ordinary people for security, stability and normalcy. The political volcano called Israel/Palestine continues to simmer, always ready to burst. Society in Israel/Palestine will inevitably have to find its own creative ways of collapsing this system of oppression, that ought to be thrown onto the trash heap of history.

Notes

1 The Peres Center Israeli Innovation Center: https://www.peres-center.org/en/the -israeli-innovation-center/explore/

2 ACRI, Physicians for Human Rights and Kav Laoved (Workers' hotline) appeal to HCJ on 3.5.2020. The IDF response (14.5.2020) reveals that the app was launched in April 2019 (before Covid-19) and that it was meant to improve the services and 'save time and bureaucracy'. The IDF emphasised that the app was for voluntary use, setting up a Gmail address for people to unsubscribe if they wish.

3 For more on illegal crossings as a continuous phenomenon, and particularly the phenomenon of 'children of the junction', see Omri Grinberg's ethnography of the crossings (Grinberg 2016).

4 Giora Eiland interview on democratTV, 21 December 2020 [in Hebrew, my notes]. See also Cronin (2021).

5 AnyVision operations in the OPT are relatively marginal as most of its sales and operations are directed at international markets. See Statt (2020).

6 Cohen (2000) notes that the Palestinians retaliate and use the platforms to express contempt, defiance, and resistance to the methods of the GSS.

7 Surveillance relation to the practice of extorting collaboration was revealed when 43 graduates of the illustrious unit 8200 of the IDF announced that they objected to 'using information to harm innocent people, to politically persecute Palestinians and to break Palestinian society through recruiting collaborators and inciting one part of society against the other'. In their letter of dissent, the graduates named the practice of extorting information from Palestinian LGBT people using 'outing' as intimidation. See Cohen (2014).

References

Abdel-Wahab, A. (2021). 'Gaza between Occupation, Division and Covid-19, Confronting Total Collapse', *Al Shabaka*, 14 January. https://al-shabaka.org/co mmentaries/gaza-between-occupation-division-and-covid-19-confronting-total -collapse/

Algazi, G. (2006). 'Offshore Zionism', *New Left Review* 40. https://newleftreview .org/issues/ii40/articles/gadi-algazi-offshore-zionism

Allegra, M., A. Handel and E. Maggor (2017). *Normalizing Occupation: The Politics of Everyday Life in the West Bank Settlements*. Bloomington: Indiana University Press.

B'tselem (2021). 'A Regime of Jewish Supremacy from the Jordan River to the Mediterranean Sea: This is Apartheid'. https://thisisapartheid.btselem.org/eng/ #1

Barnea, A. (2021). 'It Is an Extreme Step, But This Is the Way to Eradicate Crime in Arab society', *Ynet*, 19 January.

Bellin, E. (2004). 'The Robustness of Authoritarianism in the Middle East: Exceptionalism in Comparative Perspective', *Comparative Politics* 36(2): 139–57.

Ben-Natan, S. (2020). 'Citizen-Enemies, Military Courts in Israel and the Occupied Territories 1967–2000'. Unpublished dissertation. Tel Aviv: Tel Aviv University.

Ben-Natan, S. (2021). 'The Dual Penal Empire: Emergency Powers and Military Courts in Palestine/Israel and Beyond', *Punishment and Society* 23(5): 741–63. https://doi.org/10.1177/14624745211040311

Bendel, N. (2020). 'Bennett's NSO Initiative "Dangerous and Unusual" According to the Ministry of Justice', *Haaretz*, 31 March. https://www.haaretz.co.il/health /Covid-19/.premium-1.8728980 [in Hebrew].

Berda, Y. (2019). *Living Emergency: Israel's Permit Regime*. Stanford: Stanford University Press.

Bobbio, N. (1989). *Democracy and Dictatorship: The Nature and Limits of State Power*. Minneapolis: University of Minnesota Press.

Carr, D. (2020). 'Understanding the LRAD, the "Sound Cannon" Police Are Using at Protests, And How to Protect Yourself from It', *Pitchfork*, 9 June. https://pi tchfork.com/thepitch/understanding-the-lrad-the-sound-cannon-police-are-usi ng-at-protests-and-how-to-protect-yourself-from-it/

Cronin, D. (2020). 'Has Israel Weapons Industry Really Declared War on a Virus?', *Electronic Intifada*, 11 April. https://electronicintifada.net/blogs/david-cronin /has-israels-weapons-industry-really-declared-war-virus

Cohen, H. (2020). 'Give the Occupation a Like: What Can Be Learned from

GSS Operators' Facebook Pages', *Haaretz Magazine*, 29 September [in Hebrew].

Cohen, G. (2014) '43 8200 Graduates Announced That They Refuse Military Reserve Duty', *Haaretz*, 12 September [in Hebrew].

Davidson, C. M. (2022). 'The United Arab Emirates: Evolving Authoritarian Tools', in Ö. E. Topak, M. Mekouar and F. Cavatorta (eds) *New Authoritarian Practices in the Middle East and North Africa*. Edinburgh: Edinburgh University Press, pp. 320–39.

Dayan, H. (2009). 'Principles of Separation Regimes: Apartheid and Contemporary Israel/Palestine', in M. Givoni, A. Ofir and S. Hanafi (eds) *The Power of Inclusive Exclusion: The Israeli Regime in the Occupied Palestinian Territories*. New York: Zone Books, pp. 281–321.

Dayan, H. (2011). 'Israel against Democracy'. *Amsterdam Law Forum* 3(3): 89–91.

Efrat, E. (2006). *The West Bank and Gaza: A Geography of Occupation and Disengagement*. London: Routledge.

Etkes, D. and A. Has (2016). 'The Price of [Settlements] Diversity', *Theory and Criticism* 47: 261–78 [in Hebrew].

Feldman, Y. (2013). *The Lab: An Investigative Documentary on the Israeli Military Industry*. Details at: https://www.gumfilms.com/projects/lab

Fraenkel, E. (1944). *Military Occupation and the Rule of Law: Occupation Government in the Rhineland, 1918–1923*. London: Oxford University Press.

Fraenkel, E. (1941). *The Dual State*. New York: Oxford University Press.

Galili, N. (2021). 'Covid-19 Provided Israel Another Reason to Choke Gaza', *Haaretz*, 16 March. https://www.haaretz.co.il/opinions/.premium-1.9624054 [in Hebrew].

Gil, Y. (2021) 'The Shout in Balfour', *The Seventh Eye*, 17 January. https://www.the7eye.org.il/402496 [in Hebrew].

Gisha updates on Gaza permit denials (2021). https://gisha.org/publication/11683

Golkar, S (2022). 'Deep Society and New Authoritarian Social Control in Iran after the Green Movement', in Ö. E. Topak, M. Mekouar and F. Cavatorta (eds) *New Authoritarian Practices in the Middle East and North Africa*. Edinburgh: Edinburgh University Press, pp. 92–111.

Gross, A., K. Michaeli and O. Ben Naftali (2005). 'Illegal Occupation: Framing the Occupied Palestinian Territory', *Berkeley Journal of International Law* 23(3): 554–614.

Grinberg, O. (2016). 'Radical Indeterminacies, Affirmations and Subversions of the Separation Wall – The Case of the Palestinian Children of the Junction', *Journal of Borderlands Studies* 31(3): 319–37.

Gordon, N. (2008). *Israel's Occupation*. Los Angeles: University of California Press.

Hampel, Y. (2020). 'What Should You Do When You Meet a Water-Cannon Vehicle at a Demonstration', *+972 Local call*, 20 July. https://www.mekomit.co.il/ps/103578 [in Hebrew].

Has, A. (2019a). 'The Checkpoints Improved, and the Palestinians Do Not Feel They Are Led to the Milking Anymore', *Haaretz*, 24 May [in Hebrew].

Has, A. (2019b). 'Crumbs of Mercy, Why Were the Checkpoints Built This Way to Begin With?', *Haaretz*, 26 May [in Hebrew].

Has, A. (2021). 'The Occupation Statistics as an Intelligence Tip', *Haaretz*, 3 January [in Hebrew].

Hawari, J., S. Plonsky and E. Weizman (2019). 'Seeing Israel through Palestine, Knowledge Production as Anti-Colonial Practice', *Settler Colonial Studies* 9(1): 155–75.

Hever, S. (2019). 'The Nightwatchman Becomes a Mercenary', *Settler-Colonial Studies* 9(1): 78–95.

Hever, S. (2008). 'The Economy of the Occupation', The Alternative Information Center, No. 17–18.

Hever, S. (2021) 'The War that Israel Lost', *Open Democracy*, 21 May. www.opendemocracy.net/en/author/shir-hever

Human Rights Watch (2021). 'A Threshold Crossed, Israeli Authorities and the Crimes of Apartheid and Persecution'. https://www.hrw.org/report/2021/04/27/threshold-crossed/israeli-authorities-and-crimes-apartheid-and-persecution

Kabir, O. (2018). 'Edward Snowden: NSO are the Worst of the Worst', *Haaretz*, 6 November. https://www.calcalist.co.il/internet/articles/0,7340,L-3749271,00.html [in Hebrew].

Kalyvas, A. (2002), 'The Stateless Theory, Poulanzes Challenge to Postmodernism', in S. Aronowitz and P. Bratsis (eds) *Paradigm Lost, State Theory Reconsidered*. Minneapolis: University of Minnesota Press, pp. 105–43.

Kimmerling, B. (2006). *Politicide: Ariel Sharon's War against the Palestinians*. London: Verso.

Kimmerling, B. (1999). 'Religion, Nationalism and Democracy in Israel', *Constellations* 6(3): 339–50.

Kotef, H. and A. Merav (2011). 'Between Imaginary Lines: Violence and Its Justifications at the Military Checkpoints in Occupied Palestine', *Theory, Culture and Society* 28(1): 55–80.

Kubovitch, Y. (2021). 'Video Shows Strike by Israeli made Drone in Armenia during Nagorno Karabakh Fighting', *Haaretz*, 15 March [in Hebrew].

Lavie, N. and A. Jamal (2019). 'Constructing Ethno-National Differentiation on the Set of the TV Series Fauda', *Ethnicities* 19(6): 1,038–106.

Liloia, A. (2022). 'New Authoritarian Practices in Qatar: Censorship by the State and the Self', in Ö. E. Topak, M. Mekouar and F. Cavatorta (eds) *New Authoritarian Practices in the Middle East and North Africa*. Edinburgh: Edinburgh University Press, pp. 208–27.

Liss, J., I. Efrati and J. Breiner (2021). 'Ministry of Health Transferred Data of 140,000 Citizens to the GSS without their Knowledge', *Haaretz*, 15 January [in Hebrew].

Mahouzay, Y. (2016). *Between the Rule of Law and States of Emergency: The Fluid Jurisprudence of the Israeli regime*. Albany: SUNY Press.

Mazzetti, M., A.Goldman, R. Bergman and N. Perlroth (2019). 'A New Age of Warfare: How Internet Mercenaries Do Battle for Authoritarian Governments', *New York Times*, 19 March.

McMullan, T. (2019). 'Israel's Silent Cyber-power is Reshaping the Middle East', *Onezero*. https://onezero.medium.com/israels-silent-cyberpower-is-reshaping -the-middle-east-af1458d16a15

Ophir, A. and A. Azoulay (2012). *The One State Condition, Occupation and Democracy in Israel/Palestine*. Stanford: Stanford University Press.

Physicians for Human Rights (PHR) Update on Cancer Patients in the Gaza Strip during Covid Time. https://www.phr.org.il/en/cancer-patients-in-the-gaza-str ip-during-the-covid-time-update/?pr=7749

Pleyers, G. (2020). 'The Pandemic Is a Battlefield. Social Movements in the COVID-19 Lockdown', *Journal of Civil Society* 16(4): 295–312.

Rogenhofer, J.M. and A. Panievsky (2020). 'Anti-democratic Populism in Power: Comparing Erdoğan's Turkey with Modi's India and Netanyahu's Israel', *Democratization* 27(8): 1,394–412.

Segal, R. and E. Weizman (2003) *A Civilian Occupation, The Politics of Israeli Architecture*. London: Verso.

Shalhoub-Kavorkian, N. (2006). 'Counter-Spaces as Resistance in Conflict Zones: Palestinian Women Recreating a Home', *Journal of Feminist Family Therapy* 17(3–4): 109–41.

Shulman, S. (2021). 'Unit 81, the Great New Boom of Israeli IT: 100 Graduates, 50 Companies, 10 Milliard Dollars', *Calcalist Magazine*, 7 January. https:// newmedia.calcalist.co.il/magazine-07-01-21/m01.html [in Hebrew].

Statt, N. (2020). 'Microsoft to End Investment in Facial Recognition Firms after AnyVision Controversy', *The Verge*, 2 March. https://www.theverge. com/2020/3/27/21197577/microsoft-facial-recognition-investing-divest-anyvision-controversy

Tilly, C. (2007). *What Is Democracy*. Cambridge: Cambridge University Press.

Topak, Ö. E., M. Mekouar and F. Cavatorta (2022). 'Introduction', in Ö. E. Topak, M. Mekouar and F. Cavatorta (eds) *New Authoritarian Practices in the Middle East and North Africa*. Edinburgh: Edinburgh University Press, pp. 1–29.

Trochev, A. and P. H. Solomon (2018). 'Authoritarian Constitutionalism in Putin's Russia: A Pragmatic Constitutional Court in a Dual State', *Communist and Post-Communist Studies* 51(3): 201–14.

Uniacke, R. (2022). 'Digital Repression for Authoritarian Evolution in Saudi Arabia', in Ö. E. Topak, M. Mekouar and F. Cavatorta (eds) *New Authoritarian Practices in the Middle East and North Africa*. Edinburgh: Edinburgh University Press, pp. 228–51.

Weizman, E. (2017). 'The Vertical Apartheid', *Open Democracy*, 13 July. https://www.opendemocracy.net/en/north-africa-west-asia/vertical-apartheid/

Yaron, O. (2020). 'The Secret of NSO Success in Mexico: Government Corruption', *Ha'aretz*, 22 November [in Hebrew].

Yaron, O. (2020). 'The Police Directs Surfers' Traffic Through to its Secret System, Surveilling Citizens', *Haaretz*, 13 December [in Hebrew].

Yaron, O. and R. Goychman (2021). 'Cellebrite Leaves Belarus and Russia after Proof of Use of Its Product in the Nevalni Lawyer Case', *Haaretz*, 18 March.

Yesh Din (2020). 'Breaking the Silence and Physicians for Human Rights Report on Military Invasions'. https://www.yesh-din.org/en/a-life-exposed-military-invasions-of-palestinian-homes-in-the-west-bank/

Zuriek, E., D. Lyon and Y. Abu-Laban (2011). *Surveillance and Control in Israel/Palestine, Population, Territory and Power*. London: Routledge.

8

JORDAN: A PERPETUALLY LIBERALISING AUTOCRACY

Curtis R. Ryan

Introduction

Almost regardless of the topic of comparison, the Jordanian case tends to lie in the middle. On the scale of authoritarianism in the Middle East, Jordan after the 2011 'Arab Spring' was comparable neither to Egypt nor to the fragile liberal democracy of Tunisia. The Jordanian case, in fact, suggests the need to move beyond binaries: it represents neither complete authoritarian retrenchment nor genuine democratisation.

The Hashemite Kingdom of Jordan has therefore been seen as a case of 'soft' authoritarianism, or as a 'hybrid' regime (Diamond 2002; Ryan and Schwedler 2004), or as a 'liberalizing autocracy' (Brumberg 2002; Brynen 1998; Lucas 2014). I argue, however, that Jordan's hybrid system might even more accurately be regarded as a *perpetually* liberalising autocracy, in which the cycles of reform are themselves constant. In this respect, especially, Jordan can be usefully compared to Morocco, as Mekouar (2013) and Maghraoui (2022) argue. The state-controlled reform process, in short, is itself the point, not the never-achieved end goal of complete reform or liberalisation. Jordan signals constant movement and micro-levels of change, in order to essentially stay the same. There is constant movement, but not necessarily forward movement, nor necessarily meaningful change (see also, Lindsey 2020).

This chapter examines both continuities and changes in authoritarian practices in Jordan, and in resistance to those practices. Long before the Arab Spring, Jordan relied on many traditional approaches to maintaining the ruling regime: rent distribution, elite co-optation, minimal coercion and, always, a heavy reliance on international allies. But with renewed social and political mobilisation across the country during and long after the era of the Arab uprisings, Jordan has added restrictions to news media, monitored social media, and emphasised both old and new forms of 'red lines' marking the limits of acceptable political activism. This chapter examines new and old mechanisms and micro-practices of authoritarian control, reform and resistance in the Hashemite Kingdom.

Governmental Change and Reform as Autocratic Survival Strategies

The Hashemite Kingdom of Jordan is a dynastic, monarchical system, and has been since the state was created under the British Mandate and later achieved independence in 1946. The monarchical system has allowed the palace to maintain some distance between itself and the government – that is, the prime minister and cabinet ministers. Throughout its history, the monarchy has used prime ministers and their cabinets as buffers between the highest power in the state and an often-restive society. Jordanian prime ministers exist in order to be fired. In times of crisis, Jordanian kings sack the prime minister or reshuffle the cabinet. They may also dissolve parliament before the end of its term, calling for new elections. And for Jordan, new elections almost always mean new electoral laws. This too is the point. Social pressures and political opposition are effectively forced to focus on the make-up of the new government, the political tendencies of a new prime minister (for or against reform, for example), and the arcane details of the latest electoral law (Ryan 2018). Even the elections themselves can be seen as a key tool in maintaining the overall autocratic system (Lust 2006; Bustani 2016).

Even reform initiatives, including those endorsed or even promoted by Western countries or institutions, often have autocratic effects. Jordan has, for example, greatly extended its civil society over the years. But often the most influential civil society organisations are those that establish state ties, especially through sponsorships from members of the royal family. Royal NGOs and even those that are more independent are nonetheless licensed and carefully monitored, to the point that even civil society can be a tool of social control (Wiktorowicz 2000). Similarly, more recent reform efforts (also with strong international support) such as Jordan's decentralisation process (2015 and after) may be intended to deepen liberalisation and local empowerment, but in practice the Jordanian decentralisation initiative remains remarkably centralised and hence appears to be more closely linked to authoritarian upgrading than to actual liberalisation (Vollmann et al. 2020; Clark 2018).

In times of particular stress on the state from popular pressures, the Jordanian regime has tended to return not just to conventional security measures, but also to its standard arsenal of reform projects and initiatives, much like the Moroccan monarchy, as Driss Maghraoui (2022) illustrates in his chapter in this volume. In the Arab Spring period (roughly 2011 to 2013), Jordan too was affected. The kingdom never saw protests on the scale of Tahrir Square in Egypt, but Jordan is also a far smaller country. Unlike in Tunisia, Egypt, Libya and Yemen, no long-time ruler was ousted or deposed, and unlike Syria, Libya and Yemen, the country had neither a revolution nor a civil war. But this is not to say that nothing happened in Jordan during this tumultuous period in regional politics. Jordanians protested in large numbers throughout the 2011–13 period, usually in the hundreds or thousands, most calling for reform rather than revolution. Demonstrations consistently denounced corruption, called for real and lasting reform, and then differed over whether additional goals should include restoration of the social and economic safety net, or a return to political liberalisation and even democratisation. The state responded in some fairly predictable ways, sacking prime ministers and governments, reshuffling cabinets and promising a new wave of reform and change.

King Abdullah II, for example, consistently argued that the Arab Spring was an opportunity rather than a disaster, and that the wake-up call was needed to spur renewed commitment to reform. The king emphasised a new period of change in Jordan, which would include reform to the constitution, parliament, the media, and laws on parties and elections. Jordan, he argued, would represent a third way in the region between the various retrenching police states, on the one hand, and the violent implosions of the states that had descended into civil wars, on the other. Jordan would be the unique case of a powerful monarchical regime that reformed itself.[1]

Jordanians therefore prepared for another wave of slogans, marketing campaigns, and perhaps even meaningful reforms. But even by Jordanian standards, the old tactics seemed to be repeating with dizzying speed. During the first nineteen months of the regional Arab Spring, Jordan saw five prime ministers and five governments come and go. But there was, at least initially, some hope that 2011 would be as dramatic a turning point as 1989. The state did, of course, change governments repeatedly while promising new reforms and changes. But as in the earlier 1989–93 period, enthusiasm rose and eventually fell, leading to a palpable level of disappointment and disillusionment among activists, as some in the opposition tried to press the state to follow through on more than cosmetic reforms, while other parts of the opposition seemed to think that reform was as illusory in the modern era as it had been in the past.[2]

As noted above, Jordan is an autocratic state, to be sure, but it was never the full-bore police state of Ben Ali in Tunisia or al-Assad in Syria. It has been more of a hybrid regime and a perpetually liberalising autocracy. With its periodic new elections and new electoral laws, Jordan can also be seen as a kind of competitive autocracy, but only in a very limited sense. While elections, frequently revised new electoral laws and parliament all remain part of Jordanian politics, most power remains heavily concentrated within the monarchy itself. And the monarchy, in turn, initiates reforms often, but these tend to be designed to preserve, not transform, the political system. Jordanian politics remains in constant movement, just not necessarily forward movement. And as noted above: it is the movement, not the destination, that is the point. Reform programmes, new governments and cabinets, and new elections and electoral systems are all designed to buy time and to continue the process of movement without allowing for change significant enough to challenge the regime. Proponents of these measures even hope that they will not simply contain, co-opt and defuse opposition, but that they might also increase public support for the regime itself.

Jordan's version of the Arab Spring included protests that began in Dhiban and then spread across the entire country. These spawned new forms of opposition mobilisation and organisation, such as the Hirak (Yom and Khatib 2012, Yom 2014). The Hirak – a collective term referring to a set of popular protest movements – were largely youth-led and East Bank Jordanian groups that emerged in almost every city and town in the country. Most, but not all, Hirakis were East Bank Jordanian youth with tribal roots, but some of the Hirak groups also expanded to include Jordanians of varied backgrounds. Other forms of opposition emerged, not just among youth, but among influential (and politically active) older Jordanians who had spent careers working for the state, including the National Committee for Retired Servicemen (NCRS). Military veterans, in fact, acted as a kind of precursor to the Hirak, having issued manifestos making clear their discontent with the regime, even before the regional Arab Spring began (David 2010; Tell 2015).

Like the 1989 protests, the Hirak phenomenon was more disturbing to the Jordanian security elite than more traditional sources of protest in leftist, Pan-Arab or Islamist movements. But these more traditional forms of opposition also mobilised, creating at times broad opposition coalitions that spanned the usual divisions that the intelligence services had previously (and routinely) sought to exploit in order to divide the opposition. To be sure, sometimes these old divide-and-rule tactics still worked, with the General Intelligence Directorate (GID) urging some faction to abandon a planned demonstration or cut ties with a particular (often Islamist) group.

The Hashemite regime had upgraded its own security apparatus in the years before the Arab uprisings, creating a Gendarmerie force – known in Jordan as the Darak – especially for crowd control and quelling protests, in addition to the GID, the PSD (the Public Security Directorate or national police force) and, of course, the army itself. Accordingly, protesters can tell how seriously the state is concerned with their protest simply by viewing the size and scale of the security presence – not just in terms of sheer numbers, but also (potentially) in terms of their diversity – security personnel from different branches. The Darak, in fact, became almost omnipresent, especially during and after the Arab Spring era. Even Arab Spring 'reforms' seemed to reinforce the security apparatus and consolidate royal control. In 2014, the parliament passed a new counter-terrorism law that, while aimed against Jihadists, has at times been used against protesters. That is, political dissidents have sometimes found themselves charged with obscure charges of undermining the state by protesting, with cases then before the State Security Court rather than civil courts. Also in 2014, parliament gave the king full authority to appoint the main security chiefs: the heads of the General Intelligence Directorate (GID) and of the Jordanian Armed Forces. These were royal appointments in the past as well, to be sure, but now the parliament had waived its own right of consultation. Still, with some notable exceptions, the state responses to the Arab Spring-era protests were rooted in what the regime itself called 'soft security'. Many protests proceeded unhindered, while others were curbed and contained in specific geographic spaces, but unlike many other states in the region, the regime did not resort to live fire against demonstrators, and it did not employ snipers on rooftops. Yet even soft security had its limits.

There were certainly violent moments during the Jordanian Arab Spring, and these were usually connected not to official security forces of the state, but to unofficial elements that resembled the *baltajiyya* (pro-regime thugs) who had tormented protesters in other Arab states. This included a violent clash on 24 March 2011 between *baltajiyya* and unarmed, civilian protesters who had staged a peaceful sit-in near the Ministry of the Interior. The rushing and violent dispersal of this #Mar24 Movement was a turning point for many Jordanian activists, who remained understandably disillusioned thereafter with just how different or unique reform or resistance could be in Jordan (Tarawneh 2011).

International Connections and Domestic Regime Security

As a geographically small state, and one with few natural resources, no oil wealth and a generally weak economy, Jordan's domestic politics are never entirely domestic. The Hashemite kings have always relied on extensive outside support and have paid close attention to the creation and preservation of vital regional and international alliances that are designed to support Jordan, of course, but especially to ensure the survival of the Hashemite regime (Ryan 2009). From its emergence as a state, Jordan has maintained a close alliance with its former colonial power, the UK. It has also maintained an alliance with the US, from the earliest days of the Cold War to the present. This includes close bilateral ties between the two militaries as well as between the CIA and GID. The kingdom relies on financial support from the US, the UK and the EU, as well as from Japan, Canada and individual European states. It is, in fact, aid-dependent, and has no way of meeting all its annual state budgetary needs without extensive economic aid (Moore 2009). The kingdom is a de facto rentier state, with aid rather than oil providing its main budgetary resources, many of which go to support (or pay off) Jordan's vast public sector, governing bureaucracy and security services – supporting a ruling coalition that is often resistant to reform and change (Muasher 2012).

Jordan's perpetual aid dependency has also long been part of its regime survival strategy, and, as with many other states in the region, the international dimension reveals its relevance in explaining domestic politics and events, as the Introduction to this edited volume suggests (Topak et al. 2022). The Kingdom markets its own key geopolitical position and even its crises to ensure that the aid pipeline continues to support the state. Especially after its 1994 peace treaty with Israel, Jordan marketed itself as the pivotal diplomatic and communications hub in the Arab–Israeli peace process. Its large Palestinian refugee and citizen populations have also earned it external financial support, as did its Cold War stance as anti-communist bulwark in the region. Similarly, after the Cold War ended, Jordan adjusted its marketing of itself to include anti-terrorism.

Jordan developed for itself a key regional and international role as de facto forward staging and deployment area for Western powers in their declared 'Global War on Terror' and later in the bombing campaigns against ISIS or various attempts to train or supply Syrian rebel groups backed by various Western or Gulf states. When waves of Syrian refugees crossed the Jordanian border in 2011 and afterwards, Jordan gained still more financial support for its key role in aiding the global refugee crisis. This is not to say that the financial support is lucrative for the regime, or that Jordan's connections to chronic regional crises are in any way enviable, but rather that Jordan has consistently attempted to turn its many regional disadvantages into advantages and sources of outside support.

In short, the Jordanian state has always attempted to parley chronic regional crises, and its unique geopolitical position, to generate much-needed external support. And here we have a convergence not only of global and regional powers with the Hashemite regime, but also of the forms of aid itself, and indeed of Jordan's chronic fiscal crises, on the one hand, and its long pattern of securitisation and a war economy on the other. Some of Jordan's international aid is in the form of financial support, of course, but some is in the form of military aid that has strengthened the Jordanian armed forces, while also linking the army and the entire Jordanian state security apparatus into a transnational set of security relationships. The GID, for example, has extensive ties to the CIA and MI-6, and the Jordanian armed forces rely on arms, training, and exchange programmes with the US and British militaries (Kurd 2014).

The international military connection extends even to the ruling Hashemite family, as the current king, like his father before him, and like many Hashemite princes and princesses, attended the British Royal Military Academy at Sandhurst. In his influential work, Pete Moore has traced the long and complicated domestic and international history of the GID, and also noted that Jordan has in effect developed a de facto war economy that has now lasted for decades (Moore 2015, 2017, 2019). Even when Jordan itself is not at war, it remains wedged between the Israeli–Palestinian conflict to the west, the Syrian civil war to the north, and Iraq, Saudi Arabia and recurrent Gulf crises and wars to its east and south.

It would be impossible to discuss Hashemite regime survival strategies without emphasising the importance of Jordan's international allies. But while Jordan's global alliances have remained largely consistent over the decades, its regional alliances have shifted with some frequency, especially in inter-Arab relations. Within the Arab regional sphere, Jordan has increasingly relied on support from its Gulf Arab allies. This included a massive influx of cash support in 2011, when the Hashemite regime appeared especially fragile during the Arab Spring. Saudi Arabia, Kuwait, Qatar and the United Arab Emirates have provided varying levels of support over the years, but when they do, it amounts to a kind of transnational authoritarianism, as allied ruling regimes use their economic power to prop up weaker counterparts in other states – including Jordan.

The GCC states were so alarmed at the 2011 unrest in the kingdoms of Morocco and Jordan that they actually invited both states to join the Gulf Cooperation Council. While Morocco politely declined, Jordan pursued the offer, long after it seemed to vanish as matters stabilised within both of the non-Gulf Arab monarchies. But even the now-faded invitation underscores the transnational connection of these often-beleaguered monarchies, and the occasional efforts of the wealthier of these to use their petroleum wealth to assist and perhaps even save the ruling regimes of their poorer relations.

These bursts of cash have been reactive, however, with Gulf states suddenly sending large sums to prop up the Hashemite monarchy and to reduce domestic economic, social and political pressures. While Jordan has welcomed each influx of financial support, the Jordanians have also sought more consistent and less reactive forms of largesse. Yet this remains a delicate diplomatic proposition, especially since the Gulf states have their own rifts and rivalries, and hence the Hashemite monarchy tries to walk a narrow tightrope between asking for more and trying not to alienate any of its Gulf Arab allies.

While Jordan and Morocco never did end up as member states of the GCC, they did appear to engage in significant 'authoritarian learning' (Heydemann and Leenders 2011). Jordan, following the Moroccan example in 2011, therefore offered not just the usual government reshuffle and new elections, but also fairly extensive constitutional reforms (Bank and Edel 2015). Jordan's King Abdullah II in fact issued a series of 'Discussion Papers', written by the king, that were meant to prompt public discussion regarding specific aspects of reform and change. Regime opponents may not have taken these seriously, but many in the regime, and especially in the Royal

Hashemite Court, argued that this alone suggested that the Hashemite monarchy was unique among regional regimes, with no other Arab leader seeming inclined to follow this example.

After the Arab Spring: New Protests and State Responses

As early as 2013, many Jordanian government officials felt that Jordan had survived the Arab Spring, or at least its first wave, and that it had even managed to weather an enormous refugee crisis as well as intense regional security crises, wars and instability. But Jordan has seen recurring rounds of protests and slight changes in the state response to these in the years after the original Arab Spring (Moss 2014).

If regime officials were alarmed at the protests of 1989 or 2011, they were just as concerned with protests in the post-Arab Spring period. And if anything, their patience seemed to be wearing thin. In 2015, the state shifted dramatically in its stance towards its long-standing Islamist opposition. A reformist wing of the Muslim Brotherhood split from the rest of the organisation. The new Muslim Brotherhood Society formed its own exclusively national (rather than transnational) movement, cutting ties with the regional Brotherhood, and presenting itself as a loyal opposition organisation. Members of the original and larger version of the Muslim Brotherhood regarded this as a state-initiated coup to divide the Islamist opposition, and indeed many across the Jordanian opposition share that view. The two movements struggled with each other over everything from licensing to funding and office space, which may have been the exact kind of divided Islamist opposition that the state was seeking. In his recent book on the Muslim Brotherhood, Joas Wagemakers has argued that the period of confrontation and securitisation in the state's relations with the Brotherhood really began with the 1999 transition from King Hussein to King Abdullah II, with the latter seeing the challenge specifically as a security issue (Wagemakers 2020).

But in 2016 the state took a more direct role, officially recognising the newer movement as a legally licensed entity, while denying the original and larger group legal standing. Jordanian security forces moved against the older movement, closing its offices. These regime moves accelerated tensions that had only grown since at least 2010, as King Abdullah's regime attempted to crack down on the Brotherhood by dividing the Islamist opposition. Yet despite this, each version of the Brotherhood decided to eschew its frequently invoked tactic of boycotting elections, and instead both contested the 2016 elections. In 2020, they faced the same decision and again voted to compete in the parliamentary elections, despite continuing tensions with the state.

In the summer of 2018, during the holy month of Ramadan, Jordanian opposition groups called for a general strike – the first true general strike in Jordanian history – across all sectors in response to a new tax law that was part of the government's overall reform and restructuring package. But the one-day general strike was within hours beyond the hands of the original organisers as Jordanians of almost all backgrounds poured out into the streets night after night after Iftar. Again, they called for change, for eliminating new taxes on a population struggling to make ends meet, and they called for an end to corruption in public life. The protests were massive and not restricted to the capital alone. While the state maintained its general 'soft security' approach, it also deployed Darak forces in massive numbers. When the protests eventually died down, and following the ouster of the offending prime minister and his government and a royal suspension of the tax measures, the state started to draw new red lines for protests. These joined other red lines that had emerged during and after the Arab Spring.

Jordanian protesters can openly complain about and even ridicule the prime minister, the government and parliament, but calling out the monarchy – or worse, calling for the ouster of the monarchy – is a line not to cross. The first might be treated as freedom of speech and assembly, but the latter is more likely to be read as sedition. In a well-known case in 2012, for example, protesters arrested in Madaba were to be tried in civil courts, but one who burned a poster of the king was charged under Lèse-majesté laws before the State Security Court (Human Rights Watch 2012). Jordan has long maintained Lèse-majesté laws that make harming the dignity of the king a potentially treasonous offence. While the state draws the line at the monarchy, it also maintains a transnational dimension here as well. Protests and even condemnation of key allies, including even the US or the UK, may be acceptable, but insulting allies such as the Arab Gulf states is read as harming Jordan's international relations. It too counts as sedition. This can emerge in the most seemingly banal of ways.

As noted, Jordan has in the past seen cycles of openness or crackdowns regarding media via a series of laws regarding press and publications over many years. But these had usually involved print publications. In the Arab Spring era and after, the Jordanian state shifted its focus from attempting to control or contain not only physical space but virtual space as well (Schwedler

2021). As early as 2012, the state created new laws to curb online media and specifically to restrict and even close down many internet news sites. This was a sharp break in policy: before the Arab Spring, Jordan had no real restrictions regarding online content. But from 2012 onward, the state has shut down websites and monitored those that remain open. Having curbed much online media, the state then turned to social media, including legal penalties for individual posts. These measures came under the 2015 Cyber-Crimes Law, which was then revised and expanded in 2019.

Zaki Bani Irshayd, a major Islamist leader in the kingdom, was arrested in 2015 not for his efforts for the Muslim Brotherhood or even for his criticism of the state, but for posting something deemed insulting to the United Arab Emirates. More recently, in 2020, security forces detained the well-known Jordanian cartoonist Emad Hajjaj for drawing a cartoon that directly criticised the UAE normalisation deal with Israel. Hajjaj had been drawing political cartoons for years, but it was the perceived insult to a vital Gulf ally that got him in trouble with the state. Hajjaj was released after an international uproar over the case, but the point was made – again – that insulting especially Gulf allies, even in a cartoon or Facebook post, was a red line not to cross, and that the state was watching.

While Jordan cannot be regarded as a complete police or surveillance state, struggles over media and freedom of speech in print, on television and online have persisted for years. This is another theme that runs across the chapters in this volume, as the Introduction makes clear (Topak et al. 2022). Jordan has, for example, frequently changed its press and publications laws, often in an attempt to rein in criticism and dissent. In the early days of the Arab Spring, Jordan had perhaps the most open approach to the internet of any Arab country. But with new laws introduced in 2012, the state then extended its media restrictions to the internet for the first time (Tarawneh 2012). As mentioned, in 2013, Jordan closed down hundreds of websites and insisted that those that remained would have to pay significant fees to maintain their licensing status. Government officials argued that the move was needed to rein in irresponsible tabloid reporting, but reform advocates regarded this as a new red line – a virtual red line – that undercut Jordan's own carefully crafted image as open regarding the internet. Ironically, the move to ban websites came on the same day that the king issued his fourth discussion paper and announced a new pro-democracy initiative called *Dimuqrati* (7iber 2013; Ryan 2013).

Jordan's print journalists have long practised careful self-censorship when they deem it necessary. In a 2018 survey, 92 per cent of Jordanian journalists acknowledged that they practiced self-censorship (Freedom House 2019). But the new state attention to online media seemed to quickly encompass both news websites and personal (but political) posts in social media. The Jordanian state has also routinely issued 'gag orders' to the press in response to almost every crisis, large or small. The idea is purportedly to prevent widespread disinformation about sensitive topics, but the effect is more often to force Jordanians to turn to international media or simply to wild speculation on social media – the exact outcome that the state is attempting to avoid. Yet the gag orders continued, in response to countless newsworthy events, preventing Jordanian reporters from acting like actual professional journalists, and preventing the public from knowing the truth. The regime's effort to silence journalists is replicated across the region, even in countries like Morocco and Tunisia where political pluralism exists and where individual freedoms are on paper guaranteed. In their contributions to this volume both Maghraoui (2022) and Cimini (2022) provide examples of 'freedom of no speech' in both countries.

Other state moves were less in the virtual sphere and very much in the more physical sphere, and after 2011 the authorities sought to prevent any future long-term occupation of public space by protesters (Schwedler 2003, 2005, 2012, 2013). They might march and chant and demonstrate, but not turn into an 'Occupy' movement or approximate anything resembling even a fraction of Egypt's famous 2011 Tahrir protests. At times, restrictions have come even in the guise of urban beautification projects, such as the fencing in (a tall metal fence with ornate spikes) of the Fourth Circle, a key traffic interchange in Amman near the Prime Ministry. Protesters instead have tended to organise nearby in the vast parking lot of the Jordan Hospital, but not at the Prime Ministry, and not as a long-term encampment. As Schwedler notes, even getting near the Prime Ministry seems to be an increasingly difficult proposition. Similarly, protests have been blocked and contained in Amman's Abdun neighbourhood, short of their goals of getting to the US or Israeli embassies. In short, the state has steadily increased its attempts to control the geography and space available for protest both in the capital and elsewhere across the kingdom (Schwedler 2018, 2020).

To some extent after 2011, but especially after the vast 2018 Ramadan protests and demonstrations, the state has also made more of an effort to prevent what might be considered national movements. That is, state security forces have allowed protests, but not those that appear to link to other protests nationally. They seem particularly determined to prevent protest movements that might link the capital to the governorates or national movements that might cross class or ethnic lines. Activists have complained that the intelligence services seem disturbingly vigilant in preventing these national connections, detaining activists who try to work with counterparts in the governorates or even physically barring activists from one city managing to get to protests in another city. Activists in Amman, for example, complained that police blocked them from getting to Irbid to join protests there. The protesters argued that this meant that the state knew them, knew about the protest, and knew how and when they were trying to get there.[3] These newer red lines amount to a set of geographic and political restrictions attempting to thwart truly national movements of almost any type from organising or staging protest events on a national scale (Ryan 2019).

For all these efforts, waves of protest continue. In 2019, the Jordanian teachers syndicate, the largest union in the country and an organisation that emerged as a key Arab Spring reform, went on a nationwide strike. Countless Jordanian families have a member who is a teacher, but countless more have children who are students in the public education system; so almost all Jordanians were impacted by the strike in one or more ways. The teachers insisted on pay raises that had been promised at the time of the 2018 Ramadan protests, and maintained their strike for an entire month. Given the amount of time, one might have expected the public to turn against the teachers, but many and perhaps most Jordanians seemed to support the teachers throughout the lengthy strike. The state eventually acceded to most of the teachers' demands, but also seemed determined to prevent any similar event thereafter.

Yet by 2020, the state had already returned to a more aggressive stance towards the teachers, arresting the leadership of the syndicate and suspending the union entirely – in effect snuffing out one of the few concrete successes of the Arab Spring era: the creation of an independent teachers' union. But the union in many ways embodied what state security officials seemed most to fear: an organisation that truly represented citizens from every corner of the country. Just as important, it seems likely that the regime's heightened security responses to protest, activism and dissent may have been influenced by two jolts within a year of each other: one from within Jordan, one from

without: specifically, the 2018 Ramadan protests and the region-wide uprisings in 2019 in Algeria, Iraq, Lebanon and Sudan that some saw as an Arab
Spring 2.0. For Jordanian state security officials, it seems likely that all this
domestic and regional unrest – even before the Covid-19 global pandemic
– may have led to heightened securitisation across the board and a lower
tolerance for public mobilisation and dissent.

Autocracy and Dissent amid a Global Pandemic

For Jordan, and indeed for every country in the world, 2020 marked the year
of the worst global pandemic in more than a hundred years. Quarantines and
lockdowns over Covid-19 made good sense for science and public health,
but some activists worried that they might also serve as cover for retrenching
authoritarianism not only in Jordan, but also in the other autocracies of the
world. In the very early days of the global outbreak, Jordan instituted one
of the most hard-core lockdowns of any country in the Middle East, and it
seemed to work. Jordan had fewer cases than almost any other country in the
region, but like many other countries it fell victim to a second wave in the
fall of 2020. The government had called in the military to police the earlier
lockdown, but in the months afterward Jordan faced many of the problems
that other countries faced: public fatigue with quarantine, public suspicion
regarding government pronouncements and severe economic hardship. But
Jordan's economy was already in crisis even before Covid. It was, in fact, in
crisis long before the 2011 uprisings. The Covid effect, then, was to make all
these matters worse: the economic situation, social tension, the increasing
social disillusionment with the state, and the tendency of the state to rely on
securitisation as its go-to strategy regarding crises.

It was in this context that Jordan began to move to prevent further
large-scale protests, including by suspending the teacher's union for at least
a year and arresting its entire leadership. Throughout the pandemic period,
the Jordanian government had used a series of defence laws to rule effectively
via decree. At times, controversy emerged simply over state attempts to keep
people off the streets and minimise public gatherings. Health officials saw
these measures as practical and necessary to contain the pandemic, but some
Jordanians, especially on social media, questioned the motives behind public
restrictions. While some saw these as necessary in order to responsibly address
the worst health crisis the country had ever faced, many other Jordanians
worried that the defence laws, and even new Covid restrictions, were really

aimed at the opposition and at dissent, rather than for the public good. The controversy itself seemed to underscore the profound lack of faith many Jordanians have in the state and in the future of the country. Even responsible public health moves, in other words, may often read as thinly veiled authoritarianism, especially if public trust is already low.

Jordan's kings, and the Hashemite state that supports them, have always seen themselves as survivors against great odds, both domestic and regional. Jordan, they say, has survived internal and external wars, waves of refugees, international terrorism and chronic fiscal crises, and yet it remains here to tell the tale. Regime supporters therefore compare the state to its even more autocratic counterparts across the Middle East, stressing that Jordan, in this and almost all comparisons, then appears moderate and as a kind of middle case. Opponents, dissidents and reform advocates, as this chapter has made clear, see these as annoyingly repetitive and tedious arguments. Jordan, they say, should not compare itself to ruthless police states in order to look good, but should be compared to the world's major democracies, in which case it will appear autocratic and regressive.

These polarised views re-emerge in the context of every crisis, including long before and long after the Arab Spring. But recurrent waves of protests suggest that public disaffection remains high, even as reform has tended to take a back seat to securitisation efforts (al-Sharif 2013, 2014; Ryan 2015). In the post-2011 period, these included concerns with Jihadist terrorism across Jordan's borders with Syria and Iraq, but also increasingly home-grown threats from ISIS and al-Qa'ida militants even within Jordan itself. Terrorist attacks in Kerak and Irbid in 2016 underscored the state focus on security from terrorism as the pre-eminent concern.

While Jordan's domestic and border security concerns tend to be very real, and hence not just hypothetical justifications for backsliding in reform or liberalisation, reform advocates fear that securitisation of the state and of the regime will always trump efforts for more meaningful change. The state has made clear its own red lines, and it has, if anything, become more autocratic in recent years, in large part in response to these myriad challenges – from ISIS to Covid. But citizens have red lines too. And many activists argue that the state has crossed its own lines in cracking down too hard, in monitoring social media, muzzling the press, putting off or neutralising reform, and in generally securitising almost every aspect of Jordanian life.

Notes

1 Author interviews with King Abdullah II, Amman, Jordan, 21 May and 18 December 2012.
2 Author interviews with Jordanian activists, Amman, Jordan, December 2012, June 2013 and June 2014.
3 Author interviews with Jordanian activists. Amman, Jordan, June 2019 and August 2019.

References

7iber (2013). 'Internet Blocking Begins in Jordan', 2 June. http://www.7iber.com /2013/06/internet-blocking-begins-in-jordan/

Bank, A. and M. Edel (2015). 'Authoritarian Learning: Comparative Insights from the Arab Uprisings', GIGA Working Papers 274. Hamburg: German Institute for Global and Area Studies (GIGA).

Brumberg, D. (2002). 'The Trap of Liberalized Autocracy', *Journal of Democracy* 13(4): 56–68.

Brynen, R. (1998). 'The Politics of Monarchical Liberalism: Jordan', in R. Brynen, B. Korany and P. L. Noble (eds) *Political Liberalization & Democratization in the Arab World, Vol. 2: Comparative Experiences.* Boulder, CO: Lynne Rienner.

Bustani, H (2016). *Himna Mustadamna. al-Intakhabat kaada li ta'ziz ihtikar al-Sulta* ('Sustainable dominance: the elections as a tool to strengthen the monopoly of power'). *7iber*, 28 August. http://7iber.com/politics-economics/monopolizing -power-through-elections/#.V9hx8_orKhc

Cimini, G. (2022). 'Authoritarian Nostalgia and Practices in Newly Democratising Contexts: The Localised Example of Tunisia', in Ö. E. Topak, M. Mekouar and F. Cavatorta (eds) *New Authoritarian Practices in the Middle East and North Africa.* Edinburgh: Edinburgh University Press, pp. 276–95.

Clark, J.A. (2018). *Local Politics in Jordan and Morocco: Strategies of Centralization and Decentralization.* New York: Columbia University Press.

David, A. (2010). 'The Revolt of Jordan's Military Veterans', *Foreign Policy*, 16 June. https://foreignpolicy.com/2010/06/16/the-revolt-of-jordans-military-veterans/

Diamond, L. (2002). 'Hybrid Regimes', *Journal of Democracy* 13(2): 21–35.

Freedom House (2019). 'Freedom on the Net 2019: Jordan'. https://freedomhouse .org/country/jordan/freedom-net/2019

Heydemann, S. (2007). 'Upgrading Authoritarianism in the Arab World', Brookings Institution, Saban Center Analysis Paper No. 13.

Heydemann, S. and R. Leenders (2011). 'Authoritarian Learning and Authoritarian

Resilience: Regime Responses to the Arab Awakening', *Globalizations* 8(5): 647–53.

Human Rights Watch (2019). 'Jordan: Crackdown on Activists'. https://www.hrw .org/news/2019/06/04/jordan-crackdown-political-activists

Human Rights Watch (2012). 'Jordan: Drop Charges for "Undermining Royal Dignity"'. Available atr: https://www.hrw.org/news/2012/01/19/jordan-drop-charges-undermining-royal-dignity

El-Kurd, D. (2014). 'The Jordanian Military: A Key Regional Ally', *Parameters* 44: 47–55.

Lindsey, U. (2020). 'Jordan's Endless Transition', *The New York Review of Books*, 22 October. https://www.nybooks.com/articles/2020/10/22/jordans-endless-transition/

Lucas, R. E. (2004). 'Monarchical Authoritarianism: Survival and Political Liberalization in a Middle Eastern Regime Type', *International Journal of Middle East Studies* 36(1): 103–19.

Lust, E. (2006). 'Elections under Authoritarianism: Preliminary Lessons from Jordan', *Democratization* 13(3): 456–71.

Maghraoui, D. (2022). '"The Freedom of No Speech": Journalists and the Multiple Layers of Authoritarian Practices in Morocco', in Ö. E. Topak, M. Mekouar and F. Cavatorta (eds) *New Authoritarian Practices in the Middle East and North Africa*. Edinburgh: Edinburgh University Press, pp. 189–207.

Mekouar, M. (2013). 'Morocco', in P. Amar and V. Prashad (eds) *Dispatches from the Arab World*. Minneapolis: University of Minnesota Press, 135–56.

Moore, P. (2019). 'A Political-Economic History of Jordan's General Intelligence Directorate: Authoritarian State-Building and Fiscal Crisis', *Middle East Journal* 73(2): 242–62.

Moore. P. (2017). 'Jordan's Long War Economy', *The Political Economy Project*, 1 September. http://www.politicaleconomyproject.org/pepblog/jordans-long-war-economy-pete-moore

Moore, P. (2015). 'Jordan's Longest War', *Middle East Report Online*, 26 May. https://merip.org/2015/05/jordans-longest-war/

Moss, D. (2014). 'Repression, Response, and Contained Escalation under "Liberalized" Authoritarianism in Jordan', *Mobilization* 19(3): 261–86.

Muasher, M. (2011). *A Decade of Struggling Reform Efforts in Jordan: The Resilience of the Rentier System*. Washington, DC: Carnegie Endowment for International Peace.

Peters, A. M. and P. Moore (2009). 'Beyond Boom and Bust: External Rents, Durable Authoritarianism, and Institutional Adaptation in the Hashemite Kingdom of Jordan', *Studies in Comparative International Development* 44(3): 256–85.

Ryan, C. R. (2019). 'Resurgent Protests Confront New and Old Red Lines in Jordan'. *Middle East Report* 292/293: 30–4.

Ryan, C. R. (2018). *Jordan and the Arab Uprisings: Regime Survival and Politics beyond the State*. New York: Columbia University Press.

Ryan, C. R. (2015). 'Security Dilemmas and the Security State Question in Jordan', in *POMEPS Studies 11: The Arab Thermidor: The Resurgence of the Security State*, 27 February: 52–5.

Ryan, Curtis R. (2013). 'Jordan's Web Blocking Controversy', *Foreign Policy, Middle East Channel*, 20 June. http://foreignpolicy.com/2013/06/20/jordans-website-blocking-controversy/

Ryan, C. R. (2009) *Inter-Arab Alliances: Regime Security and Jordanian Foreign Policy*. Gainesville: University Press of Florida.

Ryan, C. R. (2002). *Jordan in Transition: From Hussein to Abdullah*. Boulder, CO: Lynne Rienner.

Ryan, C. R. and J. Schwedler (2004). 'Return to Democratization or New Hybrid Regime? The 2003 Elections in Jordan', *Middle East Policy* 11(2): 138–51.

Schwedler, J. (2020). 'Material Obstacles to Protest in the Urban Built Environment: Insights from Jordan', *Contention* 8(1): 70–92.

Schwedler, J. (2018). 'Political Dissent in Amman, Jordan: Neoliberal Geographies of Protest and Policing', in S. Schram and M. Pavlovskaya (eds) *Rethinking Neoliberalism: Resisting the Disciplinary Regime*. London: Routledge.

Schwedler, J. (2013). 'Spatial Dynamics of the Arab Uprisings', *PS: Political Science & Politics* 46(2): 230–4.

Schwedler, J. (2012). 'The Political Geography of Protest in Neoliberal Jordan', *Middle East Critique* 21(3): 259–70.

Schwedler, J. (2005). 'Cop Rock: Protest, Identity, and Dancing Riot Police in Jordan', *Social Movement Studies* 4(2): 155–75.

Schwedler, J. (2003). 'More than a Mob: The Dynamics of Political Demonstrations in Jordan', *Middle East Report* 226: 18–23.

al-Sharif, O. (2013). 'Jordan's Reform Agenda on Hold', *al-Monitor*. 28 October. http://www.al-monitor.com/pulse/originals/2013/10/jordan-focus-economic-security-reform-syrian-crisis.html

al-Sharif, O. (2104). 'Jordan's King Pushes to Expand Military, Intelligence Authority', *al-Monitor*. 25 August. http://www.al-monitor.com/pulse/originals/2014/08/jordan-king-constitution-amendments.html

Tarawnah, N. (2011). 'The Quick Death of Shabab March 24 and What It Means for Jordan'. *The Black Iris* (blog), 26 March. http://www.black-iris.com/2011/03/26/the-quick-death-of-shabab-march-24-and-what-it-means-for-jordan/

Tarawneh, N. (2012). 'Jordan's Internet Goes Dark', *Foreign Policy, Middle East*

Channel, 31 August. http://foreignpolicy.com/2012/08/31/jordans-internet-go
es-dark/

Tell, T. (2015). 'Early Spring in Jordan: The Revolt of the Military Veterans',
Carnegie Middle East Center, 4 November.

Topak, Ö. E., M. Mekouar and F. Cavatorta (2022). 'Introduction', in Ö. E. Topak,
M. Mekouar and F. Cavatorta (eds) *New Authoritarian Practices in the Middle
East and North Africa*. Edinburgh: Edinburgh University Press, pp. 1–29.

Vollmann, E., M. Bohn, R. Sturm and T. Demmelhuber (2020). 'Decentralisation
as Authoritarian Upgrading? Evidence from Jordan and Morocco', *Journal of
North African Studies*. https://doi.org/10.1080/13629387.2020.1787837

Wagemakers, J. (2020). *The Muslim Brotherhood in Jordan*. Cambdrige: Cambridge
University Press.

Wiktorowicz, Q. (2000). 'Civil Society as Social Control', *Comparative Politics*
33(1): 43–61.

Yom, S. L. and W. al-Khatib (2012). 'Jordan's New Politics of Tribal Dissent',
Foreign Policy, Middle East Channel. 7 August. http://foreignpolicy.com/2012
/08/07/jordans-new-politics-of-tribal-dissent/

Yom, S. L. (2013). 'Jordan: The Ruse of Reform', *Journal of Democracy* 24(3):
127–39.

Yom, S. L. (2014). 'Tribal Politics in Contemporary Jordan: The Case of the Hirak
Movement', *The Middle East Journal* 68(2): 229–47.

9

LIBYA: AUTHORITARIANISM IN A FRACTURED STATE

Ronald Bruce St John

Introduction

Over the centuries, Berbers, Vandals, Phoenicians, Greeks, Romans, Arabs, Ottomans and Italians occupied Libya in a long history of authoritarian rule. Following independence in 1951, the monarchy (1951–69) and the Qaddafi regime (1969–2011) continued this tradition of authoritarianism. After the February 17 Revolution ousted the Qaddafi regime, most of the newly created political bodies exhibited authoritarian tendencies; however, none of them established legitimacy or a national presence in a fractured state. Instead, overlapping circles of local and regional power and influence, including local councils, ethnic groups, militias, tribes and a potpourri of religious movements, flourished, using traditional and non-traditional authoritarian measures to maintain control in their spheres of influence. This chapter focuses on these circles of influence, together with the ways in which they go about exerting authoritarian control. In so doing, it highlights new political, technological, military and policing means of repression where found, including the extent to which outside powers have imported both the latest military tactics and equipment and the latest forms of social media surveillance.

The February 17 Revolution

On 17 February 2011, a heavy-handed government response to peaceful demonstrations in Benghazi led to calls throughout the country for regime change. Five weeks later, Mustafa Muhammad Abd al-Jalil, a former minister of justice under Qaddafi, announced the formation of the National Transitional Council (NTC). The NTC billed itself as the acting government of Libya; however, this was something of an illusion. During the civil war, real power rested with the local councils and militias formed to oust the Qaddafi regime (Wehrey 2018: 59–60, 174–5).

The end of the Qaddafi regime was followed by nationwide polls in July 2012 to elect a 200-member General National Congress (GNC). The Justice and Construction Party (JCP), the political arm of the Muslim Brotherhood, and the National Forces Alliance (NFA), described in the Western media as a 'liberal' political party, were the major political movements contesting the elections. The polls were doubly remarkable in that they took place only nine months after the overthrow of the Qaddafi regime, and the electorate strongly supported moderate parties, reversing a regional trend in support of Islamist groups. Of the eighty seats allocated to political parties, the NFA won thirty-nine and the JCP only seventeen (St John 2017: 303–4).

In May 2013, the GNC, besieged by Islamist militias and powerful armed groups from Misrata, passed the Political Isolation Law. It barred broad categories of officials who had served in the Qaddafi regime, estimated to number 500,000 people, from state jobs and public life for ten years. The Political Isolation Law both effectively ended the NFA as a political force and confirmed the strength of the JCP and its allies in the GNC (Pargeter 2016: 164–70, 179). With the demise of the NFA, the JCP and its Islamist allies took advantage of the absence of a more secular alternative to consolidate their grip on power (Trauthig 2019: 5–11).

In early 2014, General (later Field Marshal) Khalifa Haftar launched Operation Dignity, a military offensive targeting Islamist elements in eastern Libya. In June 2014, Libyans went to the polls to elect a 200-member House of Representatives to replace the GNC. Due to political uncertainty in Tripoli, the newly elected legislature was inaugurated in Tobruk in early August 2014. One month later, the House of Representatives confirmed a new government operating out of al-Bayda and headed by Abdallah al-Thani, a former defence minister. In the interim, the Muslim Brotherhood and affiliated Islamist elements in Tripoli united with tribal and regional interests to form Libya Dawn, a competitor to Operation Dignity. By August 2014, Libya Dawn had seized control of most of Tripoli (St John 2015: 93–8).

Government of National Accord

In December 2015, UN efforts to broker a power-sharing agreement led to the Libyan Political Agreement (LPA) (Lacher 2020: 46–9). Under its terms, the House of Representatives was designated the sole legislative authority in Libya, and the remaining members of the GNC became a consultative body, the High Council of State. A Presidency Council consisting of nine people representing various political factions exercised the functions of head of state (UNSMIL 2015). Fayez al-Sarraj, chairman of the Presidency Council and prime minister in the newly formed Government of National Accord (GNA), arrived in Tripoli in late March 2016.

Described as a peace accord, the top-down power-sharing agreement brokered by the UN was largely based on the groups, factions and individuals that Libyans held responsible for mis-managing the country after 2011 (St John 2017: 314–19, 336). A poll released in November 2013 found Libyans increasingly dissatisfied with the performance of the GNC, with the number of respondents rating its performance as poor or very poor increasing from 37 per cent in May to 60 per cent in September (NDI and JMW 2013: 12–15). Another poll released in March 2014 found that the favourability rating of all political parties and politicians had declined, continuing a trend observed in earlier surveys (NDI and JMW 2014: 21–3). With the UN-brokered GNA largely made up of institutions, political movements and individuals enjoying little respect or support from the Libyan people, it was no surprise that the GNA found it impossible to establish stability and assert legitimacy throughout the country. A similar scenario developed in Yemen, as Durac (2022) illustrates in his chapter in this volume. In Yemen too, the fragmentation of state sovereignty has led multiple actors to provide 'security' without legitimacy.

Throughout much of 2016, some militias in the west supported al-Serraj's GNA while others supported a rump National Salvation Government under Omar al-Hassi that was formed by remnants of the GNC. In the east, the al-Thani government, the House of Representatives and Field Marshal Haftar and his Libyan National Army (LNA) shared power in an uneasy, often unclear, manner. Foreign alliances further complicated the situation. Egypt, Russia, Saudi Arabia and the UAE supported Operation Dignity, and Qatar, Sudan and Turkey supported Libya Dawn. In early 2019, Haftar and his army moved south and then west, threatening to occupy Tripoli. After a prolonged siege, GNA forces in mid-2020 pushed the LNA back from Tripoli and other strategic bases in western Libya. The external dimension of the Libyan civil war is an important aspect of its development, and it also speaks to the way in which international connections, as the Introduction in this volume makes clear (Topak et al. 2022), are crucial in supporting, diversifying and permitting the deployment of authoritarian practices.

Militias

The fragmented, decentralised nature of the February 17 Revolution defined the post-revolution security environment. The NTC failed to establish authority over liberated areas, which became the domain of local power brokers. Estimates of the number of armed men who fought against Qaddafi in 2011 range from 30,000 to 100,000. Whatever the correct total, the number of active militiamen mushroomed to more than 250,000 one year later. This increase was due mostly to rent distribution in the form of payments promised by the NTC to those who could claim the status of *thuwar* (revolutionary fighters). 'As the payments grew and the militias used force to intervene in government decision-making, a sense of entitlement to benefits and a privileged political voice enshrined itself in militia discourse' (Pack, Mezran and Eljarh 2014: 1–3, 11–16, quote 3).

According to a March 2014 poll, Libyans viewed militias formed during the revolution more favourably than those formed after the revolution, but a majority had an unfavourable opinion of any armed group that did not abide by government authority. Approximately one-third of Libyans felt unsafe when travelling to daily locations, like the market, school or work, and 94 per cent supported efforts to limit the spread of firearms. Libyans felt most safe at home or in their neighbourhoods, and especially unsafe when travelling by bus or taxi. They also made a clear distinction between passing through checkpoints manned by government security forces, where 80 per cent felt safe, and those manned by *thuwar* or other militia members, where only 44 per cent felt safe (NDI and JMW 2014: 32–5).

The schism of state institutions after 2014 (Operation Dignity vs Libya Dawn) disrupted the state funding of militias; however, a UN Experts Report in June 2017 noted that other sources of income remained, including fuel smuggling, people trafficking, interference with government institutions and the local arms trade (UN Security Council 2017). Another report highlighted direct payments, letter of credit fraud and the smuggling of subsidised goods as other sources of militia income, concluding that 'it is not much of an oversimplification to state that the Libyan militias themselves are fighting primarily over money' (Pack 2019: 1).

By 2018, the numerous militias in Tripoli had coalesced into four so-called 'super militias'. In addition to providing security for the capital, these organisations used a combination of rent distribution, elite co-optation and brute coercion to dominate the government, seizing control of important ministries and central elements of the financial system (Lacher and al-Idrissi 2018: 16). As competition between the forces of Operation Dignity and Libya Dawn intensified, both sides also turned to regional and international backers, Egypt, Russia and the UAE in the case of Operation Dignity and Turkey and Qatar in the case of Libya Dawn, for up-to-date tactical training and modern weapons, including armoured vehicles, drones and high-performance aircraft, much of which had been battle tested in Syria.

Local Municipal Councils

As the NTC struggled to provide leadership to the revolution, liberated towns and cities formed local councils to collect weapons, control traffic and supply electricity and water. The structure and operation of these councils resembled the congresses and committees formed earlier by the Qaddafi regime. Most Libyans were reluctant participants in the tightly organised and strictly controlled bodies formed by Qaddafi, but they gained experience in managing local affairs which they later put to good use in rebel-controlled areas (St John 2017: 289, 291).

Faced with a series of weak central governments in 2011–15 and the ineptitude of the GNA after 2015, local councils continued to play a central role in providing local services (Lacher 2015). A nationwide poll in 2016 found that local councils provided a variety of services, including education, health, housing, infrastructure, sanitation and security services. Moreover, in part due to their status as elected bodies, local councils were the most legitimate authorities in the country (IRI/USAID 2016: 15). In contrast, a poll of five western towns conducted in 2017 found 91 per cent of those questioned felt all national governments after 2011 had failed to deliver on the aims and goals of the revolution (*Libya Herald* 18.10.2017).

A poll of fifteen municipalities released in May 2019 confirmed the results of earlier surveys. Libyans responded that local councils were well-regarded in comparison to national institutions, which were viewed negatively across the board. A majority of Libyans viewed local councils as legitimate, doing a good job, and best positioned to address local concerns, given weak central government institutions and continued conflict (IRI/USAID 2019: 26–35, 40–1, 51). After the formation of the GNA, some municipalities in the south and west continued to hold elections to select local councils. In eastern Libya, Field Marshal Haftar moved to replace elected officials with military officers loyal to him, employing a combination of rent distribution, elite co-optation and brute coercion to ensure local co-operation and compliance (Reuters 27.04.2020).

The Qaddafi regime feared civil organisations would become centres of political opposition; therefore, it systematically attacked civil society. There were no political parties, civic clubs or parent–teacher organisations in Qaddafi's Libya, and gatherings of more than three people were prohibited. One of the first responses to the February 17 Revolution was the formation by Libyans of the civil organisations long denied them. A survey of 1,022 civil society organisations in six major cities suggested there were roughly 2,000 such organisations in operation as of early 2014 (Romanet Perroux 2015: 4–5). Understandably, civil movements focused initially on democratic transition; however, they adapted quickly to the growing humanitarian crisis that followed the outbreak of violence in 2014. In so doing, civil society organisations often worked with local councils to address the growing needs of urban areas. When the pandemic surfaced, civil society organisations were well-placed to assist local councils in raising awareness and co-ordinating a humanitarian response (Elfeituri 2020: 4–5).

Religious Movements

Libya is a homogeneous Muslim society, with more than 90 per cent of the population Sunni Muslim. The Libyan people are conservative in outlook and religious in nature; however, they have never displayed any widespread appetite for radical Islam. When internal opposition from Islamist fundamentalist groups surfaced in the mid-1990s, the Qaddafi regime successfully contained it with a three-part strategy that undermined the religious authority of the *ulema* (Islamic scholars), refuted Islamist concepts and harshly treated Islamist groups (St John 2017: 254, 280).

Three days after Qaddafi was killed, NTC chairman al-Jalil initiated a roll-back of select Qaddafi-era Islamic reforms in what proved to be the outset of an assault on religious freedom and practice in Libya. In a speech in

Tripoli, he emphasised that Libya was an 'Islamic country', the Islamic religion would be the 'core of the new government', and the constitution would be 'based on the Islamic religion' (*New York Times* 24.10.2011). Less than a week later, al-Jalil stated that a Qaddafi-era law restricting polygamy was contrary to *shari'a* (Islamic canonical law) and should be abolished. His remarks appeared to condone unrestricted polygamy in a Muslim country where it had been limited and rare for decades. In February 2012, a proposed 10 per cent quota for women in the GNC was dropped to placate Islamist concerns, and in May 2012 the NTC lifted a ban on ethnic, religious and tribal parties participating in the GNC elections, again to appease Islamist interests (Pack, Mezran and Eljarh 2014: 17–24). New or revised rules, regulations and laws supporting a more authoritarian society remained a prominent feature of the revolution in the coming years.

With the end of the February 17 Revolution, authoritarian state structures and non-state religious movements repeatedly challenged the country's commitment to democracy, human rights, and civil, political and religious liberties. Using the period immediately after the GNC elections as an example, Salafists in August 2012 razed a Sufi mosque in Tripoli. In September, an attack on the US consulate in Benghazi, believed to be instigated by Ansar al-Shari'a, left the US ambassador and four other Americans dead. In December, a Coptic Christian facility in Dafiniya was attacked and two Egyptian citizens murdered. In March 2013, a Catholic priest was shot outside a Tripoli church and a major Sufi shrine was destroyed. In April 2013, Islamists attacked the French embassy in Tripoli in apparent retaliation for the French military mission against jihadists in Mali (St John 2017: 305). In the face of mounting violence, insecurity and discrimination, a Libyan analyst later characterised the overall situation as the 'tyranny of the minority' in that a minority of radicalised Libyans used harassment, intimidation and assassination to impose their will on the majority (*Libya Herald* 11.03.2015). No one was prosecuted in Libya for these and similar acts of violence, which have continued to the present day. In a recent example, Hanan al-Barassi, a prominent female dissident and outspoken critic of abuses in areas controlled by Haftar's LNA, was shot dead on a busy Benghazi street in November 2020 (*Guardian* 10.11.2020).

In February 2012, Sheikh Sadiq al-Ghariani, a Tripoli-based Islamic scholar, was appointed Grand Mufti or top religious authority in Libya. Expected to focus on religious issues and the welfare of all Libyans, al-Ghariani instead immediately involved himself in controversial social and political issues. In October 2012, he asked the minister of education to remove passages related to freedom and democracy from school textbooks. In February 2013, he issued a *fatwa* (religious edict) against a UN report opposed to violence against girls and women, stating it countered Islamic law. In May 2013, he called for an end to mixed-gender education and employment on the grounds that the mixing of sexes was immoral. In October 2013, he issued another *fatwa* directing women to wear headscarves when instructing males who had reached the age of puberty. Al-Ghariani's edicts were not followed to the letter, especially in the larger cities, but his pronouncements supported the efforts of a conservative minority to impose their definition of Islam on the majority of people in Libya, creating a milieu in which gender equality had little or no priority (St John 2017: 305–6).

While the JCP did not fare well in the July 2012 GNC elections, the Muslim Brotherhood proved adept at creating strategic alliances in the legislature, becoming the strongest voting bloc in the GNC. In the process, Libyans increasingly blamed Islamists in general and the Muslim Brotherhood in particular for the partisan bickering that fomented insecurity and blocked reconstruction (Pargeter 2016: 174–5). Secular politicians accused the Brotherhood and its affiliates of ties to extremist groups, and Salafists claimed the Brotherhood compromised Islamist principles. The civil war that followed the June 2014 elections cannot be blamed on the Muslim Brotherhood; however, causes for the post-electoral violence can be 'linked to uncompromising political stances and exclusionary politics, including the Political Isolation Law' promoted by the Brotherhood (Trauthig 2019: 3–10, quote 10).

Like many things in Libya, the Jihadist field was highly fragmented and mostly localised. The growth of Islamic State (Daesh, ISIL, ISIS), which challenged supporters of al-Qaeda and in particular the faction known as Ansar al-Shari'a, greatly concerned the Western powers. In the latter half of 2015, Operation Dignity forced Islamist militias out of Benghazi, and a militia offensive supported by American airstrikes pushed Islamic State from Sabratha. In December 2016, a coalition of militias allied with the GNA and supported by American and British special forces liberated Sirte and nearby towns. Forced out of Sirte, some Islamic State forces escaped by sea while others fled to central and southern Libya where they were unable to establish a proper base, let alone govern. Regrouped in small cells, Islamic State continued to launch attacks against the state, ranging from suicide bombings to small-scale armed attacks to kidnappings (Trauthig 2020). United States Africa Command (AFRICOM) was the most active force opposing Islamic State in the region, employing brute coercion in the form of drones and fixed-wing aircraft in intelligence gathering and strike modes.

In the post-Qaddafi era, so-called 'quietist' Salafists, followers of the Saudi cleric Rabia bin Hadi al-Madkhali, were active against Islamic State and other Islamist factions. After the fall of Qaddafi, Libyan followers of Madkhali attacked a wide range of targets, including secularists, the Muslim Brotherhood, Ibadis, Sufis and women. They also waged war on the Grand Mufti, whose teachings they considered apostate. Salafis formed anti-vice patrols to combat activities they considered un-Islamic, leading in parts of the country to a 'Salafisation' of the security sector. The predominance of Salafist norms-based policing in some areas relied on a combination of elite co-optation and brute coercion to achieve local acceptance and compliance (*New York Times* 20.02.2020). The considerable military clout of the Salafis also translated into substantial political leverage over post-2014 governments, adding another layer to an already multi-dimensional conflict (Wehrey and Boukhars 2019: 123–5, 130–2).

Tribes

Recognising the power of traditional tribal leaders and fearful they would oppose his radical reforms, Qaddafi tried to eliminate their role and influence. When those efforts failed, he reversed course and turned to them for political support, appointing members of influential tribes to powerful political, military and security posts. Later, Qaddafi created the People's Social Leadership Committee system, the first time in history the 130 tribes of Libya were organised into a quasi-national structure (St John 2017: 280–1).

After 2011, the tribes and ethnic groups of Libya mostly focused on rent distribution in the form of control of the nation's resources. With the Libyan economy totally dependent on petroleum revenues, the oil and gas deposits located in eastern Libya were the biggest prize. Tribes and other groups sought to control energy assets with a view to securing revenue and increasing political clout. In southern Libya, the struggle for assets centred on control of cities, smuggling routes, oilfields and borders. Tribal and ethnic communities in the south were heavily militarised, and their militias aggressively competed to control illicit economic activities (Lacher 2014). In the north-east, the

Awlad 'Ali Bedouin transnational confederation dominated the borderland of Egypt and Libya. In this area, the smuggling of consumer products was seen 'as a transgressive economic practice' regulated by kinship associations and 'embedded in the wider social, political and cultural connectivity of the borderland' (Hüsken 2019: 31–241, quote 9).

The February 17 Revolution damaged or destroyed state institutions, resulting in a vacuum of central government authority, legitimacy and security. In response, the tribes joined other groups in stepping in to fill the vacuum. By the end of the decade, local governance in most areas comprised a blend of local, tribal, military, social and religious councils (IRI/USAID 2019: 26). Tribal involvement in local governance accelerated after 2014 with the polarisation of central state security and increased again after 2016 when the GNA failed to establish authority and legitimacy. In the process, tribal notables, where they were able to gain control of the basic elements of security provision, such as the use of force and access to prisons, increased their participation in the security sector. 'Much anecdotal evidence suggests that tribes have reemerged and reinvented their role in the public space since the revolution, including in the domains of justice and security provision, conflict management and conflict resolution' (Cole and Mangan 2016: 5–36, quote 6). In a survey of eight municipalities conducted in 2018, Libyans identified tribes as 'important and legitimate protectors and security providers' (Al-Shadeedi and Ezzeddine 2019: 6–9, quote 6).

In the near-absence of central government, the tribes of Libya were not the only actors in a complex and fragmented state, but they dominated certain towns and areas and impacted directly on the conflict through alliances with key power brokers, notably Field Marshal Haftar and the LNA. That said, the widely-held view that Haftar's success in establishing uncontested control over eastern and later southern Libya was largely due to tribal support was inaccurate. Instead, Haftar used a combination of rent distribution (patronage), elite co-optation and brute coercion (repression) to gradually centralise control. 'Abductions and assassinations in all impunity, along with the successful repression of the region's autonomy movement, put the lie to the narrative that Haftar's rule over eastern Libya was rooted in solid tribal support. The actions of Haftar's security apparatus violated tribal conceptions of honour and exposed the impotence of established notables' (Lacher 2020: 178–9, quote 190). Haftar's rivals in western Libya, on the other hand, found it difficult to engage the tribes, both because of the urbanised outlook of the main players in Tripoli and Misrata and because of their association with the Muslim Brotherhood and affiliated Islamist groups. Moreover, power brokers in Tripoli remained suspicious of the eastern tribes, especially those that had associated with the Qaddafi regime. Tribal gatherings in 2015 did little to undermine tribal opposition in the east and south to the LPA, and after 2016 the GNA proved too weak and ineffective to create a coherent policy towards the tribes (Pargeter 2020).

Media Wars

The Qaddafi regime kept a tight grip on all electronic and print media, allowing only state-controlled outlets like the Jamahiriya News Agency (JANA) and the Jamahiriya Broadcasting Corporation. There was no freedom of speech or freedom of the press. Muhammed al-Qaddafi, the Libyan leader's eldest son, was chairman of the General Post and Telecommunications Company, a state-owned holding company in control of postal and telecommunications services in Libya. In this position, he was able to block public access to YouTube as well as a variety of independent and opposition websites.

In conjunction with the rapid expansion of civil organisations during and after 2011, broadcast, print and social media experienced an encouraging rebirth. While many of these media outlets survived only a year or two, 'approximately 50 television channels, dozens of radio stations, several daily newspapers, and nearly a dozen private weekly and monthly publications' were in business in 2014, an impressive number given the country's relatively small population (HRW 2015: 8–9, quote 9). The state operated two television channels, and several local councils funded their own channels. Private media outlets also flourished, including Salafist-controlled radio stations operating as part of Salafist efforts to displace traditional Sufi and Maliki institutions (Wollenberg and Pack 2013: 203–5).

As the decade progressed, new security laws aimed at controlling press freedom and freedom of expression multiplied. In May 2012, the NTC passed Law No. 37 which prohibited a variety of forms of political speech, including glorification of Qaddafi and his family, criticism of the February 17 Revolution and insults to Libyan institutions. The Supreme Court soon abolished Law No. 37; nevertheless, it served as a wake-up call for journalists. In February 2013, the GNC amended Law No. 195 of the Penal Code, providing prison terms for anyone who publicly insulted legislative, executive or judicial authorities. The chilling effect amended Law No. 195 had on freedom of expression was brought home in 2014 when Amara al-Khatabi, editor of the *Al-Ummah* newspaper, was found guilty under the law of defaming public officials and sentenced to five years in prison (HRW 2015: 36–7, 43).

With the political landscape increasingly chaotic, polarised and politicised, militias, armed factions, Islamists, tribes and ethnic groups exerted new forms of control over journalists, including harassment, intimidation and brute coercion. Human Rights Watch, from September 2012 to November 2014, recorded ninety-one assaults and threats against journalists, including twenty-six armed attacks against the offices of radio and television stations. The armed conflict that broke out in Benghazi in May 2014 and spread west in July of that year resulted in new forms of control over the mass media, with most privately-owned television stations supporting either Operation Dignity or Libya Dawn. After Libya Dawn seized control of Tripoli, it took over all state-owned media institutions. In response, the government in al-Bayda established a parallel state news agency as well as a new national television station (HRW 2015: 9–11).

Over time, the information battle in Libya was conducted more and more on Facebook and Twitter, although television also continued to be used to spread disinformation. The propagation of fake news was not new; the Qaddafi regime used JANA and the Jamahiriya Broadcast Corporation to spread propaganda, but the growing reliance on social media was a new technique. A survey released in May 2019 indicated that most Libyans got their news from social media or television, and it also found that well over half of them used the internet daily. Facebook was by far the most popular platform, followed by Viber, Instagram, WhatsApp and Twitter (IRI/USAID 2019: 53–5). As the ongoing conflict made its way to online spaces, all sides used social media to spread fake news. The Stanford Internet Observatory (SIO) documented one example in which Twitter in 2019 released two files of removed accounts. One file contained accounts originating in the UAE and the other accounts based in Egypt and the UAE. Both accounts contained tweets in Arabic and English supportive of Field Marshal Haftar, critical of the Muslim Brotherhood, and suggesting Turkey and Qatar were supporting terrorism in Libya (SIO 2019). On the basis of an analysis of social media, Democracy Reporting International (DRI) noted that 'online platforms continue to be important tools for war propaganda and are characterized by hate speech and misinformation'. At the same time, 'it appears that highly polarised media channels are driving online political discourse while less biased channels are lagging' (DRI 2020: 1–30, quote 26).

As part of a growing presence throughout Africa, Europe and the US, Russian-linked companies were increasingly active in Libya's information space. Yevgeny Prigozhin, a Russian oligarch with close ties to Vladimir Putin, was central to this expansion. He was known for running the Internet Research Agency and for employing Russian advisors and mercenaries through firms like the Wagner Group. In December 2018, Russian actors associated with the Wagner Group launched a social media influence operation in Libya that led to the creation of a cluster of Facebook Pages. These pages were used to boost Field Marshal Haftar and Saif al-Islam al-Qaddafi and to disparage the GNA. 'To this end, these Pages generated and shared ideologically charged content while purporting to be reliable news sources . . . Finally, despite the fact that most of the Page managers were based in Egypt, these Pages were intended to appear local and to influence Libyans' impressions of the conflict in their country, and of Haftar and Saif Gaddafi in particular' (Grossman, Bush and DiResta 2019: 1–13, quote 13).

In November 2019, the Dossier Center, a London-based investigative unit, obtained a Prigozhin-linked group document that described three additional media interventions in Libya. In the first, a Russian-linked firm took a 50 per cent stake in Aljamahiria Television, formerly the Jamahiriya Broadcasting Corporation. Aljamahiria Television and the affiliated former JANA News Agency had an extensive social media presence. According to the Dossier Center document, the Prigozhin-linked group provided technical, financial and advisory support to the television station. After the Russian firm established the joint venture, Aljamahiria Television's content changed from airing mostly Qaddafi nostalgia content to more stories supporting the LNA and criticising the GNA. Russian actors also created an anti-GNA, pro-LNA newspaper named the *Voice of the People* that had its own Facebook page and occasionally posted videos. The third Russian initiative involved consultative support for the Alhadath television station, the LNA-linked network, in an effort to improve its appearance and content. The Facebook page associated with Alhadath had around 875,000 followers (Grossman, Khadija and DiResta 2020).

Vestiges of Authoritarianism

Post-Qaddafi Libya lacked most of the political institutions associated with a working democracy, and many of the operative institutions were authoritarian in organisation and operation. Neither the National Transitional Council nor the Government of National Accord were elected in free and fair elections and thus were not democratic bodies. In contrast, the three interim transitional governments (September 2012–August 2014) were named by a freely-elected legislative body, the General National Congress, and thus were democratic in name if not always in practice. Following passage of the Political Isolation Law, the GNC rejected pluralistic policies and consensus building and became increasingly authoritarian. The al-Thani government qualified as democratic because it was named by another freely-elected legislature, the House of Representatives, a body that became increasingly authoritarian under Speaker Agila Saleh Issa. Finally, the National Salvation Government, appointed by the rump GNC, was not democratic, because the House of Representatives replaced the GNC before the National Salvation Government was appointed. In contrast, many of the local councils were democratic in that they were the product of free and fair elections. For that reason, they enjoyed high levels of legitimacy while the NTC and GNA did not.

Authoritarian regimes often undermine institutional constraints to their rule, weaken or eliminate opposition and neuter civil society. Libyan institutions that were constrained after 2011 included the Central Bank, the Constitutional Assembly, the General National Congress, the House of Representatives, the Supreme Court and other judicial bodies, the Libyan Investment Authority and the National Oil Corporation. These institutions faced repeated attacks by militias, tribes and religious movements. Civil society organisations also came under attack, the most extreme example being civil organisations promoting equal rights for women. During and after the February 17 Revolution, prominent politicians, influential clerics and traditional leaders joined forces to set the tone for a more conservative stance on the status of women in Libya, questioning their right to education, work, legal remedy, freedom of speech and human dignity.

The manipulation of electoral rules to favour a given party, movement or person is also characteristic of an authoritarian regime. As the July 2012 elections approached, the NTC repeatedly modified the rules, in large part to satisfy the complaints of the Islamist minority. After the elections, the JCP and its Islamist allies pushed the Political Isolation Law through the GNC, destroying the NFA and effectively removing some 500,000 Libyans from public life for a decade. When the Muslim Brotherhood and its Islamist allies did poorly in the June 2014 elections, as they had in the July 2012 elections, they refused to recognise the legitimacy of the House of Representatives. In all of these instances, the Muslim Brotherhood, the JCP and their Islamist allies manipulated election rules and election results in an effort to advance political goals which they could not achieve through free and fair elections.

Attempts to control the media, censor media outlets and sideline opposition journalists are other signs of authoritarianism. After a brief initial period in which media outlets flourished, Law No. 37 and, most especially, amended Law No. 195 had a chilling effect on freedom of the press and freedom of expression. Later, Operation Dignity in the east and Libya Dawn in the west moved to control broadcast and print media in areas under their sway, contributing to the polarisation and politicisation of the media landscape. At the same time, journalists throughout the country continued to be harassed, detained and jailed. While foreign news outlets like *Al Jazeera* were active in Libya from the beginning of the revolution, foreign powers began to play a more aggressive role in the second half of the last decade. Russia, Turkey, Qatar and the United Arab Emirates, among others, provided broadcast and print media outlets with advisory and financial support as well as fake news for distribution on those outlets and on Facebook, Twitter and other social media platforms.

Conclusion

A decade after the February 17 Revolution, post-Qaddafi Libya remains a fractured polity with fissures along regional, ideological, ethnic, tribal, municipal and religious lines. In addition to competing political movements in the east and west of the country, both of which are largely authoritarian in practice, non-state actors throughout Libya also have frequently resorted to authoritarianism in their competition for state resources. In so doing, state and non-state actors have relied on familiar methods of coercion, such as brute force, elite co-optation, rent distribution and media control, while also employing new methods and tools of control, ranging from state-of-the-art weapons systems and new security laws to new forms of social media manipulation. Over time, foreign actors also have increased their influence and involvement in the use of old and new methods of coercion, notably in the provision of sophisticated weapons and support for the manipulation of electronic, print and social media. National reconciliation has remained elusive, with the growing power of non-state actors a major cause of the faltering political transition. In the process, the wishes of the Libyan people have largely been ignored, and, in part for that reason, the people have become increasingly disenchanted with democratic institutions and processes.

References

Cole, P. and F. Mangan (2016). 'Tribe, Security, Justice, and Peace in Libya Today', United States Institute of Peace. *Peaceworks* 118, August. https://www.usip.org/publications/2016/09/tribe-security-justice-and-peace-libya-today

Democracy Reporting International (DRI) (2020). 'Libya Social Media Monitoring Report – Main Findings', 11 June. https://democracy-reporting.org/dri_public ations/libya-social-media-monitoring-main-findings/

Durac, V. (2022). 'Authoritarian Practice and Fragmented Sovereignty in Post-Uprising Yemen', in Ö. E. Topak, M. Mekouar and F. Cavatorta (eds) *New Authoritarian Practices in the Middle East and North Africa.* Edinburgh: Edinburgh University Press, pp. 340–57.

Elfeituri, N. (2020). 'Why Civil Society is Libya's Best Defense against the COVID-19 Pandemic', *Middle East Research and Information Project*, 23 July. https://me rip.org/2020/07/why-civil-society-is-libyas-best-defense-against-the-covid-19p andemic/

Grossman, S., D. Bush and R. DiResta (2019). 'Evidence of Russia-Linked Influence Operations in Africa', Cyber Policy Center, Freeman Spogli Institute for International Studies, Stanford University, 29 October. https://fsi-live.s3.us-we st-1.amazonaws.com/s3fs-public/29oct2019_sio_-russia_linked_influence_ope rations_in_africa.final_.pdf

Grossman, S., H. Khadija and R. DiResta (2020). 'Blurring the Lines of Media Authenticity: Prigozhin-Linked Group Funding Libyan Broadcast Media', Cyber Policy Center, Freeman Spogli Institute for International Studies, Stanford University, 20 March. https://fsi.stanford.edu/news/libya-prigozhin.

Human Rights Watch (HRW) (2015). 'War on the Media: Journalists under Attack in Libya', 9 February. https://www.hrw.org/news/2015/02/09/libya-journalists -under-attack#:~:text=(Tunis).

Hüsken, T. (2019). *Tribal Politics in the Borderland of Egypt and Libya.* New York: Palgrave Macmillan.

International Republican Institute (IRI) and United States Agency for International

Development (USAID) (2016). 'Libyan Municipal Council Research', November. https://www.iri.org/sites/default/files/wysiwyg/iri_libya_municipal _councils_presentation.pdf

International Republican Institute (IRI) and United States Agency for International Development (USAID) (2019). 'Public Opinion Survey: Fifteen Municipalities of Libya, December 31, 2018–January 31, 2019', May. https://www.iri.org/sit es/default/files/libya_poll_january_2019.pdf

Lacher, W. (2014). 'Libya's Fractious South and Regional Instability', Security Assessment in North Africa (SANA) Dispatch 3, February. http://www.smalla rmssurvey.org/fileadmin/docs/R-SANA/SANA-Dispatch3-Libyas-Fractious-So uth.pdf

Lacher, W. (2015). 'Libya's Local Elites and the Politics of Alliance Building', *Mediterranean Politics* 21(1): 64–85.

Lacher, W. (2020). *Libya's Fragmentation: Structure and Process in Violent Conflict*, London: I. B. Tauris.

Lacher, W. and A. al-Idrissi (2018). 'Capital of Militias: Tripoli's Armed Groups Capture the Libyan State', *Small Arms Survey*, Security Assessment in North Africa Briefing Paper, June. http://www.smallarmssurvey.org/fileadmin/docs /T-Briefing-Papers/SAS-SANA-BP-Tripoli-armed-groups.pdf

National Democratic Institute (NDI) and JMW Consulting (2013). 'Seeking Security: Public Opinion Survey in Libya', November. https://www.ndi.org /sites/default/files/Seeking-Security-Public-Opinion-Survey-in-Libya-WEBQU ALITY.pdf

National Democratic Institute (NDI) and JMW Consulting (2014). 'Committed to Democracy and Unity: Public Opinion Survey in Libya', March. https://www .ndi.org/sites/default/files/Libya-Committed-to-Democracy-and-Unity-ENG .pdf

Pack, J. (2019). 'How Libya's Economic Structures Enrich the Militias', Middle East Institute, 23 September. https://www.mei.edu/publications/how-libyas-econo mic-structures-enrich-militias.

Pack, J., K. Mezran and M. Eljarh (2014). 'Libya's Faustian Bargains: Breaking the Appeasement Cycle', Atlantic Council, May. https://www.atlanticcouncil.org /in-depth-research-reports/report/libya-s-faustian-bargains-breaking-the-appeas ement-cycle/

Pargeter, A. (2016). *Return to the Shadows: The Muslim Brotherhood and An-Nahda since the Arab Spring*. London: Saqi Books.

Pargeter, A. (2020). 'Haftar, Tribal Power, and the Battle for Libya', *War on the Rocks*, 15 May. https://warontherocks.com/2020/05/haftar-tribal-power-and -the-battle-for-libya/

Romanet Perroux, J.-L. (2015). 'Libya's Untold Story: Civil Society Amid Chaos', Crown Center for Middle East Studies, Brandeis University, Middle East Brief 93, May. https://www.brandeis.edu/crown/publications/middle-east-briefs/pdfs/1-100/meb93.pdf

St John, R. B. (2015). *Libya: Continuity and change.* London: Routledge.

St John, R. B. (2017). *Libya: From Colony to Revolution.* London: Oneworld.

al-Shadeedi, A.-H. and N. Ezzeddine (2019). 'Libyan Tribes in the Shadows of War and Peace', Clingendael, CRU Policy Brief, February. https://www.clingendael.org/publication/libyan-tribes-shadow-war-and-peace

Stanford Internet Observatory (SIO) (2019). 'Libya: Presidential and Parliamentary Elections Scene Setter', Cyber Policy Center, Freeman Spogli Institute for International Studies, Stanford University, 2 October. https://fsi.stanford.edu/news/libya-scene-setter

Topak, Ö. E., M. Mekouar and F. Cavatorta (2022). 'Introduction', in Ö. E. Topak, M. Mekouar and F. Cavatorta (eds) *New Authoritarian Practices in the Middle East and North Africa.* Edinburgh: Edinburgh University Press, pp. 1–29.

Trauthig, I. K. (2019). 'Gaining Legitimacy in Post-Qaddafi Libya: Analysing Attempts of the Muslim Brotherhood', *Multidisciplinary Digital Publishing Institute (MDPI)*, September. https://www.mdpi.com/2075-4698/9/3/65.

Trauthig, I. K. (2020). 'Islamic State in Libya: From Force to Farce?', International Centre for the Study of Radicalisation (ICSR), March. https://icsr.info/wp-content/uploads/2020/03/ICSR-Report-Islamic-State-in-Libya-From-Force-to-Farce.pdf

United Nations Security Council (2017). 'Final Report of Panel of Experts on Libya', 1 June. https://www.undocs.org/S/2017/466

United Nations Support Mission in Libya (UNSMIL) (2015). 'Libyan Political Agreement', December. https://unsmil.unmissions.org/sites/default/files/Libyan%20Political%20Agreement%20-%20ENG%20.pdf

Wehrey, F. (2018). *The Burning Shores: Inside the Battle for the New Libya.* New York: Farrar, Straus & Giroux.

Wehrey, F. and A. Boukhars (2019). *Salafism in the Maghreb: Politics, Piety, and Militancy.* Oxford: Oxford University Press.

Wollenberg, A. and J. Pack (2013). 'Rebels with a Pen: Observations on the Newly Emerging Media Landscape in Libya', *Journal of North African Studies* 18(2): 191–210.

10

'THE FREEDOM OF NO SPEECH': JOURNALISTS AND THE MULTIPLE LAYERS OF AUTHORITARIAN PRACTICES IN MOROCCO

Driss Maghraoui

Introduction

A rticle 25 of the 2011 Moroccan constitution clearly refers to the principle of freedom of expression and evokes guarantees about 'freedom of thought, opinion, and expression in all its forms'. The constitutional text also refers to 'freedom of creativity and publishing in the domains of literature, art and scientific research', while it bans 'any violation of the privacy of personal communication unless via a judicial order in due cases'. In article 28, the constitution states that 'the freedom of the press is guaranteed. It may not be restricted by any form of prior censorship. Everyone has the right to express and publish news, ideas, and opinions, freely and without limitation, save that which is explicitly set forth in law'. In general, the constitution gives civil society important legislative tools through which to express opinions, evaluate public policies and propose changes to official resolutions. In addition, the Moroccan public sphere today is sprinkled with various media outlets, twenty-eight different newspapers, seventeen private radio stations, ten TV stations and at least fifteen regional and thematic radio stations (OJD 2022).

However, the constitutional basis of freedom of speech has not prevented the Moroccan state from clamping down on journalists. Through different strategies, newspapers in Morocco are not allowed critical reporting about the state, especially when it is directed against the *Makhzen*, a term associated with the palace, its inner circle and close associates. In the 2021 World Press Freedom Index compiled by Reporters Without Borders (2021), Morocco ranked 136th, an important sign of a major crisis negatively affecting journalism and freedom of speech in the country. In recent years, practically all independent newspapers have disappeared from news-stands, while the very few journalists who take the risk of confronting the state are subjected to different forms of harassment through the instrumentalisation of a judiciary system which has become increasingly under political control. The crackdown on journalists started to become more evident in the context of the coverage of the Rif protests, and since then it has further amplified.

An increasing number of Moroccans are expressing themselves and their grievances via social media, because official venues are either under different forms of state control or repressed, while critical voices within the political elite are almost absent. Thus, political statements critical of the government and even the King have appeared in different ways and styles in social media. In many ways, these new outlets are a direct reversal of the logics of the 'red lines' (Smith and Loudyi 2005) that have so far framed the Moroccan public sphere. In fact, writing about topics and issues considered taboo, such as religion, the King or the nation, is viewed as 'lacking respect'. As a result, the Moroccan state has focused on silencing critical voices that are expressed in social media, especially if these are reaching to popular segments of the society.

This chapter probes the ways in which a semi-authoritarian regime or 'hybrid-regime' like that of Morocco, similar to the Jordanian monarchy, as Ryan (2022) outlines in his chapter in this volume, attempts to keep control of the public space by relying on various strategies, such as the instrumentalisation of the judiciary system, the invasion of the private spheres of individuals, and more subtle economic sanctions to crack down on critical newspapers. The state is also using new technologies to pursue surveillance, control and the silencing of critical voices. These strategies resemble the ways in which other states in the Middle East and North Africa and beyond have used to pressure social actors or intimidate journalists by instrumentalising internet service or mobile infrastructure providers (Jones 2019; Leber and Abrahams 2019). These practices have also included surveillance software developed by foreign technology companies in advanced industrialised countries to monitor and control citizens' online activities.

Since 2011 a new kind of scholarship has emerged focusing on how social media in the Middle East helped different social groups to organise and mobilise action at street level (Sakr 2013) or, contrariwise, how it further exacerbated state power through different forms of intimidation and surveillance practices. Different observers in the MENA region have recently looked at the new 'tech-enabled authoritarianism', which basically implies the use of technology by authoritarian regimes to shape the behaviour of their citizens through surveillance, repression and the establishment of services that increase political control (Topak 2017; Bouziane 2017, 2018; Sherman 2019; Bouziane et al. 2020). Identifying, scrutinising and suppressing individuals in a techno-public sphere is the most apparent manifestation of tech-enabled authoritarianism, which can manifest itself also through individual surveillance through the use of hidden microphones, cameras and sophisticated spyware. Techno-authoritarianism can also involve misinformation campaigns destined to tarnish the reputation of individuals and to silence or threaten opposing and critical voices.

I would like to argue here that the evocation of 'new strategies of control' or practices, and the more recent form of techno-authoritarianism in the Moroccan context, should not distract us from the reality that long-established methods continue to be in use. In many ways it simply means that there are additional upgraded 'tools' that have come to supplant pre-existing strategies in the new context following the February 20th movement of 2011–12. I argue that technical tools are in fact intertwined with well-established legal and financial strategies and a more recent instrumentalisation of private sex lives. Technical surveillance seems to have reached the most intimate space of individuals and therefore violates the basic principle of privacy. New variants of control appear in response to changing times, and in parallel they evolve by appropriating new instruments. These strategies have been more specifically implemented against several critical journalists, as well as civil society actors, and are unfolding in a context of burgeoning authoritarian impulses, reminiscent of what has typically been referred to as the 'années de plomb' (years of lead), a common phrase referring to the period of human rights abuse under Hassan II from the 1970s to the 1990s. For many progressive observers and democratic voices, such as the exiled journalists Ali Lmrabet, Aboubkar Jamaii and Ahmed Reda Benchemshi, the signs of optimism associated with the 2011 constitution have given way to a feeling of disillusionment regarding the potential for political transformation and democratisation in Morocco. Implicit in my analysis is, first, how the political regime is consistently adapting its strategies to an evolving environment and how these technologies and strategies are intended to have a restrictive but not necessarily effective outcome on critical discourses and freedom of speech, as the politics of resistance are emerging in different forms in a new public sphere. This aspect is particularly significant because the control of media, including social media, is still an established authoritarian practice that has evolved over time to keep pace with technological developments rather than a completely new one, as the Introduction to this volume argues (Topak et al. 2022).

The wording of the title of this chapter intentionally attempts to combine in contradictory ways the notion of 'freedom' and 'no speech', because it captures in a single phrase the realities of what two observers have called the 'kingdom of illusions' (Gozlan and Andelman 2011). The discursive strategy of playing on words with reference to liberal and democratic ideals in different 'texts', but actually engaging in practices that are the opposite in real 'contexts', is at the core of the various problems Moroccans are faced with, starting with the inherent contradictions that exist between what the Moroccan constitution states in terms of words (freedom) and the actual practices (no speech) that are imbedded in the everyday realities of individual Moroccans. This chapter deals with what I call the different layers of the strategies of control that rely on multiple practices, the most important of which is a legal 'arsenal' that I turn to in the next section.

The Legal Strategy

Regardless of its shortcomings, the 2011 Moroccan constitution presented the judiciary, in articles 107 and 108, as 'independent of the legislative power and the executive power' (Madani et al. 2012). Implicit in this theoretical formulation is the fact that an independent justice system is tantamount to the independence of jurisdictions and the judges. At the core of the independence of jurisdictions is a constitutional basis that renders unlawful the interference of public powers in judiciary procedures. But this theoretical formulation of the Moroccan judicial system fails to pass the test of the realities and the cases that, more recently, have involved different social and political actors, as it does in other cases too, notably Egypt, where, as Jumet (2022) discusses in her contribution to this volume, legalistic tools are employed to securitise the regime. It appears that Morocco has gradually moved towards a form of 'authoritarian constitutionalism' that law scholars like Roberto Ortega have evoked. Authoritarian constitutionalism implies that regimes engage in different forms of control and illiberal practices with the instrumentalisation of a constitutional text that is discursively inspired by the language of liberal democracy. As one observer put it:

> authoritarian constitutionalism refers to a very sophisticated way in which ruling elites with an authoritarian mentality exercise power in not fully democratic states. In this case, the regime's liberal democratic constitution, instead of limiting the power of the state and empowering those who would otherwise be powerless, is used for practical and authoritarian ideological function. (Niembro Ortega 2016)

If Moroccan official discourse insists on the 'democratic achievements' of the 2011 constitution, legal experts, human rights groups and organisations point to the reality that there are growing practices that are symptomatic of the unlimited power of the state and the resulting powerlessness of individuals with critical voices, especially among journalists or civil society activists.

National and international organisations, such as the *Association Marocaine des Droits de l'Homme* as well as Human Rights Watch, Freedom House or Amnesty International, have regularly invoked the dysfunctions of the Moroccan judicial system by insisting on how the penal code has effectively been constructed to undermine the improvements that were part of the initial democratic spirit of the 2011 constitution. More specifically, they point out to how the courts have systematically given prison sentences to journalists who have crossed the 'red lines'. As we will see below, this took place through a series of speedy trials, weak cases with poorly corroborated accusations, and long-term sentences.

It is important to note that in 1979, Morocco endorsed the International Covenant on Civil and Political Rights (ICCPR). The covenant established clear rules for the protection of non-violent criticism of state officials and clarified the policies according to international law. But the strategy of the Moroccan state is to establish a legal ambiguity so that the lines between the principle of 'freedom of expression' can be blurred with the act of 'committing a crime' permitted under a legal framework (Böckenförde 2016). From a different perspective, critics of the judicial system in Morocco point to the more constitutional and institutional basis of the problems of the justice system. With more specific implications for journalists, the basis for sanctions towards freedom of the press became in fact multiple and vague under the 2011 constitution. Indeed, article 41 allowed more restrictions on newspapers and journalists when they venture to write about the 'sacred values' evoked in the constitution. The reference to 'sacred values' can create another ambiguity which can be instrumentalised to further restrict freedom of the press and subject the writings of journalists to the discretion of the judge (Bendourou 2014).

An important aspect of authoritarian constitutionalism is the discrepancies within the legal framework and lack of judicial independence, something that affects most countries in the region, including Tunisia, as Cimini (2022) discusses briefly in her chapter in this book. In Morocco, journalists are confronted with the discrepancy between the July 2016 Press and Publications Code, which was supposed to eliminate prison sentences and guarantee some form of free speech, and the penal code, which established prison as a penalty for various speech-related offences. On 24 July 2017, the Moroccan parliament approved, in record time and with limited opposition, a bill that made the Moroccan equivalent of the Attorney General at the *Court de Cassation* the new head of the Public Prosecutor's Office.

Under the umbrella of the Interior Ministry and the Ministry of Communications, the bill effectively transferred the powers of the prosecutor's office from the Ministry of Justice to the King's Attorney General at the *Court de Cassation*, and subsequently the office became independent from any parliamentary oversight or government involvement. The principle of the independence of the judiciary – celebrated in official discourse – is clearly questionable when confronted with the July 2017 'reform' bill that came out in the specific context of suppression of a major social movement in the Rif region (Mouna 2018; Wolf 2019).

The outcome of these deficiencies in the judicial system was apparent in several cases against journalists. The sheer numbers of targeted individuals suggest that there is a systematic crackdown on critical voices that dare to cross the 'red lines'. For example, between September 2019 and February 2020, the Moroccan state indicted at least ten people in relation to social media posts critical of the monarch. The Moroccan Association for Human Rights and Human Rights Watch pointed out that the individuals who faced trial include political and social actors voicing powerful critical views, such as exposing a corrupt political elite, dealing with issues that involve palace politics, or being critical of policies put forward by the monarchy and strategic in terms of the stability of the monarchy.

On 23 February 2018, fifteen agents of the National Brigade of the judicial police arrested Taoufik Bouachrine, director of a popular and

independent newspaper, *Akhabar AlYawm*, on account of provocative edito-
rials like 'Governing is not a promenade by the sea', in which he criticised the
silence of the King in the context of the Rif social movement. Accused of rape,
attempted rape and human trafficking, Bouachrine was sentenced to twelve
years in prison before seeing his sentence increased to fifteen years on appeal.
According to several national and international legal experts, the whole legal
process Bouarchrine went through was in violation of the presumption of
innocence and established journalistic ethics. Before the trials, there was a
well-orchestrated campaign in some of the media outlets – presumably under
state control – to engage in a process of 'lynching' the journalist, calling him
at times a serial criminal and a pervert. The four women initially designated as
victims subsequently refused to be involved and declined to file a complaint.
One of the key witnesses, Afaf Bernani, alleged she was under pressure to be a
witness. Afaf later stated: 'I have never filed a complaint against Bouachrine.
It was the BNPJ [National Brigade of the Judiciary Police] who summoned
me and the minutes prove it . . . I was the subject of various pressures to
prosecute Bouachrine.'[1] Afaf was clearly accusing the police of falsifying her
statement, and as a result was sentenced to six months in prison for 'falsification and defamation'. The case of Bouachrine is revealing not only in terms of
the problems associated with the legal system in Morocco, but also in relation
to the instrumentalisation of sexuality, a theme which will be developed later
in this chapter.

In 2019, the international organisation Amnesty International called
for the immediate release of the journalist and declared that his imprisonment was a 'matter of freedom of expression'. In addition, a United Nations
Human Rights Council working group announced that Bouachrine's case
suffered from a 'lack of evidence' coupled with 'witness intimidation' and
that the journalist was the target of 'arbitrary detention' and 'judicial harassment'. In a clear statement of support to Bouachrine and condemnation of
the Moroccan authorities, Mohamed Sektaoui, head of the Moroccan branch
of Amnesty International, said that 'we believe that Bouachrine's imprisonment is a matter of freedom of expression', and that he 'is paying a high price
for his right to peacefully express critical opinions' (abc24 2019). The accusations were denied by the Moroccan authorities.

The case of Mr Omar Radi is also revealing about the systematic crackdown on critical journalists. Radi, who was well-known for his articles on
corruption among state dignitaries, was detained in July 2020. Mr Radi was

accused of espionage because of his relationship with European diplomats and job-related activities with a British consulting company. But according to Eric Goldstein, the Middle East and North Africa director at Human Rights Watch, 'bringing apparently bogus charges against critical journalists is now clearly part of the Moroccan government's playbook for stifling dissent', and there is 'no evidence that Radi did anything besides conduct ordinary journalistic or corporate due diligence work' (Human Rights Watch 2020).

The official reaction to the Radi case came on 2 July 2020 in a statement by Morocco's Education Minister, Saaïd Amzazi, who declared that the 'kingdom of Morocco has been the subject of an unjust international defamation campaign, [and] insists on obtaining an official response from this organisation [Amnesty International] which claims to defend human rights: a response that includes all the evidence material which it would have used to harm Morocco'. The Minister of State in charge of Human Rights, El Mostapha Ramid, and the Minister of Foreign Affairs, Nasser Bourita, affirmed in a joint press conference that the Kingdom of Morocco 'will take the necessary measures to defend its national security, as well as to enlighten national and international public opinion about these rejected allegations' and that it 'reiterates its categorical rejection of the latest Amnesty International reports, given that they are dictated by an agenda unrelated to the defense of human rights as universal values' (Guerraoui 2020).

The Financial Strategy

Being 'press enterprises', newspapers are essentially subject to the potential financial constraints that are attached to their 'business' from a political economy perspective (Benchenna et al. 2017). One of the effective practices limiting free speech, at least in print media, is through a kind of financial asphyxiation exercised on independent newspapers. There are major problems in Morocco regarding how the media are funded and ultimately supported or rendered financially bankrupt. The strategy basically relies on using the economic leverage of an entrepreneurial conservative elite to promote more mineable newspapers and journalists and simultaneously financially asphyxiate those that are regularly reporting on the dysfunctions of the state and are calling for socio-economic, legal and political reforms. It is important to note that sometimes the lines, between this entrepreneurial elite and the political elite who are in the inner circles of the decision-making process are blurred. With control over the advertising funds that constitute the financial basis of different news outlets, this economic/political elite can very often determine their long-term financial sustainability and survival. It is basically a simple equation: if a newspaper starts publishing critical discourse about the state, especially about the closest circles of power, advertisers, whether coerced or out of sheer fear of state retaliation, would automatically pull their advertisement. By contrast, if newspapers are apolitical or selective about the political elite they target (typically party members of the Islamist PJD), they are more likely to benefit from the financial largesse of business companies.

What might be new about the economic strategy controlling the newspapers in Morocco is that it is different from the strategy of Hassan II's direct censorship, especially in the early years of his reign. It has become more evident that state advertisers or private companies are coerced into boycotting independent newspapers. Accordingly, at least 'three newspapers attributed the end of their existence to this form of economic control: the weekly *Journal* in January 2010, *Al Jarida Al Oula* in May 2010 and *Nichane* in October 2010' (Benchenna et al. 2017: 34). This strategy has in fact gradually intensified to an extent that today, we can safely state that there are limited financial possibilities for an independent newspaper to survive. There are no published critical print newspapers readily available on the newsstands in the streets of Rabat or Casablanca.

As a classic example, *Le Journal* was completely hampered by lawsuits and advertising boycotts because of its critical reporting about the government and the closest circles of power. As Mr Aboubakr Jamaï put it:

> I was sentenced to pay around 250,000 Euros which I was unable [to pay] and I waited until the bailiff came to my house to take away my home furniture . . . and what was truly fatal to the institution [the journal] was the economic boycott and if you are interested in a democratic and independent press, you have to understand that it cannot exist without an economic model.[2]

This argument about the practice of financial asphyxiation raised by Jamaï in March 2013 remained valid in 2017, as it was clearly expressed in a special report by the Moroccan news website Le Desk and Reporters without Borders. The report confirmed that 'the opaqueness of the Moroccan media market is also linked to the way the advertising market functions. The lack of fairness in the allocation of advertising helps to sustain an opaque environment that escapes public control and in which popular newspapers can be the victims of boycotts' (RSF 2017). In the same report we discover that closest circles of the Moroccan regime and royal household have significant investments in the media. It seems that advertisers are rationally and instinctively more attracted to news outlets that present the most positive reporting about the Kingdom.

The reliance of the Moroccan authorities on a financial strategy also manifests itself in different ways, as in the case of the historian and journalist Maati Mounjib. On 19 September 2015, the Ministry of Interior accused Mounjib of 'corruption' and 'financial irregularities' during his management of a research centre. As evoked in an official newspaper outlet, Mounjib 'is subject to a procedure of closing the borders following a judicial order regarding financial irregularities', according to a press release from the Government and the Ministry of the Interior. According to the official discourse, he 'is subject to a procedure of closing the borders in accordance with judicial orders in connection with a file relating to financial irregularities of the time when he managed the company "Center Ibn Rochd for studies and communication"' (*Le Matin* 2015). The newspaper *Le Matin* corroborated the official discourse of the state by adding that the 'ministry reaffirms that the statements of the person concerned are devoid of any foundation, recalling that this case is being investigated by the judicial police under the supervision of a competent general prosecutor's office' (*Le Matin* 2015). Amnesty International seized upon the Mounjib case and called on the Moroccan government 'to stop abusing criminal law or administrative regulations on the receipt of foreign funding as a means to target independent human rights associations or journalists'.

Intimate Spaces and the Trap of Sexuality

Using sex and the intimate space of individuals to suppress opposition forces is not uncommon within both democratic and authoritarian settings. In Russia, for example, the practice of *kompromat*, which is part of a secret process of gathering compromising materials on different diplomats, was a common practice during the Cold War, and more recently under the presidency of Vladimir Putin (Soldatov 2017). In its December 2016 report on Morocco, the UN Human Rights Committee (HRC) was already concerned about the 'illegal infringements of the right to privacy in the course of surveillance operations conducted by law enforcement and intelligence agencies targeting journalists, human rights defenders and perceived opponents of the government'.³ What is new in the more recent Moroccan political context, however, is the instrumentalisation of the private sphere of individuals through the use of technology (Topak 2019). This is not specific to the Moroccan context, as we have witnessed similar practices in Turkey, for example. But given the relatively conservative Moroccan cultural context, it was highly unusual to make the private and sexual life of individuals public, let alone to send recorded videos of an individual making love with his partner and send it to close friends or even threaten that individual with it being posted online (Mansouri 2020). This is exactly what some journalists have had to live through as they experienced an unjustified intrusion into their most intimate lives through technical and logistical means. Is it a coincidence that these individuals happen to be among the voices most critical of the political system in Morocco?

Taoufik Bouachrine was sentenced, on charges of rape and other offences, to a twelve-year prison term in November 2018 and on 25 October 2019. The sentence was increased to fifteen years after the journalist appealed to the public prosecutor. Bouachrine was the publisher of a relatively critical newspaper. Throughout the trials, he maintained his innocence and insisted that the sentence was politically motivated. The journalist was found guilty of human trafficking, abuse of power for sexual purposes, rape and attempted rape. The charges against Bouachrine were based on testimonies and resulted, more specifically, from fifty secretly recorded videos that were confiscated by the police from his office. The sheer number of videos was therefore a clear sign that his newspaper office was monitored and constantly watched using highly sophisticated cameras. While the Moroccan authorities insisted that it was an act of human trafficking and abuse of power and rape, the defence team insisted that the videos were fake or at best showed 'consensual relations'. It is important to insist once again that four women who were referred to by the prosecution as victims ultimately refuted their having had any involvement. One of them was later condemned to six months in prison because she alleged that the police falsified her testimony, and the other three did not want to appear in court.

On 30 September 2019, a 28-year-old Moroccan journalist, Hajar Raissouni, was sentenced in a court in Rabat to a year in prison on the basis of charges that she 'had an illegal abortion and sexual relations outside marriage', while her fiancé, Prof. Rifaat al-Amin, received a one-year sentence for alleged complicity (Human Rights Watch 2019). In a major breach of the privacy of the accused, the prosecutor publicly released personal details about her sexual and reproductive life. In a letter that she sent from prison, Hajar described the charges as 'fabricated'. She also explained that the abortion never took place and that the whole ordeal could be part of a crackdown by the Moroccan authorities directly related to her articles in the more independent daily newspaper *Akhbar al Yaoum*. Hajar was covering the social movement in Rif in the northern part of the country. In the language of Raissouni's lawyer, Muhammad Sadkou, the verdict was 'regressive', and the judge's decision was a sign that 'the Moroccan state's claims to respect international conventions that guarantee rights and freedoms were lies that are detached from reality'. In the classic political style of the monarchical regime, Hajar Raissouni, her fiancé and her medical doctor received a 'royal pardon' on 16 October 2019, following widespread criticism and international mobilisation from human rights groups, who regarded her case as an attack on freedom of speech.

The case of Fouad Abdelmoumni, member of the board of directors of the NGO Transparency Maroc, is another example of how 'sexual blackmailing' has become part of a systematic attempt to keep critical voices silent (Turner 2021). Abdelmoumni is one of the civil society leaders in Morocco who has been constantly critical of corruption, repression of press freedom, and the overall policies of the so-called *makhzen*. In March 2021, Abdelmoumni presented powerful testimony on YouTube in which he spoke about the fact that he was a victim of what he called 'revenge porn'.[4] In his testimony, Abdelmoumni recounted how in February 2020 close members of his family and several close friends received video sequences of him having sex with his own partner. The videos were illegally recorded in his private bedroom through devices introduced into his air conditioner. Ironically, in the Moroccan constitutional context, sending videos could also be interpreted as a threatening message, insinuating to Abdelmoumni that he could be charged under article 490 criminalising sex outside marriage according to the Moroccan penal code.

Abdelmoumni's testimony came to corroborate previous statements by other social actors that the Moroccan regime was trying to silence dissidents through practices violating the privacy of individuals (Human Rights Watch 2021).[5] In an article in the British weekly *The Economist* with the revealing title 'Sex, lies and videotapes', Abdelmoumni even claimed that at least a dozen people of different ideological stripes had been the target of an insulting campaign that, according to him, seemed to involve the state security apparatus (*The Independent* 2021).

Alternative Voices and Strategies of Resistance

As domestic and international civil society organisations attempt to show the dire situation of freedom of expression in Morocco and the state's continuous stifling of press freedoms, the public sphere seems to witness emerging forms of resistance. This is happening in the context of growing social demands and economic problems affecting the regime's public image. Otherwise, if the intended outcome of repression and prosecution is to silence the critical voices of journalists, we see a new public space emerging which is critical of the social and economic conditions, and of the political system. As Moroccan authorities use the penal code to inflict prison sentences on individuals for their forthright criticisms, a growing number of Moroccans are relying on new media channels to express their grievances with a more critical and audacious political discourse. It is, first, evident that the internet has offered an alternative public sphere that has opened up the space for different voices regardless of their educational level or social origins. A new public sphere comes hand in hand with new ways of engaging in contentious forms of politics relying on humour, caricatures, or songs. These new forms of expression in fact started to become more apparent with the February 20th movement. But if contentious politics associated with this movement initially involved an educated youth, they gradually evolved to include other social categories.

Most notable among these alternative voices are the ultras, as they are associated with fan activism. As in other contexts in the Middle East (Close 2019), the ultras were able, in various ways, to create new consciousness and raise key socio-economic issues in straightforward language that expressed the marginalised youth's growing anxiety. In a single song such as '*fi-bladi dalmouni*' (Being oppressed in my own country), we hear a powerful and condensed discourse about social and economic marginality and exclusion. The ultras are highly critical of the state, and consistently address strong messages to the Moroccan authorities. Their slogans and songs reflect the world of urban marginality of a city like Casablanca (Bourkia 2018). The discourse of the ultras about poverty and socio-economic marginality has regularly coincided with another form of expression relying on language that came directly from the popular songs of Moroccan rap singers.

One of the most powerful critical statements came via a rap song by a Moroccan rapper, Mohamed Mounir, and two of his friends. Known also as Gnawi, Mounir released a video on 29 October which showcased a song known as 'a'cha cha'b'[6] (Long live the people). In the song, Gnaoui was blatant about exposing Morocco's economic problems, social inequality, youth problems and, more importantly, a frustration with the monarch in a language that was familiar to the poorest segment of the society because it epitomised a growing public anger. Mounir was detained, Moroccan officials arguing that his detention was provoked by the previous appearance of a video that represented an 'insult against public officials', an act that is indictable by law and that can result in a two-year prison sentence. But as a form of defiance Mounir in fact clearly announced that he had expected to be taken to jail, and he was eventually given a one-year prison sentence. The arrest of the three rappers became part of a pattern of state practices in which more Moroccans, including some activists, and even teenagers, were within five weeks, by the end 2019, arrested and charged with crimes relating to social media posts. But the crackdown triggered small-scale protests within Morocco and ultimately drew international attention, negatively affecting Morocco's image. His song, which has to date had close to 33 million hits on YouTube, became a reference point for many Moroccans regardless of their social status, as it circulated via social media.

Hunger strikes by journalists like Ali Annouzla, Maati Monjib, Soulaiman Raissouni and Omar Radi are symptomatic of a form of militant resistance against Moroccan authoritarianism and the legal system that helps to sustain it. As this chapter is being written, Radi and Raissouni are still on hunger strike and in a critical condition, while their lives are at serious risk. As Reporters Without Borders has stated, it 'is unacceptable that journalists end up putting their lives in danger to make their demands for justice heard and to recover the freedom they should never have lost'; it added that 'the Moroccan authorities must stop resorting to these arbitrary and iniquitous prosecutions that drive journalists to choose the worst methods to defend their rights' (RSF 2021b). It is symbolic that the phenomenon of hunger strikes is emerging specifically among journalists in jail, because they have run out of options. The lack of an independent legal system has been a major contributing factor to resorting to hunger strikes. Otherwise, the very idea of a hunger strike is essentially rooted in the inherent contradictions between the theory and practice of Morocco's constitution and legal practices in disciplining critical journalists.

However, the incarceration of so many journalists and political activists can be interpreted as providing a unique opportunity for them to unite against the Moroccan legal and political regime. Hunger strikes are, in fact, an extension of their political activism and resistance.

As the final lines of this chapter were being written, on 9 July 2021, a Casablanca court sentenced Raissouni to five years in prison. The Raissouni case has taken an international dimension especially after the US State Department made the following statement: 'We believe the judicial process that led to this verdict contradicts the Moroccan system's fundamental promise of fair trials for individuals accused of crimes and is inconsistent with the promise of the 2011 constitution and His Majesty King Mohammed VI's reform agenda.'[7] This statement summarises the risks that the Moroccan state is taking in terms of tarnishing its image in the context of the MENA region and possibly in terms of dealing with its Sahara issue.

Conclusion

From a historical perspective, the process of 'political reforms' that was initiated under Hassan II and marked by the so-called period of *'alternance'*, associated with the more liberal Prime Minister Abderrahman Youssoufi, was characterised by more freedom of expression than there is in the alarming situation today. The impact of hunger strikes as part of a small-scale and local resistance movement might become a point of concern for the Moroccan state, as the cases of both Radi and Raissouni are currently in the columns of the *Washington Post* (2021). The more recent crackdown on journalists is reviving a painful past about the 'years of lead', and is simultaneously tarnishing the image of the kingdom and the monarchy both internally and abroad.

Political stability in Morocco would depend on the ability of the Moroccan regime to restore some of the basic constitutional guarantees of a free press and independent civil society that were initially part of the 2011 Moroccan constitution. The Moroccan state should engage in more structural reforms of its judiciary and internal security institutions, although, as Mekouar and Derradji (2022) argue in their chapter on Algeria in this volume, major reforms might also mean an upgrade in repressive practices. A major re-organisation of the media, with guarantees of its independence as well as the establishment of robust legal structures for freedom of speech, but also against vilification in the social media, is paramount to restoring trust in the potential for reforms in Morocco.

Notes

1 See her statement in Arabic on You Tube: عفاف برناني في أول خروج لها: السجن لا
يرعبني..وهو أهون علي من شهادة الزّور وظلم بوعشرين, https://www.youtube.com/wat
ch?v=u7eD-ZFzg6s

2 See the Extract from the intervention of Aboubakr Jamaï and Ali Lmrabet during
a conference on 'Le Journal', on YouTube: *Extrait de l'intervention d'Aboubakr
Jamaï et d'Ali Lmrabet lors de la conférence sur 'Le Journal'*, https://www.youtube
.com/watch?v=ZdKbnxhRDXk

3 See the Report by UN Human Rights Committee (HRC), 1 December 2016:
Refworld | Concluding observations on the initial report of Morocco, https://
www.refworld.org/topic,50ffbce51b1,50ffbce51e7,5975bee04,0,,,MAR.html

4 L'activiste des Droits Humains marocain, Fouad Abdelmoumni victime de
'Revenge Porn', https://www.youtube.com/watch?v=oE9ZFNvVOXw

5 Human Rights Watch (HRW) argues, in its 2021 report, that Morocco intensified 'repression' against those who 'express opinions critical of the monarchy',
and that some were arrested on the basis of 'dubious accusations', such as having
'sexual relations outside of marriage'.

6 There is a symbolic aspect to the title of the song, as Moroccans are more accus-
tomed to hear *a'acha al-malik* (Long Live the King).

7 Statement made on Monday 12 July 2021 by Ned Price, spokesman of the US
State Department.

References

Abc24 (2019). 'Maroc: Amnesty appelle à la libération de Taoufik Bouachrine'.
27 February.

Benchenna, A., D. Ksikes and D. Marchetti (2017). 'La presse au Maroc: une économie très politique', *Questions de communication* 32: 239–60.

Bendourou, O. (2014). 'Les droits de l'homme dans la constitution marocaine de
2011: débats autour de certains droits et libertés', *La Revue des droits de l'homme*
6: 1–25. http://journals.openedition.org/revdh/907.

Böckenförde, M. (2016). 'From Constructive Ambiguity to Harmonious
Interpretation: Religion Related Provisions in the Tunisian Constitution',
American Behavioral Scientist 60(8): 919–40.

Bourkia, A. (2018). 'Ultras in the City. A Sociological Inquiry on Urban Violence in
Morocco', *The Philosophical Journal of Conflict and Violence* 2(2): 321–33.

Bouziane, Z. (2017). 'The Authoritarian Trap in State/Media Structures in Morocco's
Political Transition', *The Journal of North African Studies* 22(3): 340–60.

Bouziane, Z. (2018). 'Comparative Study of Broadcast Regulators in the Arab
World', *International Journal of Communication* 12(1): 4,401–20.

Bouziane, Z., A. El Kaddoussi and M. Ibahrine (2020). 'The Uneasy Journey of the Moroccan Press', in N. Miladi and N. Mellor (eds) *Routledge Handbook of Arab Media*. London: Routledge.

Cimini, G. (2022). 'Authoritarian Nostalgia and Practices in Newly Democratising Contexts: The Localised Example of Tunisia', in Ö. E. Topak, M. Mekouar and F. Cavatorta (eds) *New Authoritarian Practices in the Middle East and North Africa*. Edinburgh: Edinburgh University Press, pp. 276–95.

Close, R. (2019). *Cairo's Ultras: Resistance and Revolution in Egypt's Football Culture*. Cairo: American University in Cairo Press.

Derradji, I. A. and M. Mekouar (2022). 'Maintaining Order in Algeria: Upgrading Repressive Practices Under a Hybrid Regime', in Ö. E. Topak, M. Mekouar and F. Cavatorta (eds) *New Authoritarian Practices in the Middle East and North Africa*. Edinburgh: Edinburgh University Press, pp. 30–50.

Gozlan, M. and D. A. Andelman (2011). 'Morocco: In the Kingdom of Illusions', *World Policy Journal* 28(3): 101–12.

Guerraoui, S. (2020). 'Bourita: Amnesty's Spying Charges against Morocco Unfounded', *Middle East on-line*, 15 July. https://middle-east-online.com/en/bourita-amnesty%E2%80%99s-spying-charges-against-morocco-unfounded

Human Rights watch (2019). 'Morocco: Trial Over Private Life Allegations', 9 September. https://www.hrw.org/news/2019/09/09/morocco-trial-over-private-life-allegations

Human Rights Watch (2020). 'Morocco: Espionage Case against Outspoken Journalist', 21 September. https://www.hrw.org/news/2020/09/21/morocco-espionage-case-against-outspoken-journalist

Jones, M. O. (2019). 'Propaganda, Fake News, and Fake Trends: The Weaponization of Twitter Bots in the Gulf Crisis', *International Journal of Communication* 13(1): 1,389–415.

Jumet, K. D. (2022). 'Authoritarian Repression Under Sisi: New Tactics or New Tools?', in Ö. E. Topak, M. Mekouar and F. Cavatorta (eds) *New Authoritarian Practices in the Middle East and North Africa*. Edinburgh: Edinburgh University Press, pp. 73–91.

Leber, A. and A. Abrahams (2019). 'A Storm of Tweets: Social Media Manipulation during the Gulf Crisis', *Review of Middle East Studies* 53(2): 241–58.

Le Matin (2015). 'Le Ministère de l'Intérieur s'explique', 11 October. https://lematin.ma/journal/2015/le-ministere-de-l-interieur-s-explique/233154.html

Madani, M., D. Maghraoui and S. Zerhouni. (2012). *The 2011 Moroccan Constitution: A Critical Analysis*. International Institute for Democracy and Electoral Assistance (IDEA) Stockholm, Sweden. https://www.idea.int/publications/catalogue/2011-moroccan-constitution-critical-analysis

Mansouri, H. (2020). 'Maroc. Cette strategie sexuelle qui lamine les journalists', *Orient XXI*. https://orientxxi.info/magazine/maroc-cette-strategie-sexuelle-qui-lamine-les-journalistes,3987

Mouna, K. (2018). *Identité de la marge. Approche anthropologique du Rif.* Brussels: Peter Lang.

Niembro Ortega, R. (2016). 'Conceptualizing Authoritarian Constitutionalism', *Law and Politics in Africa, Asia and Latin America* 49(4): 339–367.

OJD-Maroc, Organisme Marocain de Justification et de Diffusion (2022). https://www.ojd.ma/Chiffres

Reporters Sans Frontières (2017). 'Hunger Strike Is Last Resort for Some Imprisoned Moroccan Journalists. Pluralism Is More Than Figures. RSF and Le Desk Release Media Ownership Monitor – Morocco Findings', 15 November. https://rsf.org/en/news/pluralism-more-figures-rsf-and-le-desk-release-media-ownership-monitor-morocco-findings

Reporters Sans Frontières (2021a). *2021 World Press Freedom Index*. https://rsf.org/en/ranking/2021

Reporters Sans Frontières (2021b). 'Hunger Strike Is Last Resort for Some Imprisoned Moroccan Journalists', 15 April. https://rsf.org/en/news/hunger-strike-last-resort-some-imprisoned-moroccan-journalists

Ryan, C. (2022). 'Jordan: A Perpetually Liberalizing Autocracy', in Ö. E. Topak, M. Mekouar and F. Cavatorta (eds) *New Authoritarian Practices in the Middle East and North Africa.* Edinburgh: Edinburgh University Press, pp. 152–70.

Sherman, J. (2019). 'The Long View of Digital Authoritarianism', *New America*, 20 June. https://www.newamerica.org/weekly/long-view-digitalauthoritarianism

Smith, A. and F. Loudiy (2005). 'Testing the Red Lines: On the Liberalization of Speech in Morocco', *Human Rights Quarterly* 27(3): 1,069–119.

Soldatov, A. (2017). 'Putin's Private Hackers', *The World Today* 73(1): 36–7.

The Independent (2021). 'Sex, Lies and Videotape, Morocco's Regime Is Accused of Blackmailing Critics', 30 January. https://eminetra.com/sex-lies-videotapes-the-moroccan-regime-has-been-accused-of-threatening-critics-middle-east-and-africa/339086/

The Washington Post (2021). 'Morocco's Jailed Journalists Deserve the Biden Administration's Attention', 30 April. https://www.washingtonpost.com/opinions/global-opinions/moroccos-jailed-journalists-deserve-the-biden-administrations-attention/2021/04/30/fa3459cc-a905-11eb-8c1a-56f0cb4ff3b5_story.html

Topak, Ö. E. (2017). 'The Making of a Totalitarian Surveillance Machine: Surveillance in Turkey Under AKP Rule', *Surveillance & Society* 15(3/4): 535–42.

Topak, Ö. E. (2019). 'The Authoritarian Surveillant Assemblage: Authoritarian State Surveillance in Turkey', *Security Dialogue* 50(1): 454–72.

Topak, Ö. E., M. Mekouar and F. Cavatorta (2022). 'Introduction', in Ö. E. Topak, M. Mekouar and F. Cavatorta (eds) *New Authoritarian Practices in the Middle East and North Africa.* Edinburgh: Edinburgh University Press, pp. 1–29.

Turner, J. (2021). 'Sexual Blackmailing of Activists Gains Strength in Morocco', *Topnewstoday*, 6 February. https://topnewstoday.live/2021/02/06/sexual-black mailing-of-activists-gains-strength-in-morocco-international/

Wolf, A. (2019). 'Morocco's Hirak Movement and Legacies of Contention in the Rif', *The Journal of North African Studies* 24(1): 1–6.

11

NEW AUTHORITARIAN PRACTICES IN QATAR: CENSORSHIP BY THE STATE AND THE SELF

Alainna Liloia

Introduction

The small state of Qatar has garnered a level of notoriety for its rogue foreign policy and what other GCC countries view as a refusal to play by the rules. Whether making a home for exiles from organisations marked as 'terrorist' by the United States, aligning itself with Islamist political parties in the region or offering tacit support for the commentary championing populist resistance in other Middle Eastern nations by the state-owned news network *Al Jazeera*, Qatar has irked its Gulf neighbours to the point of rift (twice) while stubbornly refusing to back down. Particularly since the 2011 Arab uprisings, the Qatari state has sought to represent itself as a progressive force for change in the region, and create distance between itself and other autocratic regimes in the region that have responded to dissent with harsh and repressive measures. However, despite implementing new domestic political reforms and aligning its foreign policy discourse with the hegemonic Western paradigms of democracy and human rights, the state has continued to engage in authoritarian measures at home to maintain and enforce its power, and has limited the implementation of democratic political reforms.

These and other factors make the topic of authoritarianism in Qatar a particularly interesting, albeit puzzling, case for political pundits and scholars alike, who have sought to understand Qatar's seemingly contradictory domestic and foreign policies. Moreover, the topic of Qatar's foreign policy has received renewed attention in popular media and academic scholarship since the 2017 Gulf crisis, which involved Saudi Arabia, the UAE and other Arab nations enacting a blockade against Qatar and accusing the state of sponsoring terrorism, among other accusations. In the twenty-first century, Qatari rulers have faced new challenges to consolidating their domestic rule and building a positive reputation for international consumption, particularly as new forms of social media communication and the expansion of the digital sphere have made it more difficult to control the dissemination of national narratives among domestic and international audiences. This chapter contributes to filling a gap in current scholarship on authoritarianism in Qatar by examining the state's use of new authoritarian measures, particularly digital media censorship, to fulfil its domestic and foreign policy agendas and consolidate its social and political power.

Specifically, the chapter examines how Qatar is developing new authoritarian practices to construct and control the narratives produced by national media and monitor the spread of information to international audiences.[1] It analyses how new digital authoritarian methods, in conjunction with existing state restrictions on civil society organising and the censorship of public and social media, have placed parameters on freedom of expression that effectively foster an environment of self-censorship among media organisations, journalists and social actors.[2] It argues that the Qatari state is utilising new forms of media censorship and surveillance and continued monitoring of civil society organisations towards three aims, namely: to craft a positive and progressive national narrative for domestic and international consumption; to control and dominate national political discourse; and to prevent dissenting voices from gaining public traction.

To contextualise Qatar's contemporary development of authoritarian practices, the next section will provide an overview of the state's use of authoritarian measures prior to 2011, particularly restrictions on the development of civil society and censorship of public media, to maintain social stability and prevent or quash dissent. In addition, it will analyse the disparities in the implementation of authoritarian measures on Qatar's national and migrant populations towards this end, and the role of socio-economic and political structures in shaping the state's authoritarian methods.

Preventative Authoritarian Methods[3]

Qatar is somewhat exceptional as a case study for authoritarianism due to the moderated nature of its repressive authoritarian measures and the lack of organised political or social resistance throughout the nation's history. While dissenting opinions and frustrations with the government inevitably exist among Qatar's population, these have rarely manifested in the form of organised social or political opposition in the country. In fact, Qataris often express performative loyalty towards the government and pro-government sentiment, at least publicly, and show little interest in engaging in resistance. This differentiates the Gulf nation from other Middle Eastern nations with organised social resistance movements, such as Saudi Arabia, and those with active political opposition parties and groups, such as Egypt and Bahrain. Qatar's authoritarian methods have been largely preventative, and reactive measures utilised commonly by other authoritarian regimes in the region, such as arrests, detentions and exiles, have been utilised very selectively by Qatari rulers in comparison. Since Qatar's founding in 1971, its authoritarian measures have been aimed instead at preventing dissenting views from gaining visibility and public traction and at precluding the possibility of organised resistance, largely through restrictions on the development of civil society organisations and censorship of media and publishing. Since 2011, these methods have persisted and have been supplemented by new restrictions, policies and forms of enforcement.

Restrictions on civil society organising in Qatar include requiring all civil society organisations (CSOs) to be approved by the Ministry of Social Affairs, which has full discretion to grant or refuse a licence, and requiring CSOs to pay exorbitant registration fees and annual fees to the state (State of Qatar 2004). In addition to being prohibited from establishing a civil society organisation independent of the state, Qatari law prohibits CSOs from partnering with any foreign organisations without approval of the Minister of Social Affairs (State of Qatar 2004, Article 31). The minister also has the legal power to dissolve any association that engages in 'political matters' (State of Qatar 2004, Article 35). These restrictions have limited the development of a formal 'civil society' in Qatar and have resulted in existing civil society organisations being aligned closely with the interests and agendas of the state. For example, women's organisations in Qatar are often focused almost exclusively on 'professional development' and explicitly aim to contribute to the state's gendered agendas, particularly that of increasing the number of Qatari women in the workforce so as to fulfil its workforce nationalisation goals (Qatar Businesswomen Association 2019).

Media censorship in Qatar has included both blocking access to digital sites and censoring content in printed newspapers. The legal basis of the state's arbitrary forms of censorship is found in its press and media laws, which intentionally utilise broad and vague language that allows the state full discretion in determining what constitutes a violation and allows punishment of anything opposed to state interests. While Qatar has a so-called 'independent' judiciary, the Emir appoints all members of the judiciary, and there is little separation between the power of the ruling family and the judiciary. Qatar's Publications and Publishing Law of 1979 (State of Qatar 1979, Article 47) prohibits criticism of the Emir and includes a number of broad publishing restrictions characterised by ambiguous language, such as the prohibition on publishing 'any instigation for the overthrow of the system of governance, insult to such regime or damage to the superior interests of the State' and 'any material that could endanger the internal and external security of the State, including any propaganda to adopt any destructive principles'. The law also prohibits editors-in-chief from publishing anything that the Minister of Information requests they do not publish.

As is evidenced by the state's repressive restrictions on civil society organising and publishing in the nation, Qatar's use of authoritarian measures is aimed at controlling the production of political discourses and narratives and eliminating any potential threats to its own political and social power. Civil society restrictions deny legitimacy to groups perceived as challenging the state's positions or seeking to implement political or social changes, and public media laws and forms of censorship prevent views that are not aligned with the state's positions from spreading to domestic and international audiences. At the same time, it is important to note that Qatar's efforts to prevent resistance from taking root on a domestic level have also included measures to appease social actors, and the state's implementation of restrictive authoritarian measures has paradoxically been accompanied by moves towards democratisation. The efficacy of Qatar's authoritarian methods and preventative approach to social and political resistance require a level of co-operation from Qatar's population and a willingness to accept certain limitations on their personal freedoms without resistance, which has led the state to balance repression with reform throughout its history.

Cihat Battaloğlu (2018, p. 2) makes a convincing argument that Qatar's political system cannot be classified as authoritarian or democratic, but instead should be classified as remaining in a political 'Grey Zone' between authoritarianism and democracy. He contends that, while Qatar has 'managed to meet the minimum criteria of the transition process by electoral politics and constitutional reforms, along with new political rights', and has 'slightly begun to move away from authoritarianism', it has ultimately 'proved unachievable' for the country to fully actualise or implement a democratic political system (Battaloğlu 2018, p. 2). The beginning of Qatar's political reform process is often marked by the bloodless coup of 1995, during which Sheikh Hamad bin Khalifa Al-Thani replaced his father, Sheikh Khalifa Al-Thani, as ruling Emir of Qatar. Under Sheikh Hamad's rule, which lasted until 2013, notable democratic reforms included granting women the right to vote and run for seats in the Municipal Council in 1995, holding Municipal elections in 1999, and proposing to elect a new Advisory council (*Majilis Al-Shura*). Other reforms included abolishing the Ministry of Information and its censorship office in 1998 to allow greater freedom of expression, establishing a Judicial Council in 1999 to increase judicial independence, and adopting a new Permanent Constitution in 2005.

The pattern of Qatar's political history since 1995 has been characterised by the balanced use of authoritarian measures and democratic reforms in an effort to maintain social stability, consolidate the power and rule of the ruling family, and bolster international credibility. While initial reforms under Sheikh Hamad's rule were interpreted on a domestic and international level as evidence that Qatar was moving away 'from autocratic, one-man rule to a democratic liberal government', moves towards democratisation slowed after 2005, and many initial reforms have not been fully implemented or implemented at all (Yetim 2014, p. 393). For example, while the Qatari constitution recognises women as equal citizens under the law and prohibits discrimination on the basis of gender, women still face a number of restrictions under Qatari laws and policies. Family law requires Qatari women to obtain permission from their guardians to get married, and policies of the Interior Ministry require unmarried Qatari women under 25 to obtain guardian permission to travel abroad (Aldosari 2016). While a married Qatari woman is not required to obtain permission from a guardian to travel, husbands can prevent their wives from travelling by appearing before a court. Qatari women may also be denied marital support if they work or travel without permission from their husbands. Moreover, as discussed above, while the constitution guarantees freedom of expression, freedom of the press and freedom of assembly, top-down restrictions on civil society organising and media censorship and press laws have prevented these from being fully realised. Thus, despite moves towards democratisation, the Qatari state has continued to engage in authoritarian measures that restrict democratic freedoms and has been unwilling or unable to fully implement a democratic political system.

Furthermore, Qatar's governing style and economic and political structures of state patronage have played an important role in preventing social or political resistance among the national population. The regime's control over most of the nation's wealth, namely through public ownership of most of the oil and gas industries and a system of state patronage in which the benefits of oil wealth are distributed by the state to its citizens, have resulted in a lack of separation between the interests of the state and the private interests of the ruling family (Battaloğlu 2018, pp. 74–5). The ruling family also maintains unchecked decision-making power, and there is a lack of accountability for rulers. The extent to which the state has made a bargain with its citizens in the form of an exchange of oil wealth benefits for loyalty is often debated. While scholars have debunked reductionistic views of the Gulf countries solely as rentier states that buy citizen loyalty (Yamada and Hertog 2020), it is nonetheless important to recognise the role of state patronage in preventing dissent or resistance and maintaining social stability. The continued influence of tribal affiliation and tribal-based systems of rule in determining socio-economic and political status also plays an important role in consolidating the power of the ruling family and legitimising their rule. By and large, the ruling family is recognised as a legitimate authority by the Qatari population, and the distribution of welfare benefits has, to some extent, disincentivised Qataris from engaging in dissent or upsetting the status quo.

Qatar's economic and political system has deeply shaped the authoritarian strategies Qatari rulers have chosen to adopt (and those they have not) and has played a role itself in preventing political or social dissent in the nation. The state's balancing of authoritarian measures with democratic reforms alongside the distribution of economic benefits since 1995 is, in many ways, aimed at maintaining the status quo, or the relative social stability and ruling legitimacy that has been enjoyed by the ruling family. The state's measured use of authoritarianism thus reflects its efforts to consolidate its power without stirring up social unrest, as Qatari rulers aim to eliminate potential pathways to dissent and to identify and prevent threats to their political power and legitimacy from manifesting in the form of social or political resistance.

While the political system of state patronage may incentivise loyalty to the government to some extent among Qatari citizens by providing economic stability and even wealth, the situation of non-nationals is often radically different. In fact, Qatar's use of authoritarian methods has taken on a completely different form in relation to the state's migrant population. Expatriates compose the majority of Qatar's population and 95 per cent of the workforce (Human Rights Watch 2019b). The expat population mainly comprises Western business professionals seeking to profit from lucrative professional opportunities in industries like oil and gas, cultural heritage and academia, and low-wage migrant workers (often of South Asian origin), who commonly work in industries like construction and food services. With Qataris representing a minority of the population (about 11 per cent) (Snoj 2019), the nation's large expatriate population has been viewed by the state since its founding as a cultural and political threat, and Qataris themselves have expressed concerns about a loss of cultural identity in the wake of an increasingly large expat population (Liloia 2019). A document issued by the state in 2014 (Qatar Ministry of Development, Planning and Statistics 2014, p. 10) lists several risks which stem from continued increases in the expat population, including the fact that 'some Qataris may feel crowded out of services' and the 'potential for traditional Qatari Arab and Islamic cultural values and identity to be diluted'.

In pursuit of its economic and social agendas, the latter of which includes constructing a unifying national and cultural identity and maintaining social stability among the country's national population, the Qatari state has imposed a discriminatory legal system, characterised by racialised and class-based capitalist structures imported from the West, on the country's population of migrant workers. Commonly referred to as the *kafala* system, the system of laws and policies determining the rights, or lack thereof, of migrant workers has afforded migrant workers a temporary legal status and lack of recourse for violations of their rights. Keeping migrant workers in a state of 'permanent temporariness' serves to prevent them from fully participating in society or accessing the legal, economic and political benefits of citizenship

(Vora 2013; Ahmad 2017; Lori 2019). The exclusion and marginalisation of migrant workers are also intended to prevent a labour or resistance movement from taking root among Qatar's migrant population. Considering the fact there are more than 2 million migrant workers in Qatar out of a population of about 2.6 million (Cousins 2020), widespread resistance among the migrant population could certainly pose a threat to the state's social stability. However, due to a lack of socio-economic privilege, a temporary legal status and continued legal discrimination, migrant workers remain in a precarious position in which resistance could lead to a loss of income, deportation, or other legal consequences.

The precarious situation of migrant workers in the Gulf is not wholly different from that of informal, temporary or hourly low-wage workers in seemingly 'democratic' Western nations like the United States, the UK and Canada, raising questions about the negative impacts of capitalist structures worldwide and the relationship between global capitalism and authoritarianism. Moreover, migrant workers' socio-economic marginalisation and exclusion mirrors that inflicted historically and currently on racial minorities in the United States and constitutes a form of authoritarian discipline and control not exclusive to non-Western contexts. In fact, the racialised and class-based labour systems found in the Gulf are modelled closely after those of Western nations and were imported largely by Western corporations (Hanieh 2011). For example, it was Western oil companies that implemented segregated housing schemes and paternalistic welfare programmes in Gulf oil towns in the twentieth century (Vitalis 2006; Alissa 2013; Fuccaro 2013).

Qatar's development of preventative authoritarian measures and the preservation of socio-economic and political structures that incentivise loyalty to the Qatari government have played an important role in maintaining social stability throughout the nation's history and preventing resistance movements from taking root. In the wake of the 2011 uprisings, Qatar has continued to limit the development of an active civil society and engage in traditional methods of censorship, while also implementing new authoritarian practices in an effort to prevent its own 'Arab Spring' from occurring and to craft a progressive national narrative for international consumption. The next section analyses Qatar's development of new authoritarian practices in a post-2011 context, focusing on the state's digital authoritarian strategies and new media laws and policies.

New Authoritarian Methods

What is particularly interesting about Qatar's approach to authoritarianism in a post-2011 context is the moderated nature of its approach in comparison to other Arab regimes, such as Egypt, the UAE and Saudi Arabia. In a form of what scholars have dubbed authoritarian learning (Heydemann and Leenders 2011; Hall and Ambrosio 2017), Qatari rulers adopted similar tactics to those utilised by other Arab regimes to quash dissent in the wake of the 2011 Arab uprisings towards the aim of preventing a similar resistance movement from occurring in Qatar. Such tactics included the arrests of prominent activists and journalists, media censorship and legislation and social media surveillance. Yet, the number of arrests and the length of imprisonment for most activists or journalists in Qatar pale in comparison to those in countries like Saudi Arabia, Egypt and Bahrain, and media censorship appears somewhat less extreme than in neighbouring Gulf states like the UAE and Saudi Arabia, with the allowance of a greater degree of measured criticism of the Qatari state in certain publications. This is likely due to Qatar's goal of maintaining a positive reputation in the international sphere and avoiding the criticism of human rights abuses continually levelled at nations like Saudi Arabia in international media and by international human rights organisations. In order to craft a positive and progressive national narrative for international consumption and distinguish itself from other 'autocratic' Arab regimes while also maintaining control over domestic political discourses, the Qatari state measures the perceived benefits of censorship and other authoritarian measures against their potential consequences and engages in performative measures to bolster its international reputation.

Performative shifts in the state's treatment of migrant workers since 2011 are a prime example of Qatari rulers' efforts to peddle a progressive narrative to the international community. The economic marginalisation of migrant workers, alongside impoverished and inhumane working and housing conditions, has attracted harsh criticism from the international human rights community, particularly in light of the exploitation of migrant workers in the construction of the 2022 World Cup stadiums. As a result, the state has strategically balanced the preservation of discriminatory laws and policies with performative reforms of the migrant labour system. In 2017, the Qatari state entered a co-operation programme with the International Labor Organization aimed at reforming the *kafala* system, and has gradually introduced reforms since then, including new protections for domestic workers and the introduction of a minimum wage (Human Rights Watch 2019a). In 2019, the Qatari government responded to a strike among migrant workers working on the construction of the World Cup stadiums with promises of further reform (Ghani 2019). More reforms were implemented in 2020, including abolishing the requirement of employer permission to change jobs (Human Rights Watch 2020). However, employers are still responsible for processing migrant workers' visas and employment authorisation and can report their employees for 'absconding'. Moreover, Qatar's National Human Rights Committee remains responsible for investigations of human rights abuses and is made up of government-appointed members, leading to a lack of accountability for the government in protecting migrant workers' rights. The reforms implemented appear to be largely performative, as there remains a lack of effective legal and political structures and processes for ensuring the rights of the migrant population.

Ironically, the Qatari state's attempts to brand itself as a progressive nation with a commitment to hegemonic Western paradigms of human rights have also led to the development of new authoritarian measures.[4] Particularly since the uprisings of 2011, the Qatari state has enacted new authoritarian measures in the digital sphere in an effort to control the narratives disseminated to domestic and international audiences and the political discourses of social actors. These have included censorship of digital content, surveillance of social media, and new media laws and policies. State ownership of the country's sole internet provider, Qtel, allows the state to engage in arbitrary censorship of digital content and websites. The state's censorship of media content has inevitably resulted in an environment of self-censorship, where journalists are careful not to publish material that would be deemed inappropriate or controversial by the state. The fear of having material blocked and losing the ability to publish is often enough to prevent material that elevates opinions opposed to those of the state from being published in the first place.

As scholars have argued in reference to digital authoritarianism, technology can simultaneously function as 'a tool of both empowerment and control' (Jones 2015, p. 2,014) with the digital sphere functioning as both a space for regimes to expand their repressive measures and a space for social resistance and activism (MacKinnon 2011; Jones 2015). However, those who choose to use social media as a tool of resistance often do so at a high cost, as governments surveil and jail those who are viewed as a threat to their power

(MacKinnon 2011, p. 33; Jones 2015, p. 257). Marc Owen Jones (2015, pp. 260–1) argues that government surveillance on social media platforms and a fear of being watched has led to a breakdown of trust among social actors, who fear the government's repression and sometimes each other. In the case of Qatar, the breakdown of trust between the state and social actors is central to the state's effective implementation of digital authoritarian methods, as a fear of retaliation causes social actors, media organisations and journalists to engage in self-censorship. This allows the state to exercise a level of control over the spread of information within and outside of Qatar and effectively diminish its own role in directly censoring content, while continuing to peddle a progressive narrative of the state to domestic and international audiences.

In addition to utilising digital media censorship and surveillance to discipline social actors into self-censorship, the state's arrest of journalists and activists for publishing or voicing sensitive opinions has exacerbated individuals and organisations' fears of publishing anything that does not align with the state's positions or even posting it on social media. Qatari state arrests since 2011 have included bloggers, human rights activists and journalists (Gulf Centre for Human Rights 2016). In 2011, the blogger Sultan al-Khalaifi was arrested and detained for about a month, probably, and ironically, for his blogs criticising media censorship by the Qatari state. In 2012, the prominent poet Mohamed Rashid Al-Ajami was sentenced to life in prison for 'inciting to overthrow the ruling regime' and 'insulting the Emir', though he was released in 2016 (World Alliance for Citizen Participation and Gulf Center for Human Rights 2013, p. 5). In 2013, two Qatari activists, Muhammad Issa Al-Baker and Mansour bin Rashed Al-Matroushi, were arrested and detained for less than a month for sending a 'threatening' letter to the French embassy in Doha to criticise the country's planned military intervention in Mali. Other arrests included that of Krishna Upadhyaya and Gundev Ghimire in 2014, two British human rights researchers investigating the conditions of migrant workers working on the construction of the stadiums for the World Cup 2022, and a BBC journalist team in 2015 investigating the same topic (Lobel 2015). The researchers were only detained for nine days, and the BBC team for two nights. The Qatari state's arrests are strategic in the sense that they 'make an example' of a small and select number of journalists and activists to instil fear in others and prevent them from publicly voicing or publishing their dissenting opinions or criticisms of the Qatari government. This contributes to producing an environment of self-censorship and is intended to ensure the state maintains control over the flow of information within and outside of the state.

Qatari media censorship has also reflected strategies to control national political narratives and present a progressive image of the state to the international community, which include balancing media censorship with the allowance of a certain level of media coverage questioning or criticising the Qatari government. The Qatari state strategically allows a certain level of criticism of Qatari government policies, particularly in English-language news coverage, to contribute to the construction of a progressive image of the nation as valuing freedom of expression. A report by The Gulf Centre for Human Rights (2016, p. 11) on civil society restriction in Qatar notes that, while the English-language press has covered certain human rights issues and criticised Qatari policy without consequence, Arabic-language coverage has largely stayed away from criticism of the state for fear of censorship and backlash, though it is unclear if this is due to 'direct pressure from the authorities or the business interests of newspaper owners'.

The state-owned media network *Al Jazeera* has played a key role in the state's branding efforts in the aftermath of the 2011 uprisings. Balancing criticism of 'autocratic' regimes with careful criticism of Qatari policies and other areas of public contention, *Al Jazeera*'s media coverage has aided and continues to aid in crafting the state's desired image, particularly as a nation with an active civil society and a commitment to free speech and expression. Though the state-owned mass media network reportedly operates independently from the Qatari government, its content often aligns closely with state policies and hegemonic narratives produced by the state, and criticism of the state remains limited and cautious. The state's efforts to craft a progressive image of the nation as valuing free speech also included a 2012 draft law approved by the Advisory Council that would prohibit criminal penalties for press offences, including criticism of Qatari rulers, though it retained financial penalties for publishing or broadcasting material that could 'throw relations between the state and the Arab and friendly states into confusion' or 'abuse the regime or offend the ruling family or cause serious harm to the national or higher interests of the state' (Human Rights Watch 2012). The law appears to be another case of performative commitment to change without actual implementation, as it has yet to take effect.

Despite the apparent disparity in the content of English and Arabic-language reporting and the state's limited allowance of political criticism in English-language coverage, it is evident that both remain subject to state censorship. There are lines that journalists and media organisations cannot cross without consequence. One illustration of this unfortunate reality was the shutdown of the online English-language media outlet *Doha News* by Qatari state security forces in November of 2016, lasting until 2020 (Wazir 2016). The daily news website was not a surprising target for state censorship, as it had often provided coverage of human rights issues and other controversies not normally found in the state-run media. Speculation as to what triggered the shutdown identified the publication of an article in the summer of 2016 by an anonymous Qatari man who wrote about the struggles of living as a gay man in Qatar. Since its reopening in 2020, *Doha News* continues to compete with outlets with closer ties to the state like *Al Jazeera* and the *New Arab/Al Araby Al Jadeed*.

In addition to existing laws, Qatar has implemented new media laws in recent years, including a cybercrime law issued in 2014 and a security amendment issued in 2020. The recent development of cybercrime legislation is not unique to Qatar, but rather is part of a trend throughout the Middle East since the uprisings of 2011 (Hakmeh 2018). In an effort to prevent online activism, Arab states have implemented or updated their cybercrime legislation to build a stronger basis for repressing dissent in the digital sphere. All the GCC countries, along with Egypt, Tunisia, Jordan and others, have implemented or updated their cybercrime laws since 2011. While the Council of Europe Convention on Cybercrime (or the Budapest Convention) laid out a means of classifying what constitutes a cybercrime in 2001, the GCC states were not party to the convention and have adopted a different approach in their own legislation, characterized by broad provisions that 'criminalize a wide spectrum of content' (Hakmeh 2018, p. 11).

Qatar's new cybercrime legislation is no exception. Rather, the Cybercrime Prevention Law issued in 2014 criminalises the spread of 'false news', for which it provides a broadened and ambiguous definition encompassing anything that could threaten the 'safety' of the country or 'undermine' Qatar's 'social values' or 'general order' (State of Qatar 2014). Furthermore, the state issued a security amendment to the state's penal code in 2020 focused on 'false news', stipulating a penalty of imprisonment for up to five years, a fine of up to 100,000 riyals, or both for broadcasting, publishing or re-publishing 'rumors, statements, false or malicious news or propaganda, at home or abroad, with the intention of harming national interests, provoking public opinion, or violating the social system or public order of the state' (Gulf Centre for Human Rights 2020). A more severe version of the amendment was published in the newspaper *Al-Raya* prior to the amendment's official release, but the newspaper issued an apology after intense social backlash against the law, saying it had been obtained from 'unofficial sources', leading to speculation that the government amended the law in response to the backlash.

The broad and ambiguous language of Qatar's new media laws allows for prosecution of nearly anything deemed a threat to state interests. This is intended to instil fear just as much as, if not more than, it is intended to lead to actual prosecutions. These cybercrime laws serve the purpose of providing a legal basis for punishment of dissenting opinions in the cybersphere as well as that of reminding the population of Qatar that they are being watched and could be punished if they publicly voice their criticism of the government. The vague and ambiguous language is not only a legal tactic; it is a fear tactic. Shutting down social media accounts of those who speak out on contentious issues is another tactic that has been utilised by the Qatari government, which was seen in 2019 when the police allegedly called the women running a Twitter account named 'Qatari Feminists' for starting a social media campaign about feminist issues in Qatar and told them to shut down the account (Al Bawaba 2019). They willingly complied. The fear of being watched is a very real fear, and new cybercrime laws intend to leverage that fear to increase self-censorship and prevent dissenting views from gaining public traction. Social actors, journalists and media organisations are forced to evaluate what they can get away with and what they cannot, and to determine whether publishing or posting opinions or information that does not align with the state's positions or representations is worth the potential risks, which include legal and professional consequences. Additionally, the imprisonment of activists and journalists who engage in activities deemed a threat to the state, and the censorship of content that does not align with state narratives, serves as a warning of the reality of these consequences.

Producing an environment of self-censorship serves the state's agenda extremely well, because it allows the state to avoid repressive disciplinary measures and international criticism while maintaining a level of control over the national narratives produced and disseminated at home and abroad. The ultimate goal for Qatari rulers is not to need to imprison or censor anyone because everyone is censoring themselves, allowing Qatar to tout freedom of expression and human rights while continuing to passively restrict national political discourses and dissenting voices. Beyond fostering an environment of self-censorship to diminish the state's role in censoring content, the Qatari state incentivises performative loyalty to itself by granting benefits to those who tout the state's agendas, which include professional opportunities and lucrative positions, civil society licences for organisations, and state funding for various academic and professional projects. This results in social actors and organisations not only censoring themselves, but also playing a central role in the production of state propaganda.

Western academics and journalists residing in Qatar provide a prime example of this phenomenon. The fact that academics often write for publications owned by the state or accept grant money from the Qatari government or government-affiliated institutions to conduct their research results in the continued production of scholarship and popular media content that reinforces Qatari state narratives and agendas. While some may be found on Twitter boldly professing their criticisms, many continue to self-censor and carefully curate their content on social media and in their journalistic and academic publications. As a Western scholar who plans to conduct fieldwork in Qatar in the future, I myself questioned whether or not writing this chapter could have negative professional consequences for me and weighed the benefits against the potential risks. For many, self-censorship is not only a necessary means of professional survival; it is an appealing pathway to professional success.

Conclusion

As this chapter has demonstrated, Qatar has strategically implemented new authoritarian practices, particularly new forms of media censorship and control in the digital sphere, to foster an environment of self-censorship among journalists, individuals and organisations. These practices aim to contribute to the state's political and social agendas, namely crafting a progressive national narrative for domestic and international consumption, maintaining control over the parameters of national political discourse, and preventing dissenting views and opinions from gaining traction. Ironically, Qatar's implementation of authoritarian measures in the digital sphere and beyond is aimed primarily at prevention so that the state will not find it necessary to engage in more repressive authoritarian measures to quash resistance or dissent. Learning from the example of other regimes during the Arab uprising, the Qatari state aims to prevent an uprising from taking root in the first place and to maintain a progressive image in the eyes of international actors by striking a balance between implementing authoritarian restrictions and granting democratic freedoms. In other words, the state is continually grappling with the question of how much freedom is enough freedom to appease the domestic population and the international community without threatening the power or rule of the Qatari state.

Furthermore, while the Qatari state strategically censors the outgoing and incoming flow of information in the digital sphere, it remains unable, and to some extent unwilling, to fully control public discourses. There are limits to what the state will do, as it continues to weigh the benefits of censorship against those of appeasing its national citizens and constructing a progressive national narrative. There are also limits to what the state can do, at least reasonably, as public dialogue continues and connections continue to be forged and information shared in the digital sphere across transnational borders in spite of the state's censorship efforts. In addition, it is important to note that even those working under the auspices of state-sanctioned organising have found ways to push the boundaries of the dominant political discourse and the state's top-down narratives. For example, in the form of women's business organisations like the Qatar Businesswomen Association (QBWA), and even student-run clubs like the 'Future Is Female' organisation at Georgetown University Qatar, Qatari women have begun to push the boundaries of state narratives on 'women's empowerment' and elevate more progressive interpretations of women's rights in their own public discourses and organising activities, and have forged connections with international feminist movements and organisations.

The case of authoritarianism in Qatar thus raises important questions about the limits of state-imposed media censorship and the extent to which states can discipline us into censoring ourselves. To what extent does being watched and surveilled, at the threat of personal and professional consequence, cause us to implement forms of discipline and control on ourselves, and what remains outside of the state's control? Moving forward, scholarship on authoritarianism in the Middle East must grapple with these questions, allowing for a critical analysis cognisant of the complexities of authoritarianism and censorship in an increasingly digitised world.

Notes

1 Many other contributions in this book discuss governmental attempts to construct and control media narratives. See, for instance, Morocco (Maghraoui 2022), Jordan (Ryan 2022), Turkey (Topak 2022) and the UAE (Davidson 2022).

2 Cf. particularly other Gulf states examined in this book: Saudi Arabia (Uniacke 2022), the UAE (Davidson 2022) and Bahrain (Shebabi 2022).

3 On the different forms of continuities beween old and new authoritiarian practices, see the 'Established Authoritarian Practices' section in the Introduction, which provides an overview of key examples from the book chapters (Topak et al. 2022).

4 For another example in the region, see Israel (Dayan 2022) in this book.

References

Ahmad, A. (2017). *Everyday Conversions: Islam, Domestic Work, and South Asian Migrant Women in Kuwait*. Durham, NC: Duke University Press.

Al Bawaba (2019). 'Did Qatar Govt. Force Feminists to Close Their Accounts on Twitter?', *Al Bawaba*, 8 August. https://www.albawaba.com/node/did-qatar-clo se-accounts-feminists-twitter-1302206

Aldosari, H. (2016). 'The Personal is Political: Gender Identity in the Personal Status Laws of the Gulf Arab States', The Arab Gulf States Institute Washington. http://www.agsiw.org/wp-content/uploads/2016/08/Aldosari_ONLINE_upda ted.pdf

Alissa, R. (2013). 'The Oil Town of Ahmadi since 1946: From Colonial Town to Nostalgic City', *Comparative Studies of South Asia, Africa and the Middle East* 33(1): 41–58.

Battaloğlu, C. (2018). *Political Reforms in Qatar: From Authoritarianism to Political Grey Zone*. Berlin: Gerlach Press.

Cousins, S. (2020). 'Migrant Workers Can't Afford a Lockdown', *Foreign Policy*, 8 August. https://foreignpolicy.com/2020/04/08/qatar-south-asian-migrant-wor kers-cant-afford-coronavirus-lockdown-world-cup-2022/

Davidson, C. M. (2022). 'The United Arab Emirates: Evolving Authoritarian Tools', in Ö. E. Topak, M. Mekouar and F. Cavatorta (eds) *New Authoritarian Practices in the Middle East and North Africa*. Edinburgh: Edinburgh University Press, pp. 320–39.

Fuccaro, N. (2013). 'Shaping the Urban Life of Oil in Bahrain: Consumerism, Leisure, and Public Communication in Manama and in the Oil Camps, 1932–1960s', *Comparative Studies of South Asia, Africa and the Middle East* 33(1): 59–74.

Ghani, F. (2019). 'Renewed Calls for Qatar to Address Treatment of Migrant Workers', *Al Jazeera*. https://www.aljazeera.com/features/2019/9/19/renewed-c alls-for-qatar-to-address-treatment-of-migrant-workers

Gulf Centre for Human Rights (2016). 'Qatar, Civil Society and Human Rights: Lack of Civil Society Space Hinders Work of Human Rights Defenders', May. http://www.gc4hr.org/report/view/39

Gulf Centre for Human Rights (2020). 'Qatar: Serious Fears for Freedom of Expression after Amendments to Penal Code Published', 21 January. https:// www.gc4hr.org/news/view/2309

Hakmeh, J. (2018). 'Cybercrime Legislation in the GCC Countries', *Chatham House – International Affairs Think Tank*, 4 July. https://www.chathamhouse.org/2018 /07/cybercrime-legislation-gcc-countries

Hall, S. G. F. and T. Ambrosio (2017). 'Authoritarian Learning: A Conceptual Overview', *East European Politics* 33(2): 143–61.

Hanieh, A. (2011). *Capitalism and Class in the Gulf Arab States*. New York: Palgrave Macmillan.

Heydemann, S. and R. Leenders (2011). 'Authoritarian Learning and Authoritarian Resilience: Regime Responses to the 2Arab Awakening', *Globalizations* 8(5): 647–53.

Human Rights Watch (2012). 'Qatar: Revise Draft Media Law to Allow Criticism of Rulers', *Human Rights Watch*, 30 October. https://www.hrw.org/news/2012/10 /30/qatar-revise-draft-media-law-allow-criticism-rulers

Human Rights Watch (2019a). 'Qatar: Migrant Workers Strike over Work Conditions', *Human Rights Watch*. https://www.hrw.org/news/2019/08/08/qa tar-migrant-workers-strike-over-work-conditions

Human Rights Watch (2019b). 'World Report 2019: Rights Trends in Qatar', *Human Rights Watch*, 17 January. https://www.hrw.org/world-report/2019/co untry-chapters/qatar

Human Rights Watch (2020). 'Qatar: Significant Labor and Kafala Reforms', *Human Rights Watch*. https://www.hrw.org/news/2020/09/24/qatar-significant -labor-and-kafala-reforms

Jones, M. O. (2015). 'Social Media, Surveillance, and Cyberpolitics in the Bahrain Uprising', in A. Shehabi and M. O. Jones (eds) *Bahrain's Uprising: Resistance and Repression in the Gulf*. London: Zed Books, pp. 239–62.

Liloia, A. (2019). 'Gender and Nation Building in Qatar: Qatari Women Negotiate Modernity', *Journal of Middle East Women's Studies* 15(3): 344–66.

Lobel, M. (2015). 'Arrested for Reporting on Qatar's World Cup Labourers', *BBC News*, 18 May. https://www.bbc.com/news/world-middle-east-32775563

Lori, N. (2019). *Offshore Citizens*. Cambridge: Cambridge University Press.

MacKinnon, R. (2011). 'Liberation Technology: China's "Networked Authoritarianism"', *Journal of Democracy* 22(2): 32–46.

Maghraoui, D. (2022). '"The Freedom of No Speech": Journalists and the Multiple Layers of Authoritarian Practices in Morocco', in Ö. E. Topak, M. Mekouar and F. Cavatorta (eds) *New Authoritarian Practices in the Middle East and North Africa*. Edinburgh: Edinburgh University Press, pp. 189–207.

Qatar Businesswomen Association (2019). *Qatar Businesswomen Association – About Us*. https://qbwa.qa/

Qatar Ministry of Development, Planning and Statistics (2014). 'National Development Planning and Implementation: Human Development, Sustainable Development and National Well-being'. http://www.un.org/en/ecosoc/newfun ct/pdf14/qatar_nr.pdf

Ryan, C. (2022). 'Jordan: A Perpetually Liberalizing Autocracy', in Ö. E. Topak, M. Mekouar and F. Cavatorta (eds) *New Authoritarian Practices in the Middle East and North Africa*. Edinburgh: Edinburgh University Press, pp. 152–70.

Shehabi, A. (2022). 'The Authoritarian Topography of the Bahraini State: Political Geographies of Power And Protest', in Ö. E. Topak, M. Mekouar and F. Cavatorta (eds) *New Authoritarian Practices in the Middle East and North Africa*. Edinburgh: Edinburgh University Press, pp. 51–72.

Snoj, J. (2019). 'Population of Qatar by Nationality in 2019', *Priya DSouza Communications*, 15 August. https://priyadsouza.com/population-of-qatar-by -nationality-in-2017/

State of Qatar (1979). 'Law No. 8 of 1979 on Publications and Publishing'. https:// www.almeezan.qa/LawView.aspx?opt&LawID=414&language=en

State of Qatar (2004). 'Law No. 12 of 2004 on Private Associations and Foundations'. https://www.almeezan.qa/LawView.aspx?opt&LawID=3956&language=en

State of Qatar (2014). 'Qatar – Law No. 14 of 2014 Promulgating the Cybercrime Prevention Law'. https://www.ilo.org/dyn/natlex/natlex4.detail?p_lang=en&p _isn=100242

Topak, Ö. E. (2022). 'An Assemblage of New Authoritarian Practices in Turkey', in Ö. E. Topak, M. Mekouar and F. Cavatorta (eds) *New Authoritarian Practices in the Middle East and North Africa*. Edinburgh: Edinburgh University Press, pp. 296–319.

Topak, Ö. E., M. Mekouar and F. Cavatorta (2022). 'Introduction', in Ö. E. Topak, M. Mekouar and F. Cavatorta (eds) *New Authoritarian Practices in the Middle East and North Africa*. Edinburgh: Edinburgh University Press, pp. 1–29.

Uniacke, R. (2022). 'Digital Repression for Authoritarian Evolution in Saudi Arabia', in Ö. E. Topak, M. Mekouar and F. Cavatorta (eds) *New Authoritarian Practices in the Middle East and North Africa*. Edinburgh: Edinburgh University Press, pp. 228–51.

Vitalis, R. (2006). *America's Kingdom: Mythmaking on the Saudi Oil Frontier*. Stanford, CA: Stanford University Press.

Vora, N. (2013). *Impossible Citizens: Dubai's Indian Diaspora*. Durham, NC and London: Duke University Press.

Wazir, B. (2016). 'Mysterious Shutdown Plagues Popular News Site in Qatar', *Columbia Journalism Review*, 9 December. https://www.cjr.org/watchdog/doha_news_censorship_journalism.php

World Alliance for Citizen Participation and Gulf Center for Human Rights (2013). 'The State of Qatar Submission to the UN Universal Periodic Review 19th Session of the UPR Working Group'.

Yamada, M. and S. Hertog (2020). 'Introduction: Revisiting Rentierism – With a Short Note by Giacomo Luciani', *British Journal of Middle Eastern Studies* 47(1): 1–5.

Yetim, M. (2014). 'State-led Change in Qatar in the Wake of Arab Spring: Monarchical Country, Democratic Stance?', *Contemporary Review of the Middle East* 1(4): 391–410.

12

DIGITAL REPRESSION FOR AUTHORITARIAN EVOLUTION IN SAUDI ARABIA

Robert Uniacke

Introduction

In February 2013, the Saudi Minister of Culture and Information Abdulaziz Khoja admitted to the Saudi daily *Al Watan* that the authorities were struggling to cope with the Kingdom's surging use of Twitter (*Albawaba* 2013). The platform was booming, growing by up to 600 per cent per year according to some reports and challenging the authorities' ability to censor and block content (GSN 2012a). Like those who hailed the liberating potential of social media during the 2011 Arab uprisings, some labelled Twitter as a new Saudi parliament: a watershed moment in a tightly-controlled political system centred on the ruling Al Saud family (Worth 2012).

In the years that followed, however, the world watched as the Kingdom turned the tides on this trend, transforming Saudi Twitter into a platform populated by pro-regime influencers and automated 'bots' creating the illusion of popular regime support. The rise to de facto power of Crown Prince Mohammed bin Salman (MbS) has tightened authoritarian rule and sparked scandals on a global level – not least the high-profile murder of dissident Jamal Khashoggi. Mass arrests have targeted princes, intellectuals, clerics, merchants and activists amid unprecedentedly pervasive surveillance, as authorities search for current or potential dissenters who may challenge MbS's hold on power (GSN 2021a). Saudi Arabia may have been an authoritarian state since its inception in 1932, but there are new dynamics at play in this personalised centralisation of power under MbS, as well as in the repressive practices used to maintain it.

What accounts for this rapid evolution of authoritarian rule in Saudi Arabia? The chapter aims to show that mounting repression and digital surveillance are bound up with MbS's attempts to transform the Kingdom into a global technology hub. As the regime conducts tactical social and economic liberalisation to rebrand the Kingdom and draw in international investment, it perceives internal threats: from immediate political opponents (including conservatives, liberals and sidelined royal family elements) to the more long-term evolution of that liberalisation into political demands from the populace. In response, MbS is transforming Saudi Arabia into a new kind of authoritarian state in which conformity and loyalty to his vision is expected, enforced and engineered through the abundance of data on citizens derived from high levels of communication technology use. To do this, he seeks to situate Saudi Arabia squarely within global technological trends rather than on their peripheries, binding the Kingdom to the latest possibilities and tools in repressive practice and thereby allowing it to form its own kind of digital authoritarianism that fits its 'security' needs while reaping the economic benefits. As such, in Saudi Arabia the transnational technology economy, from quasi-state Chinese companies to Israeli spyware firms to US multinationals, is helping to facilitate the evolution of an authoritarian regime from one of royal consensus to one of personalised, centralised authority.

The chapter begins with an overview of the mechanics of contemporary Saudi authoritarianism, with a focus on the rise of MbS. It then turns to the global trends in information technology harnessed by MbS to help consolidate his rule, situating Saudi Arabia in the context of repressive opportunities like big data-enabled authoritarianism and surveillance tools. It then considers three broad case studies of how these authoritarian practices are manifesting in the Kingdom today: data localisation, spyware and social media weaponisation. To conclude, it considers the implications of the above for our understanding of contemporary authoritarianism in an Arab monarchic system like Saudi Arabia. The intended contribution aims to consider the implications of contemporary repressive practice in Saudi Arabia, as unveiled by journalist- and civil society-led investigations, for academic understandings of authoritarian rule. It also hopes to shed light on some of the emerging research in the field.

Saudi Authoritarian Trends in Historical and Theoretical Perspective[1]

We begin from an understanding that an authoritarian regime, to borrow from Jebnoun, relies 'on restricting political participation and denying society or its representative institutions . . . the ability to protest against crucial decisions adopted by a small, restricted group' (2014: 1). This leaves little space to argue that Saudi Arabia has ever had anything but an authoritarian regime. Since 1932, Saudi state-building has focused on maintaining and enhancing the Al Saud family's position as the centrepiece of the state by institutionalising tribalism and patronage networks around the Al Saud. However, the rise of MbS has shifted our definition's variables: namely, how political participation is restricted and repressed, and who makes up the small, restricted group. In the Saudi case, the two are very much linked: from MbS's perspective, the forceful shrinking of Saudi Arabia's already narrow political sphere to allow for more efficient decision-making and comprehensive economic reform both requires and raises opportunities for new methodologies of repression. We must hence consider *why* Saudi authoritarian practice is changing, before turning to *how* it is changing.

As Al-Rasheed (2018: 2) has noted, the literature on Saudi Arabia tends to oscillate between the extremes of imminent state collapse and structural regime resilience. Arguments for the latter have generally formed around the rentier state model. However, a number of studies have sought to enhance or move beyond the rentier lens. Indeed, a survey of Saudi Arabia's historical revolutionary subversions, coup attempts, and traditions of radicalism and leftist politics during the second half of the twentieth century makes clear that that rent distribution has not secured political quiescence in the Kingdom (Okruhlik 1999; Bsheer 2018). Notably, Hertog argues that oil wealth actually increased incentives for political challengers to capture the state before the regime was ultimately able to stem much political contestation with large-scale patronage (Hertog 2018: 79). Bsheer goes further, suggesting that the Saudi regime is best understood as one of 'dominance without hegemony'; the state may be able to suppress dissent and 'to delimit the rules and boundaries of discursive and material practices', but it has simultaneously failed to capitalise on these delimitations to influence citizens for the regime's benefit, showing that the state 'struggles to fashion subjects along its evolving national ideals' (2020: 28). Bsheer also points out that, rather than being based on an exchange of oil wealth for political deference, Saudi authoritarianism has in many ways 'always been based on violence – and the extreme threat thereof – coupled with religious legitimation, in return for subordination in all realms of life: economic, political, social, and cultural' (2018). A useful framing of this concept comes from Nazih Ayubi, who has described such states as 'fierce', they being 'structurally weak and therefore [having] repeatedly to use (rather than to threaten to use) open violence and force (as well as intrigue and conspiracy) to ensure direct control and domination (and not simply hegemony)' (1995: 394).

This combination of patronage with brute force has been evident in the rise to power of MbS, who has seized the coercive apparatus of the state to transform Saudi authoritarianism from a consensus model to centralised authority. After the assassination of King Faisal in 1975, politics played out in a negotiated balance between senior royals and clerics, who themselves carved out spheres of influence binding them to certain sections of the economic elite. Seznec has conceptualised this system as the 'diamond'; each senior prince branched out and projected influence and patronage over a particular group (the civil service, the merchant class, minor princes and religious conservatives), which would in turn go to the centre of the diamond to resolve disputes and access the state (2014: 143–4). The royal family therefore acted as the ultimate arbiter between Saudi constituencies in a sprawling system that consolidated ultimate power in the hands of the Al Saud while facilitating outreach to key constituencies. It was in this way that the Al Saud co-opted and defused potential threats, effectively institutionalising corrupt practices in a symbiotic relationship between a central grouping of princes and a surrounding elite. Since 1975, then, Saudi Arabia has appeared to embody Michael Herb's (1999) assessment that a strategy of divide and rule, hinging on in-family power distribution, helps hold together a relatively stable autocratic system in the sense that quarrels are internally managed. This system also permitted a level of dissent among privileged groups – those whom the regime had an interest in co-opting – while heavily repressing those it did not, including the eastern Shia minority and women. This was the context in which figures like Jamal Khashoggi were allowed to operate.

When King Salman came to the throne in 2015, he began to accelerate a process that would dismantle this system with his son at the helm. Tumbling oil prices spurred a resolve to transform not only a system that bogged down policymaking and held back much-needed reform initiatives, but the broader society, to prepare the populace for a post-oil future with less lavish spending on the welfare state and fewer public sector jobs. The national economic strategy that followed in 2015 – Vision 2030 – would come to define MbS's ruling brand. In an interview intended to outline progress in the strategy (*Saudia* 2021), the Crown Prince explicitly linked the Vision to the need for changes in governing structure, saying that Saudi Arabia had been held back by its governmental structures; the previously weak central state was to be strengthened, with strategy, public policy and economic decision-making to be conducted at the centre.

To impose this systemic and societal change, MbS initiated a purge that would reconfigure Saudi authoritarianism from its elite-based horizontal leaning to a personalised regime built around himself (Brown 2017). In November 2017, princely opposition was neutralised and pacts with the merchant elite up-ended when nearly four hundred princes and oligarchs were rounded up in the Ritz Carlton hotel in Riyadh and beaten, blackmailed and stripped of billions of dollars for state coffers (Chulov 2020). In turn, repression of dissent from society at large also intensified. The regime's red lines for the acceptability of debate had shifted; citizens were now expected to voice loyalty to MbS and the Vision, and criticism of this new direction could be interpreted as dissent. Yet while the former 'diamond' elite were in the regime's immediate grasp, targeting transnational political dissidents, as well as the need to enforce loyalty in and defuse threats from the population, required more efficient technological methods.

Before turning to these new modes of repression, it is important to recognise that some points of authoritarian continuity defined the way in which MbS succeeded in sweeping to power. Underpinning the purge were two authoritarian tactics with precedent in the Kingdom and wider region: the rallying of ideological forces to frame the political shift as a necessity for the integrity of the nation, and the capture of the security services.

Firstly, the regime coalescing around MbS sought to monopolise Saudi identity into a nationalist, MbS-focused brand, partly to help curtail the powers of the religious establishment and partly to imbue corruption allegations with the nationalist edge of treachery against the nation. As Alhussein (2019) points out, this top-down assertion of a new nationalism to promote a new Saudi Arabia demonstrates notable continuity with historic attempts to harness ideological forces to rule the Kingdom; in the 1980s, the regime responded to the 1979 Grand Mosque siege by wholeheartedly backing an official religious establishment, to polish its religious credentials, rally grass-roots support and appeal to Saudi citizens. After this policy backfired with Jihadi Salafism turning to challenge the regime, a steady shift began to a more secular nationalism under King Abdullah (2005–15). Then, with the ascendance of King Salman and the appointment of MbS as Crown Prince, the promotion of nationalism accelerated. Nationalism in the Kingdom today is part and parcel of speeding the rise of MbS: 'it unites the population around the new leadership' and 'creates legitimacy for significant domestic reforms and regional confrontations that, in turn, further consolidate the power of the new system' (Alhussein 2019). A key indicator of this shift is seen in the lexicon of loyalty to the country: state propagandists have mostly dropped the label 'Westernisation' as an accusation of subversion against national values that reflects religiously-infused notions of cultural conquest, instead adopting the more nationalist term 'traitor' to disparage the full range of regime threats, from women's rights activists to those in the Ritz Carlton accused of corruption (Alhussein 2019). Indeed, a central feature of this rallying nationalist narrative became anti-corruption. Seen as a popular cause among Saudi youth, the anti-corruption campaign effectively turned the structural power of the old system against it in a campaign tinged with nationalistic overtones (GSN 2018a). Establishing an Anti-Corruption Commission (named Nazaha, or integrity) personally chaired by MbS, the Ritz Carlton crackdown expanded to lower-ranking princes and officials, collecting billions more dollars for state coffers (GSN 2020a). The accusations of treachery deployed against these figures were widely disseminated by pro-regime social media influencers, whose role will be discussed later.

In his anti-graft purge, MbS employed a second tactic: seizure of the state's coercive apparatus. In 2015, MbS established a new security force out of a Royal Guard brigade known as 'al-Ajrab'. The 5,000-strong unit was formed to deal with opposition to the MbS-led project both within the royal family and without (*Alhurra* 2021). Reporting directly to MbS, members of al-Ajrab were mobilised to kill Jamal Khashoggi, forcibly return Saudi dissidents abroad, detain women's rights activists and carry out the 2017 purge of oligarchs and opposing royals. Al-Ajrab's rise was followed by MbS's capture of all domestic security and intelligence services in 2017, as well as the placing of the prosecution service under the royal court (*Human Rights Watch* 2020).

Despite the crackdown, resistance and dissent have remained alongside public displays of approval and support. Potential dissent still emanates from the religious establishment, threatened merchant families, and even Al Saud members who remain loyal to former crown prince Mohammed bin Nayef (GSN 2018b, 2020b). The regime also appears to perceive threats in broader society, manifested in the arrests of activists proposing the same liberalising reforms as the regime but out of kilter with the regime narrative and top-down approach – for example, the activist Loujain al-Hathloul spent three years in prison after she was detained alongside a dozen other activists for campaigning to allow women to drive, a reform that was conducted only weeks after their detention. Former liberal voices, including those who had moved on from activism, have also been targeted for their potential for dissent (GSN 2020c). Evident in this pre-emptive approach is the regime's fear that liberalisation has the potential, if not tightly controlled, to escalate into political demands and a public reassessment of the fundamental basis of Al Saud rule. The liberalisation defined by Vision 2030 is therefore a tightly controlled process by which only MbS is allowed to chart the direction for change. Saudis are now expected to express almost absolute conformity with regime red lines and policy – an effective dissolution of politics. Along with the aforementioned methods, digital repression plays a growing role in coercing this conformity. The international technological trends that the Vision holds necessary for economic transformation also offer new opportunities for gathering insights on citizens, shaping narratives and infiltrating the lives of possibly threatening dissidents. These global trends first require attention before considering how they manifest in repressive practices in the Kingdom.

Saudi Arabia and Global Trends in Authoritarian Technology

The procurement and deployment of new authoritarian tools in Saudi Arabia is far from unique.[2] Rather, they are embedded in international trends in technology and data proliferation that, in Saudi Arabia, are simultaneously hailed as centrepieces of economic transformation and harnessed to repress the tensions that arise from it. As identified by Deibert (2020: 10), there are three main elements to digital surveillance that, crucially, entwine the public and private sectors. These are state-conducted data procurement and analysis; the 'datafication' economy in which customers access 'free' services in return for data access; and 'auto surveillance' by which internet users share personal information and metadata through daily activities that are then collected, analysed and sold by a variety of public and private actors.

This public–private line has become increasingly blurred as states seek out data collected for commercial purposes, and a surveillance economy builds up around this amassing of information. In tandem with the growth of 'surveillance capitalism' (Zuboff 2019) in which data is gathered and used by international technology corporations to predict and modify human behaviour, the post-9/11 prioritisation of security over privacy undermined efforts to regulate the industry and initiated increasing government efforts to use this data for surveillance purposes. In other words, as Nyst argues, many governments have embraced 'information abundance' in cyberspace, following a 'realization that such data provide powerful insights into the private thoughts, movements and political persuasions of a country's population, and the recognition that . . . surveillance can capture them' (Nyst 2018: 11). Applied to the Saudi context, ubiquitous sharing of personal data in online activities, driven by mounting levels of internet penetration, device proliferation, and social media use in the past decade, have expanded the surveillance capabilities available to MbS. Covertly installing malicious spyware on a dissident's phone allows for targeted espionage into a particular regime threat, but exploiting information abundance allows for social engineering and surveillance practices at a significant scale.

However, there are ways in which fully exploiting information abundance is in tension with long-held authoritarian practice. The tactic, in essence, relies on permitting data to flow freely, allowing useful information (such as evidence of dissent) to present itself to security services. To Saudi authorities, this presents a risk that the ground given to identify dissenters and benefit the economy could morph into a mobilisation tool at the hands of their enemies, akin to the use of social media during the 2010–11 Arab Uprisings to coordinate protests, build solidarity and take to the streets.

Global forces in cyber governance have helped Saudi authorities contend with these perceived threats, with the Kingdom seeking to augment its priorities for digitally-focused economic transformation with repressive practices incorporated from authoritarian powerhouses – what some scholars may call 'authoritarian learning' (Heydemann and Leenders 2011).[3] On the one hand, the Chinese government has been a global standard-bearer for 'cyber-sovereignty', holding that a national government should control all internet activity within its state's physical borders to help deal with the 'cybercrime and cyber terrorism' afflicting cyberspace (Zaagman 2020; Yeli 2017). However, this is fundamentally at odds with the multi-stakeholder model advocated by Saudi Arabia's allies in the United States (Rosenbash and Chong 2019). A proponent of this model would argue that the Saudi government's overtures to cyber-sovereignty is preventing it from reaping the full benefits of technology-driven economic diversification, as limiting the free flow of data across borders raises costs and lowers efficiency (Soliman 2021).

These contradictory forces demonstrate the tensions implicit in the process of adapting authoritarian rule for a changing world; in short, how to adopt, adapt and harness global political, economic and technological forces to sustain and enhance local authoritarian rule. Facing this challenge, MbS's government is endeavouring to exploit the economic and security benefits of a digital transformation while limiting the potential for 'liberating technologies'. Heavy state surveillance, espionage and social media weaponisation allow the Saudi government to manage the threats arising from technological and social change.

As the domestic need for surveillance has grown amid the centralisation of political power, fears of dissent and opportunities for data-driven monitoring, an international surveillance market has met the Saudi regime's demand. Companies from the United States, the United Kingdom, European Union member states, China and Israel, among many others, offer services from spyware to facial recognition to Deep Packet Inspection (allowing for large-scale monitoring of internet flow). As one specialist describes the variety of sources Saudi Arabia has drawn upon for these services and opportunities, China's 'Huawei is helping the government build safe cities . . . Google is establishing cloud servers, UK arms manufacturer BAE has sold mass surveillance systems, NEC is vending facial recognition cameras, and Amazon and Alibaba both have cloud computing centres in Saudi Arabia and may support a major smart city project' (Feldstein 2019: 14). This market is underpinned by the fact that, in practice, technology companies often face limited governmental restrictions on exports of surveillance and cyber-espionage technologies, or corporations often find ways to circumvent them; in 2017, the British firm BAE Systems sold a cryptanalysis system – to access encrypted communications – to the Saudi government through a Danish subsidiary after the UK government attempted to prevent the tool's sale on 'national security' grounds.

Drawing these tools to Saudi Arabia is also a legal framework in which surveillance technologies' marketed use is differently interpreted; while firms usually advertise hacking software and surveillance tools as serving counter-terrorism and law enforcement purposes (with export licences granted on this understanding), the scope of counter-terrorism is broad in Saudi Arabia. The Kingdom's 2014 counter-terror law defined terrorism as including 'any act carried out either by an individual or collective criminal project . . . with the purpose of disrupting public order; harming the security and stability of the community; risking national unity . . . harming the reputation or status of the country' (*American Bar Association*). A 2017 update added additional articles to further deter criticism of MbS's policies.

Crucially, Vision 2030's wording signals that MbS does not intend for Saudi Arabia to be a passive player in the transnational technology and surveillance industries. It not only pledges to reap the benefits of modern technologies, but to establish the Kingdom as a global leader. The plan is to position Saudi Arabia as a node in technological trends, a country that maximises 'investment capabilities by participating in large international companies and emerging technologies from around the world', with a particular focus on private sector partnerships to enhance Saudi digital infrastructure (Vision 2030: 43, 44, 57). Co-operation with leading companies is held as an important way to transfer 'knowledge and technology' to Saudi Arabia and ultimately 'localize' industries for a post-oil future (ibid. 48). In this way, the regime hopes to bind itself to rapidly accelerating technological advances, with the hope that this contributes to fending off the fate of other Arab regimes in the 2010–11 Arab Uprisings which underestimated the mobilising potential of new technologies. It is in this context of international procurement that the Saudi government seeks and obtains repressive capability.

Mass Surveillance: Big Data and Localisation

In order to make the most of the abundance of data Saudi citizens share online, the government has sought to localise data infrastructure to allow for authorities' access to citizens' data. Couching its efforts in the language of Saudi Arabia as a future technology hub, the Kingdom has sought out partnerships with international technology corporations like Amazon and Google to store data in the Kingdom while forming domestic regulations that mandate Saudi authorities to access and surveil this data. A 2020 draft document released by Saudi's National Cybersecurity Authority (NCA) outlines requirements that service providers 'use telecommunication infrastructure, including international connectivity points through operators licensed in KSA' and store certain data 'at the request of the competent authorities in the KSA' (*NCA* 2020). While similar concepts are used by the European Union's

European General Data Protection Regulation (GDPR) with a focus on user privacy, the priority here is on law enforcement and cyber-sovereignty, again displaying authoritarian governments' ability to adapt global trends for local repressive means (Soliman 2021).

Given high-profile examples of repression in the Kingdom, recent revelations that technology companies have agreed to base data centres in Saudi Arabia have drawn alarm from civil society organisations. In late 2020, Google announced it had signed an agreement with Aramco to base a Google Cloud region in the Kingdom. The parent company of Snapchat, a messaging app focused on picture and video clip sharing popular in the Gulf, was pegged as a client for the service. Google responded that the service was limited to business rather than consumer data, and Snapchat denied any data would be stored in the Kingdom. Nevertheless, the developments show the way in which Saudi Arabia seeks to co-opt international technology companies and attract infrastructural development on its own terms, aiming to play an active role in technology trends to retain and deepen access to Saudi citizens' information. Indeed, the Saudi government has a track record of enforcing quid pro quo arrangements to maintain Saudi-based servers, allowing visibility into internet traffic; in 2010, the government threatened to ban Blackberry devices until the company placed its servers in the Kingdom.

Other possible future impacts of MbS's interest in harnessing the power of big data are manifested in his plans for Neom, a futuristic city-state to serve as the centrepiece for the Kingdom's brand of digital diversification. Its main urban development, named 'the Line', is intended to exhibit the 'internet of things' – the network of data-sharing devices, including heart-rate monitors and facial recognition cameras (Bostock 2021). As planned, the 'smart city' would harvest enormous amounts of data as the core of the city's functionality. In this endeavour, the Saudis are seeking out co-operation with China; through its Digital Silk Road, agreed with the Saudis in 2017 with a focus on smart city technology, the Chinese government and state-linked companies seek to develop digital infrastructure enabled for big data control in Saudi Arabia, offering its model of massive surveillance that has given birth to increasingly intrusive practices like the social credit system in China (*Arab News* 2017; *Hoover Institution* 2021). Key to this model is a synergy between the Chinese government and Chinese technology companies, exhibiting a level of centralised control that is likely attractive to MbS, as even data nominally owned by private companies is accessible and actionable by the repressive state.

It is important to note that the feasibility of Neom has been called into question. It is noteworthy, though, that the pillar of Vision 2030's international brand – a project that MbS has invoked as constituting his 'pyramids' – hinges on mobilising the full power of technology-enabled authoritarianism. This is not only, to echo Khalili and Schwedler (2010), intended to systematically search the population for criminal elements, but also to form accurate profiles of every detail of citizens' lives for longer-term repression and social engineering.

Tapping the International Surveillance Economy: Spyware and Other Technologies

China is just one source of technological solutions for enhancing Saudi authoritarian rule. For deeper investigation of perceived regime threats beyond mass data surveillance, the Saudi regime has procured spyware technology from a range of countries with which to hack political opponents. This hacking is perhaps better theorised as what al-Rawi (2019: 1,306) calls 'online political jamming', flowing both horizontally, as offensive cyber-operations against other states, and vertically (top-down) against a state's own citizens 'to monitor, disrupt, and curb dissent and political activism' (2019: 1,313).

Leading these efforts has been Saud al-Qahtani, head of the Royal Court's Centre for Studies and Media Affairs (CSMA) and sometimes described as MbS's 'cyber-expert'. Al-Qahtani is known for his role in Jamal Khashoggi's murder and for pursuing Saudi dissidents based abroad. These operations have required the procurement of spyware, malicious software installed to targets' devices to achieve an intimate level of espionage, tracking activity including messages and microphone and camera data. Investigative journalists have found that al-Qahtani sought to retain the services of the Milan-based Italian 'offensive security' outfit Hacking Team as early as 2012 (*Bellingcat* 2019). By 2014, this technology had been turned on Saudi Arabia's eastern Shia minority in Qatif Governorate – a site of protests in 2011; the Saudi Interior Ministry concealed Hacking Team hacking spyware in an Android news app named 'Qatif Today' (Marquis-Boire et al 2014). In line with the aforementioned attempts to integrate into the industry rather than simply procure from it, the Saudi government reportedly obtained a stake in Hacking Team through intermediaries in 2018.

As targeted repression expanded from long-oppressed minorities to dissidents opposing MbS's rise to power, the state has procured increasingly sophisticated tools with more creative ways of accessing user devices. Particularly as dissidents' threat perceptions mount, spyware has been deployed in more covert ways to trick threat-aware targets. A high-profile example is the hacking of Canada-based dissident Omar Abdulaziz in 2018. According to Citizen Lab, Abdulaziz was sent a text message that purported to inform him of an upcoming delivery after he made a purchase on Amazon. Clicking on the 'exploit link' infected Abdulaziz's phone with Pegasus, an internationally marketed spyware product from the Israeli firm NSO Group (Marczak et al 2018). Later reports claimed that the CSMA's access to Abdulaziz's communications revealed his co-ordination with Khashoggi (reportedly hatching plans to resist the state's social media weaponisation) only months before the latter's murder in Istanbul by Saudi agents (Kirkpatrick 2018). In 2020, a Citizen Lab investigation found that Pegasus deployment had been further upgraded to an invisible zero-click exploit, allowing Saudi authorities to target even the most tech-savvy journalists, activists and dissidents on a large scale (Marczak et al. 2020).

NSO's Pegasus product is so powerful that the Israeli government classifies it a weapon, accordingly subjecting it to export controls. However, Israeli media have reported that the government has overseen, if not facilitated, NSO's work with the Saudi government, attending meetings between NSO officials and Arab state representatives. While the Israeli state pushes a security agenda, NSO benefits financially; an individual interviewed by *Haaretz* claimed that 'a product that you sell in Europe for $10 million you can sell in the Gulf for 10 times that' (Levinson 2020). This blurred line between private interest and state agenda is also manifested in the fact that Pegasus has a 'suicide' mechanism if it finds itself in Israel, Iran, Russia, China and the United States – the Israeli government likely does not want the nominally private sector tool falling into adversaries' hands or angering its allies. Outside these countries, the tool has been widely employed to crack down on dissent.

Weaponising and Infiltrating Social Media

In the space of ten years, Saudi Twitter has evolved from a forum for relatively free discussion and limited critique of government policy to an effective weapon for authoritarian rule. Researchers have closely tracked this process, highlighting the various tactics used by state actors or their hired hands to shape discourse on the platform. Many of these efforts focus on steering the topic of conversation in a regime-friendly direction and crowding out inconvenient narratives. Hashtag gaming, for example, seeks to create the illusion of popular support and nationalist fervour by posting a large quantity of tweets with a particular hashtag (Abrahams 2019). To this end, Saudi-linked actors have deployed large numbers of inauthentic accounts (bots) alongside regime loyalists (known as the 'electronic flies') to disparage enemies online, manipulate trends and spread false information – most notably on the outbreak of the Qatar dispute in 2017 (Nimmo 2018). Bots were also deployed to create the impression of popular discontent within Qatar itself by 'gaming' hashtags critical of Qatari leadership (Jones 2019). Hashtag hijacking, meanwhile, crowds out opposition narratives by twisting a hashtag's original message (Abrahams 2019).

The extent to which this pro-regime activity is driven by inauthentic botnets or human actors is a central debate among researchers. Much academic and journalistic attention has focused on bots as the vanguard of Saudi information operations. While serving the state's agenda, a key element of these operations again lies in the state's co-operation with the private sector. In 2019, for instance, Twitter announced a mass take-down of inauthentic accounts involving 'automated tools' run by the private Saudi digital marketing firm Smaat. However, some researchers have challenged the understanding that bots overwhelmingly dictate these pro-regime trends, instead drawing attention to the discursive impact of 'Cyber Knights', or influential social media influencers, small groups of which (281 accounts in this case) drove 80 per cent of Twitter discourse in the period after Khashoggi's murder (Abrahams and Leber 2020). These accounts often serve as a vector for disseminating hyper-nationalist discourse, heaping praise on MbS in tweets laden with Saudi flags alongside images of the prince. With this in mind, some have called for more nuanced approaches to state-backed information operations like those pervasive on Saudi social media, pointing to the participatory nature of disinformation as 'collaborative work' involving both human and non-human elements (Starbird et al. 2019).

To be sure, the Saudi government has a track record of co-opting thought leaders and using influencers to spread pro-regime narratives on social media. Amassing millions of followers across popular Saudi social media platforms like Twitter, Instagram and Snapchat, many influencers serve as hyper-nationalist figureheads, hailing regime policy and attacking dissent. These individuals' links to government are often quite evident, while plausibly deniable for the regime. As an example, one popular Snapchat influencer named Ali al-Shibani posts content glorifying the Saudi security forces' heroism and religiosity; while al-Shibani is not a Ministry of Interior employee, he regularly posts the ministry's announcements and appears to have special access to cover raids and campaigns (Al Omran 2020a). Indeed, government ministries are increasingly partnering with influencers to push their agendas. A Shura Council member recently raised concern over the large amounts of state funds being used to pay influencers to crowd out any criticism of particular departments' performance (Al Omran 2020b). To polish the Saudi government's brand overseas, especially given attempts to attract tourism and investment, the government also regularly funds international lifestyle influencer stars to visit the Kingdom and sing its praises on social media – what Human Rights Watch (2020) has called 'image laundering'. But while drawing in these figures is a question of cash, there are also indications that authorities employ repressive practices to force influencers to become propagandists. Having, like prominent Saudi self-made businessman influencer Mansour al-Rugaiba, collected legions of followers to follow the ups and downs of their entrepreneurism, influencers find that their discursive reach can draw the attention of government officials (Al Omran 2020b). Abdulaziz claimed to have spoken with over thirty influencers who faced blackmail by state authorities to force them to spread propaganda; having hacked their phones with spyware and obtained private content, the officials reportedly threatened to leak the material online and disgrace the individual unless they complied (GSN 2020b).

When 'influence' manifests in a manner deemed a threat to the regime, Saudi authorities have equally been able to turn the tide and weaponise social media platforms. Dissidents amass significant followings on Twitter, but many remain anonymous to avoid detection. In 2019, the United States Justice Department charged two Saudi Twitter employees with accessing the data of more than 6,000 Saudi Twitter users including government critics, after being recruited by Saudi agents. The spies sought out the IP addresses and email addresses of dissidents, information that could allow agents to identify and locate even anonymous critics (GSN 2019). By placing state representatives at the centre of the company's operations, Saudi authorities again displayed a drive to position themselves within global technological trends to oversee and control them rather than passively consume. In addition to direct infiltration, authorities have myriad ways of keeping watch over the social media space, which has also involved developing connections with international companies competent in the latest forms of social media analysis. In 2015, McKinsey and Company, a long-term government partner and driver of Vision 2030, submitted a report identifying three prominent social media influencers leading online criticism of austerity measures – one was later detained.

This near-complete integration of social media into the regime's coercive apparatus has wide-ranging implications. The state's infiltration of nominally private accounts, combined with ubiquitous 'electronic flies' amplifying voices of nationalistic influencers branding enemies of the nation as traitors, has imbued social media platforms with more subtle forms of surveillance than the state's direct watch alone. The replacement of civil discourse with an expectation of loyalty, as well as the threat of identification and condemnation by the regime's online allies, discourage the sharing of dissenting views and encourage participatory self-censorship – the feeling of being 'watched' transforms a platform designed for expression into a virtual panopticon. To quote Nyst, the obscurity of these tactics is central to their success: 'hiding the existence or true nature of online monitoring ensures that citizens are made to feel as if they exist under perpetual observation, increasing the likelihood that they will self-align to state-sanctioned expression and behaviour' (2018: 12). Indeed, the roaring success of a new platform for Saudis disaffected with Twitter, Clubhouse (where young participants engage in debates on topics as diverse as cannabis legalisation and intra-regional inequality), has been overshadowed by fears of the capacity of the state to co-opt the platform, for example through accessing user data. Hyper-nationalist discourse has also taken hold online; a room discussing women's rights activist Loujain al-Hathloul escalated into participants branding others as traitors and threatening to take screenshots of the names of attendees to report them to authorities (Al Omran 2021).

The Saudi government has employed other technologies to channel these nationalistic sentiments into active intra-community policing and surveillance practices between citizens. Such repressive tactics have precedent in authoritarian regimes the world over, as well as in Saudi Arabia itself; autocrats often develop large-scale informant networks in society. But in Saudi Arabia the practice has been institutionalised and technologically enabled, packaging the result as a futuristic, convenient way to ensure community security. Kulluna

Aman ('we are all security') is a phone application developed by the Saudi Ministry of Interior to, in the words of a promotional video for the app, 'turn a citizen into a security man' to protect the nation. Inviting citizens to participate in 'preserving stability', the video instructs citizens to report anything suspicious they see in their day-to-day lives. Taken alongside regular statements from authorities imploring citizens to remember Saudi Arabia's broad interpretation of terrorism, Kulluna Aman is a technological solution of participatory surveillance expanding repression beyond the social media space alone, aiming to discourage any form of mobilisation by creating a constant sense of surveillance by one's fellow citizens.[4] This provides a more efficient and scalable approach to long-term authoritarian monarchic practice; as Cavatorta (2007; 193) argues, these systems have regularly used 'a strategy of co-optation based on dividing and ruling' existing and potential opponents.

Conclusion

States in the Middle East and North Africa region have long relied on foreign companies and consultants to assist in developing local repressive practices (Khalili and Schwedler 2010). This occurred in the context of what Fred Halliday has called 'differential integration' (2005: 267) – the process by which the MENA region was incorporated into the world economy prior to the discovery of oil from a position of relative structural weakness. As such, regional states were consumers of repressive technologies, from prison construction to police capabilities. On the one hand, Saudi Arabia shows some continuity with Halliday's observation. It is a case study of the impact these externally derived high-tech tools of repression can have on the internal politics of authoritarian states, endowing security services with the ability not only to identify dissidents and remove them from the public sphere, but to construct mechanisms of participatory surveillance and potentially track, predict and manipulate the minutiae of public feelings and activities with the help of vast quantities of data. Ayubi might describe MbS's adoption of these technologies as part of a process to 'strengthen' the regime and state simultaneously, with the 'strong state' being an upgrade of the 'fierce': a truly hegemonic state that can enforce compliance and be 'more capable of achieving, through state planning, policies and actions, the kinds of changes in society that their leaders have sought' (1995: 450).

Yet it is also a case study of an authoritarian state that aims to depart from this imbalance; by pushing to transform the Kingdom into a hub and convergence point for a range of technological trends from China to Israel, MbS hopes to keep his authorities on the cutting edge of emerging techno-logical forces and shape them for local repressive practice.

Pursuing this approach is likely to breed mounting repression in the future. As established, the repression central to the process of centralising authority and driving techno-economic change spurs political pressures that, in turn, require increased repression. This stands to create a vicious circle of increasingly sophisticated and wide-ranging authoritarian repression in Saudi Arabia. Depending on the extent to which the Crown Prince succeeds, his clear ambition for the Kingdom to ascend as a regional power may also see these capacities exported to counter-revolutionary regional allies in the future.

Notes

1 For an overview of histories of repression in other MENA regimes examined in this book see the section in the Introduction 'Established Authoritarian Practices' (Topak et al. 2022).
2 See the 'Digital Surveillance' section in the Introduction (Topak et al. 2022) for similar digital practices in other MENA regimes examined to varying degrees, particularly other Gulf states such as the UAE (Davidson 2022) and Bahrain (Shehabi 2022), and the other regional powers Egypt (Jumet 2022) and Turkey (Topak 2022).
3 See also the 'Authoritarian Learning and Alliances' section in the Introduction (Topak et al. 2022) for an overview of similar trends in other MENA regimes.
4 For other cases of informant/cyber-informant work in other MENA regimes, see the 'Authoritarian Practices Shaping Civil Society and the Media' section in the Introduction, and particularly the cases from Israel/Palestine (Dayan 2022), Iran (Golkar 2022), Turkey (Topak 2022) and Bahrain (Shebabi 2022).

References

Abrahams, A. (2019). 'Regional Authoritarians Target the Twittersphere', *Middle East Report* 292(3). https://merip.org/2019/12/regional-authoritarians-target -the-twittersphere/

Abrahams, A. and A. Leber (2020). 'Framing a Murder: Twitter Influencers and the Jamal Khashoggi Incident', *Mediterranean Politics* 26(2): 247–59.

Al Omran, A. (2020a). 'Top Saudi Lawyer Jailed over Twitter Libel', *Riyadh Bureau*, 25 December. https://www.riyadhbureau.com/p/saudi-twitter-libel

Al Omran, A. (2020b). 'Manly Instincts', *Riyadh Bureau*, 2 February. https://www.ri yadhbureau.com/p/manly-instincts.

Al Omran, A. (2021). 'Loud Voices', *Riyadh Bureau*, 5 March. https://www.riyadhb ureau.com/p/saudi-clubhouse

Al-Rasheed, M. (2018). 'Introduction: The Dilemmas of a New Era', in M. Al-Rasheed (ed.) *Salman's Legacy: The Dilemmas of a New Era in Saudi Arabia.* Oxford: Oxford University Press, pp. 1–28.

Al-Rawi, A. (2019). 'Cyberconflict, Online Political Jamming, and Hacking in the Gulf Cooperation Council', *International Journal of Communication* 13: 1,301–22.

Alarabiya (2019). 'The 'Center of al-Awamiyah' Injects Fresh Hope in Saudi Arabia's al-Qatif', 1 February. https://english.alarabiya.net/features/2019/02/01/The-Ce nter-of-al-Awamiyah-injects-fresh-hope-in-Saudi-Arabia-s-al-Qatif

Albawaba (2013). 'السعودية تقر بصعوبة مراقبة تويتر', 14 February. https://www.albawaba .com/ar/%D8%A3%D8%AE%D8%A8%D8%A7%D8%B1/%D8%A7%D9 %84%D8%B3%D8%B9%D9%88%D8%AF%D9%8A%D8%A9-%D8 %AA%D9%82%D8%B1-%D8%A8%D8%B5%D8%B9%D9%88%D8 %A8%D8%A9-%D9%85%D8%B1%D8%A7%D9%82%D8%A8%D8 %A9-%D8%AA%D9%88%D9%8A%D8%AA%D8%B1-470675

Alhurra (2021). 'من 'السيف الأجرب' إلى 'فرقة النمر'.. جنود ولي العهد السعودي الغامضين, 28 February. https://www.alhurra.com/saudi-arabia/2021/02/27/%D8%A7% D9%84%D8%B3%D9%8A%D9%81-%D8%A7%D9%84%D8%A3%D8 %AC%D8%B1%D8%A8-%D9%81%D8%B1%D9%82%D8%A9-%D8 %A7%D9%84%D9%86%D9%85%D8%B1-%D8%AC%D9%86%D9%88 %D8%AF-%D9%88%D9%84%D9%8A-%D8%A7%D9%84%D8%B9 %D9%87%D8%AF-%D8%A7%D9%84%D8%B3%D8%B9%D9%88 %D8%AF%D9%8A-%D8%A7%D9%84%D8%BA%D8%A7%D9%85 %D8%B6%D9%8A%D9%86

Alhussein, E. (2019). 'Saudi First: How Hyper-nationalism Is Transforming Saudi Arabia', *European Council on Foreign Relations*, 19 June. https://ecfr.eu/publicat ion/saudi_first_how_hyper_nationalism_is_transforming_saudi_arabia/

American Bar Association (2019). 'Saudi Arabia: Counterterror Court Targets Activists'. https://www.americanbar.org/content/dam/aba/administrative/hum an_rights/justice-defenders/saudi-court-targets-activists.pdf

Arab News (2017). 'Riyadh, Beijing Launch "Digital Silk Road" Initiative', 15 December. https://www.arabnews.com/node/1209226/saudi-arabia

Ayubi, Nazih (1995). *Over-stating the Arab State.* New York: I. B. Tauris.

Bellingcat (2019). 'Lord of the Flies: An Open-Source Investigation into Saud Al-Qahtani', 27 June. https://www.bellingcat.com/news/mena/2019/06/26/lord-of-the-flies-an-open-source-investigation-into-saud-al-qahtani/

Bostock, B. (2021). 'Saudi Arabia's $500 Billion Megacity Neom Is Creating Plans to Harvest an Unprecedented Amount of Data from Future Residents', *Business Insider*, 24 March. https://www.businessinsider.com/neom-saudi-smart-city-data-surveillance-plans-experts-2021-3

Brown, N. (2017). 'The Remaking of the Saudi State', Carnegie Endowment for International Peace, 9 November. https://carnegieendowment.org/2017/11/09/remaking-of-saudi-state-pub-74681

Bsheer, R. (2018). 'A Counter-revolutionary State: Popular Movements and the Making of Saudi Arabia', *Past and Present* 238(1): 233–77.

Bsheer, R. (2018). 'How Mohammed bin Salman Has Transformed Saudi Arabia', *The Nation*, 21 May. https://www.thenation.com/article/archive/how-mohammed-bin-salman-has-transformed-saudi-arabia/

Bsheer, R. (2020). *Archive Wars: The Politics of History in Saudi Arabia*. Stanford: Stanford University Press.

Cavatorta, F. (2007). 'More than Repression: The Significance of Divide et Impera in the Middle East and North Africa – The Case of Morocco', *Journal of Contemporary African Studies* 25(2): 187–203.

Chulov, M. (2020). '"Night of the Beating": Details Emerge of Riyadh Ritz-Carlton Purge', *The Guardian*, 19 November. https://www.theguardian.com/world/2020/nov/19/saudi-accounts-emerge-of-ritz-carlton-night-of-the-beating

Cronin, S. (2013). 'Tribes, Coups and Princes: Building a Modern Army in Saudi Arabia', *Middle Eastern Studies* 49(1): 2–28.

Davidson, C. M. (2022). 'The United Arab Emirates: Evolving Authoritarian Tools', in Ö. E. Topak, M. Mekouar and F. Cavatorta (eds) *New Authoritarian Practices in the Middle East and North Africa*. Edinburgh: Edinburgh University Press, pp. 320–39.

Dayan, H. (2022). 'Israel/Palestine: Authoritarian Practices in the Context of a Dual State Crisis', in Ö. E. Topak, M. Mekouar and F. Cavatorta (eds) *New Authoritarian Practices in the Middle East and North Africa*. Edinburgh: Edinburgh University Press, pp. 131–51.

Deibert, R. J. et al. (2020). 'Online Surveillance, Censorship, and Encryption in Academia', *International Perspectives* 21(1): 1–36.

Feldstein, S. (2019). 'How Much Is China Driving the Spread of AI Surveillance?'. Carnegie Endowment for International Peace. https://www.jstor.org/stable/pdf/resrep20995.7.pdf?ab_segments=0%252Fbasic_search_gsv2%252Fcontrol&refreqid=excelsior%3Ad796ca8ca5c49986245b719baa89b28b

Halliday, F. (2005). *The Middle East in International Relations: Powers, Politics and Ideology*. Cambridge: Cambridge University Press.

Herb, M. (1999). *All in the Family: Absolutism, Revolution, and Democracy in the Middle Eastern Monarchies*. Albany: State University of New York Press.

Hertog, S. (2018). 'Challenges to the Saudi Distributional State in the Age of Austerity', in M. Al-Rasheed (ed.) *Salman's Legacy: The Dilemmas of a New Era in Saudi Arabia*. Oxford: Oxford University Press, pp. 73–96.

Heydemann, S. and R. Leenders (2011). 'Authoritarian Learning and Authoritarian Resilience: Regime Responses to the "Arab Awakening"', *Globalizations* 8(5): 647–53.

Hoover Institution (2021). 'Xiao Qiang On China's Model Of Digital Authoritarianism | Episode 2102', 11 February. https://www.hoover.org/research/xiao-qiang-chin as-model-digital-authoritarianism-episode-2102

Human Rights Watch (2020). 'Saudi Arabia: "Image Laundering" Conceals Abuses', 2 October. https://www.hrw.org/news/2020/10/02/saudi-arabia-image-launder ing-conceals-abuses#

Golkar, S. (2022). 'Deep Society and New Authoritarian Social Control in Iran after the Green Movement', in Ö. E. Topak, M. Mekouar and F. Cavatorta (eds) *New Authoritarian Practices in the Middle East and North Africa*. Edinburgh: Edinburgh University Press, pp. 92–111.

Jebnoun, N. (2014). 'Rethinking the Paradigm of "Durable" and "Stable" Authoritarianism in the Middle East', in N. Jebonoun, M. Kia and M. Kirk (eds) *Modern Middle East Authoritarianism: Roots, Ramifications, and Crisis*. New York: Routledge, pp. 1–24.

Jones, M.O. (2019). 'Propaganda, Fake News, and Fake Trends: The Weaponization of Twitter Bots in the Gulf Crisis', *International Journal of Communication* 13: 1,389–415.

Jumet, K.D. (2022). 'Authoritarian Repression Under Sisi: New Tactics or New Tools?', in Ö. E. Topak, M. Mekouar and F. Cavatorta (eds) *New Authoritarian Practices in the Middle East and North Africa*. Edinburgh: Edinburgh University Press, pp. 73–91.

Khalili, L. and J. Schwedler (2010). *Policing and Prisons in the Middle East: Formations of Coercion*. London: Hurst.

Kirkpatrick, D. (2018). 'Israeli Software Helped Saudis Spy on Khashoggi, Lawsuit Says', *New York Times*, 2 December. https://www.nytimes.com/2018/12/02/wo rld/middleeast/saudi-khashoggi-spyware-israel.html

Levinson, C. (2020). 'With Israel's Encouragement, NSO Sold Spyware to UAE and Other Gulf States', *Haaretz*, 25 August. https://www.haaretz.com/middle-east -news/.premium-with-israel-s-encouragement-nso-sold-spyware-to-uae-and-ot her-gulf-states-1.9093465

Marczak, B., J. Scott-Railton, N. Al-Jizawi, S. Anstis and R. Deibert (2020). 'The Great iPwn Journalists Hacked with Suspected NSO Group iMessage "Zero-Click" Exploit', *Citizen Lab*, 20 December. https://citizenlab.ca/2020/12/the-great-ip wn-journalists-hacked-with-suspected-nso-group-imessage-zero-click-exploit/

Marczak, B., J. Scott-Railton, N. Al-Jizawi, S. Anstis and R. Deibert (2018). 'The Kingdom Came to Canada: How Saudi-Linked Digital Espionage Reached Canadian Soil', *Citizen Lab*, 1 October. https://citizenlab.ca/2018/10/the-ki ngdom-came-to-canada-how-saudi-linked-digital-espionage-reached-canadian -soil/

Marquis-Boire, M., J. Scott-Railton, C. Guarnieri and K. Kleemola (2014). 'Police Story Hacking Team's Government Surveillance Malware', *Citizen Lab*, 24 June. https://citizenlab.ca/2014/06/backdoor-hacking-teams-tradecraft-an droid-implant/

National Cybersecurity Authority (NCA) (2020). 'Cloud Cybersecurity Controls'. https://nca.gov.sa/files/cloud_cybersecurity_controls_draft_en.pdf

Nimmo, B. (2018). 'Robot Wars: How Bots Joined Battle in the Gulf', *Journal of International Affairs* 71(1.5): 87–96.

Okruhlik, G. (2019). 'Rentier Wealth, Unruly Law, and the Rise of Opposition: The Political Economy of Oil States', *Comparative Politics* 31(3): 295–315.

Nyst, C. (2018). 'Secrets and Lies: The Proliferation of State Surveillance Capabilities and the Legislative Secrecy Which Fortifies Them – An Activist's Account', *State Crime Journal* 7(1): 8–23.

Rosenbach, E. and S. M. Chong (2019). 'Governing Cyberspace: State Control vs. The Multistakeholder Model', *Belfer Center for Science and International Affairs*, August. https://www.belfercenter.org/publication/governing-cyberspace-state-c ontrol-vs-multistakeholder-model

Saudia (2021). لقاء ولي العهد الأمير محمد بن سلمان بقناة السعودية بمناسبة مرور 5 سنوات على 'إطلاق رؤية،السعودية'. https://www.youtube.com/watch?v=eriiLN1XIa0&t=3380s

Seznec, J. F. (2014). 'Political Control in Saudi Arabia: The Avoidance of Democratization', in N. Jebonoun, M. Kia and M. Kirk (eds) *Modern Middle East Authoritarianism: Roots, Ramifications, and Crisis*. New York: Routledge, pp. 142–58.

Soliman, M. (2021). 'In the Middle East, Cyber Sovereignty Hampers Economic Diversification', *Middle East Institute*, 6 January. https://www.mei.edu/publicat ions/middle-east-cyber-sovereignty-hampers-economic-diversification

Shehabi, A. (2022). 'The Authoritarian Topography of the Bahraini State: Political Geographies of Power and Protest', in Ö. E. Topak, M. Mekouar and F. Cavatorta (eds) *New Authoritarian Practices in the Middle East and North Africa*. Edinburgh: Edinburgh University Press, pp. 51–72.

Starbird, K., A. Arif and T. Wilson (2019). 'Disinformation as Collaborative Work: Surfacing the Participatory Nature of Strategic Information Operations' *Proceedings of the ACM on Human–Computer Interaction* 3: 127.

The Independent (2017). 'Inside the Saudi Town That's Been Under Siege for Three Months by Its Own Government', 4 August. https://www.independent.co.uk/news/world/middle-east/saudi-arabia-siege-town-own-citizens-government-kingdom-military-government-awamiyah-qatif-a7877676.html

Topak, Ö. E. (2022). 'An Assemblage of New Authoritarian Practices in Turkey', in Ö. E. Topak, M. Mekouar and F. Cavatorta (eds) *New Authoritarian Practices in the Middle East and North Africa.* Edinburgh: Edinburgh University Press, pp. 296–319.

Topak, Ö. E., M. Mekouar and F. Cavatorta (2022). 'Introduction', in Ö. E. Topak, M. Mekouar and F. Cavatorta (eds) *New Authoritarian Practices in the Middle East and North Africa.* Edinburgh: Edinburgh University Press, pp. 1–29.

Vision 2030. https://www.vision2030.gov.sa/v2030/overview/

Worth, R. F. (2012). 'Twitter Gives Saudi Arabia a Revolution of Its Own', *New York Times*, 20 October. https://www.nytimes.com/2012/10/21/world/middleeast/twitter-gives-saudi-arabia-a-revolution-of-its-own.html

Yeli, H. (2017). 'A Three-Perspective Theory of Cyber Sovereignty', *PRISM* 7: 1, 21 December. https://cco.ndu.edu/PRISM-7-2/Article/1401954/a-three-perspective-theory-of-cyber-sovereignty/

Zaagman, E. (2020). 'The Age of Cyber Sovereignty?', *War on the Rocks*, 18 August. https://warontherocks.com/2020/08/the-age-of-cyber-sovereignty/

Zuboff, S. (2019). *The Age of Surveillance Capitalism: The Fight for a Human Future at the New Frontier of Power.* New York: PublicAffairs.

Gulf States Newsletter (GSN) sources

GSN (2012a). 'Gulf Countries Use Fear and Technology to Crack Down on Dissent', *Gulf States Newsletter,* 22 March (920). https://www.gsn-online.com/article/gulf-countries-use-fear-and-technology-crack-down-dissent

GSN (2021a). 'Saudi Arabia: Riyadh Seeks a Modus Vivendi with Biden', *Gulf States Newsletter*, 18 February (1120). https://www.gsn-online.com/article/saudi-arabia-riyadh-seeks-modus-vivendi-biden

GSN (2018a). 'Saudi Arabia: Autocratic Tendencies Define Disrupter-in-chief MBS's agenda', *Gulf States Newsletter*, 22 March (1056). https://www.gsn-online.com/article/saudi-arabia-autocratic-tendencies-define-disrupter-chief-mbss-agenda

GSN (2020a). 'Saudi Arabia: Bani Salman Leadership Projects Ruthless Ambition as Oil Prices Crash, Virus Spreads', *Gulf States Newsletter*, 19 March (1099).

https://www.gsn-online.com/article/saudi-arabia-bani-salman-leadership-proje
cts-ruthless-ambition-oil-prices

GSN (2018a). 'Saudi Arabia: Autocratic Tendencies Define Disrupter-in-chief
MBS's agenda', *Gulf States Newsletter*, 22 March (1056). https://www.gsn-on
line.com/article/saudi-arabia-autocratic-tendencies-define-disrupter-chief-mbss
-agenda

GSN (202b). 'Bin Salman Clan Clamps Down Further on Royal Rivals and Other
Saudi Dissidents', *Gulf States Newsletter*, 3 July (1106). https://www.gsn-online
.com/article/bin-salman-clan-clamps-down-further-royal-rivals-and-other-saudi

GSN (2020c). 'Threats from Jihadists to Liberals Dog Saudi Security Agenda', *Gulf
States Newsletter*, 9 January (1095). https://www.gsn-online.com/article/threats
-jihadists-liberals-dog-saudi-security-agenda

GSN (2019). 'United States: Three Saudis Accused of Spying via Twitter', *Gulf States
Newsletter*, 18 November (1092). https://www.gsn-online.com/article/united-st
ates-three-saudis-accused-spying-twitter

13

THE EVOLUTION OF THE SUDANESE AUTHORITARIAN STATE: THE DECEMBER UPRISING AND THE UNRAVELLING OF A 'PERSISTENT' AUTOCRACY

Yousif Hassan

Introduction

As in many other Middle East and North Africa (MENA) countries, authoritarianism has been the most prevailing reality in Sudan. Since independence in 1956, different authoritarian regimes have ruled Sudan for more than fifty-two years. Following the December 2018 uprising that ousted Omar al-Bashir after three decades of autocratic rule, Sudan adopted a new hybrid mode of governance (civilian-military) for a four-year transitional period. Less than two years into the transitional period, post-uprising Sudan is, however, gradually drifting away from democratisation and inching closer to a new form of authoritarian governance.

Integrating scholarship across the fields of comparative politics (Bellin 2012; Brynen et al. 2012b; Butcher and Svensson 2016; Liu 2015), security and surveillance studies (Akbari and Gabdulhakov 2019; Deibert 2015; Jones 2019; MacKinnon 2011; Michaelsen 2017; Topak 2019; Uniacke 2020) and international relations (Agathangelou and Soguk 2014; Alnasseri 2018; Brynen et al. 2012a; Lawson 2015), this chapter examines the authoritarian practices of the Bashir Islamist regime and explores the evolving means of authoritarian control following the December 2018 uprising.

Bashir used several authoritarian practices to control the population, including torture, targeted killings, censorship, digital surveillance, repressive security laws, ethno-politics, foreign alliances, militias and paramilitary groups. One of the most coercive policies was known as *Tamkeen* (empowerment), which enabled the Bashir Islamist party to have a strong hold on the state. *Tamkeen* policies sought to weaken civil society organising and political mobilisation by deliberately purging public institutions, the army, the police and the judiciary of career bureaucrats perceived as disloyal (Hassan and Kodouda 2019). These policies also included targeting private companies with oppressive economic measures to drive them out of business. In many cases, senior members of the Bashir Islamist party and the security apparatus seized control of these businesses.

After three decades of *Tamkeen*, Sudan had a fragmented political opposition, a powerful coercive apparatus and a fragile civil society. Thus, many scholars argued that it was unlikely to transition to democracy. They also argued that the regime would survive, and Sudan would continue to have weak prospects for a popular uprising similar to those in other MENA countries. However, civil society was eventually able to bring the authoritarian military regime down, for reasons rooted in the very authoritarian nature of Bashir's autocracy. The lack of autonomy within the security apparatus and proliferation of paramilitary groups and militias led to increasing divisions within the regime's coercive apparatus. The fragility of alliances built on ethnic and tribal conflicts weakened the political underpinnings of the regime. The shift in the strategic political alliances in the MENA region resulted in the withdrawal of support to the regime by Arab Gulf states and directly affected its fiscal health. Furthermore, the *Tamkeen* policy alienated Sudanese society, fuelled the organisational capacity of groups in civil society and strengthened the legitimacy of opposition political parties and their ability to form broad political coalitions.

Since the beginning of the transitional period in August 2019, many of the oppressive laws and coercive practices of the ousted regime have been abolished, such as the state of emergency, public order laws, press censorship and the power of arbitrary arrest by the former National Intelligence and Security Services (NISS). At the same time, several other oppressive practices have evolved and continue to persist.[1] For example, the Rapid Support Forces (RSF), a paramilitary group established by Bashir, is now part of the power-sharing agreement in the transitional period and has expanded its operation to different parts of the country. The RSF leader (appointed General by Bashir despite his lack of military background) Mohamed Hamdan Dagalo, also known as *Hemetti*, is the Deputy Chairman of the Transitional Sovereign Council (TSC). The RSF operates with impunity, targeting and detaining activists, despite passing laws that prohibit arrest by authorities other than the police. Ethnic conflicts have escalated while activists and citizens from these conflict areas continue to be targeted and killed by militias known for their ties with the military elite in the transitional government including the RSF. The military elite in the TSC are blocking efforts to dismantle the Bashir legacy, still control state resources such as gold mining and the military-security industrial complex (Gallopin 2020), and continue to have the country's telecommunication infrastructure under their purview. Internet surveillance practices by the TSC threaten freedom of expression as activists continue to face systematic state harassment, intimidation and arrest for their online activities (Freedom House 2021).

In short, competing power structures seeking to dominate the transition and influence its outcome characterise the current transitional period. As the struggle intensifies between the civilian and military elite and the balance of power continues to tilt increasingly towards the military side, the prospects for authoritarianism and the return to coercive practices will increase.

Authoritarianism and Political Violence in Sudan

Two years after independence, Sudan experienced its first post-colonial authoritarian era with the autocratic regime of General Ibrahim Abboud (1958–64). Abboud came to power at a time of economic crisis and a bitter political struggle between the major political parties at the time, the Umma Party, the People's Democratic Party (PDP), both predominantly based on religious principles, and the National Unionist Party (NUP), a Sudanese nationalist party. The Umma Party was in negotiations with the NUP to form a new government coalition and leave its existing coalition with the PDP. However, news of meetings between PDP and NUP party leaders and Nasser's regime in Cairo caused great concern for Prime Minister Abdallah Khalil, of the Umma Party. Out of fears of an increased Egyptian political influence in Sudan, Khalil started discussions about a military takeover with army generals (Hasan 1967; Holt 1961). Following a bloodless military coup, Gen. Abboud suspended the constitution, dissolved parliament, abolished political parties, banned all political activities and prohibited public gatherings. Newspapers and other media were banned, and a state-controlled media was established by the regime. Abboud also dissolved workers' unions and frequently closed down universities as an epicentre of political mobilisa-tion. Although Abboud's authoritarian practices would pale compared to those Nimeiry and Bashir later exercised, nevertheless his regime depended on coercion to survive. Abboud concentrated all powers in the Supreme Council of the Armed Forces (SCAF), with himself at the head of the coun-cil, the state, as well as a Prime Minister. The SCAF had both legislative and executive powers. The Abboud regime also introduced for the first time *'preventative arrest'* (Berridge 2015, p. 15), tortured members of political parties, and hanged young officers from the Infantry School for their attempt to overthrow the regime in December 1959. During the Abboud regime, the conflict in southern Sudan intensified following Abboud's pursuit of forced Islamisation and his Arabisation agenda in the south (Poggo 2002). This set the stage for future authoritarian regimes to exploit the southern question by enacting oppressive policies to control the population in both northern and southern Sudan. Following liberalising measures by the Abboud regime, the political opposition was able to organise through trade unions and profes-sional associations, which have been a vital tool of social mobilisation ever since. Eventually, the political opposition used the developing political crisis in southern Sudan to ignite the October Revolution of 1964 and effectively adopted the general strike strategy to end Abboud autocracy.

The second democratic period witnessed increased political polarisation, which culminated in the prohibition of elected members of the Sudanese Communist Party (SCP) from participating in parliament. The party was eventually dissolved, and this led one faction of the SCP to argue that liberal democracy could not coexist with progressive politics in Sudan. After failing to secure majority support for their position in the central committee of the SCP, this faction supported a military coup by the Free Officer Movement headed by then-Colonel Jaafar Nimeiry in May 1969. Claiming to preserve the legacy of the 1964 October Revolution, the military junta established the Revolutionary Command Council (RCC) and vowed to implement a radical political agenda. However, divisions within the RCC prompted Nimeiry to fire pro-communist members within the RCC. Expelled members of the RCC staged a coup d'état against Nimeiry, briefly arresting him, but he came back in a counter-coup and extra-judicially executed them. He also hanged senior members of the SCP accused of participating in the coup. This was the first time civilians were executed for opposing the regime. Over the course of his authoritarian rule, Nimeiry jailed leading politicians, eliminated political parties and later established a one-party system using his own created party called the Sudanese Socialist Union (SSU). State coercion during the Nimeiry regime was upgraded to a new level, with the torturing and killing of opposition figures and political leaders. Nimeiry established the State Security Organization (SSO) in 1978 to combine the functions of internal and external security. While the SSO fuelled public outrage for its barbaric practices (Berridge 2015), it became critical to the survival of the regime. Nimeiry's authoritarian practices included violent crackdowns and mass executions of opponents. For example, his regime carried out, among other atrocities, the aerial bombardment of supporters of the Umma Party, killing an estimated 1,200 people in their stronghold of Aba Island.

In the later days of his rule, Nimeiry shifted alliance to the religious right, bringing in both the Islamic Charter Front (ICF), a Sudanese offshoot of the Muslim Brotherhood, and the Umma party into his SSU. He declared *Shari'a* laws – also known as September laws – in 1983, which are based on hotly debated interpretations of *Shari'a*. This included the invention of new crimes such as the 'intention to commit fornication' and expansion of the definition of crimes that would receive harsh punishment such as public flogging and amputation of hands. Nimeiry used the penalty of apostasy to execute opposing political figures such as Mahmud Muhammad Taha, a liberal Islamic reformer who had criticised September laws and Nimeiry's policies. The September laws were means whereby to discipline citizens by instilling the fear of prosecution under *Shari'a* laws for opposing Nimeiry's policies. For example, Nimeiry established 'Instantaneous Justice Courts' under September laws that bypassed the regular judiciary system, and handed out sentences and penalties with no regard for due legal procedures. Between 1984 and 1985 more than a hundred people had their hands amputated in these courts. In fact, Nimeiry, with ICF justification, appointed himself *Imam* of the Sudan and used *bay'a* (oath of allegiance) to strengthen his political-religious legitimacy.

Although the conflict between the North and South originated in lack of development and marginalisation of the South, the September laws were the culmination of the historical and systematic oppressive practices of Islamisation and Arabisation of the Christian south by the state, raising irreconcilable issues, since independence, of national identity, Sudan's relationship with the Arab and Muslim world, and Sudan's African roots and heritage (Deng 1995). This resulted in the civil war in the South in

1983. Fuelled by the rising cost of living, corruption, economic crisis and the civil war, political parties and civil society were able to mobilise, ultimately ousting Nimeiry in the 1985 Intifada. Like other MENA dictators, Berridge (2015) argues, Nimeiry relied on networks of patronage, which included senior generals, bureaucrats and members of opposition parties, to preserve his regime.

Authoritarianism under Bashir's Islamist Regime

Following the 1985 Intifada, Sudan entered into a third period of democratic rule after a one-year transitional period. However, the legacy of the Nimeiry regime continued to haunt the post-transitional period. This legacy included the failure to dismantle the SSO and abolish the September laws, with both proving helpful for setting the stage for Bashir's authoritarian rule. After the 1985 Intifada, the ICF and Sudan's branch of the Muslim Brotherhood were re-formed into the Islamic National Front (INF) headed by Hassan al-Turabi. The INF participation in the Nimeiry regime had allowed its members to infiltrate the major security services, including the SSO. State access also allowed the INF to dominate the financial and banking sector with the adoption of the Islamic banking system. By the time of the 1985 Intifada, the INF was well organised and financially strong, with access to critical parts of the state and its banking system (Berridge 2015). The inability to negotiate a peace agreement with the Sudanese People Liberation Movement/Army (SPLA/SPLM) in the South, the worsening economic crisis and the failure to dismantle the institutions of the Nimeiry regime contributed to the end of the democratic experience when the INF staged a military coup d'état masterminded by al-Turabi. The coup was executed by INF members in the military under the leadership of then-Brigadier General Omer al-Bashir in June 1989 (Burr et al. 2003).

The following three decades saw Bashir consolidate his power, transforming the INF into his own National Congress Party (NCP), and establishing a personalist autocratic governing model (Hassan and Kodouda 2019). Bashir used several authoritarian strategies to remain in power and prolong the lifetime of his regime, including *Tamkeen* oppressive practices, ethno-politics and foreign alliances.

Tamkeen and state coercion

Tamkeen policy and state coercion need to be looked at in tandem in the case of Sudan. The early period of Bashir regime was dominated by al-Turabi as both the spiritual figure and political leader of the regime. At the heart of al-Turabi's strategy was *Tamkeen* policy. The idea behind *Tamkeen* was to transform Sudan, politically, economically, socially and culturally, into an Islamist state, ensuring a strong hold on all critical functions of the state, and preventing future uprisings, social movements and military coups. In short, the main objective of *Tamkeen* policy was to ensure that the regime could stay in power indefinitely. Bashir's *Tamkeen* strategy was built on a combination of brute coercion (Bellin 2012) and elite co-optation (Mekouar 2014) by extending access to state resources to his protégés, Islamists, and his own NCP.

Embedded within *Tamkeen* are a number of oppressive measures to control the public space, reconstruct Sudan's identity, discipline the population and transform Sudanese society using political Islam (Burr et al. 2003; Lo 2019). In the early days of *Tamkeen* policy, the regime used *jihad* as a religious battle cry for political mobilisation in the civil war against the South. Looking for stable financial resources, the real objective behind the *jihad* was to reclaim areas with oil fields in the South that were under control of the SPLM/SPLA (Lo 2019). The regime also targeted unions and civil society organisations so as to limit their organisational capacity. For instance, it cracked down on the railroad workers union in Atbra, dismantling the union and laying off 4,000 railroad workers in one day in 1991. The city of Atbara is the birthplace of the labour movement in Sudan and known for its railroad worker union organising and a history of resistance to both colonial and post-colonial regimes.

Bashir built one of the most notorious security apparatuses in the MENA region, the National Intelligence and Security Service (NISS), to stifle political dissent and enforce *Tamkeen* policies. The NISS controlled both economic and public life in the country. The NISS controlled the public space through media surveillance and security laws. For example, newspapers in the country needed security clearance from the NISS to be able to publish. Bashir also continued the legacy of September laws and passed additional legislation to discipline the population. The most notorious of these laws is the public order law, which claims to enforce Islamic traditions in Sudanese society.

Women were subjected to public flogging and other oppressive measures such as enforcing the hijab.

Tamkeen was a broad project to control society by rewarding loyalists and systematically punishing dissidents. Lo (2019) argued that through the politics of *Tamkeen*, al-Turabi justified violating the very spirit of freedom that he claimed was the characteristic distinguishing Sudanese Islamists from their contemporaries in the Muslim world.

Ethno-politics

Bashir's approach was different from those of other authoritarian leaders in the MENA region, in the sense that he deliberately sought a police state strategy that strengthened the capabilities of the security apparatus but weakened its autonomy. These strategies included: (1) fragmenting internal security institutions; (2) militarising the security apparatus; (3) creating militias in different parts of the country; and (4) establishing paramilitary groups such as the RSF.

Hassan and Kodouda (2019) argue that Bashir's personalistic strategy relied mainly on weakening the state and society to consolidate his power. One of the ways Bashir achieved this was by leveraging the historical ethnic conflicts in the country. Bashir's rule coincided with an unprecedented escalation of ethnic conflicts in different areas, including Darfur, Blue Nile and Nuba Mountains. Bashir leveraged the fragile tribal situation in Darfur to build tribal alliances and strengthen his grip on resistance movements in the margins, enabling tribal leaders loyal to his regime to operate with impunity to control political dissent and quell opposition. He also created paramilitary groups and militias that cracked down on civil society as well as fighting the armed resistance in these marginalised parts of the country. For example, the major paramilitary group, the RSF, is a state-controlled offshoot of the Janjaweed. The Janjaweed is a militia made up mainly of members of nomadic 'Arab' tribes that have been at odds with the African tribes in Darfur. The RSF also includes mercenaries from neighbouring countries in western Sudan who share tribal links with the Janjaweed.

Bashir autocracy marked a significant transformation in Sudan's ethnic politics, as religious ideology and ethnic sentiments were used for both political mobilisation and state coercion. With the rise of political Islam and ethnic conflicts spreading across the country, the struggle over the question of Sudan's national identity intensified. The conflict between secularism and religion has occupied an increased space in popular political discourse, and in fact continues to dominate the transitional period.

Foreign alliances[2]

Bashir had sought regional and international alliances with states like Iran, Qatar, Saudi Arabia, Egypt, the UAE and Turkey. He also increased intelligence and security co-operation with the United States post-9/11 and relied heavily on foreign alliances to finance and protect his regime (Yom and Gause 2012), but this was ultimately one of the factors that led to his demise.

Regionally, the regime's previous ties with Iran and the Muslim Brotherhood have always added tension to its relationship with Egypt and other key Arab Gulf countries. After the secession of South Sudan, severe economic crises hit Sudan as a result of the loss of revenues from the oil-rich South and the shift in geopolitics in the region and internationally. Under mounting financial pressure in 2015, Bashir cut ties with Iran and joined the Saudi coalition supplying thousands of troops to fight the war in Yemen. However, he refused to follow Saudi Arabia and Emirates after they isolated Qatar or cut ties with Turkey in 2017. As a result, Turkish and Qatari engagement increased in Sudan. For example, Turkey signed a deal to redevelop the Red Sea port of Suakin and reportedly was going to build a naval dock (Stevis-Gridneff and Said 2019). However, Bashir made a series of strategic mistakes by playing rivals off against each other, costing him the support of both sides.

Internationally, the regime sought Western alliances and co-operation to prolong its life and maintain its oppressive apparatus and grip on power. It was challenging for Bashir to maintain international legitimacy, for many reasons, including (1) arrest warrants against him issued by the International Criminal Court for war crimes and crimes against humanity (ICC 2010) and (2) the US listing of Sudan in the State Sponsor of Terrorism list. However, Bashir was able to navigate the turbulent waters of international relations by providing concessions to co-operate with the United States on the so-called War on Terror, and assist the EU in its efforts to stop the flow of refugees and international migrants from Africa (Alamin 2018; Baldo 2017; Kingsley 2018). For example, the NISS participated in regional and international security operations led by US intelligence agencies (Blanchard 2019; Tossell 2020; United States Department of State 2017). In addition, the RSF was supported by the EU to carry out operations of migrant control

(Tubiana et al. 2018). On the one hand, this co-operation strengthened the fiscal health of the security apparatus of the regime and enhanced its oppressive capabilities (Baldo 2017; Kingsley 2018; Tubiana et al. 2018). On the other, it legitimised the Bashir regime through the EU making Khartoum the centre for counter-smuggling collaboration (Kingsley 2018) and establishing the Khartoum Process, a platform for international migration conferences that included European Union officials and their counterparts from several African countries. Investigative reports such as Kingsley (2018) suggest that the level of co-operation included agents of the NISS interrogating Sudanese political dissidents seeking asylum in Europe who were candidates for deportation, with no monitoring or legal due process by European officials.

Digital Surveillance

Many studies of the Arab Spring show that authoritarian regimes have widened their coercive practices and increased their investments in new authoritarian tools such as new security laws targeting internet activities, social media and digital and communication surveillance (Leber and Abrahams 2019; Topak 2019; Uniacke 2020; Yom and Gause 2012). Internet blackouts, online censorship and fake news have become the main practices authoritarian regimes employ to stifle political dissent and prevent social and political mobilisation (Akbari and Gabdulhakov 2019; Deibert 2015; Jones 2019; Khondker 2011; Leber and Abrahams 2019; Topak 2019).

In the case of Sudan, the Bashir regime had built digital capabilities for online surveillance and security operations in response to the rise of social media and online forms of political activism. For example, internet and digital rights organisations such as Citizen Lab, Freedom House and NetBlocks reported digital surveillance practices by the regime and its security apparatus. Citizen Lab confirmed that the Bashir government had possessed digital surveillance technology and used internet filtering technology to censor the internet (Dalek et al. 2018). Freedom House and NetBlocks reported frequent blocking of social media apps such as WhatsApp, Facebook, Twitter, Periscope and Instagram by internet service providers to disrupt social media mobilisation. The NCP and NISS created the 'Cyber Jihad' unit, which engaged in practices of online censorship, targeted activists on social media and spread propaganda and fake news online (Lamoureaux and Sureau 2019). The 'Cyber Jihad' unit has frequently manipulated internet content and social media discussions to advance the agenda of Bashir and his NCP Islamist party. Practices of communication surveillance by the 'Cyber Jihad' unit also included hacking the phones of activists and opposition leaders. In addition, Lamoureaux and Sureau (2019) confirmed that the NISS was engaged in a multitude of digital media surveillance practices such as 'blocking, controlling, jamming and slowing down certain websites, and hacking private accounts' (p. 39). The NISS controls the information and communication technology (ICT) infrastructure in the country both commercially through private companies' investments and at the state level. The NISS had a tight grip on the telecommunications providers and significant involvement in their hiring processes embedding NISS agents within their operations. The Telecommunications and Post Regulatory Authority (TPRA) was responsible for setting the limits to the allowed content on the internet and operated a state-sponsored online censorship programme through its internet service control unit. The regime created TPRA to replace the National Telecommunications Corporation as a new regulatory body and placed TPRA under the control of the Ministry of Defence. Furthermore, the regime enacted the Law on Combating Cybercrimes in 2018, which is based on the highly restrictive Informatics Offenses Act of 2007, and criminalises online activists, journalists and ordinary citizens for legitimate content that can be viewed by the state as disturbing public morality or public order, offending the reputation of the state or threatening national security (Hunt 2012; Ministry of Justice 2020).

The regime began taking notice of the threat of new communication technologies and social media mobilisation following the emergence of youth movements, particularly after the rise of *Girifna*, a Sudanese youth-led political movement that relied on the use of social media for political mobilisation. However, social movements in the country consistently challenged the limits and effectiveness of the regime's digital media surveillance. For example, *Nafeer*, a Sudanese youth-led humanitarian initiative, organised via social media, was able to overcome the NISS attempts to control the digital public space and suppress its online activities, and continued its operation of volunteering and relief activities in Sudan by 'mobilizing a larger networked support system based on social media links' (Lamoureaux and Sureau 2019). Furthermore, the increased oppression of women during the Bashir regime led women's groups to seek alternative spaces such as social media for freedom of expression and public life. Ali (2019) argues that in the context of structural inequalities in Sudan based on class, location, ethnicity and gender that shape women's experience, and more so under Bashir, online women's groups provided important social and political mobilisation platforms around specific issues, political struggle and alternatives forms of expression. These groups were targeted by the regime security apparatus and their members repeatedly faced repression.

Social Movement Suppression during the December Uprising

In December 2018, Bashir introduced emergency austerity measures that triggered anti-government demonstrations across the country, which turned into calls for Bashir to step down. The popular uprising included groups from across the social spectrum and different parts of the country. Bashir responded with brute force but failed to stop the protests from spreading. The security forces mounted a fierce crackdown on protesters, killing dozens, but the protest movement continued to gain momentum. In fact, it grew in part in response to the repressive practices of the security apparatus, which increased both solidarity and anger among the protesters. The Sudanese Professionals Association (SPA) emerged as the organising body of the protests and issued *The Declaration of Freedom and Change*, which was signed by the Forces of Freedom and Change (FFC), a broad coalition of political parties and civil society organisations, demanding the immediate and unconditional fall of Bashir and his regime. The declaration demanded an immediate transfer of power to a civilian government and laid down the path to a transitional period leading to a democratically elected civilian government. Failing to control the protests with brute force, Bashir declared a state of emergency, banned all unauthorised gatherings and provided the security forces and RSF with sweeping powers to quell the protests. This did not deter protesters, and after more than six months of non-violent insurrection the protest movement was able to stage a large sit-in protest outside the military headquarters that eventually resulted in the ouster of one of the most enduring and coercive regimes in the MENA region. Sudanese Armed Forces (SAF) defectors protected civilians and helped sustain the sit-in during the first few days, while protesters came under daily heavy gunfire from the security forces and the NCP militias attempting to break the sit-in. Over the next few days of the sit-in protest, security forces killed twenty-two people in attempts to clear it. Bashir was ousted on 11 April 2019 by the Sudanese Armed Forces (SAF) and replaced with a Transitional Military Council (TMC). Immediately, the TMC suspended the country's constitution, closed its borders and airspace and declared a three-month state of emergency. However, many of the TMC members were members of Bashir's security council and closely linked to the regime's atrocities and human rights violations in Darfur, Nuba Mountains and Blue Nile.

The protesters challenged the legitimacy of the TMC and demanded the unconditional transfer of power to a civilian-led transitional government. Under mounting pressure from the protest movement, three members of the TMC resigned on 25 April. However, the TMC refused to meet the demands of the protest movement. On the other hand, the FFC entered into a series of negotiations with the TMC about the transfer of power and the arrangement of the transitional period, which was a strategic mistake on the FFC's part. The TMC strategy was to prolong the negotiations while using repressive tactics to weaken the momentum of the social movement. The TMC made several attempts to break the sit-in during the negotiations where more than twenty people were killed, including soldiers from SAF who were protecting civilians in the sit-in area.

The TMC deliberately undermined the negotiations, leading to an impasse. For example, after a series of prolonged negotiations, an agreement on principles about the transitional period was reached. The proposed agreement at the time included a three-year transition period, a civilian cabinet, and a 300-member all-civilian transitional legislative body where the FFC would have two thirds of the seats and the TMC would appoint the remaining third. The agreement also included a Transitional Sovereign Council (TSC) made up of civilian and military members, but the issue of control over the TSC prevented the agreement from being finalised. Furthermore, amid the increasing violence instigated by NCP militias and NISS, the TMC suspended the talks for 72 hours, demanding the removal of roadblocks and barricades that the protesters had put up. This led the FFC to launch a successful two-day general strike to pressure the TMC to resume negotiations.

After months of intense negotiations, on 3 June, the TMC decided to break the sit-in. Forces of the NISS, RSF and militias of the NCP attacked the peaceful protest, committing the worst massacre since the start of the demonstration by opening fire, torching tents and killing hundreds of people. According to reports from the Sudanese Physicians Association and Physicians for Human Rights, 112 people were killed, between six and seven hundred people were injured and more than seventy cases of rape were reported (BBC 2019; Dahab et al. 2019; Fricke 2020). The TMC withdrew from all agreements reached with the FFC during the previous negotiations. The TMC also shut down internet access in the country for thirty-six days. Internet blackouts had previously occurred a few times during the protests in January, February and April 2019 (NetBlocks 2018, 2019a,b). However, after the 3 June massacre and internet blackout, the protest did not die down, and the social movement was able to organise through different tactics used in previous protests to expand networked activities offline (Ali 2019; Kadoda and Hale 2015; Lamoureaux and Sureau 2019). For example, the protest movement shifted to different communication strategies such as short messages and phone-to-phone communication to organise and spread information. The TMC's repressive actions continued to backfire, leading to the historic mass demonstration of 30 June 2019. Organised without internet and social media access in the country, the 30 June demonstration was the most decisive mass mobilisation event during the uprising. This event forced the TMC return to the negotiating table and a transitional power-sharing agreement was reached on 5 July 2019, with the mediation of the African Union.

Authoritarianism and Transition in Sudan

Authoritarianism is a dynamic concept with wide-ranging conceptualisations. While these conceptions seem to be centred on elections, political parties, or framing authoritarianism as state-level practice, recent scholarship in political science has opened up new ways to think about contemporary authoritarianism. For example, Glasius (2018) looks at authoritarianism from an accountability preceptive. She defines authoritarianism as the 'active practices of *accountability sabotage*'. From this perspective, transitional periods are not immune to authoritarianism. In fact, the current transition in Sudan, like previous ones, is complicated by what the former spokesman of the TMC admitted about dismantling the Bashir regime. He pointed out that it could take decades to eliminate the legacy of Bashir, suggesting a project well beyond the planned transition. This raises concerns about the prospects of democracy in Sudan.

The transitional period to date has three main characteristics: fragility of the transitional institutions, divergence of key democratisation processes and uncertainty of economic recovery (Berridge 2020; Khalifa 2020). The constant reproduction of crisis reflects the level of polarisation and division among the FFC and political elite as well as the contradictions in the power-sharing agreement. The military elite are gradually consolidating their power and strengthening their grip on the TSC, which is led by the military elite for what was supposed to be the first two years of the transitional period.

Sudan is currently attempting to carry out democratisation, but it is also facing many challenges that are not unique to Sudan. Scholarship on transitional challenges in the MENA countries (Liu 2015) outlines core elements that affect the progress of transitions including: (1) conflict between secularism and Islam; (2) military intervention; and (3) geopolitical factors. This is evident in the case of Sudan, as the demands of two major rebel factions for a secular state in post-uprising Sudan threaten the stability of the transitional period after they refused to sign the Juba Peace Agreement (Dahir 2020). The Sudan Liberation Movement/Army and Sudan People Liberation Movement/Army (North) are both demanding the right of self-determination in lieu of establishing a secular state and abolishing the *Shari'a* laws (a.k.a. the September laws). None of the transitional or elected governments that came after the ousted regime of Nimeiry was able to dismantle Nimeiry's legacy of *Shari'a* laws.

On the other hand, the TSC was established in the transitional constitution as a symbolic head of the state with no executive power. However, the military elite in the TSC continue to violate the transitional constitution, control key political processes such the peace process, stall the creation of a transitional parliament and block institutional reform of policing, the security apparatus and the judiciary system, among others. Additionally, Hemetti, the most notorious militia leader during the Bashir regime and known to the international media as the strongest man in Sudan, is consolidating his power during the transitional period through the establishment of the RFS as a legitimate organisation with immense financial resources from gold mining, supplying of troops to the war in Yemen, human trafficking in sub-Saharan Africa, and a growing business empire investing in health, food and entertainment, among other sectors (Gallopin 2020).

The struggle is increasingly intensifying between the competing power structures of the transitional period. For its part, the military elite in the TSC exploits the divisions among the political elite while increasingly aligning themselves with regional actors such as Egypt, Emirates and Saudi Arabia, seeking to intervene in the political process and influence the outcome of the transitional period (Custers 2020; Tisdall 2019). With the armed forces, paramilitary groups, security and intelligence services, information and communication technology (ICT) sector, and the military-security industrial complex, under the control of the military elite (Gallopin 2020), authoritarian practices in Sudan are poised to intensify during the transitional period, threatening any real prospects of democratisation and meaningful institutional building and reform.

Authoritarian learning and the politics of transition

Heydemann and Leenders (2011) argue that there are two symmetrical processes working in parallel in the unfolding and unravelling of authoritarian regimes in the MENA region: one is at the level of societies where the protest movement deploys a repertoire of contention tactics that work in its favour. The second is the learning process of authoritarian regimes. Heydemann and Leenders argue that authoritarian systems tend to learn from each other. The military elite in the TSC seem to have learned from the emerging strategies of authoritarian governance used by other MENA countries post the Arab Spring that are designed to undermine gains achieved by the recent uprisings in the region.

On the one hand, they are attempting to counter the impact of social media in political mobilisation through social media manipulation techniques similar to those of other countries in the region (Jones 2019; Leber and Abrahams 2019; Michaelsen 2017). They are employing techniques such as the use of online propaganda, fake news, content altering, hacking of activists accounts, and use of bots to create fake social media accounts to disseminate misinformation. In addition, the transitional government passed highly criticised amendments to the Law on Combating Cybercrimes of 2018. The changes introduced in the new amendments have left in place many of the repressive provisions of the Bashir regime. In fact, the amendments increase penalties for many activities specified in the original law. While internet freedom has generally improved under the transitional government, however, the reforms to the cybercrime laws and telecommunication regulations do not address practices of digital surveillance in post-uprising Sudan. According to the latest report from Freedom House on the state of the internet (Freedom House 2021), Sudan still lacks internet freedom and ranks among the worst countries in the world. For example, the army announced the appointment of a new cybercrime military commissioner to monitor and document online 'insults' by journalists and activists against the army and seek criminal persecution for any violation (Biajo 2020). Furthermore, the TSC has moved TPRA from the Ministry of Information and brought it under its direct control. This decision signals the desire of the military elite in the TSC to continue the practices of digital surveillance of the ousted regime and ensure their control over the information and communication infrastructure in the country.

On the other hand, new security laws are being passed following the footsteps of countries such as Egypt (El Gizouli 2020). For example, after the assassination attempt against the new Prime Minister of the transitional cabinet, the TSC, the cabinet and the FFC passed a new law to establish a new internal security apparatus separate from the newly reformed General Intelligence Service (GIS) to track, monitor and pre-empt the activities of terrorist groups linked to former NCP and Islamists in the country. El Gizouli (2020) points out that this new security apparatus will likely be designed in a similar fashion to its Egyptian counterpart and 'serve the dual function of appropriation and repression'. According to the new law, the definition of what constitutes a terrorist action includes any organisation with objectives opposed to the December uprising. El Gizouli (2020) argues that this is an ambiguous formula taken directly from the playbook of repressive regimes, highlighting the threat such formulation poses to civil liberties and reconstituting authoritarian practices as part of the transitional authority.

However, there are still as many reasons to remain optimistic as there are causes for concern during the current transitional period. For example, the resilience of social movements, and the sense of optimism among civil society actors with the tenacity of political parties and union-based organising (Berridge 2015), might in fact limit the possibility of an authoritarian comeback, at least in the near future. This was evidently stronger in the December uprising, in contrast to during past popular uprisings. The December uprising was the longest mass demonstration movement, lasting for more than six months. Protests in both previous uprisings, of October 1964 and April 1985, lasted three and nine days respectively before regime change. One other key difference is that civil movement resistance seems to be stronger in the marginalised parts of the country than in previous uprisings. For example, cities such as Ad-Dmazin, the capital city of Blue Nile state, Al-Fashir, the capital city of Northern Darfur, and Atbara in the north-east, were key sites for the December uprising. Indeed, this is no surprise given that these are the areas that were hit the hardest by the oppressive practices of Bashir's Islamist regime. All of these points underscore a stronger level of determination by the social movement and a renewed commitment towards democratisation in the country.

Conclusion

Authoritarianism in Sudan has evolved along with the changing nature of political struggle in the country. For example, Abboud took over against a backdrop of political rivalries between religious-right parties and Sudanese nationalists, while Nimeiry took over during a political struggle between the religious right and the left. Both the authoritarian Abboud and Nimeiry set up 'liberalised autocracies'. Brumberg (2002) argues that in liberalised autocracies the ruler's strategy is to pit opposition groups against one another in ways that give rulers room for manoeuvre and limit the opposition's capacity to co-operate for regime change. The degree to which an autocratic regime would accommodate the different social and political forces depends on the 'arbitrating role of the ruler' (Brumberg 2002: 61). This was evident during the Nimeiry regime, which aligned with different political groups in the country at different political moments. Nimeiry was able to survive through a series of shifting political alliances during his rule, ranging from the Communist Party and the political left in 1969 to southern regionalists in 1972 and, later, to the ICF and religious-right political parties in 1977. Both Nimeiry and Abboud opened up spaces of state-controlled liberties while subjecting the accommodation of the different social forces to their own arbitration. Nevertheless, both used state coercion to manage their respective versions of liberalised autocracies.

On the other hand, Bashir came to power with the rise of political Islam in the MENA region. Bashir's autocracy was more clearly built on the ideological and political support of the Islamist NCP as the basis for his *Tamkeen* policy. Bashir's authoritarian practices can be understood within the context of the evolution of authoritarianism in Sudan. Previous repressive regimes in Sudan provided the foundation and infrastructure from which Bashir's coercive security apparatus evolved. For example, the Nimeiry regime provided the foundation for the authoritarian rule of Bashir and his NCP party. Earlier in his autocracy, Bashir relied on members of the security apparatus associated with the INF and embedded within the Nimeiry regime. Furthermore, the Sudan civil war and the tension between secularism and the religious and spiritual underpinnings of Sudanese society were exploited by the authoritarian regimes as a means of authoritarian control. The civil war was positioned as a religious war and used to mobilise Northerners, especially those in riverain Sudan, against other parts of the country including the South. This also provided the pretext for Bashir to open up more military fronts and engage in ethno-politics and militarisation of the margins of the country to control opposing political groups. Ultimately, the failure to dismantle Nimeiry's legacy during the transitional period following the 1985 Intifada created an environment ripe for Bashir's authoritarian regime. However, both Nimeiry and Bashir ended up creating a personalistic style of autocracy that left them without allies and accelerated their demise towards the end of their rule.

Unfortunately, the current transitional period exhibits characteristics similar to those of the previous transitional period. For example, dismantling Bashir's legacy has proven to be an arduous task for the social movement during the transitional period thus far. The military elite are interested in keeping this legacy in order to strengthen their control over the state and reassert themselves as legitimate political actors with greater political influence. Mansouri (2016) argues that the democratisation process in the MENA region is still in its infancy, considering how deeply autocracies have penetrated the political process across the region. With the military elite controlling the critical functions of the state, the transitional period looks more and more like an 'enforced power-sharing' arrangement. Brumberg (2002) argues that 'enforced power-sharing can form an alternative to either full democracy or full autocracy, particularly when rival political, social, ethnic, or religious groups fear that either type of rule will lead to their political exclusion' (p. 61). In other words, this type of arrangement, if it continues, may lead to the current transitional period becoming the basis for a transition into a soft or semi-authoritarian governance model in Sudan. While it is still early in post-uprising Sudan to make any sort of conclusive political prediction about the future of the country, however, examining the different models of authoritarian rule that took hold in the Sudanese context might help in providing an understanding of the authoritarian practices in the current transitional period.

Notes

1 See also the 'Established Authoritarian Practices' section in the Introduction, which provides an overview of key examples of authoritarian continuities from the book chapters (Topak et al. 2022).

2 For other examples of international alliances, see the 'Authoritarian Learning and Alliances' section in the Introduction, which provides key examples from the book (Topak et al. 2022).

References

Agathangelou, A. M. and N. Soguk (2014). *Arab Revolutions and World Transformations*. London: Routledge.

Akbari, A. and R. Gabdulhakov (2019). 'Platform Surveillance and Resistance in Iran and Russia: The Case of Telegram', *Surveillance & Society* 17(1/2): 223–31.

Alamin, M. (2018). 'Sudan Militia Demands EU Payment for Blocking African Migrants', *Bloomberg*, 13 April. https://www.bloomberg.com/news/articles/20 18-04-13/sudan-militia-demands-eu-payment-for-blocking-african-migrants

Ali, N. M. (2019). 'Sudanese Women's Groups on Facebook and #Civil_ Disobedience: Nairat or Thairat? (Radiant or Revolutionary?)', *African Studies Review* 62(2): 103–26.

Alnasseri, S. (2018). *Arab Revolutions and Beyond: The Middle East and Reverberations in the Americas*. London: Palgrave Macmillan.

Baldo, S. (2017). 'Border Control from Hell: How the EU's migration partnership legitimizes Sudan's "militia state"' [analysis]. https://reliefweb.int/report/sudan /border-control-hell-how-eus-migration-partnership-legitimizes-sudans-militia -state

BBC (2019). 'Sudan Crisis: What You Need to Know', *BBC News*, 16 August. https://www.bbc.com/news/world-africa-48511226

Bellin, E. (2012). 'Reconsidering the Robustness of Authoritarianism in the Middle East: Lessons from the Arab Spring', *Comparative Politics* 44(2): 127–49.

Berridge, W. J. (2015). *Civil Uprisings in Modern Sudan: The 'Khartoum Springs' of 1964 and 1985*. New York: Bloomsbury Academic.

Berridge, W. J. (2020). 'Briefing: The Uprising in Sudan', *African Affairs* 119(474): 164–76.

Biajo, N. (2020). *Sudan Army's Plan Is to Return to 'Dark Days', Journalists Say | Voice of America – English*. Voice of America, 6 August. https://www.voanews.com/pr ess-freedom/sudan-armys-plan-return-dark-days-journalists-say

Blanchard, L. P. (2019). *Sudan's Uncertain Transition* (CRS Report CRS Report for Congress, R45794). Library of Congress. Congressional Research Service. Library of Congress. Congressional Research Service. https://www.hsdl.org/?ab stract&did=

Brumberg, D. (2002). 'Democratization in the Arab World? The Trap of Liberalized Autocracy', *Journal of Democracy* 13(4): 56–68.

Brynen, R., P. Moore, B. Salloukh and M.-J. Zahar. (2012a). *Beyond the Arab Spring:*

Authoritarianism & Democratization in the Arab World. Boulder, CO: Lynne Rienner.

Brynen, R., P. Moore, B. Salloukh and M.-J. Zahar. (2012b). 'New Horizons in Arab Politics', in *Beyond the Arab Spring: Authoritarianism & Democratization in the Arab World.* Boulder, CO: Lynne Rienner, pp. 1–13.

Burr, M., R. O. Collins and J. M. Burr (2003). *Revolutionary Sudan: Hasan Al-Turabi and the Islamist State, 1989–2000 Hasan Al-Turabi and the Islamist State, 1989–2000.* Leiden: Brill Academic.

Butcher, C. and I. Svensson (2016). 'Manufacturing Dissent: Modernization and the Onset of Major Nonviolent Resistance Campaigns', *Journal of Conflict Resolution* 60(2): 311–39.

Custers, D. (2020). 'Sudan's Transitional Process in the Face of Regional Rivalries'. *Middle East Centre,* 20 November. https://blogs.lse.ac.uk/mec/2020/11/20/sud ans-transitional-process-in-the-face-of-regional-rivalries/

Dahab, M., N. Abdelmagid, A. Kodouda and F. Checchi (2019). 'Deaths, Injuries and Detentions During Civil Demonstrations in Sudan: A Secondary Data Analysis', *Conflict and Health* 13(16).

Dahir, A. L. (2020). 'Sudan Signs Peace Deal with Rebel Alliance', *The New York Times,* 16 August. https://www.nytimes.com/2020/08/31/world/africa/sudan -peace-agreement-darfur.html

Dalek, J., L. Gill, B. Marczak, S. McKune, N. Noor, J. Oliver, J. Penney, A. Senft and R. Deibert (2018). *Planet Netsweeper* [Research Report]. The Citizen Lab – Munk School of Global Affairs & Public Policy, University of Toronto. https:// citizenlab.ca/2018/04/planet-netsweeper/

Deibert, R. (2015). 'Cyberspace under Siege', *Journal of Democracy* 26(3): 64–78.

Deng, F. M. (1995). *War of Visions.* Washington, DC: Brookings Institution Press.

El Gizouli, M. (2020). Will the New Sudan follow Egypt's Authoritarian Path? *Middle East Eye,* 25 March. http://www.middleeasteye.net/opinion/will-new-su dan-follow-egypts-authoritarian-path

Freedom House. (2021). *Sudan: Freedom on the Net 2020 Country Report.* https://fr eedomhouse.org/country/sudan/freedom-net/2020

Fricke, A. (2020). *'Chaos and Fire': An Analysis of Sudan's June 3, 2019 Khartoum Massacre.* Physicians for Human Rights' (PHR). https://phr.org/our-work/res ources/chaos-and-fire-an-analysis-of-sudans-june-3-2019-khartoum-massacre/

Gallopin, J.-B. (2020). *Bad Company: How Dark Money Threatens Sudan's Transition.* The European Council on Foreign Relations (ECFR). https://ecfr.eu/publicati on/bad_company_how_dark_money_threatens_sudans_transition/

Glasius, M. (2018). 'What Authoritarianism Is . . . and Is Not: A Practice Perspective', *International Affairs* 94(3): 515–33.

Hasan, Y. F. (1967). 'The Sudanese Revolution of October 1964', *The Journal of Modern African Studies* 5(4): 491–509.

Hassan, M. and A. Kodouda (2019). 'Sudan's Uprising: The Fall of a Dictator', *Journal of Democracy* 30(4): 89–103.

Heydemann, S. and R. Leenders (2011). 'Authoritarian Learning and Authoritarian Resilience: Regime Responses to the "Arab Awakening"', *Globalizations* 8(5): 647–53.

Holt, P. M. (1961). *A Modern History of the Sudan*. London: Weidenfeld & Nicolson.

Hunt, N. (2012). 'Report: Need for Press Freedom Reform in Sudan', *International Media Support*, 12 November. https://www.mediasupport.org/report-need-for-press-freedom-reform-in-sudan/

ICC. (2010). *Second Warrant of Arrest for Omar Hassan Ahmad Al Bashir*. https://www.icc-cpi.int/Pages/record.aspx?docNo=ICC-02/05-01/09-95

Jones, M. O. (2019). 'Propaganda, Fake News, and Fake Trends: The Weaponization of Twitter Bots in the Gulf Crisis', *International Journal of Communication* 13: 1,389–415.

Kadoda, G. and S. Hale (2015). 'Contemporary Youth Movements and the Role of Social Media in Sudan', *Canadian Journal of African Studies/Revue Canadienne Des Études Africaines* 49(1): 215–36.

Khalifa, A. A. (2020). *Sudan's Transition: Challenges and Opportunities*. The Washington Institute, 1 June. https://www.washingtoninstitute.org/policy-analysis/view/Sudan-Transitional-Government-Economy-Peace-Building

Khondker, H. (2011). 'Role of the New Media in the Arab Spring', *Globalizations* 8(5): 675–9.

Kingsley, P. (2018). 'By Stifling Migration, Sudan's Feared Secret Police Aid Europe', *The New York Times*, 23 April. https://www.nytimes.com/2018/04/22/world/africa/migration-european-union-sudan.html

Lamoureaux, S. and T. Sureau (2019). 'Knowledge and Legitimacy: The Fragility of Digital Mobilisation in Sudan', *Journal of Eastern African Studies* 13(1): 35–53.

Lawson, G. (2015). 'Revolution, Non-violence, and the Arab Uprisings', *Mobilization* 20(4): 453–70.

Leber, A. and A. Abrahams (2019). 'A Storm of Tweets: Social Media Manipulation during the Gulf Crisis', *Review of Middle East Studies* 53(2): 241–58. 9.45.

Liu, Z. (2015). 'Middle East Upheavals and Democratic Transition of Arab Countries', *Journal of Middle Eastern and Islamic Studies (in Asia)* 9(2): 38–72.

Lo, M. (2019). 'Turabi's Islamic Project: From the Rhetoric of Freedom to the Politics of Tamkeen', in M. Lo (ed.) *Political Islam, Justice and Governance*. New York: Springer, pp. 249–303.

MacKinnon, R. (2011). 'China's "Networked Authoritarianism"', *Journal of Democracy* 22(2): 32–46.

Mansouri, F. (2016). 'Prospects for Democratization in the Middle East Post-Arab Spring', in A. Saikal (ed.), *The Arab World and Iran: A Turbulent Region in Transition*. London: Palgrave Macmillan, 9–28.

Mekouar, M. (2014). 'No Political Agents, No Diffusion: Evidence from North Africa', *International Studies Review* 16(2): 206–16.

Michaelsen, M. (2017). 'Far Away, So Close: Transnational Activism, Digital Surveillance and Authoritarian Control in Iran', *Surveillance & Society* 15(3/4): 465–70.

Ministry of Justice (2020). *Law on Combating Cybercimes – Ministry of Justice – Sudan*, July. https://moj.gov.sd/files/download/204

NetBlocks (2018). 'Study Shows Extent of Sudan Internet Disruptions Amid Demonstrations', *NetBlocks*, 21 December. https://netblocks.org/reports/study -shows-impact-of-sudan-internet-disruptions-amid-demonstrations-qr8Vj485

NetBlocks (2019a). 'Social Media Access Restored across Sudan', *NetBlocks*, 26 February. https://netblocks.org/reports/social-media-access-restored-across-sudan-noy9dnB3

NetBlocks (2019b). 'Social Media Disrupted in Sudan as Protests Converge in Khartoum', *NetBlocks*, 7 April. https://netblocks.org/reports/social-media-disru pted-in-sudan-as-protests-converge-in-khartoum-peBONpAZ

Poggo, S. S. (2002). 'General Ibrahim Abboud's Military Administration in the Sudan, 1958–1964: Implementation of the Programs of Islamization and Arabization in the Southern Sudan', *Northeast African Studies* 9(1): 67–101.

Stevis-Gridneff, M. and S. Said (2019). 'As Sudan Grapples with a Post-Bashir Future, Regional Powers Circle', *Wall Street Journal*, 27 April. https://www.wsj .com/articles/as-sudan-grapples-with-a-post-bashir-future-regional-powers-circ le-11556362800

Tisdall, S. (2019). 'Sudan: How Arab Autocrats Conspired to Thwart Reformists' Hopes', *The Guardian*, 3 June. http://www.theguardian.com/world/2019/jun /03/sudanese-crackdown-comes-after-talks-with-egypt-and-saudis

Topak, Ö. E. (2019). 'The Authoritarian Surveillant Assemblage: Authoritarian State Surveillance in Turkey', *Security Dialogue* 50(5): 454–72.

Topak, Ö. E., M. Mekouar and F. Cavatorta (2022). 'Introduction', in Ö. E. Topak, M. Mekouar and F. Cavatorta (eds) *New Authoritarian Practices in the Middle East and North Africa*. Edinburgh: Edinburgh University Press, pp. 1–29.

Tossell, J. (2020). *Consolidating Sudan's Transition: A Question of Legitimacy* [CRU Policy Brief]. Clingendael – the Netherlands Institute of International Relations. https://www.clingendael.org/publication/consolidating-sudans-transition

Tubiana, J., C. Warin and G. M. Saeneen (2018). *Multilateral Damage: The Impact of EU Migration Policies on Central Saharan Routes*. The Clingendael Institute – Netherlands Institute of International Relations. https://www.clingendael.org /pub/2018/multilateral-damage/

Uniacke, R. (2020). 'Authoritarianism in the Information Age: State Branding, Depoliticizing and "De-civilizing" of Online Civil Society in Saudi Arabia and the United Arab Emirates', *British Journal of Middle Eastern Studies*, first view. https://doi.org/10.1080/13530194.2020.1737916

United States Department of State (2017). *2016 Country Reports on Human Rights Practices – Sudan*. https://www.refworld.org/docid/58ec89c54.html

Yom, S. L. and F. G. Gause (2012). 'Resilient Royals: How Arab Monarchies Hang On', *Journal of Democracy* 23(4): 74–88.

14

AUTHORITARIAN NOSTALGIA AND PRACTICES IN NEWLY DEMOCRATISING CONTEXTS: THE LOCALISED EXAMPLE OF TUNISIA

Giulia Cimini[1]

Introduction

In recent years, concern about the rise of a global tide of authoritarianism has increased (Glasius 2018; Moghaddam 2019; Diamond 2020). On the one hand, several democracies have been backsliding (Bermeo 2016), with leaders such as Erdogan in Turkey, Duterte in the Philippines, Orbán in Hungary and Modi in India regularly branded 'authoritarian'. Likewise, the deterioration of democratic institutions affects other Western countries with a long track record of upholding basic freedoms and rights, like the United States (Freedom House 2020a). On the other hand, the Middle East and North Africa (MENA), which still accounts for a significant geographical concentration of authoritarian or semi-authoritarian regimes, has largely circumvented attempts at democratisation in the last decade. In 2010–11, the much-criticised democratisation studies came back onto the agenda of scholars and policymakers for a time, challenging long-dominant assumptions of Arab authoritarian 'exceptionalism'. Yet, after only a few months, possibilities for democratic change seemed far more remote, and Tunisia remains the only democratic success in the region, though President Kais Saied's power grab in summer 2021 is challenging this.

Authoritarian drifting in established democracies and authoritarian resilience are two distinct phenomena. However, a practice perspective is an important and under-appreciated lens of analysis through which to look at new developments in both cases. This is key to examining what authoritarianism may look like in democratic settings, as well as in those contexts where democracy has not yet taken root. Several factors may account for this lack of analysis. So far as democracies are concerned, Glasius (2018) points out at least three possible explanations: firstly, the fact that 'authoritarianism' is usually conceived in negative terms as a 'shortfall of democracy without a definition in its own' with the risk of unhelpfully stretching the term; secondly, the over-emphasis on electoral malpractice, so that it overshadows other dimensions of the 'quality' of democracy; and, thirdly, the almost exclusive vantage point of the nation-state level of enquiry, which dismisses *tout court* the role played by globalisation. As Topak et al. recall in the introduction to this volume, when it comes to portraying resilient authoritarian regimes, scholars privileged structural explanations drawing attention to factors like the legacies of de-institutionalisation and identitarian ties (Heydemann 2016), rent-distribution mechanisms and elite co-optation (Brynen et al. 2013), foreign alliances (Yom and Gause 2012) and brute coercion (Bellin 2012). All these approaches follow more traditional frameworks typical of the authoritarian resilience paradigm so dominant in the 2000s after the disillusionment with the region's hopes of democratisation in the 1990s. They centred on the political role of the military, on the security apparatus, or on the exploitation of sectarian cleavages above all.

Focusing here on the MENA region, the limits of a merely structuralist approach, not least in terms of dichotomous views, are evidenced by another phenomenon: the cross-country persistence of mobilisation and social unrest regardless of regime (re)configuration. This is an indicator of a more variegated reality on the ground, which can hardly be frozen in a binary logic of authoritarianism versus democratisation. Indeed, despite a significant variance and diversity in post-2011 political trajectories, contentious moments and protest movements have never ceased to punctuate Arab politics, as clearly epitomised by what is often called the 'Arab Spring 2.0' with the 2018–19 upheavals in Sudan, Algeria, Iraq and Lebanon (Schwedler et al. 2019). Not unlike the calls to re-evaluate the micro-dynamics of struggle and dissent for a more comprehensive understanding of contemporary Arab politics (El Issawi and Cavatorta 2020) so as to capture what Heydemann (2002) calls 'politics under the radar', the detection of micro-practices of authoritarianism directly speaks to the more plausible presence of changes within continuity and that of continuities within change.

A practice-oriented approach offers valid insights for both established democracies and enduring authoritarian regimes, however different the forms they take might be: liberal autocracies (Brumberg 2002), authoritarian-democratic hybrid regimes (Stepan and Linz 2013), grey zones, semi-authoritarian entities, among a wide variety of adjectives as descriptors of different forms of polity that are neither 'classic' authoritarian nor fully democratic. But what about fully-fledged relatively new democracies?

This is, indeed, a third scenario – in addition to established democracies experiencing authoritarian tendencies and resilient authoritarian regimes – that deserves attention and that is equally lacking in the exploration of authoritarian practices. Unlike other case studies in this book, the present chapter analyses this possibility through the atypical example of Tunisia. In stark contrast to the most recent wave of democratic recession, democracy has taken hold in Tunisia (Diamond 2020). Nonetheless, the country finds itself in a peculiar situation. On the one hand, wide sectors of Tunisian society have successfully reclaimed and re-appropriated the public space, with the achievement of unprecedented levels of civil and political rights. On the other, most of the same old elites and governing methods have remained in place, notwithstanding the initial euphoria of breaking with the Ben Ali regime and the authoritarian practices it embodied. At the same time, and alarmingly, the new system has so far failed to address key aspects of social justice and economic development.

This chapter thus revolves around two main research questions. How does 'nostalgia' for the autocrat's myth play out in Tunisia's new-born democracy? To what extent do legacies of the old regime manifest themselves? The argument is that the remnants of authoritarianism are manifested in the revival of pre-existing patterns of securitisation and police abuse nurtured by a feeling of authoritarian nostalgia and the parallel discrediting of the democratic system, with both acting as direct incentives and 'negative' inducements respectively. In other words, an illusory nostalgia for strong, centralised power capitalises on the widespread malaise for unmet social welfare demands and the ambiguities in ruling elite re-composition. This sentiment resurfaces from time to time and accompanies accusations against a dysfunctional democratic system (Brumberg and Ben Salem 2020). Meanwhile, legal battles to circumvent revolutionary claims, ensure impunity for old economic and political elites and expand legal protections for security forces, alongside the heavy-handed response to some key protests against the backdrop of the securitisation mantra, all rest on the old regime's toolkit and mindset, although to a different extent.

Hence, this chapter illustrates the shortcomings and contradictions of an unclear break with the institutions and politics of the days of dictatorship. First, it will reflect on the concept of authoritarian nostalgia and the leaders playing this card. It will then focus on empirical cases like police empowerment and the heavy-handed response to some key protests, alongside other practices that, without being necessarily authoritarian, favour counter-revolutionary sentiment. It concludes with a likely generalisation of the findings from the experience of Tunisia.

The Trap of Authoritarian Nostalgia

In Tunisia, there has been no return to heavy-handed autocratic forms. Likewise, there is no unified reactionary front, nor new systematised authoritarian practices permeating all levels of governance and reducible to a single, centralised and coherent logic of action. Yet, some troubling trends have been emerging and can be described as multi-faceted authoritarian reflexes. First is the return of political currents claiming not only Bourguiba's modernist and statist heritage but also Ben Ali's legacy, which results in a proud claim to a mythical past with a fairly strong grip on the population. Second are the revival of practices and attitudes which were hallmarks of the former regime. Third is the disillusionment with the new political order on the basis of its poor socio-economic performance, that is, the failure of a much-wanted 'social' democracy to emerge and meet those demands of social justice included in the calls for 'bread' and 'dignity' of the revolutionary slogans (Teti et al. 2019). It is the cumulative effect of these aspects that hinders democratic anchoring and even fosters democratic setbacks. This failure characterises also the case of Iraq where socio-economic demands have not been met despite almost two decades of pluralist politics. In her chapter in this volume, Costantini (2022) shows that Iraqi security services manage socio-economic dissent through 'authoritarian reflexes', including both traditional violent repression and new methods of coercion.

The first trend relates to authoritarian nostalgia, which is but one of the manifestations of democratic backsliding. It refers to sentiments among citizens that idealise past periods of authoritarian rule. With nostalgia, a disappointing present is contrasted with a romanticised conception of the past, and of its strongmen. This phenomenon is not unique to Tunisia and has been observed in both transitioning and consolidated democracies. Yet, as de Leeuw et al. (2018: 5) note, the literature tapping into this nostalgic element is relatively scarce and the few extant studies tend to focus on Central and Eastern European countries and their communist-socialist legacies, virtually ignoring right-wing authoritarian regimes. As for those countries, for example, Neundorf and her colleagues (2020) have shown higher nostalgia and weaker democratic support among individuals who grew up under authoritarianism. In contrast, Al Shamary (2018) recalls other studies demonstrating that in sub-Saharan democratising countries it is especially the youth who are more supportive of authoritarianism precisely because they did not live under authoritarian constraints. During my participant observation in Tunisia since 2014, it was common to hear sentiments of nostalgia expressed by ordinary people, which could easily be summarised (and simplified) in the refrain 'We were better off when we were worse off'. Though anecdotal, these observations are corroborated by several surveys. Data from the Afrobarometer (Meddeb 2018) have documented, for instance, a decreasing rejection of one-party rule ('only' 51 per cent, down from 68 per cent in 2015) or one-man rule in the country (from 79 to 61 per cent). According to the Arab Barometer (2019), the percentage of those associating democracy with negative terms – for example, 'indecisive', 'ineffective at maintaining stability' and 'leading to weak economic outcomes' – has grown between 2010–11 and 2016–17, although it then began to drop. Notably, young people are more likely to blame their country's economic challenges on its democratic configuration (Arab Barometer 2019). At the same time, the same surveys capture a high level of support for democracy despite its 'faults' (79 per cent).

These data are not necessarily as contradictory as it may seem at first glance. Rather, they confirm the coexistence of multiple trends and preferences that the binary logic of democratisation and authoritarianism fails to account for. Unsurprisingly, dissatisfaction with government performance and the instability of the present largely contribute in explaining the roots of authoritarian nostalgia, and the support that many Tunisians provided for the summer 2021 'constitutional coup' on the part of the elected president speaks to this. With the democratic model still failing to address the redistributive claims raised in the 2011 uprisings, the people's discontent with (formal) politics significantly increased. This allows a nostalgic rhetoric to gain ground, in parallel with anti-establishment forces, narrow-minded nationalism and populist stances. In the aftermath of the 2011 pro-democracy uprisings, the clear will of the founding fathers of the Second Republic to prevent the authoritarian return of Ben Ali's style of governance – intimately associated with centralisation and personalism in the collective perception – has been constitutionalised with 'interwoven powers' invested in the heads of the executive branch: the prime minister on the one hand and the president of the Republic on the other. In recent years, some challenged the effectiveness of the semi-presidential regime adopted in the constitution, and former president Beji Caid Essebsi (2014–19) often pushed for constitutional amendments towards a 'presidentialisation' of the system. The conjunction of the slow pace of reforms enacted by newly democratic institutions with his strong presidency – legitimised by direct popular vote – has frequently pointed to the 'dysfunctions' of the new-born democratic regime for the stalemates it often causes. In other words, the core of the crisis lies in the way the political system is currently designed as it divides, and thus weakens, executive power. Such a condition echoes from time to time in a growing nostalgia for a strongman in contrast to the alleged inefficiency of corporate but polarised bodies, like parliament and government, in facing the country's economic and security challenges. In this, the 'mythology' surrounding the political, economic and social development in Ben Ali's Tunisia plays out (Cavatorta and Haugbølle 2012).

Whereas Essebsi – alternatively considered the champion of Tunisian modernism and the guarantor of stability or a symbol of counter-revolution and democratic backsliding – endorsed this narrative as an incumbent, anti-establishment forces also jumped on the bandwagon. Among others, the conservative, anti-Islamist and ultra-nationalist right-wing Free Destourian Party (*Parti destourien libre*, PDL) emerged in Tunisia's political landscape in 2019–20. Its outspoken leader, the 45-year-old lawyer Abir Moussi, is the former Deputy Secretary General of the disbanded Democratic Constitutional Rally (RCD), Ben Ali's ruling party. She openly claims his heritage (I'm a *Ben Aliste*, she says) and challenges the revolutionary gains. In the 2019 parliamentary elections, the PDL came in third place after Ennahda and the personalist Heart of Tunisia party with 6.6 per cent of votes. Since then, there has been a crescendo in popular support for Moussi's party. Recent surveys on voting intentions from Tunisian polling agencies Sigma Conseil and Emrhod Consulting showed that the PDL is in a virtual dead heat with Ennahda with around 22 per cent (*The Arab Weekly* 2020). Virtually, the party has more than tripled its consensus in less than a year. On a related note, Moussi's husband is the chief of one of the many police unions that mushroomed over the course of 2011 and 2012 after having been for long banned from forming professional associations or going on strike (Sayigh 2015), and 'she's become the political spokesperson for the police unions' (Kimball 2019). It could be of secondary importance, were it not that the latter acted as strong reactionary forces. This is clearly evident in their hostility towards Tunisia's Truth and Dignity Commission, which is charged with investigating the gross human rights violations that the Tunisian State has committed since 1955 in order to provide compensation and rehabilitation to victims. Police unions have also been lobbying MPs, even by threatening to stop protecting them, for the adoption of controversial laws to their benefit, and have put pressure on judges in a number of trials involving police officers (Grewal 2018; Walsh 2019). In the midst of a pandemic, and with the parliament disagreeing on everything, a draft law seeking to expand legal protections for domestic security forces and customs officers was recently revived in the assembly by Moussi's PDL after being shelved back in 2015. By proposing sentences ranging from three months to three years in prison for anybody criticising the actions of law enforcement, the amendment caused a public outcry. It showcases an 'outdated conception of the security forces, one in which citizens should show a level of respect to law enforcement that practically borders on worship' (Dahmani 2020). Some also point to the enhancement of police powers and the politicised use of military courts against civilians as facilitating factors for a potential strongman's takeover in a still fragile democracy (Grewal 2019). This legacy and authoritarian nostalgia mutually reinforce each other. At the same time, they go hand in hand with the renewal of practices typical of past authoritarian regimes, of which the police in particular have become the protagonists, as the next section illustrates.

Old Wine in New Bottles? The Shadows of Authoritarian Tendencies

Regardless of potential strongman (or -woman) takeovers, shadows of the old regime play out in a number of distinct yet interrelated aspects. The first of these is the re-launch of old practices under the country's new 'state of exception' and the post-2015 securitisation mantra. These practices were part and parcel of the authoritarian arsenal to safeguard the previous regime and suppress dissent, and include restrictions on public gatherings, and restrictions on freedom of movement, assembly and expression, as well as broad licence for the police to arrest and detain people on security-related – or terrorism-related – charges. Second, during the spread of Covid-19 new practices emerged, but their character seems nonetheless ephemeral and not yet reducible to a single, coherent state project. Finally, it is worth reflecting upon initiatives that, without being authoritarian *per se*, nurtured a widespread sense of impunity enjoyed by old regime elites and apparatus, further reducing accountability and strengthening clientelist and personalistic networks (Mohsen-Finan 2018).

In short, Tunisia has not elaborated new authoritarian practices thus far, but rather has selectively restored some of the old ones that never entirely disappeared, especially with regard to the Ministry of the Interior (MoI), a pillar of the former authoritarian regime. Indeed, a notable difference with the past is that whereas 'authoritarianism' was previously centralised by the Presidency, Ben Ali's legacy of authoritarian rule and practices is far more scattered and outside of political control. In a way, and in parallel with the increasing weaknesses of governments and parliament, not to mention the absence of fundamental democratic institutions like the Constitutional Court, multiple competing centres of power are emerging, like police unions. Notwithstanding their fragmentation, they have increasingly become powerful actors, with little or no control from elected politicians. Under Ben Ali, Tunisia 'was commonly considered a police state *par excellence*' and one of 'the most heavily policed states in the world (Lutterbeck 2015: 1). The MoI was, to use Lutterbeck (2015)'s terms, 'presidentialised' in that it was under the direct control of the Presidency. Whereas the country's level of police density prior to 2011 is still debated and available figures were later considered to be deliberately inflated (Hanlon 2012), the generally held perception of the Tunisian police's omnipresence is a striking feature of the past regime (Lutterbeck 2015). The police were not only a tool of Ben Ali's authoritarian rule, as widely acknowledged (Camau and Geisser 2003; Hibou 2006), but became a symbol of corruption, repression and nepotism: in other words, a symbol of the regime itself. Notably, Bouazizi's self-immolation after police confiscated his merchandise was the perfect example of something familiar to many Tunisians (and Arab citizens): arbitrary and humiliating treatment by the state, personified by police officers. Unsurprisingly, police stations were a major target of the demonstrators' anger during the 2011 uprising.

The police can rightfully be considered a key reactionary force in post-2011 Tunisia. When talking about revived practices pointing to the reflexes of authoritarianism, securitising protests and policing citizens have to be mentioned. As Gordner (2019: 15) notes, mobilisations by the pro-transitional justice and anti-corruption movement *Manich Msamah* (I Will Not Forgive) 'were met with infiltration, surveillance, repression, and arrests'. In addition to nationwide movements like *Manich Msamah* or the anti-austerity and pro-dignity *Fech Nestanneou* (What Are We Waiting For?) campaign in response to the new financial law in January 2018, there were also more localised protests. Indeed, since 2015 protests have become increasingly fragmented and decentralised (Vatthauer and Weipert-Fenner 2017) on issues of under-development and mismanagement of resources, rocking especially the south-west and south-east of the country. The year 2016 marked a new critical moment of social unrest following the suicide of unemployed graduate Ridha Yahyaoui, which recalled Bouazizi's iconic self-immolation. In particular, protests spread in the interior and southern regions of Kasserine, Tatatouine and Kebili. Setting aside their local specificities, all these protracted protests see young people in precarious employment at the core of mobilisation. Securing employment and local development are key demands, and road blocks, riots and sit-ins are the main modalities of action. The way in which the police dealt with the new wave of protests hit a sensitive nerve, given the violence employed and the overall repressive attitude various police forces adopted at the local level. The disproportionate use of force was a restoration of old practices. Beyond policing people, and as part of the securitisation strategy, defamatory rhetoric was used to discredit protesters by insinuating that criminals or terrorists had infiltrated the movement, threatening the country's security (Okkez 2016). For instance, during the mobilisation against the energy corporation Petrofac on the Kerkennah Islands (Sfax region) in 2016, many accounts tell of surprise night-time police raids as counter-terrorist operations, a massive display of force with tear gas and water cannon, hardly discriminating between protesters, or between protesters and the general population (Feltrin 2018). In June 2020, the indiscriminately violent crackdown on peaceful demonstrators protesting their difficult economic situations in the southern town of Tataouine was equally alarming. Human rights violations and police abuses were common practice in authoritarian Tunisia, resulting sometimes in deaths and mostly targeting opponents of the regime. Yet, as Lutterback (2015) recalls, the system relied more on forms of 'administrative control' than on the physical disappearance or elimination of opponents. In the most recent years, harassment and abuses became increasingly random.

In Tunis, multiple cases of police violence against women, LGTB activists and lawyers were reported (The Observers 2020). According to human rights organisations, different cases of police violations, even culminating in unlawful killings, are emblematic of a wider pattern of abuse and brutality. Even more worrying is the absence of impartiality of investigative judges when the suspected crime perpetrator is a police officer, and the lack of transparency in decision-making, resulting in stalled investigations and no accountability. For example, in March 2018, a young football supporter's death made national headlines. Nineteen-year-old Omar Laabidi drowned in a canal when, after a football match, he was pushed into it by a group of policemen who ignored his claims that he could not swim (Amnesty International 2019). The hashtag '*t3alem 3oum*' (Learn to swim), recalling the alleged retort of the policeman to Omar, went viral, sparking outrage. In another case, Ayman Othmani, 19, was shot in the back during a raid by customs officers on a warehouse in Tunis, where they believe smuggled goods were stored. According to witnesses, officers surrounded Ayman after they had shot him and beat him while he was unconscious before he died from his wounds (Amnesty International 2019). All these episodes, which are by no means isolated, resume pre-existing patterns of violence and impunity.

The heavy-handed approach of police and other security forces has also been legitimised in light of the dominant securitisation mantra. As the followers of the Copenhagen School would put it, the securitisation process dramatises politicised or non-politicised issues as issues of supreme priority, that need to be dealt with using urgent and extraordinary measures, even breaking democratic rules. In this sense, terrorism has become an all-encompassing category for all sorts of mobilisation, and the securitisation mantra was easily adopted and justified after the 2015 terrorist attacks on foreign tourists at the Bardo museum in Tunis and the beach resort in Sousse. Watchdog organisations have not ceased to denounce police abuses, torture and a disproportionate level of surveillance, which all threaten democratic freedoms in the name of counter-terrorism (Amnesty International 2016; Human Rights Watch 2018). Against this backdrop, the state of emergency continuously in place since 2015 provides the government and the Interior Ministry with exceptional powers, allows the monitoring of the press, and imposes significant constraints on individuals' movements and public demonstrations, among others. In its last report on Tunisia, Freedom House (2020b) confirms that under the state of emergency thousands of people have faced severe restrictions on their freedom of movement and arbitrary arrests have continued to take place.

This permanent state of exception, long before the lockdowns and curfews imposed by the Covid-19 outbreak, spread the idea of an illusory 'normality'. What should be extraordinary circumstances have been increasingly normalised and are becoming part of ordinary life in a democratic/democratising society. When reflecting upon the diffusion of illiberal practices in many NATO and European Union countries, Laurence (2019) recalls Walter Benjamin's aphorism that 'the state of emergency in which we live is not the exception but the rule' to introduce the tricky if not dangerous effects of permanent emergencies. Unsurprisingly, these worldwide restrictions were introduced as counter-terrorism tools, particularly after 9/11 (Lyon and Haggerty 2012). Tunisia is no exception. Agamben's (2005) thought-provoking claim that the suspension of the legal order to face an existential threat is becoming the dominant paradigm of government in contemporary politics and democratic societies fits Tunisia well. The extent to which the state of exception is normalised and consolidating as a mode of governance remains an open question, but, undoubtedly, the Tunisian 'war on terror' has been frustrating many of the civil liberties acquired since 2011. What is clear, though, is that it favoured the resumption of old practices and the (re-)empowerment of actors which the previous regime was based on, like the security forces. The exogenous shock of the 2015 attacks accelerated the long-awaited reform of the security sector, but with a lighter footprint than originally intended. Indeed, the performance-driven approach typical of Security Assistance programmes aimed at modernising equipment and improving training standards overshadowed the more comprehensive Security Sector Reform that encompasses issues of governance, ethics, rule of law and human rights. On the domestic front, the terrorist threat sped up the adoption of the 2015 counter-terrorist law, which replaced the strongly criticised 2003 Anti-Terrorism Act. The latter, interestingly, had been neither abrogated nor amended after the revolution. The 'favourable' juncture after the terrorist attacks allowed the new law to see the light of day, but, despite some improvements, it has been referred to as a return to a 'police state', with regard to those provisions relating to the extension of the period of detention and the (re-)introduction of the death penalty (Human Rights Watch 2015), as well as for the wide-ranging immunity granted to investigators and for the infringements on the right to privacy (Privacy International 2019).

Whereas all the examples mentioned in the previous paragraphs directly point to the revival of old practices, with the spread of the Covid-19 some additional practices have been introduced, namely the technology for tracking citizens' movements enforcing the lockdown, the absence of judicial recourse and the delegation of measures usually prescribed by judicial authorities to security officers – like mandatory hospitalisation (Jrad 2020). On closer inspection, though, these practices are not completely new either. It is the 'exceptional' circumstances in which they were taking place that are new. While Tunisia's fledgling democracy is more likely to be threatened by the economic fallout than a securitised response to the pandemic, and despite reassurances about the temporary nature of 'exceptional' measures, the prompt deployment of anti-Covid technology to monitor the population – like drones for detection and robots to enforce the lockdown – is not exempt from criticism. As French and Monahan (2020: 8) argue, surveillance dynamics as part of the authorities' response to the pandemic strictly pertain to 'sociocultural constructions of (in)security, vulnerability, and risk'. The readiness to deploy this technology – first produced in 2015 for security uses – to patrol civilians in the streets easily fits into an existing pattern of resumed securitisation. This is all the more so given that such cutting-edge, expensive technologies are largely if not completely absent from other sectors of society, from public administration to justice, education and healthcare. For the sake of clarity, the MoI did not deploy massively remote-controlled robots, but limited this experiment to the Tunis capital, and with very few units. Known as P-Guard, they were equipped with infra-red and thermal imaging cameras and interacted with suspected violators of the lockdown (Ministry of Interior 2020). However, their employment still remains problematic.

Against this backdrop, the short-lived proposal for a draft law aimed at fighting fake news and criminalising online defamation was seen in some quarters as a renewed attempt to restrict freedom of expression and information under the guise of combating the Covid-19 emergency (Ben Mbarek and Aliriza 2020). During the pandemic, a number of bloggers and online activists were arrested and several received prison sentences for posting purportedly fake news about the coronavirus (Freedom House 2020c). Others have been prosecuted on charges of defamation and online offences following their criticism of security forces and of local public officials' poor management of the crisis (ibid.). Indeed, Decree No. 115 of 2011 – the new Press Code – provides some protection for professional journalists, but does not include bloggers. In addition to this vacuum, the most significant problem lies with the judiciary, which continues to employ laws from the Ben Ali era that have not been amended or substituted since. Hence, whereas the 2014 constitution bans censorship and enshrines the right to free expression and freedom of the press, the 'old' penal and telecommunications codes are still in place, infringing on those rights. These are exactly the practices that caused many to fear a U-turn on the progress achieved since the uprising, and that are indicative of persisting legacies from the past even in the new democratic setting.

Furthermore, it is worth noting that authoritarian reflexes resurface, leveraging specific practices and discourses, as well as highly symbolic battles that have nonetheless practical implications, not least the re-empowerment of old regime personalities. Notably, reactionary forces – meaning here old regime cronies and networks first of all – engaged in legislative battles over transitional justice. Lustration provisions and the reconciliation law are a case in point. Whereas the former aimed at safeguarding Tunisia's democracy from recalcitrant former ruling elites reclaiming the Destourian legacy of the Ben Ali or Bourguiba regimes, the latter should have helped the country to move towards genuine national reconciliation.

Lustration proposals initially enjoyed strong support from both Islamist and leftist parliamentarians in the Assembly, but were firmly opposed by the supporters of the newly-founded Nidaa Tounes party and its leader Essebsi. However, as part of a distinctive learning process connected to the 2013 critical juncture which prompted the Islamist party's readiness to negotiate (Cimini 2021), Ennahda's leadership changed course, and abandoned the pro-revolutionary demand for a lustration provision in the transitional justice law. By the end of 2013, despite significant controversy and criticism within the party's rank and file, the transitional justice law passed without the chapter on the 'immunisation of the revolution' which would have banned former regime officials from holding political office. In April 2014, when the issue re-emerged during the vote on the electoral law, a specific provision banning former RCD officials from running for office at the following elections was rejected.[2] The reconciliation law for its part inflamed public debate for two years. On 13 September 2017, Tunisia's parliament finally approved the Law on Administrative Reconciliation (Organic bill 49-2015). Initiated by president Essebsi as the 'Reconciliation in the Economic and Financial Sectors Bill' (Assembly of the Representatives of the People 2015), the original draft was intended to provide amnesty to businessmen, and to political and administrative figures of the post-independence periods. In exchange for dropping legal proceedings against them, they would have to pay a fine and return the assets allegedly earned illicitly. According to Essebsi, the bill would have served the triple purpose of cutting red tape, improving the investment environment through the regularisation of many businessmen's pending positions, and boosting national development projects through the reclaimed money. In a similar vein, Ennahda also backed this unpopular bill, suggesting that it would ultimately contribute to increasing investments in disadvantaged regions and favour job creation, while also being a building block of the consensus needed for the country's successful transition. Far from working towards 'reconciliation', such a law deeply interfered with the ongoing transitional justice process by allowing many public officials and state employees to evade it. In doing so, this law reinforced the idea of politics as the 'hostage' of specific lobbies or personalities with the old regime being still in force. Famously, in response to it, the pro-transitional justice and anti-corruption *Manich Msamah* took to the streets. This leftist and mostly youth-led movement was finally partially successful insofar as it forced parliament to repeatedly amend its proposals so that the final version of the bill ultimately granted amnesty to administrators, but, notably, not to politicians, and on condition that there was no evidence they derived personal gains from their action. Yet, the difficulty in possessing overwhelming evidence is so great that the rule can easily be circumvented, as some observers note (Brésillon 2017). This law left a widespread sense of impunity, and the triumph of a 'business as usual' logic, to the detriment of the revolutionary spirit.

To sum up, lustration provisions and the reconciliation law abide by two different logics: exclusion and inclusion of old regime personnel – be they ruling party members, administrative cadres, or businessmen above all. By extension, what is also at stake is the rejection of the practices and values they represent, so entrenched with the autocratic regime. Through rejection of the former bill and adoption of the latter, old governing practices and people become legitimised. Also, the transitional justice mechanisms are diminished in that they fail to reckon with a legacy of large-scale past abuses in order to ensure accountability. In turn, the gains of the revolution are symbolically eroded.

Conclusion

The 'regression' of democracy worldwide comes with a number of implications in both democratic and non-democratic contexts. In young democracies like Tunisia, ignoring both the existence and the causes of authoritarian nostalgia and other practices could have serious political and social repercussions, ranging from escalating anti-government or anti-system protests to further democratic backsliding. In a post-authoritarian setting like the Tunisian one, the path of reforms and policymaking should move away from past mechanisms. As a result of regime change, an equal change in elite personnel, structure and policies is expected. In practice, though, the outcomes of regime change are not always so clear-cut. Instead of looking for a clear break with the past, or a break partly fulfilled, it would be more useful to see whether and to what extent there exist 'shadows' of authoritarianism, which may materialise in a given set of practices or mindset. Tunisia is not the only country to experience strongman nostalgia, which has both historical and contemporary parallels. For example, Applebaum (2020) identifies a blend of 'cultural despair' with 'nostalgia' in established democracies, translating to what she calls the 'restorative nostalgia' typical, for example, of the Brexit campaign or Trump's 'Make America Great Again' slogan. In comparative terms, the experience of Tunisia confirms the likely unavoidable authoritarian legacy that young democracies have to deal with. It also clearly points to the fact that this legacy is all the more reluctant to recede when the legitimacy of the new system of governance is weakened. Furthermore, Tunisia displays a number of tendencies and practices observed in established democracies, like increased securitisation and police brutality. Likewise, cynicism towards democracy in the United States and Western countries seems to be stronger among younger people, alongside political apathy and an increase in toleration of authoritarianism (Foa and Mounk 2016), not unlike in this Maghrebi country.

A practice-oriented analysis is key to seeing whether, and how, authoritarian nostalgia will manifest itself in the future, without the constraints of rigid categorisation of regimes and without necessarily questioning the democratic form, but rather appreciating the different nuances it can take on. After all, no alternative form of hegemony has been developed yet in response to the crisis of 'authority' expressed by the uprisings (Schwedler et al. 2019), a fact that reminds us how matters are in flux. Future empirical work can be used for theory building and improve our understanding of post-authoritarian settings and of the conditions under which reactionary forces self-perpetuate, intersecting people's expectations (or frustration) not least according to a specific set of socio-economic variables.

Note

1 The research for this work was supported by the Gerda Henkel Foundation under the 'Security, Society and the State' programme.

References

Al Shamary, M. (2018). 'Authoritarian Nostalgia Among Iraqi Youth: Roots and Repercussions', *War on the Rocks*, 25 July. https://warontherocks.com/2018/07/authoritarian-nostalgia-among-iraqi-youth-roots-and-repercussions/

Amnesty International (2016). *Tunisia: Evidence of Torture and Deaths in Custody Suggest Gains of the Uprising Sliding into Reverse Gear*, 16 January. https://www.amnesty.org/en/latest/news/2016/01/tunisia-evidence-of-torture-and-deaths-in custody/

Amnesty International (2019). *Tunisia: Where Running from Police Can Be Deadly*, April 2019. https://www.amnesty.org/en/latest/campaigns/2019/04/tunisia-where-running-from-police-can-be-deadly/

Applebaum, A. (2020). *Twilight of Democracy: The Seductive Lure of Authoritarianism*. New York: Doubleday.

Arab Barometer (2019). *Arab Barometer V: Tunisia Country Report*. https://www.arabbarometer.org/wpcontent/uploads/ABV_Tunisia_Report_PublicOpinion_2018-2019.pdf

Assembly of the Representatives of the People (2015). *The Reconciliation in the Economic and Financial Sectors Bill* [in Arabic]. http://www.arp.tn/site/projet/AR/fiche_proj.jsp?cp=90496

Ben Mbarek, G. and F. Aliriza (2020). 'Amid Pandemic, Efforts to Restrict Freedom of Speech Continue', *Meshkal*, 20 April. http://mesh-kal.com/?p=765

Bellin, E. (2012). 'Reconsidering the Robustness of Authoritarianism in the Middle East: Lessons from the Arab Spring', *Comparative Politics* 44(2): 127–49.

Brésillon, T. (2017). 'Tunisia: Towards the Restoration of Personal Power – Constitutional Reform Announced', *Orient XXI*, 10 October.

Brumberg, D. (2002). 'The Trap of Liberalised Autocracy', *Journal of Democracy* 13(4): 56–68.

Brumberg, D. and M. Ben Salem (2020). 'Tunisia's Endless Transition?', *Journal of Democracy* 31(2): 110–24.

Brynen, R., P. W. Moore, B. F. Salloukh and M.-J. Zahar (2013). *Beyond the Arab Spring: Authoritarianism and Democracy in the Arab World*. Boulder, CO: Lynne Rienner.

Camau, M. and V. Geisser (2003). *Le Syndrome Autoritaire. Politique en Tunisie de Bourguiba à Ben Ali*. Paris: Presses de Sciences Politiques.

Cavatorta, F. and R. Hostrup Haugbølle (2012). 'The End of Authoritarian Rule and the Mythology of Tunisia under Ben Ali', *Mediterranean Politics* 17(2): 179–95.

Cimini, G. (2021). 'Learning Mechanisms within an Islamist Party: Tunisia's Ennahda Movement between Domestic and Regional Balances', *Contemporary Politics* 27(2): 160–79.

Costantini, I. (2022). 'Silencing Peaceful Voices: Practices of Control and Repression in post-2003 Iraq', in Ö. E. Topak, M. Mekouar and F. Cavatorta (eds) *New Authoritarian Practices in the Middle East and North Africa.* Edinburgh: Edinburgh University Press, pp. 112–30.

Dahmani, F. (2020). 'Is Tunisia at Risk of Becoming a Police State Again?', *The Africa Report*, 12 October. https://www.theafricareport.com/45588/is-tunisia-at -risk-of-becoming-a-police-state-again/

de Leeuw, S., R. Rekker, R. Azrout and J. van Spanje (2018). 'A Matter of Nostalgia: How Authoritarian Traditions Shape the Distribution of Democratic Support on the Left–Right Dimension', ECPR Joint Sessions, Nicosia, Cyprus. https:// ecpr.eu/Filestore/paperproposal/b6ef9691-0b9f-4810-97e7-292c7eaa77b8.pdf

Diamond, L. (2021). 'Democratic Regression in Comparative Perspective: Scope, Methods, and Causes', *Democratization* 28(1): 22–42.

El Issawi, F. and F. Cavatorta (2020). *The Unfinished Arab Spring. Micro-Dynamics of Revolts between Change and Continuity.* London: Gingko.

Feltrin, L. (2018). 'The Struggles of Precarious Youth in Tunisia: The Case of the Kerkennah Movement', *Review of African Political Economy* 45(155): 44–63.

Foa, R. and Y. Mounk (2016). 'The Danger of Deconsolidation: The Democratic Disconnect', *Journal of Democracy* 27(3): 5–17.

Freedom House (2020a). 'Freedom in the World 2020 Finds Established Democracies Are in Decline', Press Release, 4 March. https://freedomhouse.org/article/new-report-freedom-world-2020-finds-established-democracies-are-decline

Freedom House (2020b), *Freedom in the World 2020: Tunisia.* https://freedomhouse .org/country/tunisia/freedom-world/2020

Freedom House (2020c), *Freedom on the Net 2020.* https://freedomhouse.org/count ry/tunisia/freedom-net/2020

French, M. and T. Monahan (2020). 'Dis-ease Surveillance: How Might Surveillance Studies Address COVID-19?', *Surveillance and Society* 18(1): 1–11.

Glasius, M. (2018). 'What Authoritarianism Is . . . and Is Not: a Practice Perspective', *International Affairs* 94(3): 515–33.

Gordner, M. (2019). 'Youth Politics in Tunisia: Comparing Land/Labor, Leftist Movements, and NGO-ized Elites', in S. Yom, M. Lynch and W. al-Khatib (eds) *Youth Politics in the Middle East and North Africa*, POMEPS Studies Series 36, pp. 14–19.

Grewal, S. (2018). *Time to Rein in Tunisia's Police Unions*, Project on Middle East Democracy.

Grewal, S. (2019). *Tunisian Democracy at a Crossroads*. Washington, DC: Brookings Institution.

Hanlon, Q. (2012). *Security Sector Reform in Tunisia. A Year after the Jasmine Revolution*. United States Institute for Peace: Special Report No. 304. https://www.usip.org/sites/default/files/SR304.pdf

Heydemann, S. (2002). 'La question de la démocratie dans les travaux sur le monde arabe', *Critique Internationale* 17: 54–62.

Heydemann, S. (2016). 'Explaining the Arab Uprisings: Transformations in Comparative Perspective', *Mediterranean Politics* 21(1): 192–204.

Hibou, B. (2006). *La Force de l'Obéissance: Économie Politique de la Répression en Tunisie*. Paris: La Découverte.

Human Rights Watch (2015). *An Analysis of Tunisia's Draft Counterterrorism Law*, 8 April. https://www.hrw.org/sites/default/files/related_material/memo.2015.04.08.Tunisia%20Counterterrorism%20Law.eng_.pdf

Human Rights Watch (2018). *World Report 2018: Tunisia*. https://www.hrw.org/world-report/2018/country-chapters/tunisia

Jrad, E. (2020). *Tunisia Facing COVID-19: To Exceptional Circumstances, Exceptional Measures?*, Arab Reform Initiative, 14 April. https://www.arab-reform.net/?p=10117

Kimball, S. (2019). 'Tunisia's Authoritarians Learn to Love Liberalism', *Foreign Policy*, 14 June. https://foreignpolicy.com/2019/06/14/tunisias-authoritarians-learn-to-love-liberalism/

Lyon, D. and K. Haggerty (2012). 'The Surveillance Legacies of 9/11: Recalling, Reflecting on, and Rethinking Surveillance in the Security Era', *Canadian Journal of Law and Society* 27(3): 291–300.

Lutterbeck, D. (2015). 'Tool of Rule: the Tunisian Police under Ben Ali', *The Journal of North African Studies* 20(5): 813–31.

Marsad Majles (2013a). التصويت على إنهاء النقاش العام حول مشروع القانون المتعلق بالتحصين السياسي للثورة [Vote on the closing of the general debate on the Draft Law on the Political Immunisation of the Revolution], 28 June. https://majles.marsad.tn/vote/51cd934b7ea2c47c3f3672c7

Marsad Majles (2013b). التصويت على إضافة باب متعلق بالتحصين السياسي للثورة إلى القانون الأساسي عدد 2013/12 المتعلق بتنظيم العدالة الإنتقالية [Vote to add a chapter related to the political immunisation of the revolution to the Organic Law No. 12/2013 related to organizing transitional justice], 14 December. https://majles.marsad.tn/vote/52b1eb4512bdaa7f9b90ec1f

Marsad Majles (2014). التصويت على الفصل 167 من مقترح قانون أساسي يتعلق بالإنتخابات

والإستفتاء. [Vote on Article 167 of the draft organic law relating to the elections and referenda], 30 April. https://majles.marsad.tn/vote/53613d2912bdaa078a b82503

Meddeb, Y. (2018). 'Support for Democracy Dwindles in Tunisia amid Negative Perceptions of Economic Conditions', *Afrobarometer Dispatch* 232, 3 September. https://afrobarometer.org/sites/default/files/publications/Dispatches/ab_r7_dis patchno232_support_for_democracy_dwindles_in_tunisia_1.pdf

Ministry of Interior (2020). *Ministry of Interior in Tunisia using Security Robots P-Guard to Enforce Lockdown during Coronavirus.* YouTube, 29 March. https:// www.youtube.com/watch?v=wiwSPo_GbqM&feature=youtu.be&app=desktop

Moghaddam, F. M. (2019). *Threat to Democracy: The Appeal of Authoritarianism in an Age of Uncertainty.* American Psychological Association.

Mohsen-Finan, K. (2018). 'A Return to Authoritarianism in Tunisia: After the Revolution (part I)', *Al Araby*, 17 January. https://www.alaraby.co.uk/english /comment/2018/1/18/a-return-to-authoritarianism-in-tunisia-part-i

Neundorf, A., J. Gerschewski and R.-G. Olar (2020), 'How Do Inclusionary and Exclusionary Autocracies Affect Ordinary People?', *Comparative Political Studies* 53(12): 1,890–925.

Okkez, M. S. B. (2016). 'خارطة الاحتجاجات: التحرّكات السلميّة تتواصل' [The Map of Protests: Peaceful Protests Continue], *Nawaat*, 25 January. https://nawaat.org /52/ خارطة-الاحتجاجات-التحركات-السلمية2016/

Privacy International (2019). *State of Surveillance Tunisia.* 14 March. https://privacy international.org/state-privacy/1012/state-surveillance-tunisia

Sayigh, Y. (2015). *Missed Opportunity: The Politics of Police Reform in Egypt and Tunisia*, Washington, DC: Carnegie Endowment for International Peace.

Schwedler, J., A. Said and R. Curtis (2019). 'Return to Revolution', *Middle East Report* 49: 3/4.

Stepan, A. and J. Linz (2013). 'Democratization Theory and the "Arab Spring"', *Journal of Democracy* 24(2): 15–30.

Teti, A., P. Abbott and F. Cavatorta (2019). 'Beyond Elections: Perceptions of Democracy in Four Arab Countries', *Democratization* 26(4): 645–65.

The Arab Weekly (2020). 'Tunisia Opinion Polls Show Growing Polarisation, Pessimism', *The Arab Weekly*, 8 June. https://thearabweekly.com/tunisia-opin ion-polls-show-growing-polarisation-pessimism

The Observers (2020). 'Tunis-based Rights Groups Sound Alarm over Police Violence against Women', *France 24*, 8 July. https://observers.france24.com/en /20200818-tunis-policeviolencetowardswomen?fbclid=IwAR3_1nKH1BYPO Me62NrMdYVf_Ke1mrSuRLfoNAH3mYq6I6dUEej0Sg5d60

Topak, Ö. E., M. Mekouar and F. Cavatorta (2022). 'Introduction', in Ö. E. Topak,

M. Mekouar and F. Cavatorta (eds) *New Authoritarian Practices in the Middle East and North Africa.* Edinburgh: Edinburgh University Press, pp. 1–29.

Vatthauer, J.-P. and I. Weipert-Fenner (2017). *The Quest of Social Justice in Tunisia: Socioeconomic Protest and Political Democratization Post 2011,* PRIF Reports 143. Frankfurt am Main: Hessische Stiftung Friedens- und Konfliktforschung.

Walsh, A. (2019). *Restarting Police Reform in Tunisia: The Importance of Talking About Everyday Security.* Washington, DC: Middle East Institute.

Yom, S. and G. F. Gause (2012). 'Resilient Royals: How Arab Monarchies Hang On', *Journal of Democracy* 23(4): 74–8.

15

AN ASSEMBLAGE OF NEW AUTHORITARIAN PRACTICES IN TURKEY

Özgün E. Topak

Introduction

In October 2010, *The Economist* made the following observation about Turkey: 'Turkey is heading in a good direction. It remains a shining (and rare) example in the Muslim world of a vibrant democracy with the rule of law and a thriving free-market economy.' From the AKP's election to power in 2002 until the party's heavy-handed response to the Gezi protesters in 2013, Western media and policy circles, as well as national supporters of the AKP, promoted the image of the Party as a reform model for the entire MENA. The so-called 'Turkish model' had in fact little substance from the outset. The AKP's authoritarian practices, including pressures on media, the use of politically motivated trials and surveillance of dissident or oppositional groups, were already present in the first decade of its rule, even though these and other practices have significantly expanded their reach and intensity post-2013 (see e.g. Yeşil 2016; Oğuz 2016; Topak 2017 2019; Tansel 2018; Kaygusuz 2018). The continuity in authoritarian practices under the two decades of the AKP's rule makes it difficult to designate the 'new' in new authoritarian practices. The picture is further complicated if we consider the country's authoritarian tradition. Yet, there is also something novel about the current authoritarian practices which aggressively aim to discipline all spheres of political and social life, including the online sphere, rather than only targeting selected individuals and groups. Following the model of an assemblage (Topak 2019) these practices are also continuously expanding their reach, and make new connections.

This chapter cannot provide a detailed examination of each authoritarian practice and its complex genealogy. Rather, the aim is to provide a historically-grounded and theoretically informed overview of key expanding authoritarian practices under the AKP's rule. To this end, the chapter starts by discussing the authoritarian state tradition in Turkey and how the AKP inherited this tradition. Next, it draws on Michael Mann's model of the authoritarian state and the concept of the authoritarian assemblage and examines expanding authoritarian practices in key areas including civil society, law/judiciary, police/policing and the internet.

The AKP and the Authoritarian State Tradition in Turkey

Modern Turkey inherited the tradition of top-down rule of the central authority in the absence of a strong civil society from the Ottoman Empire (Heper 2000).[1] Under the leadership of Mustafa Kemal Atatürk and following the War of Independence (1919–23), the state elites put an end to Sultanic authority and established the Turkish Republic. The Republican civil and military elites implemented a secularist-nationalistic programme of modernisation. They envisioned a homogeneous society composed of Sunni Muslim Turks with secular lifestyles. This vision excluded non-Muslims,[2] and identified Muslims as targets of reform, discipline and assimilation, and if none of these works, state repression. Kurds, the largest ethnic minority in Turkey and a predominantly Sunni-Muslim population, were perceived as 'future Turks' who could be successfully assimilated into Turkishness (Yeğen 2007), while signs of Kurdish identity, including cultural-linguistic expressions, were not tolerated. From Turkey's transition to a multi-party system in 1950, the political elites were primarily populist conservatives, but the Republican elites in the military and judiciary continued to hold veto and intervention powers (Hale 1994) which culminated in the military coups of 1960, 1971, 1980 and 1997.

The 1960 coup mainly targeted Islamists and resulted in the execution of the then prime minister Adnan Menderes. The 1971 and 1980 coups mainly targeted leftist social movements and figures. Encouraged by the global US-backed anti-leftism of the Cold War era, the military junta (1980–3) officially embraced the 'Turkish-Islamist ideology', and organised a witch-hunt characterised by 'mass arrests and systematic torture' (Can

2016: 344) as well as mass surveillance and purges of the leftists. In the 1980s, the PKK (Kurdistan Workers' Party) emerged with an agenda to establish an independent Kurdish state in south-eastern Turkey through armed insurgency. The spiral of violence, terror and conflict between the PKK and Turkish security forces resulted in the deaths of 30,000 to 40,000 individuals, while the counter-insurgency measures and the conflict environment displaced half a million to three million Kurds. From 1985 and until 2002, thirteen Kurdish majority cities in eastern and south-eastern Turkey were governed by state of emergency rule, which both restricted fundamental rights and freedoms in these areas and provided immunity to officials from criminal prosecution. The hardline security approach and the use of Gladio-type 'deep state' forces (see Söyler 2013) led to widespread human rights violations including extra-judicial executions, disappearances, torture, prosecution, arrest and imprisonment of pro-Kurdish rights defenders, human rights activists and journalists (Amnesty International 1996; HRW 2012). The 1990s were also marked by the crackdown on Islamists who were supported by the 1980s Turkish-Islamist military junta against the leftists, but later became a threat to the secularist establishment. Under the Welfare Party (RP), Islamists had a wave of electoral victories in both municipal and general elections, culminating in a RP-led coalition government in 1996. The Republican establishment reacted against Islamists with a 'postmodern coup' in 1997, removing the RP leader from power and banning the RP from politics, without establishing a military junta. The coup measures also included restrictions on and increased surveillance of religious schools and Islamist business organisations, and the closing down of some pro-Islamist media outlets as well as investigation, surveillance and/ or dismissal of suspected Islamists from public service (Hale and Ozbudun 2009: 4–5; Yeşil 2016: 64–5).

When the AKP, as the successor of the RP, came to power in 2002 it found itself in conflict with the Republican elites. Initially, the Party did not confront the latter group directly, and adopted an EU-backed democratisation agenda. It implemented a number of reforms including increased civilian control over the army, and improvements in Kurdish rights such as lifting the state of emergency rule and removing the ban on Kurdish broadcasting and language. However, the AKP's democratisation agenda soon turned out to be a strategic manoeuvre to broaden its internal and external support base in its efforts to conquer the state rather than a genuine attempt of democratisation

(Somer 2017). In the process of capturing state power from the Republican establishment, the Party particularly benefited from politically motivated trials. Claiming to be fighting against the 'deep state', the *Ergenekon* (2008) and *Sledgehammer* (2010) trials convicted hundreds of secular military officers (including the then Army Chief) on the basis of allegations that they had plotted to overthrow the government. Alongside the military officers, dissident or oppositional prosecutors, journalists, academics and civil society representatives were also targeted, many of whom were critical of both the AKP and the Gülen community. The evidence in these trials was flawed or fabricated, and defendants' rights were violated (Dogan and Rodrik 2014). Still, the pro-AKP media presented the trials as necessary steps for democratisation and labelled anyone raising concerns about the evidence and the violation of the rights of the defenders as 'coup enthusiasts' (Yeşil 2016: 98). In its effort to establish an uncontested single party rule, the AKP also made political hay from sex tapes implicating the leader of the main opposition party the CHP (Republican People's Party) and ten high-level officials of the second opposition party, the MHP (Nationalist Action Party), all of whom were forced to resign before the 2011 general elections. In these political operations, security forces used wiretapping, bugging and other forms of digital surveillance to collect data about their targets. Some of the collected digital materials were later edited to fabricate evidence against targets (Topak 2017: 538; Çelik 2020: 111).

It eventually became clear that Gülenist police and judiciary forces led these politically motivated trials and surveillance operations (Oğuz 2016: 95–6). The Gülen community is an Islamist organisation founded by Fetullah Gülen in the 1970s. On the civil society side, the community gradually possessed a large network of business and civil society organisations both at national and international levels. On the bureaucracy side, the Gülenists gradually infiltrated all levels of state bureaucracy, particularly the police, judiciary and military. The Gülenists significantly increased their powers during the AKP's first decade in power and operated as an ally of the Party in its effort to capture the state. Once capture was largely completed in 2012–13, the alliance between the two groups began to break down due to the struggle between them for full control of the state. While the two allies worked together during the repression of the 2013 Gezi protesters, their conflict broke out in the open with the Gülenist attempt to discredit Erdoğan and leading AKP cadres with leaked corruption tapes in late 2013. Their fight became violent when the Gülenist (now defined as FETÖ [Fethullahist Terrorist Organization] by the government) army officers led a coup to overthrow the AKP government in 2016 (Şık 2017).

In the aftermath of the coup attempt, the AKP declared a state of emergency[3] and carried out a wide-scale crackdown which included mass purges at all levels of the public sector, including the judiciary, police, military, universities, schools and health sector; imprisonment of journalists; and closures of civil society organisations. Beyond targeting the suspected coup plotters, the AKP took advantage of state of emergency powers to target a wide spectrum of dissidents including Kurdish parliamentarians, human rights defenders and leftist dissident academics such as Academics for Peace (Topak 2017). The latter group of over 2,000 academics criticised human rights violations, including prolonged curfews, civilian deaths and mass displacement, which had occurred during the clash between the Turkish Army and the PKK in 2016, and called for a return to the Kurdish peace process which had started in 2009 and abruptly ended in 2015. Academics for Peace were labelled 'terrorist supporters' by Erdoğan, the AKP and pro-government media. In addition, some were detained and arrested, many were tried on charges of terrorist propaganda, many were dismissed from their positions and banned from public service, and many lost their passports. The criminalisation of Academics for Peace demonstrated that 'the concept of "terrorism" has been stretched so far that it can be employed against anyone who fails to toe the party line' (Baser et al. 2017: 276). In 2017–18, Turkey's authoritarian regime deepened through transformation of the political system into an executive presidency and Erdoğan's election as the president. Even though the state of emergency was officially lifted following the presidential elections, Erdoğan continued to enjoy extensive powers, and pressures on dissident and oppositional figures and organisations increased. The global pandemic crisis from March 2020 also contributed to the deepening of authoritarianism with new laws and practices.

The Gülenist conspiracy against Erdoğan and the AKP was an internal challenge to the AKP's regime from an ex-ally with little public support. Despite possessing high levels of economic, political and coercive power, the Gülen community, as an elite Islamist organisation, did not have a popular support basis in the society. The more popular challenge to the AKP's rule came from the Gezi protesters, who protested against the AKP's increasingly Islamist, authoritarian and neoliberal policies in 2013. Starting at Istanbul Gezi Park, the protests quickly spread throughout Turkey. The police responded to protesters violently, leaving eight dead and more than 8,000 injured. In the aftermath of the Gezi protests, the AKP took steps to pre-empt another mass protest movement, and increased its authoritarianism. The Gülenist conspiracies and the resurgence of the conflict with the PKK served as further catalysts for the expansion of authoritarian practices.

To summarise, building on Turkey's authoritarian tradition, in the first decade of its rule, the AKP targeted key opposing and dissident figures in the process of establishing dominance on state bureaucracy. In the post-2013 environment, the party began to establish a mass authoritarian system which resulted in the curtailment of rights and freedoms of the entire population. According to the 2020 Freedom House Report, Turkey witnessed the second most dramatic decline in civil rights and political freedoms in the last ten years after Burundi, and is a 'not free' country (Freedom House 2020: 14).

The Authoritarian State and the Institutionalisation of Despotism

This section provides the conceptual framework for understanding Turkey's authoritarian state and its expanding authoritarian practices. Michael Mann's theory of the authoritarian state (1984, 2008) offers a useful perspective via which to think about the characteristics of an authoritarian state. According to Mann, authoritarian states possess high levels of despotic and infrastructural powers. Mann defines despotic power as 'the range of actions which the elite is empowered to undertake without routine, institutionalised negotiation with civil society' (1984: 188), and infrastructural power as 'the capacity of the state to actually penetrate civil society, and to implement logistically political decisions throughout the realm' (1984: 189). While both democratic/bureaucratic and authoritarian states are high in infrastructural power which allows them to effectively implement policies, it is the latter that uses its coercive capacity to establish 'an institutionalized form of despotism' (Mann 1984: 191). Authoritarian states are typically ruled by 'the single, hierarchically structured party' (Mann 2008: 356) which dominates civil society and suppresses dissident/oppositional forces. Mann sees surveillance, understood broadly as gathering information from the population, as a key feature of all modern states with high infrastructural powers. Even though Mann does not provide details on the relationship between surveillance and state type, it can be argued that it is the authoritarian states that use wide-scale authoritarian surveillance as a key technique of suppressing civil society and political dissent (Topak 2019).

The contemporary Turkish state has high levels of infrastructural power in areas related to coercive capacity (including authoritarian control, policing and surveillance), even though it has limited or low levels of infrastructural power in other areas of state capacity (e.g. delivery of public services, preventing corruption, taxation).[4] The contemporary Turkish state is also high in despotic powers. The current regime is characterised by 'a particular combination of supreme power of the leader, an extremely weak parliament and elections of a plebiscitary character' as well as 'total erosion of intermediary groups and institutions' (Yılmaz 2020: 266). The takeover of state bureaucracy by the AKP, and the use of state resources/power to promote the Party and its supporters and to suppress its opposers, is reminiscent of single-party dictatorships where there is 'a complete amalgamation of state and party' (Arendt 1976: 419).

The AKP's control over military, police and judiciary is worth further analysis. The AKP, with the internal help of Gülenists, and external and broad support for demilitarisation, ended Turkey's long-standing military tutelage in the first decade of its rule. Rather than contributing to democratisation, this model of 'demilitarisation', both paved the way for the 2016 failed coup by the Gülenists and resulted in an increase in authoritarianism. In the post-coup environment, more than 20,000 military officers, including close to half of all generals and admirals, were purged, and some generals were forced to retire. In addition, 50,000 new officers were recruited and new promotions were made, based on political loyalty (Yetkin 2021: 2–3). Following Turkey's transition to a presidential system, Erdoğan took a number of additional steps to further institutionalise his grip on the military. He transferred the key decision-making powers in matters of military (including security) recruitment and promotion decisions, to himself and the Defence Ministry. Similarly, Erdoğan deepened his control over the police and the National Intelligence Organisation (MİT), both of which were armed with new powers to surveil and suppress dissidents (Kaygusuz 2018: 294).

The actors of the security apparatus, in particular the police, have worked in harmony with the judiciary, which also gradually came under the control of the AKP and Erdoğan. In the first years of its rule, the AKP was threatened by the Republican judiciary, which attempted to close down the Party in 2008. In response, through the 2010 constitutional amendment, the Party changed the structure of the Supreme Board of Judges and Prosecutors (HSYK), thus bringing the judiciary under government control and facilitating the infiltration of Gülenist cadres (Özbudun 2015; Oğuz 2016: 96–7). The mass purging of alleged Gülenists from the judiciary did not contribute to an independent judiciary, because they were replaced by loyal cadres. The 2018 transition to the presidential system further deepened the political control over the judiciary. Under the new system, there is 'total control of parliamentary and presidential appointments to the judiciary' including appointments to the HSYK and the Constitutional Court (Tahiroglu 2020: 69). More recently, in January 2021, an Erdoğan loyalist prosecutor was appointed to the Constitutional Court. The Constitutional Court was not yet fully under the control of Erdoğan, because some of its sitting members, including the Court's president, were appointed by former presidents and parliaments. In some trials (including those against Academics for Peace), the Court took a surprisingly pro-human rights stance, despite not meaningfully resisting the authoritarianism overall.[5] The court's limited 'activism' came under attack from the government and Erdoğan, and some of its decisions were not implemented by the local courts. Within this context, the changing composition of the Constitutional Court in favour of Erdoğan could be regarded as the final blow to any semblance of an independent judiciary in Turkey. Meanwhile the international judicial pressure on Turkey has not produced effective outcomes. The European Court of Human Rights (ECHR) ordered the immediate releases of Selahattin Demirtaş and Osman Kavala, but the Turkish authorities refused to comply. The imprisonment of Demirtaş and Kavala is particularly significant for its wider chilling effects for the political opposition and civil society. At the time of his imprisonment in November 2016, Demirtaş was co-chair of the pro-Kurdish Party HDP (*Halkların Demokratik Partisi*). His charismatic leadership and opposition to Erdoğan's increasing authoritarianism helped the HDP to gain popularity in wider segments of the society, beyond the traditional Kurdish voters of the party. In 2015 general elections, the HDP gained a record of 13.1 per cent of the national votes, putting Erdoğan's ambitions of a one-man regime at risk. Kavala is a philanthropic businessman, known for his leadership role in pro-democracy civil society organisations. He was detained in 2017 on the basis of allegations that he organised the Gezi Park protests to overthrow the government. His indictment was 'entirely unsubstantiated', showing that that he was detained for being 'a political nuisance for Erdoğan' (Tahiroglu 2020: 76–7).

Despite all these steps for institutionalising despotism, the stability of despotism is questionable because the regime remains vulnerable to internal cracks and external challenges. To begin with, the Turkish state is not a monolithic entity. While the presidential system gave Erdoğan unmatched powers, the declining popularity of the AKP forced him to establish an alliance with the ultra-nationalist MHP to obtain a majority in the parliament. The new ultra nationalist-Islamist alliance did result in a further increase in authoritarian practices, but, at the same time, it showed the limits of Erdoğan's and the AKP's power by means of revealing its dependence on alliances. While Erdoğan is hierarchically at the top of the authoritarian alliance, there are other actors who might influence and direct authoritarian practices, and even rival Erdoğan. In this context, the increasing power of the Interior Minister Soylu is worth mentioning. Backed by the MHP, Soylu even surpasses Erdoğan in calling for and at times directing ultra-nationalist and ultra-authoritarian practices. While the state apparatus seems to be under the control of Erdoğan/the AKP and, partially, the MHP at the moment, the tradition of shifting alliances in the governing authoritarian bloc (recall Erdogan's failed alliance with Gülenists) and persisting popular opposition indicates that such control is neither absolute nor eternal.

The popular opposition to Turkey's authoritarian bloc comes from the oppositional parties supported by roughly half of the population, and political protests. In the electoral arena, the CHP won Ankara and Istanbul municipalities in the 2019 local elections, thus ending twenty-five years of AKP rule in these cities. The election outcome was significant, as it showed that the AKP could be defeated even without fair elections. During the 2019 elections, the AKP not only used intensive media propaganda, and public and private resources, but it also put political pressure on the YSK (Supreme Electoral Council) to cancel and re-run the Istanbul elections. The AKP eventually reluctantly accepted the second CHP victory in the re-run election, possibly due to national and international pressure. The Party, however, showed no tolerance towards the electoral victories of the pro-Kurdish

Party, the HDP. Revitalising the tradition of emergency rule in the Kurdish majority areas, the Party removed 102 Kurdish mayors during the official state-of-emergency period (2016–18), and another ninety-three mayors who won the 2019 local elections, replacing them with state trustees (Whiting and Kaya 2021: 2). In fact, the authoritarian practice of appointing state trustees is in the process of being generalised to the entire civil society, which can be considered a step towards the creation of a state-controlled 'deep civil society' as in Iran (see Golkar 2022 in this volume). In December 2020, the government passed a bill which allows appointment of state trustees to replace NGO executives undergoing a terror-related investigation. The new law puts activists/members of human rights NGOs at risk, because many of them are frequently investigated under the vague and broad counter-terrorism laws (see Bianet 2020).

An Assemblage of Authoritarian Practices

The above section has already discussed some key new authoritarian practices during the late AKP rule, such as practices to establish total political control over the judiciary, the politically motivated trials targeting the opposition and civil society, and the practice of appointing state trustees. This section provides further detail on new authoritarian practices in three key domains: protest, policing and internet surveillance. Before moving forward, however, it is important to establish the conceptual framework for understanding the expanding authoritarian practices in Turkey. These practices follow the model of an authoritarian assemblage. The authoritarian assemblage can be understood as a generalised version of 'the authoritarian surveillant assemblage' (Topak 2019). While the authoritarian surveillant assemblage is specifically about authoritarian surveillance practices, the authoritarian assemblage may include any authoritarian practice. There are three key features in the authoritarian assemblage: expansion of authoritarian practices, connections among authoritarian systems/practices, and direction/control of authoritarian practices by the authoritarian state:

1. *Expansion of authoritarian practices.* The authoritarian assemblage expands through incorporating new practices, technologies, actors and laws. Consider the system of internet surveillance. Within this system, particularly since 2013, there has been an unprecedented expansion of laws (i.e., to allow greater surveillance and censorship powers), actors

(e.g. the social media monitoring unit, AkTrolls, cyber-informants) and technologies (e.g. new monitoring and hacking tools), which have resulted in new practices for surveilling and disciplining dissidents. Similar arguments can be made about other systems such as the protest policing system and mass media system, which have expanded their reach with new actors, laws, technologies and practices.

2. *Connections among authoritarian systems/practices.* The systems of the authoritarian assemblage do not expand their reach in isolation, but by forming new connections with each other. For instance, the protest policing system is increasingly combined with the internet surveillance system, in that the latter targets protesters and their potential supporters in the online sphere. Government-controlled mass media also operate as a complementary system by discrediting protesters and their demands in news reports. Formal and informal collaborators and informants can take part in multiple systems. For instance, they may report dissidents' social media posts, or gather data on employees in a public institution.

3. *Direction/control of authoritarian practices by the authoritarian state.* Unlike the more decentralised versions of the assemblage (see Haggerty and Ericson 2000), the authoritarian assemblage and its diverse systems and practices are controlled and co-ordinated by the central authoritarian state. Expanding Mann's theorisation of infrastructural power, this control and co-ordination capacity of the authoritarian state can be regarded as a key component of the state's authoritarian infrastructural power. The Turkish state has high levels of this infrastructural power, as its capacity to bring together diverse systems, actors and practices to suppress dissent demonstrates.

The protest policing system

Turkey has a tradition of authoritarian policing against protesters,[6] who are often perceived as enemies rather than dissidents (Uysal 2016: 220). The authoritarian protest policing apparatus was empowered during the AKP's first decade with amendments to the Anti-Terror Law in 2006 and the Police Powers and Duties Law in 2007. As in many other MENA and Western contexts, these revisions respectively broadened the scope of terrorism to incorporate a wide range of oppositional activities, and gave police extended powers to stop and search, fingerprint and use lethal force

(Berksoy 2013). The new law resulted in a substantial increase in policing, surveillance and arrests in Kurdish and Alevi majority neighbourhoods and cities of Turkey which are automatically categorised as 'suspect' regions by the security forces (Yonucu 2017). Prior to the Gezi protests, police responded heavily to the Tobacco Workers' protests in 2010 and May Day Demonstrations in 2013. Authoritarian policing, though, peaked during the Gezi protests. The police adopted a 'zero-tolerance' approach (Atak and della Porta 2016) characterised by excessive use of tear gas, water cannon and plastic bullets, as well as beatings of protesters. The police response was driven by their negative perception of the protesters, which was shared and fuelled by the government and the pro-government media. This perception was built on the us v. them divide, 'where the "us" stands for the national, the local, the sacred, the religious, the "authentic people" of society, and the "them" represents the arrogant, privileged "other" who are alien to [their] own people and culture' (Atak and della Porta 2016: 619; Uysal 2016: 221).

Significantly, Erdoğan and the pro-government media labelled the Gezi protesters a 'bunch of looters' and 'extremists' who were trying to harm the Turkish economy and Turkey's moral values. In this context, the pro-government media published fake news to discredit the democratic demands of the protesters and deepened the us v. them divide. The major fake news included the claim that protesters drank alcohol in a mosque and that they violently assaulted a woman and her baby because she was wearing a head-scarf. The pro-government media did not provide any credible evidence to prove these claims. In fact, counter-evidence eventually surfaced. The CCTV footage showed that no confrontation took place between the head-scarfed woman and the protesters, and the imam of the mosque stated that the protesters did not drink alcohol in the mosque, but rather used the mosque as a medical centre for injured protesters. Because the effectiveness of fake news is not judged by its level of correspondence to factual reality but by its emotional appeal to the intended audience, fake news played an instrumental role in consolidating the AKP's Islamist/right-wing support base against the protesters. In fact, the government increasingly made use of similar fake news in post-Gezi protests.[7] For instance, in the 2019 Women Day's March, pro-government sources, possibly AkTrolls (see below), used social media to claim that the protesters whistled and booed Ezan [Adhan] whereas in reality the protesters whistled and booed the police (see Karabag

2019). The use of fake news by mass media and social media to discredit the protesters illustrates how the protest policing system is combined with mass media and social media systems under the format of authoritarian assemblage.

Another key feature of assemblage is the exponential growth of systems of suppression, and this feature can also be observed in the post-Gezi updates to the protest policing system. Like other MENA regimes examined in this book, Turkey responded to the threat of social protests by upgrading its authoritarian apparatus.[8] The 'Internal Security Package' was passed in 2015, giving the police extended powers to conduct strip searches, use lethal weapons, wire-tap and engage in preventative arrests (Oğuz 2016: 101; Topak 2019: 461). The powers of the Turkey's National Intelligence Agency (MİT) were similarly extended around the same time. The 2014 amendments to the MIT law gave the MIT new surveillance and operational powers. In particular, it was given the right to gather every kind of information from public and private entities without a court order. The same law also allowed the MIT to undertake operations on matters relating to terrorism, internal security and external security with the permission of the Council of Ministers, which was controlled by the then Prime Minister Erdoğan. In fact, Erdoğan's control over the MIT gradually became almost total (Oğuz 2016: 100–1; Kaygusuz 2018; 294).

The recent response to the Boğaziçi students is illustrative of the last stage of the protest policing system under the authoritarian assemblage. In January 2021, Erdoğan appointed the academic Melih Bulu, a former AKP parliamentary candidate, as rector of Boğaziçi University, one of the top universities in Turkey. Bulu is the first externally appointed rector to the Boğaziçi since the 1980s military regime.[9] Boğaziçi students began to stage demonstrations to protest against Bulu's appointment and demanded his resignation. The police dispersed the protesters with excessive force on campus. The following day, the police raided students' homes, arresting and detaining at least twenty-eight students and seizing their computers and smartphones. Despite police violence, the students continued their protests, which were supported by others (mainly students from other universities) in different parts of the country, leading to another 560 arrests (HRW 2021). Meanwhile, the online activities of students came under surveillance. Some students were arrested for their Twitter and Clubhouse posts. The social media arrests demonstrated, once again, the interaction between the protest policing system and the internet surveillance system. Perhaps expectedly, the mass media system also took part. Following Erdoğan's framing of students as 'members of terror organizations' and alien to the 'national and moral values of the society' (DW 2021), a smear campaign against the students was launched in the pro-government mass media. LGBTQ+ student protesters were particularly targeted with hate speech (HRW 2021).

The Boğaziçi protests showed both the strength and the limitations of the authoritarian assemblage. On the one hand, the authoritarian assemblage quickly and violently responded to the protesters by bringing together various repressive systems, actors and practices. On the other, it failed to obtain legitimacy and pre-empt dissent. Despite the efforts of authorities to link students to terror organisations, they could not find any evidence for this in the materials and social media posts they seized. Despite the efforts of government and the pro-government media to discredit the protesters, the legitimate demands of students for a democratic university gathered sympathy and support from large segments of society. According to an opinion poll, 67 per cent of the population, including 17 per cent of AKP voters, found the students to be righteous and 62 per cent found police response excessive (Konda 2021). Perhaps more importantly, despite the government's efforts to pre-empt any public opposition since the Gezi protests, the Boğaziçi protests showed that the authoritarian regime can be questioned and even challenged.

The internet surveillance system

Deibert's (2015) categorisation of first, second and third generations of internet controls provides a useful framework for understanding Turkey's expanding internet surveillance system. According to Deibert, the first generation of controls includes straightforward blocking of websites through internet filtering technology (2015: 65). The second-generation controls involve creation of new technical and legal frameworks to monitor and access citizens' internet transactions such as emails and social media posts, often without court approval (Deibert 2015: 66–8). Finally, the third-generation controls include offensive tactics to surveil and intimidate internet users and make government propaganda, including the use of hacking tools and mobilisation of pro-government social media agents (such as hackers and trolls) (Diebert 2015: 68–71).

As in some other MENA regimes,[10] Turkey's internet surveillance system has gradually evolved to incorporate second- and third-generation controls, although first-generation controls have continued and even expanded their reach. The government passed the Internet Law (Law No. 5651) in 2007 and since then has censored thousands of websites via the Telecommunications Directorate (TIB). The Gezi protests and the release of corruption tapes by the Gülenists in 2013 led government to expand its censorship powers. By 2013, a majority of mainstream media organisations were already under the direct or indirect control of the government, leading to either pro-government propaganda or self-censorship (see Arsan 2013). By 2018, more than 90 per cent of all newspapers and televisions had come under government control (RSF 2018). In the absence of an independent mass media, internet and social media became the main venues for government criticism, most notably during the the Gezi protests, when these venues played key roles in exposing police brutality and mobilising the protesters. In 2014, the government amended the internet censorship law to enable 'fast banning of websites . . . access by the TIB to logs of all user activities on the internet, URL and IP blocking, and a new government-controlled ISP union' (Akgül and Kırlıdoğ 2015: 11). Meanwhile, surveillance of social media posts of citizens (in particular Twitter posts), already occurring pre-2013 on a small scale, has intensified, leading to frequent social media arrests based on charges including 'spreading terrorist propaganda', 'inciting the public to hatred, animosity and agitation' 'insulting religious values' and 'insulting the President' (Freedom House 2018).

The post-2016 coup attempt Decree Laws further increased the government's surveillance powers (Yeşil et al. 2017; Topak 2019: 463). Decree Law 670 allowed access to all forms of data from private and public entities, including digital communications data, in coup-related investigations. Decree Law 671 allowed the BTK (which replaced the TIB) to access any form of digital communications data from network providers on matters of national security and public order. Finally, Decree Law 680 increased the surveillance powers of the Turkish National Police by enabling its Cybercrimes Department to access internet data of suspects without court approval for twenty-four hours, thus extending the unwarranted wire-tapping practice of the police to the internet realm.

In the post-coup state of emergency context, these 'second-generation' controls were expanded together with 'first-generation' controls, including internet shutdowns and restrictions and content removals. These included regional internet shutdowns in Kurdish majority cities and temporary throt-

tling of social media and WhatsApp, both of which were implemented to
pre-empt mobilisation of protests about arrests and removals of Kurdish politicians from their posts. Additionally, the government blocked access to drive
services when the emails of a government official were leaked (Yeşil et al. 2017:
14–15). Meanwhile Turkey has consistently been ranked among the top
countries for content removal requests from Twitter and Facebook (Freedom
House 2018) and the number of blocked domain names and websites has
increased (İFÖD 2019: 2). By 2019, 21,000 addresses, composed of news
websites and links, Twitter and Facebook accounts and posts and YouTube
videos, were blocked to 'protect national security and public order'. Most of
these addresses were publicising 'government criticism and alternative views
on the Kurdish issue, and broadcasting news which were not covered by the
mainstream media during the conflict with the PKK' (İFÖD 2019: 17). In
the post-2016 context, social media arrests were also intensified, and they
began to produce totalitarian effects. According to the 2018 survey by the
Reuters Institute, 65 per cent of internet users in Turkey fear prosecution if
they post political views online (Reuters Institute 2018: 13). The depth of
totalitarian control of public speech is measured not only by self-censorship,
but also by the obligation to express pro-government opinions. Indeed,
Turkish citizens, at least some of them, began to post pro-government statements on social media to prove that they were not suspects and to advance
in their careers. In a number of interviews published in the daily newspaper
Cumhuriyet (Avşar 2018), a doctoral candidate stated that when she closed
down her social media account while writing her thesis, she got a warning
from her supervisor, who explained that the Dean's Office views non-active
social media users as potential suspects who are hiding something. She added
that pro-government social media posts became an advancement criterion in
her university.

Social media surveillance is being conducted by various actors, including the Social Media Monitoring Unit of the Turkish National Police and
citizen cyber-informants who are encouraged to report dissident social media
users to the authorities. Many social media accounts are being investigated
on the basis of cyber-snitching reports, and the monetary rewards for cyber-
snitching have exponentially increased (Yeşil et al. 2017: 16; Topak 2019:
464–6). In fact, reminiscent of historical totalitarian regimes, and as in some
other MENA regimes examined in this book,[11] the informant/collaborator
surveillance in online and offline spheres has reached a point where it has

begun to function as an entire system of control which supplements other systems including internet surveillance, protest policing and judicial control systems (see Topak 2019: 466–7). In addition to these actors of 'second-generation' controls, AkTrolls and intelligence officers have been targeting dissident social media users, representing the 'third-generation controls', in Diebert's terms. AkTrolls were formed soon after the Gezi protests to spread pro-government propaganda, including fake news, on social media and to surveil and intimidate dissident social media users. In addition to using fake accounts, AkTrolls have increasingly used automated bots (Saka 2019). In June 2020, Twitter suspended more than 32,000 Troll accounts linked to Russian, Chinese and Turkish government propaganda, 7,340 of which were AkTrolls. According to analysis by the Stanford Internet Observatory (Grossman et al. 2020), most of these accounts were linked to the youth wing of the AKP, while some involved local AKP politicians and others were fabricated personalities. These accounts were found to create re-tweet rings to make AKP propaganda (on both domestic and foreign affairs), and discredit and criminalise opposition parties (particularly the HDP and CHP). To complement AkTrolls' offensive practices, Turkish security and intelligence actors have increasingly been using advanced monitoring, gathering, blocking and hacking technologies. These included Deep Packet Inspection (DPI) technology delivered by Sandvine/Procera (a company based in Canada and the United States) and Finfisher/FinSpy produced by a German company (CitizenLab 2018; Topak 2019: 463).

In July 2020, the government passed a Social Media Amendment (No. 7253) to the Internet Law to further increase censorship and surveillance practices. The amendment mandates social media platforms, including Facebook, Instagram, Twitter, Periscope, YouTube and TikTok, to open representative offices in Turkey, store users' data in Turkey, and fully comply with removal and block requests of the Turkish authorities or face fines and bandwidth restrictions. As of March 2021, YouTube, Twitter and Facebook agreed to appoint local representatives after facing fines. It remains to be seen to what extent they will comply with other obligations of the amendment. The amendment also (ab)uses 'the right to be forgotten' to enable content removals from social media platforms, websites and search engines. In a democratic setting, the right to be forgotten can be used by citizens to protect themselves from unfair stigmatisation. In Turkey, this right has mainly been used by AKP politicians and pro-AKP individuals to remove news involving their involvement in corruption, and criticism of their policies (see e.g. Cumhuriyet 2021).

Conclusion

The Turkish state has a tradition of using authoritarian practices to govern society. The AKP rule marked the gradual expansion of authoritarian practices, both traditional (such as pressures on dissidents) and new (such as internet surveillance). These practices are organised around the model of the authoritarian assemblage in that they expand their reach and form new connections with each other. This chapter has provided a brief analysis of some key control systems (including political, judicial, protest policing, mass media and social media) and their associated authoritarian practices, ranging from new controls over the judiciary, appointments of trustees and fake news to social media trolling. There are other systems and practices deserving to be analysed to provide a fuller picture of the Turkish authoritarian assemblage, but these could not be examined in this piece owing to word limitations.[12] The expansion of the authoritarian assemblage is, however, not an indication of its durability or longevity. The authoritarian regime continues to be challenged by the democratic forces of Turkey, whose origins go as deep as the authoritarian ones in the history of Turkey.

Notes

1 Such traditions have also existed in other MENA regimes examined in this book. See particularly the 'Established Authoritarian Practices' in the Introduction (Topak et al. 2022) for an overview of how authoritarian state traditions have resulted in the implementation of established authoritarian practices across diverse MENA contexts.

2 Prior to the formation of the Turkish Republic, the Committee of the Union and Progress subjected Armenians to mass deportations and killings (the Armenian Genocide) during the First World War. Following Turkey's War of Independence against the invading Greek and other Western forces, the new Republic and Greece signed a compulsory population exchange agreement, and exchanged the Orthodox Christian population in Turkey for the Muslim population in Greece.

3 Other states of emergency examined in the book include those in Egypt (Jumet 2022), Sudan (Hassan 2022) and Tunisia (Cimini 2022). See also the 'Legalizing Authoritiarian Practices' section in the Introduction (Topak et al. 2022).

4 Cf. White and Herzog (2016). Unlike White and Herzog (2016), I define coercive capacity as a category of infrastructural power.

5 Notably, the court refused to review the state of emergency decrees.

6 The vast majority of protesters have been leftists and socialists, public employees, Kurds and unionists (Uysal 2016: 154–5).

7 On fake news and overall repression of media and journalists in other MENA regimes, see the 'Authoritarian Practices Shaping Civil Society and the Media' section in the Introduction (Topak et al. 2022), particularly the cases of Morocco (Maghraoui 2022), Bahrain (Shebabi 2022) and Egypt (Jumet 2022).

8 See the 'Protests and Policing' section in the Introduction (Topak et al. 2022).

9 In 1992, the state controls over rector appointments were softened with the partial re-introduction of rector elections by the faculty. The Higher Education Council (YÖK) became responsible for presenting the top three candidates to the President, who then appointed one of them as the rector. Overall, this semi-authoritarian format of rector appointments did not cause much controversy, because the YÖK and the Presidents in general respected the university votes. In 2016, the government used the state of emergency situation as an excuse to cancel rector elections altogether and give full powers to the President to appoint rectors.

10 See the 'Digital Surveillance Section' in the Introduction [Topak et al. 2022] for an overview from this book. Notable examples include the Gulf States, such as Saudi Arabia (Uniacke 2022), and the other regional powers Egypt (Jumet 2022) and Iran (Golkar 2022).

11 See particularly the chapter on Iran (Golkar 2022) for a 'deep' and institutionalised version of informant surveillance. See also Saudi Arabia (Uniacke 2022) and Israel (Dayan 2022) for other examples of cyber-snitching.

12 For instance, there is the urban control/surveillance system which has been updated by the mobilisation of the neighbourhood watchmen (*bekci*) since 2016.

References

Akgül, M. and Kırlıdoğ, M. (2015). 'Internet Censorship in Turkey'. *Internet Policy Review* 4(2): 1–22.

Arendt, H. (1976). *The Origins of Totalitarianism*. Orlando: Harvest.

Arsan, E. (2013). 'Killing Me Softly with his Words: Censorship and Self-Censorship from the Perspective of Turkish Journalists', *Turkish Studies* 14(3): 447–63.

Atak K. and D. Della Porta (2016). 'Popular Uprisings in Turkey: Police Culpability and Constraints on Dialogue-Oriented Policing in Gezi Park and Beyond', *European Journal of Criminology* 13(5): 610–25.

Amnesty International (1996). *Turkey: No Security without Human Rights*. https://www.amnesty.org/en/documents/EUR44/084/1996/en/

Avşar, S. (2018). 'Sosyal medyada "yazma" korkusu . . . "İstiyorum ama yazarsam hayatım mahvolacak"', 11 February. https://www.cumhuriyet.com.tr/haber/sosyal-medyada-yazma-korkusu-istiyorum-ama-yazarsam-hayatim-mahvolacak-924602

Baser, B., S. Akgönül and A. Erdi Öztürk (2017). '"Academics for Peace" in Turkey: A Case of Criminalising Dissent and Critical Thought via Counterterrorism Policy', *Critical Studies on Terrorism* 10(2): 274–96.

Berksoy, B. (2013). *Military, Police and Intelligence in Turkey: Recent Transformations and Needs for Reform*. İstanbul: TESEV.

Bianet (2020). 'NGO Bill Will Lead to Closure of Many Associations'. https://bianet.org/english/human-rights/236450-ngo-bill-will-lead-to-closure-of-many-associations

Can, B. (2015). 'Human Rights, Humanitarianism, and State Violence: Medical Documentation of Torture in Turkey', *Medical Anthropology Quarterly* 30(3): 342–58.

Cimini, G. (2022). 'Authoritarian Nostalgia and Practices in Newly Democratising Contexts: The Localised Example of Tunisia', in Ö. E. Topak, M. Mekouar and F. Cavatorta (eds) *New Authoritarian Practices in the Middle East and North Africa*. Edinburgh: Edinburgh University Press, pp. 276–95.

Çelik, B. (2020). 'Turkey's Communicative Authoritarianism', *Global Media and Communication* 16(1): 102–20.

CitizenLab (2018). 'Bad Traffic: Sandvine's PacketLogic Devices Used to Deploy Government Spyware in Turkey and Redirect Egyptian Users to Affiliate Ads?'. https://citizenlab.ca/2018/03/bad-traffic-sandvines-packetlogic-devices-deploy-government-spyware-turkey-syria/

Cumhuriyet (2021) 'Erişim engeline dönüşen "unutulma hakkı", muhalifler için sansür, siyasiler için geçmişin "aklanması"'. https://www.cumhuriyet.com.tr/haber/erisim-engeline-donusen-unutulma-hakki-muhalifler-icin-sansur-siyasiler-icin-gecmisin-aklanmasi-1805067

Dayan, H. (2022). 'Israel/Palestine: Authoritarian Practices in the Context of a Dual State Crisis', in Ö. E. Topak, M. Mekouar and F. Cavatorta (eds) *New Authoritarian Practices in the Middle East and North Africa*. Edinburgh: Edinburgh University Press, pp. 131–51.

Deibert, R. (2015). 'Authoritarianism Goes Global: Cyberspace under Siege', *Journal of Democracy* 26(3): 64–78.

Doğan, P and D. Rodrik (2014). *Yargı, Cemaat ve Bir Darbe Kurgusunun İçyüzü* [Courts, Community and the Inside Story of a Fictive Coup]. Istanbul: Destek.

DW (2021). 'Erdoğan'dan Boğaziçili gençlere: Öğrenci misiz, terörist misiniz?' https://www.dw.com/tr/erdoğandan-boğaziçili-gençlere-öğrenci-misiz-terörist -misiniz/a-56442021

Freedom House (2018). 'Freedom on the Net 2018 – Turkey', 1 November. https:// www.refworld.org/docid/5be16af3c.html

Freedom House (2020). *Freedom in the World 2020.* https://freedomhouse.org/sites /default/files/202002/FIW_2020_REPORT_BOOKLET_Final.pdf

Golkar, S. (2022). 'Deep Society and New Authoritarian Social Control in Iran after the Green Movement', in Ö. E. Topak, M. Mekouar and F. Cavatorta (eds) *New Authoritarian Practices in the Middle East and North Africa.* Edinburgh: Edinburgh University Press, pp. 92–111.

Grossman, S., F. Akis, A. Alemdaroğlu and J. A. Goldstein (2020). 'Political Retweet Rings and Compromised Accounts: A Twitter Influence Operation Linked to the Youth Wing of Turkey's Ruling Party'. Internet Observatory Cyber Policy Center. Stanford. https://fsi-live.s3.us-west-1.amazonaws.com/s3fs-public/202 00611_turkey_report.pdf

Göztepe, E. (2018). 'The Permanency of the State of Emergency in Turkey: The Rise of a Constituent Power or Only a New Quality of the State?', *Zeitschrift für Politikwissenschaft* 28(4): 521–34.

Haggerty, K. and R. Ericson (2000). 'The Surveillant Assemblage', *British Journal of Sociology* 51(4): 605–22.

Hale, W. (1994). *Turkish Politics and the Military.* London and New York: Routledge.

Hale, W. and E. Ozbudun (2009). *Islamism, Democracy and Liberalism in Turkey: the Rise of the AKP.* London: Routledge.

Hassan, Y. (2022). 'The Evolution of the Sudanese Authoritarian State: The December Uprising and the Unraveling of a "Persistent" Autocracy', in Ö. E. Topak, M. Mekouar and F. Cavatorta (eds) *New Authoritarian Practices in the Middle East and North Africa.* Edinburgh: Edinburgh University Press, pp. 252–75.

Heper, M. (2000). 'The Ottoman Legacy and Turkish Politics', *Journal of International Affairs* 54(1): 63–82.

HRW [Human Rights Watch] (2012). *Time for Justice: Ending Impunity for Killings and Disappearances in 1990s Turkey.* https://www.hrw.org/report/2012/09/03 /time-justice/ending-impunity-killings-and-disappearances-1990s-turkey

HRW [Human Rights Watch] (2021). *Türkiye: Protestocu Öğrenciler Hakkında Ceza Davası Açılabilir.* https://www.hrw.org/tr/news/2021/02/18/377883

İFÖD [İfade Özgürlüğü Derneği] (2019). *An Iceberg of Unseen Internet Censorship in Turkey.* https://ifade.org.tr/reports/EngelliWeb_2019.pdf

Jumet, K. D. (2022) 'Authoritarian Repression Under Sisi: New Tactics or New Tools?', in Ö. E. Topak, M. Mekouar and F. Cavatorta (eds) *New Authoritarian Practices in the Middle East and North Africa.* Edinburgh: Edinburgh University Press, pp. 73–91.

Karabag, G. (2019). '"Camide içki içtiler"; "Başörtülü bacımıza saldırdılar"; "Ezanı ıslıkladılar": Siyasi amaçlı gerçek dışı iddialar', *Medyascope.* 11 March. https://medyascope.tv/2019/03/11/camide-icki-ictiler-basortulu-bacimiza-saldirdilar-e zani-islikladilar-siyasi-amacli-gercek-disi-iddialar/

Kaygusuz, Ö. (2018). 'Authoritarian Neoliberalism and Regime Security in Turkey: Moving to an "Exceptional State" under AKP', *South European Society and Politics* 23(2): 281–302.

Maghraoui, D. (2022) '"The Freedom of No Speech": Journalists and the Multiple Layers of Authoritarian Practices in Morocco', in Ö. E. Topak, M. Mekouar and F. Cavatorta (eds) *New Authoritarian Practices in the Middle East and North Africa.* Edinburgh: Edinburgh University Press, pp. 189–207.

Mann, M. (1984). 'The Autonomous Power of the State', *European Journal of Sociology* 25(2): 187–213.

Mann, M (2008). 'The Infrastructural Power of the State', *Studies in Comparative International Development* 43: 355–65.

Oğuz, Ş. (2016). '"Yeni Türkiye" nin siyasal rejimi' [The political regime of 'New Turkey'], in T. Tören and M. Kutun (eds) *Yeni Türkiye? Kapitalizm, Devlet, Sınıflar* [New Turkey? Capitalism, State and Classes]. Istanbul: SAV, pp. 81–127.

Özbudun, E. (2015). 'Turkey's Judiciary and the Drift toward Competitive Authoritarianism', *The International Spectator* 50(2): 42–55.

Reuters Institute (2018). *Digital News Report 2018.* http://media.digitalnewsreport.org/wp-content/uploads/2018/06/digital-news-report-2018.pdf?x89475

RSF (2018). *Doğan Media Group Sale Completes Government Control of Turkish Media.* https://rsf.org/en/news/dogan-media-group-sale-completes-government-control-turkish-media

Saka, E. (2019). *Social Media and Politics in Turkey: A Journey through Citizen Journalism, Political Trolling, and Fake News.* New York: Lexington.

Shehabi, A. (2022). 'The Authoritarian Topography of the Bahraini State: Political Geographies of Power and Protest', in Ö. E. Topak, M. Mekouar and F. Cavatorta (eds) *New Authoritarian Practices in the Middle East and North Africa.* Edinburgh: Edinburgh University Press, pp. 51–72.

Somer, M. (2017). 'Conquering versus Democratizing the State: Political Islamists and Fourth Wave Democratization in Turkey and Tunisia', *Democratization* 24(6): 1,025–43.

Söyler, M. (2013). 'Informal Institutions, Forms of State and Democracy: The Turkish Deep State', *Democratization* 20: 2, 310–34.

Şık, A. (2017). *İmamın Ordusu* [The Army of the Imam]. Istanbul: Kırmızı Kedi.

Tahiroglu, M. (2020). 'How Turkey's Leaders Dismantled the Rule of Law', *The Fletcher Forum of World Affairs* 44(1), 67–96.

Tansel, C.B. (2018). 'Authoritarian Neoliberalism and Democratic Backsliding in Turkey: Beyond the Narratives of Progress', *South European Society and Politics* 23(2): 197–217.

The Economist (2010). 'A Country's Welcome Rise', 21 October. https://www.econ omist.com/node/17309065

Topak, Ö. E. (2017). 'The Making of a Totalitarian Surveillance Machine: Surveillance in Turkey under AKP Rule', *Surveillance & Society* 15(3/4): 535–42.

Topak, Ö. E. (2019). 'The Authoritarian Surveillant Assemblage: Authoritarian State Surveillance in Turkey', *Security Dialogue* 50(5): 454–72.

Topak, Ö. E., M. Mekouar and F. Cavatorta (2022). 'Introduction', in Ö. E. Topak, M. Mekouar and F. Cavatorta (eds) *New Authoritarian Practices in the Middle East and North Africa.* Edinburgh: Edinburgh University Press, pp. 1–29.

Uysal, A. (2016). *Sokakta siyaset: Türkiye'de protesto eylemleri, protestocular ve polis.* Istanbul: Iletisim.

Yılmaz, Z. (2020). 'Erdoğan's Presidential Regime and Strategic Legalism: Turkish Democracy in the Twilight Zone', *Southeast European and Black Sea Studies* 20(2): 265–87.

Yeğen, M. (2007). 'Turkish Nationalism and the Kurdish Question', *Ethnic and Racial Studies* 30(1): 119–51.

Yeşil, B. (2016). *Media in New Turkey: The Origins of an Authoritarian Neoliberal State.* Champaign, IL: University of Illinois Press.

Yeşil, B., E. K. Sözeri and E. Khazraee (2017). 'Turkey's Internet Policy after the Coup Attempt', Internet Policy Observatory. http://globalnetpolicy.org/wpcon tent/uploads/2017/02/Turkey1_v6-1.pdf

Yetkin, M. (2021). 'Erdoğan restructures Turkish military up to political needs'. Yetkin Report, 2 September. https://yetkinreport.com/en/2021/09/02/erdogan-restructures-turkish-military-up-to-political-needs

Yonucu, D. (2017). 'The Absent Present Law: An Ethnographic Study of Legal Violence in Turkey', *Social & Legal Studies* 27(6): 716–33.

Uniacke, R. (2022). 'Digital Repression for Authoritarian Evolution in Saudi Arabia', in Ö. E. Topak, M. Mekouar and F. Cavatorta (eds) *New Authoritarian Practices in the Middle East and North Africa.* Edinburgh: Edinburgh University Press, pp. 228–51.

White, D. and M. Herzog (2016). 'Examining State Capacity in the Context of Electoral Authoritarianism, Regime Formation and Consolidation in Russia and Turkey', *Southeast European and Black Sea Studies* 16(4): 551–69.

Whiting, M. and Z. Kaya (2021). 'Autocratization, Permanent Emergency Rule and Local Politics: Lessons from the Kurds in Turkey', *Democratization*, doi: 10.1080/13510347.2021.1871602.

16

THE UNITED ARAB EMIRATES: EVOLVING AUTHORITARIAN TOOLS

Christopher Davidson

Introduction

The United Arab Emirates is widely known for its hydrocarbon wealth, globally focused sovereign wealth funds, high-profile 'soft power' investments (Nye 2004), and – post-Arab Spring – its extraordinarily intense efforts to re-shape regional politics. As such, its international relations and international political economy dynamics have attracted considerable scholarly attention. Notably, much has been written on the UAE's historical ties to Britain, its subsequent multi-faceted relationship with the United States and its increasingly formal links to Israel. Likewise, considerable attention has been paid to the UAE's unwaveringly firm stance against Iran and its perceived proxies (including Yemen's Houthi movement), its opposition to the transnational Muslim Brotherhood and its actions against putatively Islamist-enabling Qatar.

Moreover, with the UAE being a high GDP per capita 'rentier state' with a relatively small number of citizens and a substantial expatriate workforce (Beblawi 1987), there has also been a strong focus on the nitty-gritty of its authority structures and rulers' contemporary statecraft. Due emphasis, for example, has been placed on the increasing political dominance of Abu Dhabi (the largest and wealthiest of the UAE's constituent emirates) (Davidson 2007, 2009); the rise of Abu Dhabi's crown prince, Muhammad bin Zayed Al-Nahyan (a.k.a. 'MBZ') (Roberts 2020; Juneau 2020; Davidson 2006); the ostensibly central and acquiescence-ensuring role of hydrocarbon-financed welfare and employment-based 'social contracts' or 'ruling bargains' (Lucas 2014; Krane 2019); the careful co-option of tradition and religion (Davidson 2008); and the – rather limited – range of 'authoritarian upgrading' efforts (Heydemann 2007; Cavatorta 2010; Hinnebusch 2012), including elections for the largely powerless Federal National Council (Burton 2019).

As yet, however, comparatively little has been written on the ways in which MBZ's regime – presiding over a resource-rich and relatively techno-logically advanced state (with a consequently high capacity for repression) – has been developing a range of new authoritarian tools to strengthen further its position. After all, although the UAE never experienced mass protests in 2011 and has been able to avoid the sort of austerity drives seen in Saudi Arabia and other Gulf states in the wake of the 2014 oil price crash, MBZ has nonetheless faced sporadic calls for reform from a small but vocifer-ous element of the local population, and on occasion even explicit domestic criticism – especially with regard to official stances on political Islam and, more lately, Israel (Freer 2017; Davidson 2013; Reuters 2020; Council for Foreign Relations 2020).

Drawing on a range of primary and secondary sources (including official government data, state press releases, judicial documentation, reports from international and non-governmental organisations and articles in the inter-national and local media), this chapter situates such developments within a suitably constructive framework of evolving Gulf authoritarianism,[1] and seeks to provide a systematic and empirically rich analysis of some of these new authoritarian instruments. In particular, covering tools that could be considered both legally-based and more obviously coercive – and those that could be deemed both 'direct' and 'indirect' – the chapter reviews the recent tightening-up of the UAE's media and free-speech-related legislation, the apparent introduction of increasingly sophisticated cyber-surveillance tech-niques and (most dramatically) the creation of a multi-layered and mostly foreign-staffed 'praetorian guard'. Finally, in the context of such tools being transferable or exportable to other authoritarian settings, the chapter consid-ers the likely impact of the UAE's evolving authoritarianism elsewhere in the Gulf and the wider Arab region.

Legacy Media: Upgrading Controls[2]

With parallels to the UAE's historic and much-discussed restrictions on national non-governmental and civil society organisations, and against a backdrop of consistently poor World Press Freedom Index scores (Reporters Without Borders 2019), the Abu Dhabi regime appears to have adopted most of the UAE's earlier tried and tested controls on domestic media organisations. First and foremost, beyond the official *Wakalat Anba'a al-Emarat* (a.k.a. 'Emirates News Agency'), the majority of national and local media organisations remain either de facto state- or ruling-family-owned (*Guardian* 2007; *National* 2016), or are instead very heavily supervised by specific government authorities. In particular, the UAE's now forty-year-old Law on Governing Publications and Publishing (described by Freedom House as 'one of the most restrictive [media laws] in the Arab world') (Freedom House 2020a) still requires all domestic media organisations to be government-licensed, all publications to be submitted for censorship, and all newspapers to 'publish free of charge material of public interest sent by the ministries'.[3] Moreover, it states that 'the person of the president of [the federation] or the rulers of the emirates may not be criticized'; that 'any material which includes an incitement to, and is harmful to Islam, or the system of government in the country, or harms the country's interests or the basic systems on which the society is founded shall be prohibited'; and that 'material containing shameful information on the person of the president of an Arab, Muslim country or a country with friendly ties may not be published' (UAE Federal Law 1980).

Meanwhile, despite frequent statements from senior Emirati spokesmen on the need for improved media freedom and more critical journalism (Emirates News Agency 2017), MBZ's regime has clearly also sought to strengthen systems based on some degree of anticipated (or actual) repression. As the US Department of State notes of the situation, 'the government owns most newspapers, television stations, and radio stations . . . all media conforms to unpublished government reporting guidelines . . . the government also influences privately owned media through the National Media Council, which directly oversees all media content' (US Department of State Bureau of Democracy, Human Rights, and Labor 2020).

In most cases, existing or revised legislation seems to have been a sufficient deterrent. Editors and publishers in the UAE are understood to be mindful of all laws, and to 'commonly practice self-censorship due to fear of government retribution' ((US Department of State Bureau of Democracy, Human Rights, and Labor 2020), while many of the country's expatriate journalists are thought to 'have little incentive to engage in risky critical or investigative journalism' (Freedom House 2019). In particular, a 2015 law on combating discrimination and hatred seems to have added fresh restrictions for media outlets, stating that 'no words or action which may incite to commit the crime of blasphemy or defamation of religions . . . may be debated on the right of freedom and expression' (UAE Federal Law 2015), while a 2016 law has effectively provided the Abu Dhabi-based National Media Council with even greater control over UAE media output and media-related policies (UAE Federal Law 2016). For those instances in which the laws themselves have not been enough of a deterrent, there is of course considerable evidence that MBZ's regime has also continued to use more straightforward coercive tactics. In December 2015, for example, a Jordanian expatriate working as a culture reporter for an Abu Dhabi-based newspaper was arrested and then charged with 'insulting state symbols' following allegations he had been criticising the UAE, Egypt and Israel (Human Rights Watch 2017); and in July 2017 the popular *Arabian Business* magazine was banned for a month following its publication of an article criticising the UAE's real estate sector (Committee to Protect Journalists 2017).

Online Free Speech Tightening

Given the much-discussed accelerating internet access and social media penetration rates in the UAE and the other Gulf states (Internet Telecommunications Union 2018) – and of course the supposedly high-profile role played by online platforms during 2008's April 6 movement in Egypt, 2009's Green movement in Iran, and then the Arab Spring (Hussain 2015; Khiabany 2015; Rahimi 2015) – the co-option and control of such new technologies has unsurprisingly been taken very seriously by the Abu Dhabi regime, with evidence that its leaders have gone to considerable lengths to try to keep at least one step ahead of any organised cyber dissent.

Most obviously, as with their command over 'legacy' media outputs (though in this case aimed primarily at individuals rather than organisations), the UAE authorities have attempted to use existing or revised legislation to encourage online self-censorship and, where necessary, to justify actual censorship. Notably, 2012's federal Law on Combating Cybercrimes stipulates very heavy penalties for those who 'establish or administer or run a website or publishes on a computer network or any information technology means [anything] which would promote or praise any programs or ideas which would prompt riot, hatred, racism, sectarianism, or damage the national unity or social peace or prejudice the public order and public morals' (UAE Federal Law 2012).

Reinforcing such legislation, the past few years have also seen citizens and residents being issued with numerous prominent warnings on social media usage. In June 2017, for example, the UAE's public prosecutor office warned that any social media activity expressing sympathy for Qatar – following the launching of a UAE- and Saudi Arabia-led diplomatic and economic embargo on the putatively Muslim Brotherhood-supporting state – would be punishable by imprisonment or fines of up to $136,000; and in April 2018, the UAE's Telecommunications Regulatory Authority tweeted a statement cautioning all residents that the posting or spreading of 'fake news' on social media was punishable by imprisonment or fines of up to $272,000 (*Gulf News* 2018). In September 2019, the ruler of Dubai (who also serves as the UAE's vice-president, prime minister and minister for defence) then also advised social media users not to tarnish the country's image on the basis that 'the reputation of the UAE is not for public use by those who seek more followers ... we shall not accept that a number of online users taint the legacy of the late Sheikh Zayed bin Sultan Al Nahyan that he established on the values of credibility, love and respect' (*Khaleej Times* 2019); and a month later he published a list of ten social media 'guidelines' which, *inter alia*, called for Emirati users to 'represent their country online to reflect the Founding Father Sheikh Zayed bin Sultan Al-Nahyan's image and ethics, the UAE's accomplishments, and humanitarian initiatives' (UAE Government 2020).

Meanwhile, there is extensive evidence that MBZ's regime has also engaged in more straightforward coercive tactics. In November 2014, for example, an Emirati activist who had been using Twitter to campaign for the release of his father and other political prisoners was sentenced to three years imprisonment by the Supreme Court after being accused of 'damaging institutions' and 'communicating with external organisations to provide misleading information' (Human Rights Watch 2017a,b; Reuters 2019c); in February 2015 three Emirati sisters who had similarly been using Twitter to demand the release of their brother were reportedly arrested and 'held in secret detention and with no contact with the outside world' until their eventual release three months later (Bloomberg 2015; Amnesty International 2015); and in August 2018 an Omani student studying in the UAE was reportedly apprehended following a number of controversial tweets and then later sentenced to life imprisonment (Human Rights Watch 2020).

Cyber-surveillance Techniques[4]

Accompanying such conventional legislation-based and 'offline' coercive strategies, there are now strong indications that the Abu Dhabi regime has also sought and developed more direct and powerful means to censor, surveil and even manipulate social media and other cyberspace communication platforms. Indeed, as a particularly wealthy state with access to considerable resources and the ability to hire specialist personnel, the UAE seems to have been able to successfully harness some of the very latest technologies and methods and – for the time being at least – to have kept the upper hand. In this context, Andreas Krieg has noted that 'to regain control over a global public sphere in cyberspace, [MBZ and the crown prince of Saudi Arabia] have resorted to cyber subversion' (Middle East Eye 2019), while the *New York Times* has observed how Abu Dhabi's leaders have managed to build 'a hypermodern surveillance state where everyone is monitored' (*New York Times* 2020b).

Notably, beyond the much-discussed blocking of critical or potentially controversial websites and platform content and the extensive 'deep packet' inspection of personal emails and other internet data carried by state-owned servers (Freedom House 2020b; Howard and Hussein 2013; *Wall Street Journal* 2018), in recent years the UAE also appears to have been purchasing (and deploying) some of the most sophisticated cyber-surveillance software packages in the world. In 2010, for example, it was revealed that the UAE authorities had earlier acquired a service supplied by a US firm to allow its telecommunications providers to fake secure connections and thus position themselves as the 'men in the middle' during users' web transactions (Davidson 2013). In 2012 it was then understood that the UAE had bought spyware from an Israeli company founded by former members of the Israeli Intelligence Corps; and in May 2016 the *New York Times* noted that invoices from an Italian spyware manufacturer indicated that the UAE had become their second-biggest customer (after Morocco) (*New York Times* 2016). Moreover, in June 2017 a joint investigation by BBC Arabic and a Danish newspaper alleged that a Danish subsidiary of a major British multinational had been exporting a surveillance package called *Evident* to the UAE and several other authoritarian states. According to a former employee, the software allowed for the interception of 'any Internet traffic . . . if you wanted to do a whole country, you could . . . you could follow people around . . . they were capable of decrypting stuff as well' (BBC 2017).

With these and other such purchases and hires soon seeming to deliver results, as early as 2009 the UAE authorities appear to have been able to install advanced spyware on Blackberrys (which at the time were widely used for their encrypted 'BBM Messenger' social media service). Following claims from users that a 'performance enhancing patch' provided by Emirati telecommunications providers had begun to slow their devices, Blackberry's Canadian manufacturer launched an investigation and released a patch of their own to uninstall the rogue update, explaining that 'independent sources have concluded that the [UAE] update is not designed to improve performance of your BlackBerry Handheld, but rather to send received messages back to a central server' (BBC 2009). Furthermore, by the end of the year the UAE was understood to have established a new Development Research Exploitation Analysis Department (known by its acronym, 'DREAD') which, in the name of counter-terrorism, was understood to have been 'exploring vulnerabilities in Windows computers and transferring files to servers operating out of [MBZ's crown prince's court]' (Reuters 2019e). Revealed by a Reuters special investigation, in 2012 DREAD had then launched its signature 'Project Raven', which was believed to be staffed by a team of former US intelligence officers and to be 'helping the UAE engage in surveillance of other governments, militants and human rights activists critical of the monarchy', and in late 2015 the department was moved under the umbrella of an Emirati cyber technology company with substantial government contracts (which at the time was sharing a building with the UAE's National Electronic Security Authority). According to several of DREAD's former employees, by this stage Project Raven's staff had had access to an 'arsenal of cyber tools, including a cutting-edge espionage platform known as Karma [used to hack into] the iPhones of hundreds of activists, political leaders and suspected terrorists'. Moreover, they claimed that those working on the project had even managed to turn 'a prosaic household item, a baby monitor, into a spy device' and that 'senior National Electronic Security Authority officers were [being] given more control over daily functions'. Adding further detail, another former staff member who previously worked for the US National Security Agency has described how the project had eventually developed two missions: 'a purple briefing', which was 'a purely defensive mission, protecting the government of the UAE from hackers and other threats'; and a 'black briefing', which was 'the offensive, operational division of the National Electronic Security Authority and will never be acknowledged to the general public'. As she recalled of the latter, 'some days it was hard to swallow, like [when you target] a sixteen-year-old kid on Twitter . . . but it's an intelligence mission, you are an intelligence operative . . . I never made it personal' (Reuters 2019b,d,e; *New York Times* 2019a).

Also, in the UAE (and perhaps linked to Project Raven), in 2013 evidence of the Israeli spyware was discovered on the devices of prominent Emirati human rights activist Ahmad Mansour Al-Shehhi, with researchers at Citizen Lab at the University of Toronto's Munk School of Global Affairs describing it as 'the most sophisticated spyware they had ever uncovered on a mobile device' (*New York Times* 2019a). Similarly, in March 2016 Citizen Lab determined that the Italian spyware was being used to target Al-Shehhi's emails, tracing it in the first instance to 'a UAE conglomerate owned by a member of the Abu Dhabi ruling family', and shortly afterwards it was reported that the UAE had been using the same spyware to target 1,100 others. In May 2016 it was then claimed that another form of spyware was being used against members of a London-based UAE human rights organisation, in addition to approximately 400 others (including 24 Emirati Twitter users, at least three of whom were arrested shortly after surveillance began) (*New York Times* 2016). More recently, in December 2019, US officials with knowledge of a classified intelligence assessment described how a new UAE-designed text and video messaging service with millions of downloads (the majority being in the UAE) could potentially be used by 'the government of the United Arab Emirates to try to track every conversation, movement, relationship, appointment, sound and image of those who install it on their phones'. Though the UAE's Telecommunications Regulatory Authority denied these claims, a forensic digital investigation carried out by the *New York Times* concluded that the software was 'a cleverly designed tool for mass surveillance, according to the technical analysis and interviews', and that its developers were linked to a data mining firm operating from the same building as the National Electronic Security Authority – by then rebranded as the Signals Intelligence Agency (*New York Times* 2020a).

As well as its use of sophisticated cyber-surveillance software, there is also evidence that MBZ's regime has been among the pioneers of more experimental 'bot' technology and 'troll farming' techniques. As Ben Nimmo, Marc Owen Jones, Andrew Leber and Alexei Abrahams demonstrate in their ground-breaking work (Nimmo 2018; Jones 2019a, Leber and Abrahams 2019; Abrahams and Leber 2020), these have aimed to shape – and in some cases subvert – entire global social media debates. In summer 2017, for example, it was reported that thousands of bots had been spreading anti-Qatar messages following the UAE and Saudi-led embargo. As Jones noted, 'what these bot armies represent is not an organic outpouring of genuine public anger at Qatar or [its Al-Thani ruling family], but rather an orchestrated and organized campaign' (Jones 2019a). Scrutinising 200,000 relevant tweets from this period, Leber and Abrahams drew similar conclusions, observing 'the mass production of online statements via automated "bot" accounts' and 'manipulation . . . aimed at securing organic participation from supportive publics' (Leber and Abrahams 2019).

In August 2019, Facebook then stated it had had to close 350 accounts 'linked to marketing firms in Egypt and the United Arab Emirates' which had been 'phishing messages promoting the UAE [state]' (Reuters 2019a); while in September 2019 Twitter claimed it had had to suspend more than 4,000 UAE-based accounts tweeting 'content directed at Qatar and Yemen' along with an additional 270 UAE- (and Egypt-) linked accounts believed to have been operated by a private company that had been 'targeting Qatar, Iran and other countries as well as amplifying messaging supportive of the Saudi government' (ABC 2019). As Jones described at the time, there seemed to have been 'a global influence campaign in several languages using a mixture of human-operated (trolls) and automated accounts (bots) . . . they criticised the Brotherhood, Qatar, praised [the crown prince of Saudi Arabia], the Yemen War etc.' (Jones 2019b).

Praetorian Guards

Notwithstanding the Abu Dhabi regime's extensive efforts to centralise control over the UAE's conventional military, security and intelligence-related organisations, there seems to have been a strong emphasis on upgrading the most elite units while ensuring they remain separate from other command structures. In this sense, MBZ appears to have been developing one of the most advanced and distinct examples of contemporary *cohors praetoria* or 'praetorian guards' (as per the special bodyguard divisions assigned to protect the Roman emperor during the imperial period).

After all, in recent years Abu Dhabi has witnessed a wave of successful army officer-led coups d'état (most notably in Sudan and Egypt), and has undoubtedly recognised the benefits of maintaining contemporary 'armies to watch the army' (Hertog 2011), or, as James Quinlivan has put it, the need for 'parallel force units ... equipped in the same manner as regular army units ensur[ing] that the regular military will consider them in any balance-of-power calculation' (Quinlivan 1999).

Despite the UAE never previously having had a functional equivalent of neighbouring Saudi Arabia's proto-military National Guard (or even the Saudi Royal Guard bodyguard unit), MBZ's evolving praetorian arrangements in some respects seem like those of Saudi Arabia. Notably, beyond upgrading infrastructure and training for its Amiri Guard (which is ultimately controlled by one of MBZ's half-brothers and has duties comparable to the Saudi Royal Bodyguard unit's) (*National* 2020), in 2011 the Abu Dhabi regime is understood to have inaugurated a new Presidential Guard force. Including a Special Operations Command, a small aviation wing and (since March 2016) its own 'national service academy', the approximately 5,000–13,000-strong force has been likened by some to the US Marines (Roberts 2020); but has also been described as 'operating outside the conventional framework of traditional armed forces' and as being focused on 'regime defence functions' as well as having a 'combat formation' (Emirates News Agency 2016). Though little data is available on the UAE's exact deployments in Yemen, it appears that the Presidential Guard has been playing a significant role in the conflict, thus providing its units with considerable front-line experience while also establishing itself as an especially MBZ-loyalist force and thus a potent parallel to the regular armed forces (Roberts 2020; Salisbury 2020).

As with Saudi and other Gulf state rulers, MBZ has unsurprisingly been keen on employing foreign advisors.[5] Since 2010, for example, the Amiri Guard is understood to have been receiving training from 'a non-governmental American company that trains the US Secret Service to protect the American president' (*National* 2020), and the Presidential Guard currently receives training from the US Marines (as per a $150 million Foreign Military Sales agreement with the US government) (*Middle East Eye* 2015). Dwarfing these agreements, however (and unlike in Saudi Arabia), most of Abu Dhabi's recent foreign hires appear to have been brought in as independent contractors. As David Roberts notes, some of these men have been allowed to accumulate real power over promotion and selection issues as part of an effort 'to break with the past to instil the beginnings of a meritocratic officer selection system'. In this category (among reportedly 'dozens' of retired Australian, British and American officers), a former Australian general currently heads the Presidential Guard while a former British Royal Marine has responsibility for placing other expatriate officers (Roberts 2020; *New York Times* 2019b; *Telegraph* 2010).

More remarkable, however, and seemingly without an equivalent in Saudi Arabia (or indeed any of the other Gulf states), has been the entirely foreign-staffed 'secret desert force' set up by Blackwater founder Erik Prince, as revealed by a May 2011 *New York Times* investigation. Intended to be 800-strong and based in a $500 million complex in Abu Dhabi's interior, it was understood to have initially comprised Columbian and South African soldiers who had been entering the UAE posing as construction workers. Significantly, it was believed to be operating outside any formal chain of command, and – according to papers associated with the project – its *raison d'être* was to conduct special operations missions inside and outside the country, defend oil pipelines and skyscrapers from terrorist attacks and 'put down internal revolts'. Moreover, according to interviewed former employees of the force, 'the UAE's rulers, viewing their own military as inadequate, also hoped that the troops could blunt the regional aggression of Iran, the country's biggest foe'. Further to these objectives, there were also indications that Prince was under strict instructions to hire no Muslim mercenaries, on the basis that 'Muslim soldiers . . . could not be counted on to kill fellow Muslims', and suggestions that the force needed to be prepared for possible 'crowd-control operations where the crowd is not armed with firearms but does pose a risk using improvised weapons such as clubs and stones' (*New York Times* 2011).

Since its founding, the force appears to have grown substantially, and likely now numbers over 1,800 men. Though reportedly no longer involving Prince, it still appears to be shrouded in secrecy, with 'Emirati leaders' rarely paying visits, with westerners understood to be serving as its de facto trainers and commanders, and with no social media activity permitted by any of its members. As for the soldiers themselves, the majority now seem to be Latin American (rather than South African), with most being 'battle-tested' Columbians alongside smaller contingents of Panamanians, Salvadorans and Chileans (*New York Times* 2015). Indeed, by summer 2013 the number of Columbian recruits was so high that the Columbian government formally complained to Abu Dhabi over the 'exodus' of its 'highly trained' security sector professionals (*Financial Times* 2013). With the situation seemingly unresolved and relations deteriorating further, the Columbian minister of defence then began to protest to the media that 'his best soldiers were being poached', while his government tried (unsuccessfully) to broker an agreement with Abu Dhabi to 'stanch the flow' (Bloomberg 2015; *New York Times* 2015).

With regard to operational activities, perhaps unsurprisingly the force seems to have spent most of its time 'on base' in Abu Dhabi, with those involved in the project describing 'years of monotony at the desert camp' and 'rising every day at 5 am for exercise and military training – including shooting practice, navigation and riot control'. However, there is now evidence that at least some of its units have been tested out in a variety of challenging international roles. UAE-hired Columbians, for example, are known to have been providing anti-pirate security on commercial cargo vessels, while in November 2015 it was revealed that around 450 'hand-picked' members of the force had earlier been deployed to Yemen. Understood to have been receiving bonus payments of $1,000 a week (on top of their regular $2,000–$3,000 monthly salaries), the latter appear to have been serving as advance 'Emirati' patrols – wearing UAE military uniforms and dog-tags – and to have repeatedly been involved in front-line combat (*New York Times* 2015; *Times* 2015). In December 2015, most notably, it was heavily reported that two Western commanders (a former British army officer and an Australian mercenary) had been 'leading a team of Colombian soldiers secretly employed by the United Arab Emirates' that had been killed 'during an ambush outside the south-western city of Taiz while attempting to capture al-Amri military base' (*Times* 2015; *Guardian* 2015).

Conclusion

Focusing on three of the most prominent sets of new authoritarian tools being deployed by the UAE, this chapter has demonstrated the extent to which MBZ's regime has been prepared to face perceived new threats with a range of new and increasingly sophisticated instruments and methods. Certainly, in this context – with its sweeping media and free speech-tightening legislation and sophisticated cyber-surveillance techniques – the UAE appears to have joined the front ranks of high-tech 'networked authoritarian' states. Indeed, the UAE case seems to tally strongly with Rebecca MacKinnon's original China-specific definition of 'authoritarian regimes [that] can adapt to the Internet, even using networked technologies to bolster legitimacy', and similarly with the subsequent observations of Katy Pearce and Sarah Kendzior (focusing on Azerbaijan) and Nathalie Maréchal (focusing on Russia) (MacKinnon 2011; Pearce and Kendzior 2012; Maréchal 2017; Leber and

Abrahams 2019). Moreover, the UAE's evidently extensive efforts to extract data on its citizens from a diverse range of sources (including telephones, computers and various social media platforms) provides a good authoritarian example of the 'surveillant assemblage' (Haggerty and Ericson 2000; see Topak 2019, 2022).

Meanwhile, notwithstanding elements of 'authoritarian learning' from Saudi Arabia (Heydemann and Leenders 2011), the structure and modus operandi of Abu Dhabi's multi-layered and mostly foreign-staffed praetorian guard is undoubtedly unprecedented for the Gulf states, and indeed most of the Arab world. Certainly, MBZ's 'secret desert force' seems to have much more in common with the sort of 'neo-sultanistic' private militias observed in earlier authoritarian settings elsewhere, including those operated by Rafael Trujillo in the Dominican Republic (Hartlyn 1998), by François Duvalier in Haiti (Snyder 1998) and by Ferdinand Marcos in the Philippines (Thompson 1998).

Though these new tools may not easily spread or replicate to the UAE's neighbours – not least given the considerable resources, investment and planning required – it seems possible some aspects may eventually transfer, especially if Abu Dhabi's regime remains stable and the country maintains its relative prosperity. After all, there is considerable evidence that Saudi Arabia and other Gulf states have not only been adopting aspects of the UAE's media and free-speech-tightening legislation, but also many of its sophisticated (and bought-in) cyber-surveillance techniques (*Guardian* 2020; *New York Times* 2018). In parallel, of course, many Gulf and other Arab rulers are likely monitoring MBZ's praetorian arrangements closely, and it seems reasonable to assume that at least some will be considering the need for similarly elite-level, foreign-staffed private militias.

Furthermore, even if the UAE does not seem to be explicitly engaged in full-blown autocracy promotion, and clearly lacks a 'unified, coherent set of foreign policies that constitute intentional efforts to promote a particular regime type abroad' (Tansey 2016), there is nonetheless little doubt that Abu Dhabi has invested considerable energy in pushing something a little narrower onto other states, both in the Gulf and the wider Arab region. Indeed, beyond simply representing an effort to 'prudentially defend the surrounding political order' in the wake of the unsettling 2011 Arab uprisings (Brownlee 2017), Abu Dhabi's continuing support for anti-Islamist military strongmen (such as Egypt's Abdel Fattah El-Sisi and Libya's Khalifa Belqasim

Haftar), and its significant pressure on other monarchies (such as Bahrain and Kuwait) to join in with outlawing the Brotherhood, have perhaps been less about any wholesale autocracy promotion and more about a UAE-led 'diffusion of repression' based on MBZ's signature policies (Darwich 2017). Certainly, unlike in the old days of 'political petrolism' or 'checkbook diplomacy', in which wealthy states such as the UAE used to dispense aid or provide diplomatic support to indigent Arab regimes more or less regardless of their internal politics (*Washington Post* 1977; Peck 2010; Schlumberger 2005), there now seems a distinct expectation to do things Abu Dhabi's way – at least regarding political Islam – or face the consequences.

Notes

1 See also the book chapters on other Gulf States [Bahrain (Shehabi 2022), Qatar (Liloia 2022) and Saudi Arabia (Uniacke 2022)] where similar authoritarian practices exist to varying degrees.
2 See also the 'Authoritarian Practices Shaping Civil Society and the Media' section in the Introduction for other cases of media repression in various other MENA regimes (Topak et al. 2022).
3 For other examples of continuation of repressive authoritarian practices in MENA countries, see the 'Established Authoritarian Practices Section' in the Introduction. See also the 'Legalising Authoritarian Practices' section for the implementation of repressive laws by other MENA regimes to curb dissent (Topak et al. 2022).
4 See the 'Digital Surveillance' section in the Introduction (Topak et al. 2022) for similar digital practices in other MENA regimes to varying degrees, particularly in other Gulf States, Saudi Arabia (Uniacke 2022) and Bahrain (Shebabi 2022).
5 See the 'Authoritarian Learning and Alliances' section in the Introduction (Topak et al. 2022) for similar international linkages of other MENA regimes such as Bahrain (Shebabi 2022) and Saudi Arabia (Uniacke 2022.)

References

ABC (2019). 'Twitter Shuts Down Thousands of International Accounts Tied to Political Spam', 20 September.

Abrahams, A. and A. Leber (2021). 'Framing a Murder: Twitter Influencers and the Jamal Khashoggi Incident', *Mediterranean Politics* 26(2): 247–59.

Amnesty International (2015). 'UAE: Release Sisters Secretly Detained for Three Months over Tweets', 15 May.

BBC (2009). 'UAE Blackberry Update Was Spyware', 21 July.

BBC (2017). 'How BAE Sold Cyber-Surveillance Tools to Arab States', 15 June.

Beblawi, H. (1987). 'The Rentier State in the Arab World', in H. Beblawi and G. Luciani, Giacomo (eds) *The Rentier State*. New York: Croom Helm.

Bloomberg (2015). 'Recruiting Mercenaries for Middle East Fuels Rancor in Colombia', 31 December.

Bloomberg (2015). 'U.A.E. Holds Sisters on Tweets Backing Brother, Amnesty Says', 1 March.

Brownlee, J. (2017). 'The Limited Reach of Authoritarian Powers', *Democratization* 24(7): 1,326–44.

Burton, G. (2019). 'What Influence Do Advisory Assemblies Have? A Print Media Analysis of the UAE's Federal National Council, 2011–15', *Journal of Arabian Studies* 9(1): 13–32.

Cavatorta, F. (2010). 'The Convergence of Governance: Upgrading Authoritarianism in the Arab World and Downgrading Democracy Elsewhere?', *Middle East Critique* 19(3): 217–32.

Committee to Protect Journalists (2017). 'Dubai Suspends Magazine for One Month', 31 July.

Council for Foreign Relations (2020). 'What's Behind the New Israel–UAE Peace Deal?', 17 August.

Darwich, M. (2017). 'Democratization, Creating the Enemy, Constructing the Threat: The Diffusion of Repression against the Muslim Brotherhood in the Middle East', *Democratization* 24(7): 1,289–90.

Davidson, C. (2006). 'After Shaikh Zayed: The Politics of Succession in Abu Dhabi and the UAE', *Middle East Policy* 13(1): 42–59.

Davidson, C. (2007). 'The Emirates of Abu Dhabi and Dubai: Contrasting Roles in the International System', *Asian Affairs* 38(1): 33–48.

Davidson, C. (2008). *Dubai: The Vulnerability of Success*. London: Hurst.

Davidson, C. (2009). *Abu Dhabi: Oil and Beyond*, London: Hurst.

Davidson, C. (2013). *After the Sheikhs: The Coming Collapse of the Gulf Monarchies*. New York: Oxford University Press.

Emirates News Agency (2016). 'Mohammad Bin Zayed opens Presidential Guard National Service Academy', 2 March.

Emirates News Agency (2017). 'Mohammed bin Rashid Emphasises Role of Media amid Current Challenges', 12 June.

Financial Times (2013). 'Bogota Alarmed by Exodus of Colombian Soldiers to UAE', 3 June.

Freedom House (2019). 'Freedom of the Press 2017: United Arab Emirates Profile'.

Freedom House (2020a). 'Freedom of the Press: United Arab Emirates 2015'.

Freedom House (2020b). 'Freedom on the Net 2018: United Arab Emirates'.

Freer, C. (2017). 'Rentier Islamism in the Absence of Elections: The Political Role of Muslim Brotherhood Affiliates in Qatar and the United Arab Emirates', *International Journal of Middle East Studies* 49(3): 479–500.

Guardian (2007). 'Newland Hires more Telegraph Staff', 2 November.

Guardian (2015). 'Australian Mercenary Reportedly Killed in Yemen Clashes', 8 December.

Guardian (2020). 'Revealed: Saudis Suspected of Phone Spying Campaign in US', 29 March.

Gulf News (2018). 'UAE Residents Warned: Up to Dh1 Million Fine If You Do This', 30 April.

Haggerty, K. and R. Ericson (2000), 'The Surveillant Assemblage', in *British Journal of Sociology* 5: 4,605.

Hartlyn, J. (1998). 'The Trujillo Regime in the Dominican Republic', in H. E. Chehabi and J. Linz (eds) *Sultanistic Regimes*. Baltimore, MD: Johns Hopkins University Press.

Hertog, S. (2011). 'Rentier Militaries in the Gulf States: The Price of Coup-Proofing', *International Journal of Middle East Studies* 43(3): 400–2.

Heydemann, S. (2007). 'Upgrading Authoritarianism in the Arab World', Brookings Institution Saban Center for Middle East Policy, Analysis Paper No. 13.

Heydemann, S. and R. Leenders (2011). 'Authoritarian Learning and Authoritarian Resilience: Regime Responses to the Arab Awakening', *Globalizations* 8(5): 647–53.

Hinnebusch, R. (2012). 'Syria: From Authoritarian Upgrading to Revolution?' *International Affairs* 88(1): 95–113.

Howard, P. and M. Hussain (2013). *Democracy's Fourth Wave: Digital Media and the Arab Spring*. Oxford: Oxford University Press.

Human Rights Watch (2017a). 'Osama al-Najer: United Arab Emirates', 3 November.

Human Rights Watch (2017b). 'UAE: Jordanian Journalist Convicted', 17 March.

Human Rights Watch (2020). 'UAE: Omani Sentenced to Life in Tainted Trial', 9 July.

Hussein, M. (2015). 'Three Arenas for Interrogating Digital Policies in the Middle East', *International Journal of Middle East Studies*: 47(2): 366–8.

Intercept (2016). 'Spies for Hire', 24 October.

Internet Telecommunications Union (2018). 'Individuals and the Internet, 2000–2017', 1 December.

Jones, M. O. (2019a). 'Propaganda, Fake News, and Fake Trends: The Weaponization of Twitter Bots in the Gulf Crisis', *International Journal of Communication* 13(1): 1,389–415.

Jones, M. O. (2019b). 'Saudi, UAE Twitter Takedowns Won't Curb Rampant Disinformation on Arab Twitter', Monkey Cage (*Washington Post*), 25 September.

Juneau, T. (2020). 'The UAE and the War in Yemen: From Surge to Recalibration', *Survival* 62(4): 183–208.

Jumet, K. D. (2022). 'Authoritarian Repression Under Sisi: New Tactics or New Tools?', in Ö. E. Topak, M. Mekouar and F. Cavatorta (eds) *New Authoritarian Practices in the Middle East and North Africa*. Edinburgh: Edinburgh University Press, pp. 73–91.

Khaleej Times (2019). 'Sheikh Mohammed's Warning to Social Media Users in UAE', 1 September.

Khiabany, G. (2015). 'Technologies of Liberation and/or Otherwise', *International Journal of Middle East Studies* 47(2): 348–53.

Krane, J. (2019). 'Subsidy Reform and Tax Increases in the Rentier Middle East', Project on Middle East Political Science, 'The Politics of Rentier States in the Gulf', POMEPS Studies No. 33.

Leber, A. and A. Abrahams (2019). 'A Storm of Tweets: Social Media Manipulation during the Gulf Crisis', *Review of Middle East Studies* 53(2): 241–58.

Liloia, A. (2022). 'New Authoritarian Practices in Qatar: Censorship by the State and the Self', in Ö. E. Topak, M. Mekouar and F. Cavatorta (eds) *New Authoritarian Practices in the Middle East and North Africa*. Edinburgh: Edinburgh University Press, pp. 208–27.

Lucas, R. (2014). 'The Persian Gulf Monarchies and the Arab Spring', in M. Kamrava (ed.), *Beyond the Arab Spring: The Evolving Ruling Bargain in the Middle East*. London: Hurst, pp. 313–15.

Lyon, D. (2009). 'Surveillance, Power, and Everyday Life', in C. Avgerou, R. Mansell, D. Quah and R Silverstone (eds), *The Oxford Handbook of Information and Communication Technologies*; Oxford: Oxford University Press.

MacKinnon, R. (2011). 'Liberation Technology: China's Networked Authoritarianism', *Journal of Democracy* 22(2): 32–46.

Maréchal, N. (2017). 'Networked Authoritarianism and the Geopolitics of Information: Understanding Russian Internet Policy', *Media and Communication* 5(1): 29–41.

Middle East Eye (2015). 'Revealed: The Mercenaries Commanding UAE Forces in Yemen', 26 December.

Middle East Eye (2019). 'How Saudi Arabia and the UAE are Silencing Dissent', 8 February.

National (2016). 'International Media Investments Acquires Ownership of the National', 16 November.

National (2020). 'Graduation Day for Class of Elite Amiri Guards', 11 March.

New York Times (2011). 'Secret Desert Force Set Up by Blackwater's Founder', 14 May.

New York Times (2015). 'Emirates Secretly Sends Colombian Mercenaries to Yemen Fight', 25 November.

New York Times (2016). 'Governments Turn to Commercial Spyware to Intimidate Dissidents', 29 May.

New York Times (2018). 'Israeli Software Helped Saudis Spy on Khashoggi, Lawsuit Says', 2 December.

New York Times (2019a). 'A New Age of Warfare: How Internet Mercenaries Do Battle for Authoritarian Governments', 21 March.

New York Times (2019b). 'U.A.E. Pulls Most Forces from Yemen in Blow to Saudi War Effort', 11 June.

New York Times (2020a). 'It Seemed Like a Popular Chat App. It's Secretly a Spy Tool', 20 January.

New York Times (2020b). 'Mohammed bin Zayed's Dark Vision of the Middle East's Future', 9 January.

Nimmo, B. (2018). 'Robot Wars: How Bots Joined Battle in the Gulf', *Columbia Journal of International Affairs*, 19 September.

Nye, J. (2004). *Soft Power: The Means to Success in World Politics*. New York: Public Affairs.

Pearce, K. and S. Kendzior (2012). 'Networked Authoritarianism and Social Media in Azerbaijan', *Journal of Communication* 62(2): 283–98.

Peck, M. (2010). *The A to Z of the Gulf Arab States*. New York: Scarecrow.

Quinlivan, J. (1999). 'Coup-proofing: Its Practice and Consequences in the Middle East', *Security Studies* 24(2): 131–65.

Rahimi, B. (2015). 'Rethinking Digital Technologies in the Middle East', *International Journal of Middle East Studies* 47(2): 362–5.

Reporters Without Borders (2019). '2019 World Press Freedom Index: United Arab Emirates'.

Reuters (2019a). 'Facebook Says It Dismantles Covert Influence Campaign Tied to Saudi Government', 1 August.

Reuters (2019b). 'Project Raven: Inside the UAE's Secret Hacking Team of American mercenaries', 30 January.

Reuters (2019c). 'UAE Releases Activists on Eid Amnesty: Rights Groups', 8 August.

Reuters (2019d). 'UAE Used Cyber Super-weapon to Spy on iPhones of Foes', 30 January.

Reuters (2019e). 'White House Veterans Helped Gulf Monarchy Build Secret Surveillance Unit', 10 December.

Reuters (2020). 'UAE's Israel Deal Met with Arab Dismay but Quiet Welcome in Gulf', 14 August.

Roberts, D. (2020). 'Bucking the Trend: The UAE and the Development of Military Capabilities in the Arab World', *Security Studies* 29(2): 301–34.

Salisbury, P. (2020). 'Risk Perception and Appetite in UAE Foreign and National Security Policy'. Chatham House, Middle East and North Africa Programme, July.

Schlumberger, O. (2005). 'Rents, Reform, and Authoritarianism in the Middle East', 11th Triennial General Conference in Bonn, workshop on 'Transforming Authoritarian Rentier Economies', September, 22–3.

Shehabi, A. (2022). 'The Authoritarian Topography of the Bahraini State: Political Geographies of Power and Protest', in Ö. E. Topak, M. Mekouar and F. Cavatorta (eds) *New Authoritarian Practices in the Middle East and North Africa*. Edinburgh: Edinburgh University Press, pp. 51–72.

Snyder, R. (1998). 'Paths out of Sultanistic Regimes: Combining Structural and Voluntarist Perspectives', in H. E. Chehabi and J. Linz (eds) *Sultanistic Regimes*. Baltimore, MD: Johns Hopkins University Press.

Tansey, O. (2016). 'The Problem with Autocracy Promotion', *Democratization* 23(1): 141–63.

Telegraph (2010). 'Queen's Gulf Visit: Britain's Historic Ties to the United Arab Emirates', 24 November.

Thompson, M. (1998). 'The Marcos Regime in the Philippines', in H. E. Chehabi and J. Linz (eds) *Sultanistic Regimes*. Baltimore, MD: Johns Hopkins University Press.

Times (2015), 'British Mercenary Killed in Yemen', 10 December 2015.

Topak, Ö. E. (2019) 'The Authoritarian Surveillant Assemblage: Authoritarian State Surveillance in Turkey', *Security Dialogue* 50(5): 454–72.

Topak, Ö. E. (2022). 'An Assemblage of New Authoritarian Practices in Turkey', in Ö. E. Topak, M. Mekouar and F. Cavatorta (eds) *New Authoritarian Practices in the Middle East and North Africa*. Edinburgh: Edinburgh University Press, pp. 296–319.

Topak, Ö. E., M. Mekouar and F. Cavatorta (2022). 'Introduction', in Ö. E. Topak, M. Mekouar and F. Cavatorta (eds) *New Authoritarian Practices in the Middle East and North Africa*. Edinburgh: Edinburgh University Press, pp. 1–29.

UAE Federal Law No. 11 (2016). 'Concerning the Regulation and Powers of National Media Council (NMC)', 22 July.

UAE Federal Law No. 15 (1980). 'Concerning Governing Publications and Printing', 16 November 1980, articles 3, 24, 11, 39, 70–1, 76.

UAE Federal Law No. 2 (2015). 'Concerning Combating Discrimination and Hatred', 15 July 2015, article 3.

UAE Federal Law No. 5 (2012). 'Concerning Combating Cybercrimes', 13 August, article 24.

UAE Government (2020). 'Media in the UAE: Regulator of Media in the UAE'.

Uniacke, R. (2022). 'Digital Repression for Authoritarian Evolution in Saudi Arabia', in Ö. E. Topak, M. Mekouar and F. Cavatorta (eds) *New Authoritarian Practices in the Middle East and North Africa.* Edinburgh: Edinburgh University Press, pp. 228–51.

US Department of State Bureau of Democracy, Human Rights, and Labor (2020). 'United Arab Emirates 2018 Human Rights Report'.

Wall Street Journal (2018). 'Throughout Middle East, the Web Is Being Walled Off', 18 July.

Washington Post (1977). 'Practising Checkbook Diplomacy', 21 December.

Wired (2008). 'Cairo Activists Use Facebook to Rattle Regime', 23 July.

17

AUTHORITARIAN PRACTICE AND FRAGMENTED SOVEREIGNTY IN POST-UPRISING YEMEN

Vincent Durac

Introduction

Authoritarian governance in pre-2011 Yemen conformed to many of the stereotypes about the MENA region, in which a dominant president, Ali Abdullah Saleh, led a political party, the General People's Congress, which occupied a central role in political life. Saleh's position depended on a number of stratagems, ranging from co-option of elites and opposition political figures to external patronage, the co-option and/or penetration of civil society and, when necessary, the wielding of outright repression against political opponents. Saleh lost power in the aftermath of Yemen's 2011 uprising, after which a combination of external actors and domestic elites fashioned a transitional plan for the reconstruction of Yemeni politics. The fracturing of this elite bargain in the face of popular discontent and regional challenges ultimately led to civil war and external intervention in 2015 to prop up the shaky post-Saleh status quo. In post-2015 Yemen, it has become effectively meaningless to talk about the authoritarian practices of a centralised state either in response to opposition or in pursuit of regime maintenance. Rather, what has developed is a fragmented polity in which the power of the central state is severely constricted by the emergence of significant sub-state actors (with external patronage) and in which the adoption of authoritarian forms of control is no longer the monopoly of any single actor, state or non-state. This chapter will review these developments and, in particular, will examine the question of what it means to speak of authoritarian governance in a fragmented state in the course of a conflict in which the power of the central government is contested.

Areas of Limited Statehood and Heterarchical Security Orders

The aftermath of the 2011 Arab uprisings has up-ended accepted wisdom regarding sovereignty in the Middle East. With the exception of Tunisia, regimes challenged by popular mobilisation responded with violence against their citizens, leading to a militarisation of politics and societies. In many instances, popular mobilisation led to a breakdown of previously established governing practices and the fragmentation of the apparatus of the state. Regimes responded by building new authoritarian regimes out of the remains of what had previously existed often with the assistance of transnational partners. What resulted from this was the militarisation of society through the deployment of 'elevated levels of violence' by elites in fragmenting states (Stacher 2015: 260). In the case of Yemen, post-2011 violence has deepened fragmentation in a state where the writ of central government has never extended across all the territory of the country.

The new landscape has invited a number of attempts to reframe notions of sovereignty to encompass a reality that no longer accords with traditional Weberian understandings of the concept. As Borzel and Risse (2016: 149) point out, the 'ideal-typical' state enjoys sovereignty in the sense of the formal organisation of political authority within the state and the ability of public authorities to exercise effective control within the borders of their polity. However, the empirical reality is that the majority of states in the international system do not satisfy these minimum requirements of sovereignty and suffer from problems of limited statehood. In areas of limited statehood, the capacity to implement and enforce central decisions is lacking and there is no monopoly on the use of force (Polese and Hanau-Santini 2018: 379). The Republic of Yemen, as will clearly be demonstrated, belongs to this category of areas of limited statehood, not merely since the uprising of 2011 and its aftermath, but for a considerably longer period of its modern history. Nonetheless, it is important to note, as Borzel and Risse (2016: 150) observe, that areas of limited statehood where the state is absent or dysfunctional are rarely ungoverned or ungovernable places. To this extent, the concept of areas of limited statehood helps to address the deficiencies of notions such as failed and failing states which carry with them Eurocentric and normative preconceptions that states function and therefore 'fail' in the same or similar ways. In contrast, Polese and Hanau-Santini (2018: 381–2) posit the view that states may persist as 'non-sovereign actors' in settings where sub-state or transnational actors may exert functions typically pertaining to the sovereign, for instance the exercise and threat of violence. One result of this is the multi-actor and multi-level nature of security governance that results from the fragmentation of sovereignty across the region. Polese and Hanau-Santini (2018: 384) propose that these new iterations of security governance are best understood in terms of heterarchical, as opposed to hierarchical, order. Heterarchical order connotes systems with multiple and often tangled hierarchies, 'where units are variously related, generating multiple rankings according to capabilities or authority'. Heterarchy, in this understanding,

> refers to political orders which are neither anarchic nor hierarchic but where the following features are present: (a) the lack of a clear superimposition of state coercive institutions over other coercive agents; (b) the existence of an oligopoly of violence, with blurred boundaries and tasks' definition among different security actors, even within the state; and (c) the existence of different hierarchies within a given political order, linked to different rankings associated to different functions. (Polese and Hanau-Santini 2018: 384)

Thus, the concept of heterarchy complements that of areas of limited state-hood in facilitating the conceptualisation of new orders of security govern-ance characterised by the fragmentation of political authority and an unclear distribution of coercive capabilities (Polese and Hanau-Santini 2018: 384). In this context, as the Introduction to this volume makes clear (Topak et al. 2022), there is a degree of continuity with practices established before heterarchy kicked in.

The Limits of the State and Authoritarian Practice in Pre-uprising Yemen

The Yemeni state conforms almost precisely to the designation of areas of limited statehood, having never enjoyed meaningful control of all of its terri-tory. Even prior to unification, the central government had a limited record in providing services other than policing. In the south, as Mansour and Salisbury (2019) note, electricity supply did not extend beyond the cities of Aden or Mukalla until the 1980s, while in the north local services were provided through autonomous local development councils, funded through remittances, which were later incorporated into state structures. As a result, Yemen has no more than a thirty-year history of state provision of services. More significantly, the central state did not enjoy a monopoly on the use of violence. The *Small Arms Survey* reported in 2003 that Yemen's tribes held a total of over 5.5 million small arms, while tribal sheikhs personally held a further 184,000 or so. By comparison, the state held around 1.5 million (Phillips 2011: 52).

The limited reach of the state had determining impacts on the nature of the post-unification political system. The Republic of Yemen came into existence in 1990 when the Yemen Arab Republic (YAR) in the north and the formerly Marxist-Leninist People's Democratic Republic of Yemen (PDRY) in the south came together to constitute the new state. From the outset, Ali Abdullah Saleh, the former president of the YAR, dominated political life in the new republic. The constitution of the new state gave the president formidable powers, notwithstanding its formal identification as a participatory parliamentary democracy that protected liberal freedoms. Under the terms of the constitution, he was Supreme Commander of the Armed Forces, and appointed all members of the Consultative Council, the Supreme Commission for Elections and Referendums (SCER), the Supreme Judicial Council, senior government officials, and military and police officers. The President promulgated laws passed by the House of Representatives, issued presidential decrees, had the power to declare states of emergency, could request amendments to the Constitution and had the power to dissolve parliament. He also appointed the Prime Minister. Although there was an elected parliament, this was a weak institution which posed little challenge to executive power. However, in any case, formal political institutions, as Phillips observes, lacked significance in comparison with informal institutions. Formal institutions were subservient to the interests of Saleh's regime and the constitution was routinely ignored in daily political affairs (Phillips 2011: 37–8).

Instead, Saleh's regime relied on a 'complex and flexible network of tribally- and regionally-based patronage relationships' in order to perpetuate his grip on political power (ICG 2011: 10). Longley-Alley (2010) has detailed the patronage system that underpinned his rule. In effective acknowledgement of the limitations imposed by an environment where the state failed to enjoy a monopoly of violence and where social forces were strong, Saleh consistently chose co-option, compromise and divide-and-rule tactics over exclusion and direct confrontation (Longley-Alley 2010: 393). Relying on resources provided by Yemen's oil sector, on which the economy was overwhelmingly dependent, as well as the provision of access to the private sector, Saleh drew tribal elites, religious leaders, traditional merchants and technocrats into a far-reaching patronage network. However, he also set out to ensure control of the coercive apparatus of the state, notably by placing family members, and members of the Sanhan tribe to which he belonged, in positions of control of key institutions. Thus, the president's half-brother, Mohammed Saleh al-Ahmar, was Commander of the Air Force; his nephew was deputy commander of the National Security Bureau; another nephew was Head of the Presidential Guard. The country was divided into five military zones, all of which were controlled by either relatives of the President or members of the Sanhan elite (Phillips 2011: 89). Below the elite level, Saleh used the military as a vehicle for patronage in his relationship with tribal sheikhs. According to the International Crisis Group (ICG), sheikhs would become colonels without any training. As a result, there were more colonels in the Yemeni army – some 14,000 – than all other officer ranks combined. Officer status conferred significant privileges. Those involved received salaries, petrol subsidies, uniforms and supplies. They were also allotted a certain number of soldiers who worked in their service as guards, even though their salaries and benefits came from the central government budget (ICG 2013).

The coercive apparatus of Saleh's regime encompassed a number of key institutions. The Political Security Organisation (PSO), led by military officers, was the major intelligence organ of the state and the most feared internal security and intelligence organisation. The PSO reported directly to the President through the Deputy Prime Minister for Defence and Security and operated its own detention centres. One of its key responsibilities was to detect and remove any threats to the regime. To this end, it employed a number of tactics: creating dissension in rival political parties, and engaging in assassinations, kidnapping, torture and espionage. Active NGOs were particular targets, 'where they had penetrated and established allied civil bodies' (Said 1997). The PSO had an estimated force strength of 150,000 spread throughout the country. The Central Security Office (CSO) numbered at least 40,000 (although some estimates put its strength at 60,000). The CSO was equipped with a range of infantry weapons and armoured personnel carriers and was overseen by the Ministry of Interior and Yahya Saleh, one of former President Saleh's nephews. The CSO had specialist institutions, including a Counter Terrorism Unit which was created in 2002 and which was heavily backed by international actors, particularly the United States. The CSO operated in Saada against the Houthi movement and in the south against the Southern Movement (see below). It also had its own extra-judicial detention facilities. Also in 2002, the regime created a National Security Bureau (NSB), following the signing of a counter-terrorism treaty with the United States in the aftermath of the September 11 attacks (Shiban 2017). Finally, the Republican Guard, an elite unit of the Yemeni Army, included the special forces wing of the military, and was commanded by Saleh's son, Ahmed Ali Abdullah Saleh (Al-Zwaini 2012: 34–5).

As noted above, Saleh preferred to govern through patronage and co-option. However, his regime was not unwilling to deploy coercion when particular 'red lines' – unwritten but firmly-established prohibitions against certain topics – were crossed. These included the war with Houthi rebels in the north, the repression of the largely peaceful Southern Movement, the failure to contain Al-Qaeda, and the widespread corruption within the country's top leadership. Those who crossed these lines were subjected to incommunicado detention, confiscation of newspapers and news equipment, threats and harassment (Committee to Protect Journalists 2010).

Nonetheless, the Yemeni state was long seen as an 'arbitrative' state rather than a centralised power capable of authoritarianism, and the Saleh regime for many years operated through a mix of coercion and co-option with its rivals (Mansour and Salisbury 2019: 36). But, while Saleh preferred compromise, co-optation and divide-and-rule tactics rather than outright confrontation with its opponents, when challenged he was prepared to rely on the coercive apparatus of the state. This was markedly clear in his response to the emergence of opposition in the south and the north of the country. The early dominance of Saleh's General People's Congress, and the increasing disenchantment of the leaders of the Yemeni Socialist Party (the former ruling party of the PDRY) with the unification process, led to a period of instability and political violence that culminated in a brief civil war in 1994. Following failed attempts at dialogue with Saleh, southern leaders declared secession on 21 May 1994 and the establishment of a new 'Democratic Republic of Yemen'. In the conflict that ensued, between 5,000 and 7,000 lives were lost as northern forces practising a form of 'total war aimed at completely defeating the southern military' (Mansour and Salisbury 2019: 36). In July 1994 northern troops entered Aden, the former capital of the PDRY, bringing the conflict to a close. Although short, the civil war had long-lasting consequences. The victorious GPC clamped down on southern 'secession-ists', and opposition figures, especially in the south, were arrested often on the basis of little or no evidence. The northern regime confiscated lands, private homes and wealth from leading supporters of the YSP in the south and distributed these to GPC loyalists. Northern élites began to exploit the resources of the south, including the oilfields of Hadramawt and Aden port, as hundreds of socialists, dissidents and government critics left the country. The period since the end of the Cold War saw the consolidation of GPC control and that of President Salih. Although Salih lifted the state of emergency that had been declared in July 1994, there was no restoration of the 'privileges and tolerances established during the four-year liberal interlude' (Carapico 1998: 188). Elections in 1997 were boycotted by the YSP and led to a substantial victory for the GPC, which won 188 seats to Islah's 56 (Schwedler 2002: 51). Despite the YSP boycott, the elections were generally seen as relatively free and fair. Nonetheless, the dominance of the ruling party since 1994 led one writer to conclude that 'the GPC has become virtually synonymous with the state' (Day 2006: 134). The defeat of the southern forces and the subsequent treatment of the region created the conditions for the subsequent emergence of the Southern Movement (*Hirak*), which began when a group of military officers, forced into early retirement after the 1994 civil war, started to hold weekly sit-ins in towns and cities in the south to demand better treatment from the regime in Sanaa. These protests grew rapidly and by late 2007 were attracting hundreds of thousands of people (Day 2010: 8–9).

Following the civil war, the regime also began to build a more tradi-tional police state, using the intelligence services, police and judiciary to crack down on purported terrorists and internal dissent. This process was deepened with Yemeni engagement with the US-led 'war on terror', which led to US funding for the creation of new counter-terrorism and security services from around 2003 onwards (Mansour and Salisbury 2019: 37).

Ten years later, Saleh again relied on the coercive apparatus of the state to address a challenge, this time emanating from the north of the country. The Believing Youth (*al-Shabab al-Mo'men*) was a Shia Zaydi revivalist movement that emerged in the 1990s and quickly became associated with the family of Hussain al-Houthi, a charismatic figure whose rhetoric drew support while antagonising the Government. Members of the al-Houthi family claim descent from the Prophet Muhammad, and the family purports to defend Zaydi identity from dilution in a wider Sunni Islamic identity. The movement was motivated in part by what was seen as economic discrimination against the northern province of Saada, as well as the regime's tolerance of Saudi-inspired anti-Shi`a agitation in the north of the country. This included the expression, by Saudi-trained clerics, of the view that Zaydis and other Shi`as are heretics and apostates from true Islam.

Direct conflict with the regime was triggered when militants belonging to the group shouted anti-US and anti-Israeli chants in a Saada mosque in the presence of the President. Attempts at reconciliation between Saleh and al-Houthi failed and in June 2004 the regime sought to arrest him. Fighting broke out and lasted until the security forces killed al-Houthi in September 2004. However, this did not end the conflict as members of al-Houthi's family assumed prominent roles in the organisation. His brother, Abd al-Malik al-Houthi, took over the leadership, denouncing the regime's relationship with the United States, while the Government claimed that the rebels sought to establish a theocratic Zaydi state in Yemen with the support of Iran. The latter claim was much disputed in the early years of the conflict, which was largely fuelled by local grievances over economic marginalisation, market access and the lack of infrastructure in the region. There were a further five rounds of fighting between 2004 and 2010, with the loss of several thousand lives and the displacement of hundreds of thousands of people. Although a number of ceasefires were implemented, the regime did little to address the underlying causes of conflict, which were transformed from local grievances into deep-seated resentment of the regime in Sanaa.

The Impact of the 2011 Uprising and its Aftermath

On 15 January 2011, the day after Zine al-Abdine Ben Ali stepped down as president of Tunisia, several dozen students, civil society and opposition activists attended a rally in Sana'a. The protests were given significant momentum following the resignation of Hosni Mubarak in February as hundreds of activists gathered in front of the university and thousands of others took to the streets elsewhere in the country calling for similar change in Yemen (ICG 2011: 3). As the anti-regime protest movement gained traction, winning the support of the Houthi Movement and of the Southern Movement, Saleh's regime responded with violence. Activists and protesters were harassed, arrested and beaten. On 23 January, security personnel arrested Tawwakul Karman and eighteen other activists, prompting a further round of protests in Sanaa and Taiz, which led to their release. As well as attacks on the demonstrators, Saleh announced a number of economic concessions. These included pay raises and free food and gas for the military and security forces, salary increases for the lowest-paid civil servants, the reduction of income tax by half, the introduction of new subsidies and price controls, and an extension of social welfare assistance to half a million families (Boucek and Revkin 2011: 2). However, regime violence continued against the protesters. On 25 February, a teenage protester was shot and killed by police in Aden. This was followed by a dramatic escalation in the level of regime repression on 18 March, when snipers occupied the buildings that overlook University Square (or 'Taghir' – 'Change' – Square as it was called by protesters) in Sana'a and killed 52 peaceful protesters while wounding hundreds more (Phillips 2011). The attacks shook the base of the regime and led to a split in the security apparatus of the state. There were mass defections from the ruling party, while Saleh's long-time ally, General Ali Mohsen al-Ahmar, a distant relative and one of the most important military figures in the country, joined the opposition, offering the protection of his troops to the protesters. With the possibility of full-scale civil war looming, external actors became involved. Led by Saudi Arabia, the Gulf Cooperation Council devised a plan for the transfer of power from President Saleh to his Vice-President, Maj.-Gen. (later Field Marshal) Abd al-Rabbuh Mansur al-Hadi and a power-sharing government between the GPC and a coalition of opposition parties (the Joint Meeting Parties or JMP), to be followed by a national dialogue process to explore possible solutions to Yemen's multi-faceted crises. The five permanent members of the UN, as well as the EU, supported the GCC Initiative. After months of prevarication, Saleh finally stepped down in November 2011. In January 2012 parliament passed a controversial law granting immunity from prosecution to Saleh and his family. His close aides were given limited protection from prosecution for 'politically motivated' crimes other than terrorist offences. This was followed by the election of Hadi to the presidency in February 2012. Under the terms of the GCC Initiative, he ran unopposed and his candidacy was supported by the GPC and the opposition coalition. However, under Hadi, the transitional process in Yemen yielded little progress. A National Dialogue Conference held in Sana'a was charged with addressing a wide range of political issues, including constitutional reform, the southern question and the situation in the Houthi stronghold of Saada. However, the conference was weakened by the fact that it had no meaningful representation from the south.

In particular, both the Hirak and the Houthis opposed Hadi's proposal of a six-region solution to the question of the federal structure of Yemen. Throughout this period, while Houthi political representatives took part in the transitional process, their fighters continued to expand their territorial control. Having secured control of the province of Saada during the course of the 2011 uprising, they moved south. By January 2014 battles raged across the north of the country, from the border with Saudi Arabia to the gates of the city of Sana'a. Socio-economic distress fuelled the expansion of the Houthis, as the transitional government led by Hadi failed to address corruption or to enact meaningful reforms. As the government lost legitimacy, the Houthis were able to mobilise support beyond their immediate support base in opposition to it. In September 2014, Hadi introduced a cut in fuel subsidies in order to secure financial aid from the IMF and the World Bank. The protests that ensued gave the Houthis the excuse to enter and take control of Sana'a by September 2014.

The Houthi seizure of Sana'a was made possible in part by a dramatic shift in political dynamics. In its initial phases, Saleh and his supporters accepted the transitional process, on the assumption that his continued leadership of the GPC would allow him to maintain influence in public life. However, as Hadi gradually moved to exclude Saleh and his family from positions of influence, under pressure from the international community, this position changed. By 2014, an utterly unexpected reconfiguration of forces had developed as Saleh and the Houthis entered into an alliance of convenience based on their newly shared opponents, who now dominated public life, in the form of Hadi and the JMP. The Houthi expansion was greatly aided by the co-operation, or at least non-resistance, of forces loyal to former president Saleh.

By February 2015, Hadi had fled to Aden in the south, and in March 2015 external actors intervened once more, when Saudi Arabia and the United Arab Emirates (UAE) led a military intervention, which dramatically escalated the conflict. The coalition includes a number of other Arab states, the most significant of which is the United Arab Emirates (UAE). The US, the UK and France also supported the intervention, which had as its core objectives the defeat of the Houthi movement, which many believe to be sponsored by Iran, and the restoration of Hadi to power. By 2017, the country had effectively become fragmented into a number of zones of control. Houthi forces controlled the north-west; UAE-backed forces became the most important security actors in the southern governorates; in the northern-central governorates and in northern Hadramawt to the east, military and security actors associated with the main Islamist opposition party *Islah* performed most security and military functions.

The Fragmentation of Sovereignty and Authoritarian Practice in Post-2015 Yemen

The conflict in Yemen has had a number of critical impacts. Apart from the loss of life and the devastating humanitarian consequences of the war, it has deepened pre-existing fragmentation and made possible the emergence and consolidation of an array of state-like actors contesting for power and resources and each associated with a diversity of authoritarian practices which are deployed in the course of that contest. Both deepening fragmentation and the diversification of authoritarian practice have been accentuated in different ways by the engagement of external actors in the Yemeni conflict, as will be discussed further below.

Deepening fragmentation

The conflict in Yemen since 2015 has served only to deepen the level of fragmented sovereignty which pre-existed, characterised by a proliferation of state-like actors, a diversity of security actors and an associated diversification of authoritarian practice. Ardemagni and Sayigh (2018) propose that three 'governments' now exist within the countries territorial boundaries: Hadi's internationally recognised government, which has been based in Aden since the Houthi takeover of Sana'a; the 'parallel government' established by the Houthis in the north of the country; and, the Southern Transitional Council (STC), proclaimed by southern secessionists in 2017 in Aden, which has significant support from the militias backed by the UAE. Salisbury (2017) goes further, describing Yemen as a 'chaos state' where central government has either collapsed or lost control of large segments of the territory over which it is nominally sovereign, and where a political economy has emerged in which groups with varying degrees of legitimacy co-operate and compete with one another. In this analysis, Yemen more closely resembles a series of mini-states at varying degrees of war with one another than a single state engaged in a binary conflict. These state-like actors assert that authority is conferred on them in different ways. Hadi's administration draws on his election to the presidency in February 2012 and on a resolution of the UN Security Council in April 2015 that named him as Yemen's legitimate president. The Houthis, having seized control of state institutions in late 2014, signed a deal with Hadi's administration that gave them a route to participation in government. In February 2015, they issued a 'constitutional declaration' that established new bodies, including a transitional executive, known as the Supreme Revolutionary Council. The Hadi government and the Houthis each have their own parliaments, consisting of members elected in 2003 (Mansour and Salisbury 2019: 12). In addition, the signing of the Riyadh Agreement in November 2019 to end conflict between forces supporting Hadi's government and southern secessionists backed by the UAE appeared to have the effect of confirming the legitimacy of the STC. The signing of the deal, which was attended by the crown prince of Saudi Arabia and the crown prince of the UAE, effectively constituted recognition of the UAE-backed STC by Saudi Arabia and the UN (Ardemagni 2019).

Diversification of authoritarian practice

The fragmentation of sovereignty that characterises post-2015 Yemen has had a direct impact on patterns of authoritarian practice. The Houthis, the internationally recognised government and the southern secessionists have each been associated with the deployment of authoritarian and repressive practices in dealing with real or potential dissent.

The Houthis

The takeover of the capital by the Houthis in September 2014, in partnership with former president Saleh, left them in effective control of major state security institutions, including the defence and interior ministries as well as elite military units and their stockpiles of weaponry. The 'hybrid' forces of the Houthis and the remnants of forces under the command of the pre-war interior and defence ministries, along with other state institutions, constitute a significant security actor. According to Mansour and Salisbury, up to 70 per cent of the army, police and 'paramilitary formations' in Yemen joined the Houthi–Saleh alliance during the early days of the conflict. This force still has an estimated 180,000–200,000 armed men under its control, less than half the official figure for the YNA. The Houthis also enjoy significant, if often overstated, support from Iran. According to the UN Panel of Experts on Yemen, Iran was in non-compliance with Security Council Resolution 2216 due to its failure to prevent the transfer of Iranian-made short-range ballistic missiles to the Houthis. Later in 2018, the Panel again reported that Iran was in breach of the international arms embargo by supplying the Houthis with advanced weaponry (Durac 2019: 670).

Authoritarian practices, repression and human rights abuses have become commonplace in areas under Houthi control. Al-Iriani and Transfield (2019) have described the development of a 'police-state' which generates widespread fear of its security structures and repressive police institutions, and in which dissent is not tolerated. The Houthis have assigned supervisors to institutions and communities, including police stations, to ensure their loyalty. These supervisors can arrest anyone who shows opposition to the de facto government; they collect intelligence and report to their superiors on anyone or anything suspected of being a threat. In the areas that they control Houthi forces arbitrarily detain critics and opponents as well as journalists, human rights defenders and members of the Baha'i community, subjecting opponents to incommunicado detention, unfair trials and enforced disappearance. According to the Yemeni human rights NGO *Mwatana*, the Houthis were responsible for 125 cases of 'arbitrary detention' in 2019 (Mwatana 2019). In July 2019, the Sana'a-based Specialised Criminal Court sentenced thirty academics and political figures to death on charges, including espionage for the coalition led by Saudi Arabia and the UAE (Amnesty 2019).

The internationally recognised government and southern forces
Hadi's internationally recognised government relies on the Yemeni National Army (YNA), formed from the rump of the military and bolstered by mass recruitment of tribal and other fighters, whose forces number around 450,000–500,000. However, this estimate includes a large number of so-called 'ghost' soldiers: fictitious or absentee names listed on the military payroll to enrich commanders, as noted earlier. Most YNA forces are concentrated in the Al Jawf, Mareb and northern Hadramawt governorates and represent the dominant force in the city of Taiz. The YNA also oversees the fight at fronts on the Saudi–Yemeni border, and in Hajja governorate in north-western Yemen. The YNA was also present in Aden until August 2019, retains positions in Lahj, Abyan and Shabwa, and its brigades fight along the Red Sea coast (Mansour and Salisbury 2019: 23). However, the YNA is noted for its weak capabilities despite receiving training, salaries and weapons

from Saudi Arabia. The main legitimising factor behind its forces is their affiliation with Hadi's internationally recognised government.

A diversity of forces associated with the Southern Movement have emerged in the course of the conflict. The Southern Resistance Forces (SRF) are overseen both by the UAE and the secessionist Southern Transitional Council. Unlike the YNA, the SRF has proved an effective force in the conflict with the Houthis. Since 2016, the UAE has been training, equipping and exercising effective command and control over a range of paramilitary forces in southern Yemen, some of whom are notionally under the control of Hadi's government but are effectively overseen by UAE commanders, while the STC also claims control of these forces (Mansour and Salisbury 2019: 24). However, not only have the SRF proved capable in battle with the Houthis, they have also clashed with forces under the control of Hadi's government. In August 2019, SRF units led by the STC seized control of military bases and government institutions previously held by the Hadi government, in what the government described as a UAE-led coup, illustrating not only the limited power that the government exercised over these forces but also an emerging divergence in the strategies employed by Saudi Arabia and the UAE respectively in the country. As Ardemagni (2018) points out, the UAE has developed a whole set of economic and geopolitical interests arising out of its presence in southern Yemen and its patronage of local actors. She argues that UAE strategy has developed from a concern to address the threat of jihadi actors to increasing its geopolitical influence in the Horn of Africa and the Indian Ocean (Ardemagni 2018).

Forces associated with the STC have committed human rights violations and are thus also viewed critically by many in the south (Al-Iriani and Transfeld 2020). In particular, the existence of a network of secret prisons was revealed. Dozens of people have been 'disappeared'. According to Amnesty International, the UAE, operating in shadowy conditions in southern Yemen, appears to have created a parallel security structure outside the law, where egregious violations continue to go unchecked (Amnesty 2018). *Mwatana* documented fifty-six arbitrary detentions carried out by government forces, and twenty-four cases of arbitrary detention by UAE-backed Southern Transitional Council forces in the governorates under its control (*Mwatana* 2019). Aden has been described as 'lawless' and characterised by arbitrary arrests and detentions, and enforced disappearances and torture, while light and semi-heavy weapons are available in the hands of ordinary citizens who found themselves at the mercy of brigades and armed militias 'comprising a rough mix of extremists, thugs, and former prisoners, who operate outside state control' (Said 2019).

The impact of external actors

The fragmentation of sovereignty and the diversification of authoritarian practice in Yemen have deepened in several important respects as a result of the policies and interventions of external actors, much as in Libya, as St John (2022) discusses in this volume. As has been noted earlier, the Houthis have received military assistance from Iran. However, the scale of this has been dwarfed by the scale of support received by Saudi Arabia and the UAE from its Western allies. British arms sales to Saudi Arabia have amounted to at least £4.7 billion since the start of the conflict, while, in April 2017 the United States signed a $110 billion commitment to supply military assistance to the Saudis. In addition, all sides to the conflict have relied extensively on the use of unarmed aerial vehicles – or 'drones'. In February 2020, the UN Panel of Experts on Yemen concluded that Iran was supplying the Houthis with advanced weaponry and high-tech components for the production of weapons, including missiles and drones (Nadimi 2020). Their opponents in the Saudi-led coalition rely on larger Chinese-made drones to surveil and target Houthi leaders. In 2018, a coalition drone strike killed one of the Houthis' leading members, Saleh al-Samad (Rieni 2019). In addition, the anti-Houthi coalition has relied on foreign mercenaries from a variety of countries in the course of the conflict. These include Eritrean and Sudanese fighters as well as forces from Colombia, Panama, Chile and El Salvador.

Conclusion

Yemen has never really known a state that extended its control over all of the territory in the ideal-type of the Weberian model. However, since the 2011 uprising, and particularly following the outbreak of an internationalised civil war in 2015, sovereignty has been even more fragmented. As a result, in the case of Yemen, authoritarian practices no longer take the form of a centralised state relying on its coercive apparatus in order to quell a domestic insurgent. Rather, they constitute the practice of a diversity of actors enjoying de facto sovereignty and legitimacy to varying extents, from the internationally recognised, if highly challenged, 'government' of Hadi to the Ansar Allah movement and an array of southern actors. There has been both continuity with the authoritarian practices of the Saleh regime and the adoption of novel practices and techniques, particularly in the period since the intervention of external actors in 2015. Saleh's intelligence services routinely relied on kidnapping, torture and assassination of political opponents and the repression of civil society activism. Since 2015, both the Houthis and their opponents have engaged in surveillance of political opposition and human rights defenders, arbitrary detention, torture and the use of the death penalty. To this, external actors have added new forms of authoritarian practice, notably the use of drone technology forces to target prominent Houthi leaders and reliance on foreign mercenaries. All of this deepens the political crisis in the country and makes its resolution even more intractable. Despite this, the international consensus is directed towards the 'restoration' of an untenable, perhaps non-existent, status quo ante which is dependent on irrelevant considerations of state sovereignty and which wilfully substitutes an idealised notion of sovereign state practice for the reality of fragmented sovereignty and fragmented authoritarian practice

References

Al-Iriani, M. and M. Transfeld (2020). '(Human) Insecurity in a Fragmented State', Yemen Polling Center. https://www.yemenpolicy.org/human-insecurity-in-a-fragmented-state%e2%80%8b/

Al-Zwaini, L. (2012). 'The Rule of Law in Yemen: Prospects and Challenges', *Hague Institute for the Internationalisation of Law*. https://www.kpsrl.org/publication/the-rule-of-law-quick-scan-in-yemen-prospects-and-challenges

Amnesty International (2019). 'Yemen 2019'. https://www.amnesty.org/en/countries/middle-east-and-north-africa/yemen/report-yemen/

Amnesty International (2018). 'Disappearances and Torture in Southern Yemen Detention Facilities Must Be Investigated as War Crimes'. https://www.amnesty.org/en/latest/news/2018/07/disappearances-and-torture-in-southern-yemen-detention-facilities-must-be-investigated-as-war-crimes/

Ardemagni, E. (2019). 'Yemen: The Southern Secessionists Enter the State'. https://www.ispionline.it/it/pubblicazione/yemen-southern-secessionists-enter-state-24325

Ardemagni, E. (2018). 'The UAE's Security-Economic Nexus in Yemen', Carnegie Endowment for International Peace. https://carnegieendowment.org/sada/76876

Ardemagni, E. and Y. Sayigh (2018). 'Patchwork Security: The New Face of Yemen's

Hybridity', Carnegie Middle East Center. https://carnegie-mec.org/2018/10/30/patchwork-security-new-face-of-yemen-s-hybridity-pub-77603

Börzel, T. and T. Risse (2016). 'Dysfunctional State Institutions, Trust, and Governance in Areas of Limited Statehood', *Regulation and Governance* 10(2): 149–60.

Committee to Protect Journalists (2010). 'In Yemen, Brutal Repression Cloaked in Law'. https://cpj.org/reports/2010/09/in-yemen-brutal-repression-cloaked-in-law/

Day, S. (2010). 'The Political Challenge of Yemen's Southern Movement', Carnegie Endowment for International Peace Middle East Program 108. *carnegieendowment.org/files/yemen_south_movement.pdf*

Durac, V. (2019). 'The Limits of the Sectarian Narrative in Yemen', *Global Discourse* 9(4): 655–73.

International Crisis Group (2011). 'Popular Protest in North Africa and the Middle East (II): Yemen between Reform and Revolution', *Middle East/North Africa Report* 102. http://www.crisisgroup.org/en/regions/middle-east-north-africa/iran-gulf/yemen/102-popular-protest-in-north-africa-and-the-middle-east-II-yemen-between-reform-and-revolution.aspx

International Crisis Group (2013). 'Yemen's Military-Security Reform: Seeds of New Conflict?', *Middle East/North Africa Report* 139. https://www.crisisgroup.org/middle-east-north-africa/gulf-and-arabian-peninsula/yemen/yemen-s-military-security-reform-seeds-new-conflict

Longley A. (2010). 'The Rules of the Game: Unpacking Patronage Politics in Yemen', *Middle East Journal* 64(3): 385–409.

Mwatana for Human Rights (2020). 'Without Accountability: Human Rights Situation in Yemen 2019'. https://reliefweb.int/report/yemen/without-accountability-human-rights-situation-yemen-2019

Mansour, R. and P. Salisbury (2019). 'Between Order and Chaos: A New Approach to Stalled State Transformations in Iraq and Yemen', Chatham House. https://www.chathamhouse.org/2019/09/between-order-and-chaos

Nadimi, F. (2020). 'The UN Exposes Houthi Reliance on Iranian Weapons', The Washington Institute for Near East Policy. https://www.washingtoninstitute.org/policy-analysis/un-exposes-houthi-reliance-iranian-weapons

Phillips, S. (2011). 'Chapter Five: The Regime', *Adelphi Series* 51(420): 87–104.

Polese, A. and R. Hanau Santini (2018). 'Limited Statehood and Its Security Implications on the Fragmentation Political Order in the Middle East and North Africa', *Small Wars and Insurgencies* 29(3): 379–90.

Reini, J (2019). 'Cheap Drones Are Changing the Calculus of War in Yemen', *GlobalPost*, 3 June. https://www.pri.org/stories/2019-06-03/cheap-drones-are-changing-calculus-war-yemen

Saif, A. K. (1997). 'The Politics of Survival and the Structure of Control in the Unified Yemen 1990–97', MA dissertation, Department of Politics, University of Exeter. http://al-bab.com/albab-orig/albab/yemen/unity/saif1.htm#Instituti onal

Said, O. (2019). 'The View from Aden: A Shadow State between the Coalition and Civil War', *Arab Reform Initiative*. https://www.arab-reform.net/publication /the-view-from-aden-a-shadow-state-between-the-coalition-and-civil-war/

St John, R. B. (2022). 'Libya: Authoritarianism in a Fractured State', in Ö. E. Topak, M. Mekouar and F. Cavatorta (eds) *New Authoritarian Practices in the Middle East and North Africa*. Edinburgh: Edinburgh University Press, pp. 171–88.

Salisbury, P. (2017). 'Yemen: National Chaos, Local Order', Chatham House. https://www.chathamhouse.org/2017/12/yemen-national-chaos-local-order

Shiban, B. (2017). 'A Short History of Counter-Terrorism in Yemen', in M.-C. Heinze (ed.) *Addressing Security Sector Reform in Yemen: Challenges and Opportunities for Intervention During and After Conflict*. Centre for Applied Research in Partnership with the Orient (CARPO). https://carpo-bonn.org/en /addressing-security-sector-reform-in-yemen-2/

Stevenson, T. (2019). 'Saudi's Coalition in Yemen: Militias and Mercenaries Backed by Western Firepower', *Middle East Eye*, 28 March. https://www.middleeasteye .net/news/saudis-coalition-yemen-militias-and-mercenaries-backed-western-fire power

Topak, Ö. E., M. Mekouar and F. Cavatorta (2022). 'Introduction', in Ö. E. Topak, M. Mekouar and F. Cavatorta (eds) *New Authoritarian Practices in the Middle East and North Africa*. Edinburgh: Edinburgh University Press, pp. 1–29.

INDEX